LUTHERAN QUARTERLY BOOKS

Editor

Paul Rorem, Princeton Theological Seminary

Associate Editors

Timothy J. Wengert, The Lutheran Theological Seminary at Philadelphia, and Steven Paulson, Luther Seminary, St. Paul

Lutheran Quarterly Books will advance the same aims as *Lutheran Quarterly* itself, aims repeated by Theodore G. Tappert when he was editor fifty years ago and renewed by Oliver K. Olson when he revived the publication in 1987. The original four aims continue to grace the front matter and to guide the contents of every issue, and can now also indicate the goals of *Lutheran Quarterly Books:* "to provide a forum (1) for the discussion of Christian faith and life on the basis of the Lutheran confession; (2) for the application of the principles of the Lutheran church to the changing problems of religion and society; (3) for the fostering of world Lutheranism; and (4) for the promotion of understanding between Lutherans and other Christians."

For further information, see www.lutheranquarterly.com.

The symbol and motto of *Lutheran Quarterly,* VDMA for *Verbum Domini Manet in Aeternum* (1 Peter 1:25), was adopted as a motto by Luther's sovereign, Frederick the Wise, and his successors. The original "Protestant" princes walking out of the imperial Diet of Speyer 1529, unruly peasants following Thomas Muentzer, and from 1531 to 1547 the coins, medals, flags, and guns of the Smalcaldic League all bore the most famous Reformation slogan, the first Evangelical confession: the Word of the Lord remains forever.

Living by Faith: Justification and Sanctification, by Oswald Bayer (2003).

Harvesting Martin Luther's Reflections on Theology, Ethics and the Church, essays from *Lutheran Quarterly,* edited by Timothy J. Wengert, with foreword by David C. Steinmetz (2004).

A More Radical Gospel: Essays on Eschatology, Authority, Atonement, and Ecumenism, by Gerhard O. Forde, edited by Mark Mattes and Steven Paulson (2004).

The Role of Justification in Contemporary Theology, by Mark C. Mattes (2004).

The Captivation of the Will: Luther vs. Erasmus on Freedom and Bondage, by Gerhard O. Forde (2005).

Bound Choice, Election, and Wittenberg Theological Method: From Martin Luther to the Formula of Concord, by Robert Kolb (2005).

A Formula for Parish Practice: Using the Formula of Concord in Congregations, by Timothy J. Wengert (2006).

Luther's Liturgical Music: Principles and Implications, by Robin A. Leaver (2006).

The Preached God: Proclamation in Word and Sacrament, by Gerhard O. Forde, edited by Mark C. Mattes and Steven D. Paulson (2007).

Theology the Lutheran Way, by Oswald Bayer (2007).

A Time for Confessing, by Robert W. Bertram (2008).

The Pastoral Luther: Essays on Martin Luther's Practical Theology, edited by Timothy J. Wengert (2009).

Preaching from Home: The Stories of Seven Lutheran Women Hymn Writers, by Gracia Grindal (2011).

The Early Luther: Stages in a Reformation Reorientation, by Berndt Hamm (2013).

The Life, Works, and Witness of Tsehay Tolessa and Gudina Tumsa, the Ethiopian Bonhoeffer, edited by Samuel Yonas Deressa and Sarah Hinlicky (2017).

THE PREACHED GOD

Proclamation in Word and Sacrament

Gerhard O. Forde

Edited by
Mark C. Mattes & Steven D. Paulson

Fortress Press
Minneapolis

THE PREACHED GOD
Proclamation in Word and Sacrament

Interior contents have not been changed from prior editions.

Paperback ISBN: 978-1-5064-2725-6
eBook ISBN: 978-1-5064-2726-3

The paper used in this publication meets the minimum requirements of American National Standard for Information Sciences — Permanence of Paper for Printed Library Materials, ANSI Z329.48-1984.

Manufactured in the U.S.A.

Contents

CONTENTS

Citations for Previously Published Essays

We gratefully acknowledge permission to reprint materials previously published in the following:

"Called to Freedom," *Luther Jahrbuch* 62 (1995): 13-27.

"Fake Theology: Reflections on Antinomianism Past and Present," *dialog* 22 (1983): 246-51.

"The Lord's Supper as the Testament of Jesus," *Word & World* 17 (1997): 5-9.

"The Lutheran View (of Sanctification)," in *Christian Spirituality: Five Views of Sanctification,* ed. Donald L. Alexander (Downers Grove, Ill.: InterVarsity, 1988), pp. 13-32.

"Preaching the Sacraments," *Lutheran Seminary Bulletin* 64, no. 4 (1984): 3-27.

"Public Ministry and Its Limits," *dialog* 30 (1991): 102-10.

"Something to Believe: A Theological Perspective on Infant Baptism," *Interpretation* 47 (1993): 229-41.

"When the Old Gods Fail: Martin Luther's Critique of Mysticism," in *Piety, Politics, and Ethics. Reformation Studies in Honor of George Wolfgang Forell,* ed. Carter Lindberg (Kirksville, Mo.: Sixteenth Century Journal Publishers, Inc., 1984), pp. 15-26 (*Sixteenth Century Essays & Studies,* III).

Abbreviations for Frequently Used References

BC   *The Book of Concord: The Confessions of the Evangelical Lutheran Church,* ed. Robert Kolb and Timothy J. Wengert (Minneapolis: Fortress, 2000).

BC-T   *The Book of Concord: The Confessions of the Evangelical Lutheran Church,* ed. Theodore G. Tappert (Philadelphia: Fortress, 1959).

CA   The Augsburg Confession in *The Book of Concord: The Confessions of the Evangelical Lutheran Church,* ed. Robert Kolb and Timothy J. Wengert (Minneapolis: Fortress, 2000).

CD   Karl Barth, *Church Dogmatics* (Edinburgh: T. & T. Clark, 1936-77), ET of *Kirchliche Dogmatik, 1932-1970.*

ELCA   Evangelical Lutheran Church in America

LCMS   Lutheran Church–Missouri Synod

LW   *Luther's Works* [American Edition], 55 vols. (Philadelphia: Fortress and St. Louis: Concordia, 1955-86).

WA   *Luthers Werke: Kritische Gesamtausgabe* [Shriften], 65 vols. (Weimar: H. Böhlau, 1883-1993).

WA TR   *Luthers Werke: Kritische Gesamtausgabe: Briefwechsel,* 18 vols. (Weimar: H. Böhlau, 1912-1921).

Acknowledgments

This second volume of Professor Gerhard O. Forde's collected essays, lectures, and sermons has arrived after his death August 9, 2005, at the age of 77. Forde is one of a small number of American Lutheran theologians who have made an indelible mark in theology in the United States and internationally. He did so by means of his interpretation of Luther for the modern audience, which became the way that he taught so many of us the gospel of Jesus Christ. Teaching the gospel to anyone is no easy matter, and yet Professor Forde did it frequently, simply, and with few peers. The only true theologians are the kind Luther, and Forde, called "theologians of the cross" rather than "theologians of glory." So it is that Professor Forde confessed and taught, and even in light of his own cross, clung to Christ's promise, "Because I live, ye shall live also" (John 14:19). We dedicate this book to the future work of proclaiming the radical gospel of Jesus Christ for sinners, and in gratitude for the faithful witness of Professor Forde among us.

In the production of this book we also express our thanks to Dr. Paul Rorem of Princeton Seminary, the general editor of *Lutheran Quarterly Books,* for his tireless work at publishing the best theology available to preachers, teachers, and all who lend an ear. We are thankful for the bibliography of writings that was first compiled by Dr. Joseph Burgess and Dr. Marc Kolden for their Forde *Festschrift,* and then carefully updated by Ms. Amy Marga of Princeton Seminary. We also appreciate the careful review of the manuscript by Pastor Ronald R. Darge, adjunct instructor in Religion at Grand View College.

Introduction: Taking the Risk to Proclaim

Final editing for this volume of Professor Forde's writings was interrupted by news of his death on August 9, 2005. This marks the end of a vocation as teacher of the church spanning three decades at Luther Seminary, with wide-ranging effect through thousands of preachers and teachers, not only in Lutheran churches, but throughout the church catholic. Since death and resurrection were central concerns of his teaching, his passing only makes these writings more urgent and significant to those who follow. Forde would occasionally address his congregation as the Apostle Paul did his: "You have died." Only then would he proceed to articulate what it means to preach the word of Christ to the dead, the word that raises them to new life. This collection of writings thus stands as an appropriate tribute to a teacher who thought of his work as a means to improve preaching, in word and sacrament, and by this means establish the church as the creature of that word.

This book is the third of Forde's texts published in *Lutheran Quarterly Books;* each one includes his own preaching as the goal of all his theology. Throughout his work, Forde drew upon Luther and the Lutheran Confessions as sources for Christian freedom, and in his own writing one senses the boldness of that freedom. The bright light of the distinction between law and gospel made the gospel clear and vibrant in his lectures, essays, and sermons. For years Forde lectured at Luther Seminary in St. Paul on the Lutheran Confessions, which he thought of as charters of freedom. He likened them to "manumission papers," or the Magna Carta. That meant that they were written, and so "legal," documents, but not the sort that could be called canon law. Instead, they were assurances and demonstrations of the authority by which one preached boldly, not withholding the gospel for fear that the gospel would fall into the wrong hands. In what hands did the gospel belong if not the "wrong" ones?! It is that kind of fear that led to his understanding of a "conspiracy of silence" that tempered proclamation into some kind motivation for the "free" will. When he was asked to preach at an ordination, as you will read below, he concluded his sermon with the kind of exhortation that bestows the gospel instead of another burdensome law:

> Remember above all, that the promise of the Father, the power from on high is, above all, the power of forgiveness. Don't forget to claim that also for yourself. You are not called to carry the burden of the world on your back. You are not called to be religious megalomaniacs, gurus or whatever. You are witnesses. You see, there is a real, good news here for you too. You aren't called to do it all. Just to bear witness. God will take it from there. You will be clothed with power from on high. Speak that word of forgiveness! Preach it!

He liked to "tell it like it is," and not mince words. Most especially he knew that were it not for faith — alone, that is, the kind that comes only by preaching, and preaching comes only by a preacher sent by God — then we are all dead in our sins. We do not need to wait for the expiration of our bodily breath for that to happen.

This book is an appropriate climax of Forde's published writings because it focuses on the main point of theology: word and sacrament. For bound wills, determined to establish their relationship with God on the basis of law alone, the only means of breaking through to freedom and resurrection is the proclaimed gospel. The only solution for God's absolute judgment is absolution, and that arrives only by giving the crucified Christ to sinners unconditionally. Christ was put to death for our sin and raised for our justification. So in this volume we turn again to the heart of the matter for Professor Forde: How do we cease having a wrathful God and get a God preached for us? Thinking along this same line, Oswald Bayer once stated, "Article V [of the Augsburg Confession] is the most important article in the Confession."[1] That means that although the chief article is

---

1. Oswald Bayer, *Living by Faith: Justification and Sanctification* trans. Geoffrey W. Bromiley (Grand Rapids: Eerdmans, 2003), p. 44.

justification by faith alone, it is the *means* of making that faith that keeps it from becoming one more human work. How do we get faith? We need a preacher. Such has Professor Forde been for many of us, and through these publications we expect his voice will affect another generation and more. For justification is always a matter first of death, then of resurrection from the dead. For that reason we gratefully continue Forde's work and witness by taking up the central question of this collection: What is preaching?

One of Professor Forde's most provocative and disquieting teachings states plainly that *preaching is God's election of the ungodly.* That God elects is bad enough. That God elects or chooses people while they are opposed, or ungodly, is worse. But the notion that all of this choosing by God is done by *preaching* is the worst of all — that is, until one stops merely thinking about it and actually does it. If such preaching really happens, hearers rejoice so much at the good news that one can hardly keep them quiet. But for preachers themselves the discomfort of preaching remains. After all, they are apparently being given a task that only the Holy Spirit can accomplish, and of course, the Holy Spirit blows where the Spirit wills. What theologian wants to speak at all of election today, although it is constantly on the lips of the apostles? Professor Forde's assertion does new things with the old teaching that we might still find in dogmatic textbooks. When God's choosing comes by preaching, election is no longer a preoccupation with the past, or even of speculations regarding God outside time. Instead, election is a matter of the future, indeed of what Forde calls "celebrating the future," and all at once establishes this future as given in the present for faith — alone.

In this second volume of Forde's lectures and essays, some previously published and some given here for the first time, we have concentrated attention on this assertion that God chooses his own by preaching. That makes preaching itself a sacrament, and the sacraments themselves are things to be preached. What we seek to provide in these writings is something of the way that Gerhard Forde taught others to do the kind of preaching in which God himself is done to hearers by what Christians usually call the means of grace: word and sacraments. In one way or another all of these writings concern preaching and how to improve it.

The Reformation intended the same thing, to improve preaching. "Improve" might be too mild. It was to accomplish the kind of preaching that God's kingdom demands and promises. As a historical movement this particular Reformation has largely lost its momentum, and it unfortunately did so quite quickly even in the sixteenth century. But that does not mean that Martin Luther's kind of Reformation failed because it proved unworkable or unnecessary; it was not really tried. Whenever the gospel was set out purely, that is, when it was allowed to have its unencumbered way with its hearers, it proved to be too dangerous even to most Reformers who were trying to make it their cause. The gospel, after all, condemns what the old world considers best about life, and as Luther noted in *The Bondage of the Will,*

> The world cannot bear the condemnation of that which it regards as best. Therefore, it charges the Gospel with being a seditious and erroneous doctrine that subverts commonwealths, principalities, kingdoms, empires, and religions; it accuses the Gospel of sinning against God and Caesar, of abrogating the laws, of subverting morality and of granting people the license to do with impunity whatever they please.[2]

Many of those who were initially caught up in Luther's kind of proclamation took cover in religious humanism and its moralizing notion of the church as a Christian militia that would bring in the kingdom of God. Others reverted to the old religion, which was as good as any other when it comes to reforming institutions and people, and had the advantages of long tradition, established power, and the ability to maintain the *status quo.* Some of the more experimental sorts of Reformers resorted to antinomianism. They attempted to ignore the working of the law in preaching. Law cannot accomplish repentance, they seemed to think; only the gospel makes a real impact on individual lives, so live as if there is no law! It should not surprise us that the closer one is to the pure and simple gospel, the more the fears of losing the law (or the advantages of having no law in the church) emerge, tempting the preacher and hearers alike to stop giving the gospel at all. But "when the old gods fail," as Forde put it, there is really no other place to go. The gospel is the only new thing that ever happens in this old world, otherwise all is vanity. But in order to get this gospel, preachers and hearers of God's word will necessarily engage in what Forde calls "breaking the conspiracy of silence." There is a kind of conspiracy in the church itself to keep the genie in the bottle, to make sure that we do not have too much grace or too much gospel. Forde once put it this way:

2. LW 26, 14.

A funny thing has happened to the church on its way to the modern forum. It seems to have forgotten what it was going to say! There is something of a conspiracy of silence abroad among us which seduces and entices us not to say it [the gospel], or at least not to say it too confidently.

God demands and promises an absolute preaching. Therefore, God sees to it that everything in this old world drives to the pulpit. Not just the Reformation or Martin Luther, mind you, or for that matter the systematic theology of Gerhard Forde, but everything in life drives to the pulpit. Yet, even such a statement is not quite adequate to describe either Professor Forde's theology, or the purpose of doing theology at all. In such a sentence, "the pulpit" puts a static symbol where an actual "happening" or dynamic "event" takes place — or, to use Forde's more precise language, a specific and vital "doing." In preaching, there and then, one receives the benefits of Christ in the forgiveness of sins. Forgiveness, moreover, does not merely wipe the old sinful slate clean so that one can start over. It gives a really new life because it gives a new Lord who has a new kingdom. That is, it gives a preached God where before one only had an unpreached divinity. If that is not hard enough to swallow, what is worse is that this is not speaking about two different gods. There is only one God, as Israel and Job and the church learned to confess by hard experience. But God is worshiped in two very different ways. One either spends a life trying to worship the unknown God (seeking a gracious neighbor, Forde once said), or one receives Christ. This reality forces people to speak the truth despite their fears: Christ means death to them, to their whole selves, and only then a new creation. "I" (to switch to the dangerous first person) must learn to speak of myself as two, one as good as dead and the new "I" who is made alive in faith. Such a distinction between old and new is the only way to speak worshipfully of God the Father, Son, and Holy Spirit as the one true Lord of the living.

Theology Is for Proclamation

Theology is for proclamation.[3] That means that the basic issue for any theology is finally a *hermeneutical* and *eschatological* one. Forde is quite clear,

3. G. Forde, *Theology Is for Proclamation* (Minneapolis: Fortress, 1990).

however, that by hermeneutical, he does not mean "word play." Changing metaphors in order to dodge one accusation or another (say, adding "Mother" to "Father" when praying), or by means of attracting some new fancy of the human will is not what he means by an improvement of preaching. Preaching is not the exercise of multiplying metaphors, nor is it the exercise of drawing in hearers by means of telling attractive stories. The gospel itself, and alone, must end the imprisonment of people by their own theological myths and the endless spinning-out of metaphors. This means that the work of theology must drive to the proclamation of the cross of Christ in which his benefits, *his own real self,* are given for sinners. Without this giving of Christ, only and alone, preaching has failed. In order to give Christ, the words of theology must be pushed out of the third person (God forgives) and into the first- to second-person address: "I forgive you." In this way the preacher ceases only reiterating how God redeems us (telling the old, old story), but actually *does* salvation, yes, even *does God,* to the hearer. Yet this is not as simple as it first sounds. Christ himself was accused of blasphemy for forgiving sins, which God alone can do. Christ was, in a strange sense, guilty of the charge of doing what God alone could do in forgiving sins. The preacher today should be accused in a like way, and be found guilty as charged, of forgiving sins as only God can do. But anyone who has actually done this sort of thing can tell you that once the preacher steps out of the normal role of moral exhortation, then the trouble really begins.

What actually happens when true proclamation is published in this old world? The result of this act or *doing,* as Forde calls it, is not just providing more information for the hearer, nor is it presenting a possibility for a decision, nor could we call it obedience to the rule of faith, nor is it even some analogy between image and prototype. Instead, proclamation accomplishes the death of the old sinner and the resurrection of the new saint *in faith itself.* Faith, as we learn from the Apostle Paul, comes "by hearing" (Romans 10). *Words* do these things, they provide the proper criticism of our selves, so we call this divine work *hermeneutical.* More specifically, the words we use come first from Scripture's text, and so the question of how to move from Scripture to proclamation is precisely what preachers are concerned about. Forde has offered a basic help to us in his description of "doing the text" to the hearer in a type of repetition of the original effect of the words that came to be written down, the words of Christ first and foremost, but also of the apostles who bear witness to him. But the repetition is not mere quoting of Christ's words, it is a repetition of the *function* of Christ's words. For example, in the parable of the treasure found in a field, the preacher seeks to catch what the words did to Christ's own hearers — accusing of sin and publishing the Lord's new words that bring the new kingdom. Then one turns and, using one's best critical skill, seeks to "do the text" again to hearers in the present. What that text always does is condemn and promise. It works the law and the gospel.

At the same time that we call the work of proclamation *hermeneutical,* we also learn that proclamation is *eschatological,* because what the words do is to kill and make alive. To speak this way immediately raises the main problem with preaching. Preachers are afraid that God will do exactly as promised! It sounds too risky, since it would mean that the pulpit is then even more than the fulcrum from which God moves the world. God and church are no longer interested in a mere "reformation" of church and world.

The idea that a church is reformed and always reforming, or that a society is to do the same, is now far outdistanced by true proclamation. By the preacher's words God creates a *new* world. That means we are claiming a lot for what most of the world appears to ignore. Indeed, most theologians fear preaching has become a private, rather than a publicly effective matter. It seems that preaching and religion are now only a matter of the heart, the inner and private world of individuals. But we are not asserting that hearers of God's Word merely "think," or "imagine," or believe in their inner heart that God is doing some new thing. The preacher's words will work actual weal and woe, and actually raise the dead in the real world.

Professor Forde often used the words "actual" or "real." He is not interested in what people imagine, or see from their perspectives, or for that matter what is considered *ideally* true. He has always held that the gospel is not talking about mere possibility thinking, or an actuality that is somehow established by our deeds, but it is *God's* actuality that is decidedly "down-to-earth" because of the coming of Christ in the flesh. It is frightening enough to realize that God is not interested in just talking about the world, but is already going about radically changing it. Moreover, it means that proclamation goes considerably beyond what most people seek — some means by which to move from theory to practice. For example, most agree with Marx that the point is not to *think* about the world, but to *change* it; but we are just not quite sure how to do that. The proletariat does not seem to be holding up its end of the bargain, and a revolution to-day becomes tomorrow's totalitarianism. But we are saying here that in *preaching* God changes things in the most radical way. God ends the old life and creates anew. Preaching is much more than normal human rhetoric. God will not be merely tolerated, made appealing, understood, described, or apologized for. Preaching is God's own instrument for the most radical change possible: a new creation.

Because God's work always threatens fearful sinners, who attempt to make God's Word as ineffective as their own words, God hides from us and our languages, our thoughts and explanations. Why? By hiding and withdrawing (only to come all too near in another way) God is actively taking away our free will, and its dream of immortality that falls prey to the temptation of the law itself. God kills what we hold best about ourselves. But God does so for another purpose than satiating his own wrath at sinners. It is done for what God is really after, the "proper" work of God — to give us a truly Christian freedom that trusts Christ, even against God's own all-working power in history and creation. As Forde preaches it himself, one quits fearing that God actually does give all workers in the vineyard the same no matter how long they work. Instead, one begins trusting that God is providing a new freedom that already starts peeking out in this world.

Yet, who is not afraid to fall into the hands of this living God? No one wants an *almighty* God. Maybe we could do with a cooperating God. Maybe we wouldn't mind an empathetic God who can feel our pain. Perhaps even a properly distant God looking down on us from time to time would not be out of the question. But an almighty God? No. A living God is one who does not wait for us to choose, but makes a divine choice of his own. And what does God choose in this old world? He chooses his Son, Jesus Christ. The Father that cursed Christ is nevertheless the same Father who raised him and justified his cause of forgiving those who sinned against him. That is not, after all, a "system," or a "nature," or the discovery of the invisible mind of God. Proclamation is God at work. And God's proper work, God's will, is to make creatures who trust his only begotten Son, pure and simple. When Christ comes to you by way of a preacher, it is too late to do anything but suffer God and reap the benefits of a new creation. God will not be justified outside his words, but justifies himself *in* his words, and so it is in faith itself that God alone creates something really new.

A Theology of the Cross

Theology, especially its "systematic" kind, is not for mapping out the mind of God, but for leading to the place where the Father wants to give you his very heart, his Son. We have this way of speaking today. When a grandmother wants to show you pictures of her new granddaughter she is apt to point and say, "She's my heart." Augustine used to say that persons are more where they love than where they live. But the heart, as we know, is a funny thing. It does what it wants, often defying reason. In most places in our lives this creates significant problems. But if God wants to give his heart to actual sinners, even so that he could point at us and say, "there's my heart," well then, we might have a real advantage in hearing and trusting this. God's divine heart is a powerful thing; it is not restricted to what it finds lovely. Instead of loving only what it finds attractive, it loves that which is not lovely, especially in God's own eyes. Then, when God loves something it becomes lovely. It is created anew. The Father wants to give us his heart, who is the only begotten Son, but does not wait for us to become worthy. Such self-giving is hard enough to accomplish for anybody, although some extraordinary people in this world seem able to turn values upside down and love the poor, marginalized, and forgotten. As St. Paul says, it is difficult to find people who will give their lives for another — although it does happen now and then. But God not only manages to love the underbelly of the world, God re-creates it. God's gospel word puts a new heart within us, thus ending the old and creating us new. He does this without condition — since the cross and its judgment have already happened in history. God made the unlovely to be lovely by sending a preacher. Imagine that! This is what many have called, following Luther, a theology of the cross. Even better, as Professor Forde has taught, this is what it means to undergo God's Word in the world and become a theologian of the cross.

But this has always opened a series of difficult theological questions that are not for the faint of heart. If God saves by choosing, and chooses apart from righteousness in our own selves as measured by deeds required of the law, then why did God ever bother giving the law in the first place? Was Moses all a charade? What of the distinction between Jew and Gentile, male and female, slave and free? And worse yet, if one just starts announcing the gospel indiscriminately, won't that mean absolute license given to people to do whatever they want? (That was

9

Erasmus' fear about Luther.) What happened with the law of God is re-markable indeed. God did what we deem impossible. God made his own divine law eternally *historical* by means of Christ's historical cross. The law became *once and for all*. It became something in Christ that could now be told as a story: "Once upon a time . . ." This is something the great thinkers of every sort have assumed is impossible and so they never really dared even to dream it. Freedom might be many things, but it could never be freedom from the law itself, could it? The great thinkers of the world, Christian or not, have usually thought that the law is eter-nal in the sense of existing outside time; otherwise everything, as we know it, would die. Ontology would come to an end. Being would be-come non-being. Good would become Evil. Chaos would reign. God would cease being the creator and sustainer, mostly because God himself would then have died. To say this more directly yet, there can be no dif-ference between the law and God's own being, can there? For this reason, God giving his heart in Jesus Christ is not a simple matter. It complicates things for us on earth, especially those of us who are trying hard (some-times) to live according to God's divine plan as revealed in his law. And it only gets more complicated when we kill him, and to top things off the Father adds his own curse to the mess of Christ's cross, withdrawing the Spirit, or allowing it to be given up, from the Son.

But God's heart is Christ, the incarnate Lord who is *this man* who was crucified for the sake of sinners like you and me. God's heart is not the law. God's heart, what God wills and wants at the deepest level, is not a pattern of historical development, or even abstract almightiness — even something so lofty-sounding as "salvation history," for example. It turns out that Jesus Christ incarnate is what the Father and Holy Spirit have been after throughout history (and apparently before), and they never stop wanting him. This God/man, Jesus Christ, also wants some-thing. He has a heart too — a heart that is no less than that of the Fa-ther's and the Holy Spirit's. Jesus Christ, who is no other than God-for-us, refuses to proceed without his people, his kingdom, and his new cre-ation. He prayed to the Father this way: "No one will snatch them out of my hand" (John 10: 28), and then when raised from the dead proceeded to go and get people by preaching to them just as he had before his death: "Fear not!"

The eternal law has now become temporal in this man Jesus, who never ceases being *this man* and neither does he cease being the true God.

Christ refuses to become a divine plan, or a decision of God, or an archetypal being meant for iconic participation, or even merely a model to imitate. Sometimes sinners like ourselves attempt to take the people who are in our lives and make them into something symbolic. We try to make others into a plan of our own design or into an idea we have for their lives. We do something similar when it comes to Jesus Christ. Christ is then made to bear the aspirations we have for others and ourselves — he is made the projection of our dreams and designs — especially of some type of immortality. But Christ refuses to be a blank screen for our projections, with apologies to Feuerbach's attempt to become the "second Luther." Christ refuses to be anyone but himself, Son of God and Son of Man, crucified for our sakes under Pontius Pilate, and raised on the third day by the Father in the power of the Holy Spirit. And this same *theanthropos* refuses to be himself without taking his sinners with him. One of Professor Forde's great contributions to theology is located at this place. We can see it especially clearly in his lecture on Barth's Christology. As brilliant as Barth was to take the old church dogmas, including Christ's two natures (or his three offices, or the Triune Being of God), and make them fit the *history* of the man Jesus, there remains in his effort an abstraction from our own history and away from the arrival to us of a preacher. Barth's doctrine, however much it is tuned to Christ's history, ends up *describing* Christ rather than *giving* him to the ungodly.

Theologians then end up attempting to resolve in doctrine itself the questions of why God would become a human being, or how the right doctrine helps us by drawing an analogy between Christ's humanity and our own. Theologians even end up thinking they can unite the church on the basis of agreement in such doctrines. We end up with the old problem named for Nestorius, carefully dividing God and humans so that God remains clean from human degradation, and humans hold out the hope of imitating the model of Christ in something like an *analogia relationis*. Forde, like all good theologians of the present age, has been influenced by Barth, but has a very different Christological center than Barth had. Consequently, in Forde's writings there is a different relation between theology and the preaching office itself. The answer to the human dilemma of sin is not some type of *thinking,* or the effort to reproduce a certain *feeling,* nor is it the typical notion of motivating people to produce a *doing* that is moral in nature. The law ends when Christ arrives, in his person no less.

Taking the Risk to Proclaim

So, how does Christ arrive? By proclamation, that is, the giving of his bene-fits in the words of the preacher when the preacher preaches Christ alone, and the Holy Spirit takes the words and makes a new heart. Human sin ends when the proclamation of Christ, taken from his story in the Bible, is done in the here and now. That involves a great risk for the preacher, how-ever. The risk is to speak *for* God, not *about* God. That risk is then to apply the unmitigated law as a final judgment that has already been accom-plished, and to give the unconditional gospel that has triumphed in Christ to a real human being. Why is this risky? First, because no one thinks they need it! They do not see forgiveness of sins as the solution to their life's problems. Second, if the Holy Spirit does what is promised, then a cross is laid upon the person that is no less than the death of the old self. Who wants that?

For this reason, faith that trusts and clings to this God, this man Je-sus Christ, is a real *pathos,* a struggle or suffering against the temptation to find another ground by which to trust something — even some noble idea of Christ. But there is only Him. He comes only as the one we cruci-fied and whom the Father raised. And he comes by preaching. Outside of this way of giving his heart, God's wrath and our suffering and death re-main — are keenly felt and observed — and God simply will not be found or explained in some other way. "It is what it is," as the modern saying goes. Call it fate or call it chance, you get the cards dealt to you. The al-mighty God, the Father the Creator, even the Holy Spirit with all spiritual gifts, and Jesus Christ himself is only a threat to our best parts (mind or spirit or soul) apart from Christ as he is preached and given for the for-giveness of sins. Apart from the preacher applying promises directly to you, even the narrative or story of God in Christ going to the cross for us (say, in the form of a movie) can become the worst form of accusation, demanding some culprit or explanation that must be provided by our own inner voices.

Without a preacher, things are just as Luther once described them in his lectures on Galatians (1535). We can know quite a bit about God: that he exists, that he demands things from us, and that he will be our final judge in the next life. But yet the one crucial thing remains missing if you do not have his heart, that is, what God intends specifically "for you." To one who killed Christ — either as perpetrator, bystander, or victim — this is to live in death until the preacher applies the pronoun directly, personally, historically, and presently: "I forgive you all your sins in the name of the Father, Son, and Holy Spirit."

We actually learn this kind of preaching "in a nutshell" from the sacraments. Baptism and the Lord's Supper especially teach us how to preach. Absolution, as Forde liked to say, is the only solution to the Absolute. Only then does the almightiness, immutability, and eternity of the Creator, the Father, the Holy Spirit, and Jesus Christ, become good news to us while we are yet sinners. When God promises forgiveness, his heart is not fickle. It does not change. The Father's heart wants Jesus Christ and all who belong to him, period. That is true even though this demands applying a cross to each of those whom he then raises from the dead.

In writing books (like this one), we are left with such one-step-removed statements, since theology is *talking about* something that must finally eventuate in a confession such as the Ethiopian eunuch's: "If what you are saying is true, then what is to keep me from being baptized?" This then calls out for you to *speak for* God to specific, active, personal sinners. Sometimes we say theology is "second order" talk that aims at a "first order" way of speaking. The first order does not describe or explain, but actually does things with words. Yet, what happens in the pulpit, or in proclamation (since pastors now routinely ambulate) is not the same, for example, as a man and woman making promises that create a marriage. Pulpit or proclamation is God's own doing in which old sinners are brought to death by the law and raised up as new creatures with a new Lord and kingdom in faith itself. This makes preaching unlike any other first order or "performative" discourse in the world. The pulpit, to use the geographic metaphor, is the place from which this world truly becomes old, and the new kingdom of Christ is created.

In light of Forde's call to take the risk of proclamation, the dreary and lifeless state of preaching today is alarming enough to wake the dead. That description includes the energetic, glorious, and enthusiastic versions of preaching like those the Apostle Paul experienced at Corinth. The pseudo-apostles who came preaching after Paul in that city had faces that glowed when they preached, but they failed as preachers because they tried to tone down the gospel. They asked for just a little bit of cooperation and law to be joined with Jesus Christ himself so that faith and the law would not be emptied of good works. We must admit at the most basic level that the Reformation's attempt to improve preaching is unfinished or even a

failure. But there is no "plan B." God will not rest with failure by church institutions or theological traditions on this point. After all, how will they
hear if they have no preacher?

For years Professor Forde taught the Lutheran Confessions to large
numbers of preachers-in-training. The central matter for this second volume of collected essays can be put in terms of one of the Lutheran Confessional documents, *The Augsburg Confession*. The central article of that
document is the fourth article: "Furthermore, it is taught that we cannot
obtain forgiveness of sin and righteousness before God through our merit,
work, or satisfactions, but that we receive forgiveness of sin and become
righteous before God out of grace for Christ's sake through faith . . ." The
first volume of Forde's essays, entitled *A More Radical Gospel*, was about
the chief article of faith (justification by faith alone, or the *sola fide*); this
second volume takes up the question of how such faith is *made*. Since faith
alone makes us right with the Almighty God, then how do we get that
faith? This is why the fifth article of the Augsburg Confession answers immediately: "To obtain such faith God instituted the office of preaching,
giving the gospel and the sacraments." Proclamation creates faith. And
such a new creation is, we learn, the very method God used to create this
old world in the first place. God creates by the Spirit, freely, out of nothing,
by speaking a word that comes to us from outside, and continuously —
day by day. Just as with Scripture, the Lutheran Confessions cannot be interpreted except in accord with their own meaning, their literal meaning,
and this means that faith alone saves. Further, faith comes by hearing, and
hearing comes by proclamation, and proclaimers are given (sent) by the
Holy Spirit who uses such "means" as Word and Sacraments to create faith
"where and when he wills, in those who hear the Gospel," as in Galatians
3:14: "So that we might receive the promise of the Spirit through faith." The
gospel is the promise of Christ. When you have his promise you have *him*,
death, resurrection, and all. When you have him, you have the heart of the
Father and the very person of the Holy Spirit who witnesses only to Christ.
Only with justification by faith alone as the center, source, and goal of theology can one then speak intelligibly and profitably (for the edification of
the church) about good works or what the church and its unity is, and (the
special concern of this volume), how to give baptism, the Lord's Supper,
and absolution to actual sinners without any human qualifications, including those qualifications the preacher (or hearers) might wish to place
on these means of grace.

God Electing Faith

Indeed, how does God make faith? This is always *the* question of theology. Once the commonplace of "faith" is identified (a feat in itself, since philosophy does not have this way of speaking), then how does the Holy Spirit goes about the new creation? This question involves us immediately in the further question of divine election or predestination, and so of the controverted issues of God and time, and God's eternal will. Forde has always taken Luther's most drastic sentence (at least in the eyes of most theologians) as the crux of the matter here: ". . . we have to argue in one way about God or the will of God as preached, revealed, offered, and worshiped, and in another way about God as he is not preached, not revealed, not offered, not worshiped."[4] This might seem palatable for modern tastes if one could think of this as two "points of view" held by more or less the same person, since we routinely hold disparate and even contradictory thoughts in our minds. But Luther is speaking of these two different necessities for arguing about God as having a death, a grave, in between them. That puts a whole new light on human "perspectives." It also puts a whole new light on God.

God has not bound himself to his own word, to Christ, as if by a universal law or unassailable definition of "being." God is not only the person of Jesus Christ. We speak of two wills for God, both outside and in time. Why? Because God not preached has no cross of Christ by which he bestows forgiveness on the sinners announced in the here and now by a preacher "for you." There is in God apart from Christ only the law: "do this," and judgment: "you have not done this." And finally, apart from Christ, apart from preaching, apart from God's word, there is only a deafening silence with the anticipation of a wrathful end. That is what happens to people who have no preacher. They become as one who has no hope, or they manufacture strange hopes that are echoes of their own voice or projections of their own fears and aspirations. They don't stop having a God; they just have a God-not-preached. Even Jesus Christ can be spoken about as a God-not-preached, sometimes endlessly. But Jesus Christ then becomes an idea or abstraction, a kind of cipher for what we want this God to do or the way we want this God to think of us. Christ then becomes merely our speculations of what we would expect out of God if we were running the universe.

4. LW 33: 139.

Proclamation brings an end to the not-preached God (that is already in operation with people before any preacher arrives), and applies the preached God. Preaching is no less than giving the promises in which Christ himself is present and active "for you." Proclamation gives Christ himself to people who are active opponents of Christ himself (often by pursuing their own Christ idea). This type of theology, Christology, and soteriology is the basis for what can be called Forde's theology of word and sacrament, of ministry and of the freedom of the Christian. It comes out of the question of election. Does God determine before all time who will be chosen and who will be damned, like picking out potatoes from a sack? Does God wait and take those who have chosen for themselves? Does God give encouragement, or help, or power to some in greater measure than to others, and then prefer them? Does God crown a good-faith effort, or perhaps begin a process that the person must complete? Such speculations come to an end in the actual proclamation of the gospel. That happens when we make disciples by baptizing in the name of the Father, Son, and Holy Spirit. It happens when we do as we are told, proclaiming the Lord's death in the bread and wine until he returns: "given and shed for you, for the forgiveness of sins." It happens in the absolution by the declaration of Christ's promise to actual sinners: "I forgive you in the name of the Father, Son, and Holy Spirit."

These are God's means for electing actual people in their place and time. Election happens in history. This gives unprecedented authority to the office of the ministry, which is the spiritual priesthood of all believers. But that authority is the authority of the gospel to create anew. It is not the kind of authority the world either has too much of, or not enough of, in the form of the law alone. The authority is to do the divine electing here and now. Once the public office of ministry and ordination are put in relation to the basic matter of all theology — election — then a series of modern pitfalls regarding the office and its authority can be avoided, and the real power of the office can be unleashed for the creation of the church by God's own word.

One can also avoid the series of pitfalls that have plagued much of the theology of the sacraments in the tug-of-war between what is objective and subjective in the sacraments: What does God do and what do I do when it comes to the sacrament? Instead, this focuses on the way God elects by making faith in him presently. Faith is not in an idea we have or a feeling or a moral construct. When we say "faith," we mean faith in Christ who remains always external to me, but nevertheless gives his whole self without reserve — truly uniting himself to us — in order to make us new. So in baptism Christ's word in the water gives neither a metaphor, nor a mere sign of his presence residing elsewhere, but gives "something to believe in," as Forde put it. Baptism gives a *thing* in which *Christ* comes to us so that we need not fear or disregard him. He puts himself in the water so to be grasped by a faith that is urged on every side to despise the lowliness of Christ and seek for something higher, or mystical, or more spiritual behind this little mask of creation in which God is done again to his creature.

It may surprise some that Professor Forde, known for his work in atonement, eschatology, and ecumenism, taught worship courses for many years. But proclamation includes the sacraments; in fact it is especially tied to them as the real way of preaching that otherwise gets subsumed by other forms of rhetoric that seem to move people at the moment. So Forde taught that the sacraments are something to be preached, and preaching itself is sacramental. Christ will not have it any other way, and by this means elects his sinners.

Each of the essays in this volume is profoundly pastoral. They are guided by the fundamental conviction that God does not finally need human explanation but rather proclamation. They recognize that God is at work in all creaturely activities to make people ready to receive him with joy and to permit them to embrace their genuine humanity expressed through spontaneous and carefree service to the neighbor and the world. Nevertheless, they also recognize that God must tear down sinful human life before he can build up. Wherever our self-centeredness, rebelliousness, indifference, and self-righteousness are found, God is active to recreate us as new beings, who live by fearing, loving, and trusting him. Our self-destructive and socially disruptive ways result in dead-end consequences. God lifts us up when and as we are rendered powerless by those situations in life that accuse and/or confuse us. God remakes us by claiming us as his own.

God Preached and Not Preached

The first section of this volume, "God Preached and Not Preached," acknowledges the pastoral concern that people will inevitably encounter God in their worldly experience as one who works both life and death. Of course, such a topic is not popular today — undoubtedly it never has been.

Forde's point is not to indulge in religious masochism. Rather, it is the realistic acknowledgment that the old being's inevitable encounters with God involve, like Jacob at the Jabbok, a power struggle. The old being believes that he or she is self-sufficient and that if God enters the picture he is seen as one who can be used and not feared, loved, and trusted for his own sake. Since God claims his own for himself, old beings will eventually encounter God's resistance to this hopelessly misdirected way of being. God's resistance, as Forde notes in the first essay ("Whatever Happened to God? God Not Preached"), takes the guise of the *deus absconditus*, the "hidden God," the God "not preached" precisely as distinguished from "God preached" who has come to us in the word of and about Jesus Christ.

This view, peculiar to Luther, is not a theological fossil but the actual experience of all humans, both believers and non-believers alike. All people will inescapably encounter experiences that shatter their fundamental self-confidence that their lives are manageable. Indeed, we will be led to question and doubt whether or not the universe says "yes" to us or is instead either indifferent to our plight or downright hostile to us. Here we are dealing with an experience that is not merely that of hearing the accusing voice of the law. Instead, this fundamental experience or encounter carries home the truth that we are unable to control our fate. This experience happens in the very attempt to affirm ourselves as "gods" in either our theories (science) or our practice (ethics). We are so rendered impotent before this God that in the very attempt to map or control our universe for the sake of securing our destiny we are blind to the fact that it is precisely this obsessive behavior that controls us. We are not free with regard to our fate, and we are unaware of just how bound we are.

One response that humans have to this "hidden God," who will be encountered in our experience at some point or another, is to theologize. If God could be explained in an overall system of theological truth, then we could believe that the "hidden God" we experience would be rendered harmless. We could continue on our merry way with the belief that we are ultimately affirmed by and in charge of the universe. We would not have to suffer the death — loss of control of our lives — that the "hidden God" does to us. However, we want to remove this "wild" side from God when we systematize him as an element of our theological schemes. But this in turn prohibits affirming God as merciful. Only as all-powerful can God be all-merciful — this is what we need, even if it is not what we want! Forde's point is that our theorizing about God — our "theologies of glory" — offer only false securities in the face of this "hidden God." Only preaching, delivering the word of forgiveness to sinners and speaking the promise of God's care to the insecure, can reconcile people to the absolute! What is needed in our church and society is a company of preachers who are bold enough to deliver this reconciling word with courage, conviction, and integrity, and can thus move people from servile to filial fear.

"When the Old Gods Fail: Martin Luther's Critique of Mysticism," a contribution for a George Forell Festschrift (*Piety, Politics, and Ethics*) in 1984, addresses the theme of meeting God. We meet God "for us" not in the immediacy of mystical unification but mediated in the Word that completely alters the terrain of one's life. Forde analyzes the disputed relationship that Luther had with the mystical tradition of the church. After all, Luther praised the medieval mystic John Tauler and employed mystic terms, such as *raptus*. Was Luther then something of a mystic? Forde thinks not. Forde notes that the mystic seeks to move out of the abyss of separation from God into immediate experience of unity with the divine. The mystic employs a hermeneutic that internalizes the letter of the scriptural text by allegorizing it in order to achieve an experiential knowledge of God and thus escape impersonal, bureaucratic religious rituals. Luther's discovery, however, was that the experience of God is not to be found in a system of signification of the text's exoteric or esoteric meanings but rather in what the text *does* (and not just what it allegorically signifies) to one. The "letter" of scripture does not primarily refer to a "spiritual" meaning behind the text but is an inseparable embodiment of spiritual activity that remakes the human anew — calls forth trust in God. Hence, one should not translate the text into one's own spiritual journey. That only reinforces a disembodied, enthusiastic "god-within-ism," just as mysticism does. Rather, one should cling to the external *(externum)* word that gives the new life it promises. Again, it is the "God preached" who makes the believer certain of faith in opposition to the "hidden God" that one ultimately encounters in mystic experience.

Forde brings this critical distinction to bear on Barth's Christology in the third essay, "Karl Barth on the Consequences of Lutheran Christology." As is well known, Barth complained that the Lutheran Christology's affirmation of the "communication of attributes" *(communicatio idiomatum)* between the divine and the human in Jesus Christ — including the *genus maiestaticum,* the view that the glorified humanity of Christ is everywhere present — opens the door for the Feuerbachian position that

theology at heart is anthropology. For Feuerbach, humanity (and humanity alone), properly understood, is divine. Furthermore, for Barth, Lutheran Christology is too abstract, too removed from the actual history of
God with and in Jesus of Nazareth. Forde, remarkably sympathetic to these
concerns, nevertheless argues that Barth's fatal flaw was to hold that Christology is itself insufficient to secure the field against the abstraction and
subjectivism that Barth fears. Indeed, Barth's Christology contributes to
the very problems he is trying to solve. Forde is skeptical that history can
be the "great solvent" of abstraction. Is the eternal *Gottesgeschichte* behind,
in, or above human history? Barthian Christology offers only an earthly
shadow of the eternal history of God. He also charges that Barth's appeal
to history is finally an appeal to *our* history — and thus it is itself vulnera-
ble to the charge of subjectivism. The only answer to the conundrums of
Barth's quasi-Nestorian response to Lutheran orthodoxy is proclamation
— delivering the "preached God." Barth's problem was that he tries to remove "God not preached" with theoretical Christology, but only proclamation can do that!

Doing the Word

The second section, "Doing the Word," continues the pastoral focus of this
collection of essays by specifically focusing on preaching, baptism, the
Lord's Supper, and the office of absolution. Forde is clear that the authority for these public acts comes from the authority of the Word itself. While
our culture has tended to make religion into a private matter of conscience, Forde asserts it is God himself who makes the ministry into a public office — one that "crosses the line," a vehicle through which God invades the orders of this age to set free those captivated by sin, law, and
demonic power. In the office of the ministry, the kingdom of God "stakes
out a claim," and sets up an "embassy" by which eschatological liberating
power is unleashed. Given our disputes over the nature of the public ministry, it is important to recognize that *no* other view offers a "higher" view
of ministry than that advocated by Forde, which is authorized by the
power of the Word alone.

Forde's "Preaching the Sacraments" is really composed of two lectures. "The Sacrament of Preaching" and "Preaching the Sacraments" were
first published in the *Lutheran Theological Seminary Bulletin* in 1984. Forde

argues that law and gospel are rightly divided in preaching when the sermon is not primarily didactic, but rather something that claims the listener on God's behalf. We need to "sacramentalize" the word: it gives Christ and all his blessings. Christ is *really present* in preaching! Hence, preachers need to be bold enough *to give Christ* to their hearers. Preachers are tempted to give the text a moral — translating it into our terms or allegorizing it in order to offer us something to do. We miss Luther's insight that it is the Scripture that interprets us. Preachers need to read the pericopes so as to allow themselves to be exegeted by them and then preach in a fashion that allows the text *to do its deed* to the hearers.

In the second part of this essay, Forde emphasizes that to preach the sacraments is to do a "visible word by means of an audible." The sacraments offer an alien word that counters our sin that is curved in upon itself, and permits the anxious conscience to be made secure. If one claims that the sacraments are in some sense "magical," then we must recognize that they offer *God's* magic and not ours. If one frets that "cheap grace" is offered in the sacraments, we should refocus the discussion to *radical grace* as God's sheer generosity. It concludes, as does this volume, with samples of Forde's preaching.

"Public Ministry and Its Limits" was published in *dialog* in 1991. Forde affirms that the legitimization of ministry can never be found in a historical episcopate modeled after the hierarchical patterns of this old, dying age, but rather is to be grounded in a new view of the doctrine of election. All too often predestination is mythologized as an atemporal story about God before the foundation of the world either choosing or rejecting the creatures that he would make. Forde notes that predestination only makes sense as God's action *in the living present* through the word to claim sinners as his own. Hence, he defines ministry in light of the doctrine of election as the "actual doing of divine election in the living present by setting bound sinners free through the word of the cross." God has ordained this public office for good order in the church. It is to be accountable to the public standards of the church. It does not suppose "canonical ordination" as it developed in the Eastern or Western traditions. In this regard Forde notes that Article 28 of the *Augsburg Confession* was not an apology for the traditional episcopate, but sought instead to bring bishops under the proper "eschatological limit" of the gospel. Luther's understanding of a liberating ministry cannot be properly grafted onto a tree with those sorts of episcopal roots.

"Something to Believe" was published in *Interpretation* (1993) following the influential argument of Karl Barth against infant baptism. Forde underscores baptism as providing objectivity to faith. Baptism leads us outside ourselves to an objective referent — God's promise that comes in and with this bath. Hence the necessity for baptism is grounded in the unconditional gospel as a sheer gift apart from any legality. Baptismal faith is grounded in the activity of the triune God to save. The external sign of water in sacramental action allows faith to have something to cling to. Forde contends that without such a tactile and tangible event like baptism, faith would have nothing to believe! Hence, faith is based on the irreducible externality of this specific act in opposition to any attempt to subjectivize it. It is the free gift alone, given in baptism, that destroys the self that wants to stay in control of one's life — to be one's own "god" for oneself. Baptism leads to faith and not vice versa, as most modern theologians assert. If it were otherwise, faith would end up believing in itself, its own power to believe, and so a kind of fideism. Baptism is the perfect cure for the modern, narcissistic self, which Forde views as a "black hole."

"The Lord's Supper as the Testament of Jesus" was published in *Word and World* (1997). In that essay Forde retrieves Luther's well-known construal of the Lord's Supper as "testament" — as in "last will and testament." Such a testament offers an inheritance to its rightful heirs. The Lord's Supper is misunderstood when it is conceived of as our prayer, action, or sacrifice. Instead, the Lord's Supper is Christ's institution that makes the church by carrying out the will of Jesus diachronically, extending his will through time, delivering his promise and gifts to his own.

"Absolution: Systematic Considerations" has never been published, but was delivered as a lecture at Luther Seminary. Forde draws on the theme developed in the first essay of this volume, that absolution — as a pastoral activity — is the "answer" to the problem of the absolute, the old being's rejection of its power. Absolution is an irresistible word that recreates the new being. He develops this theme with regard to Luther's "bound will" masterfully interpreted not as an abstract, anthropological speculation, but as the actual, attempted "power struggle" that the old being inevitably wages with the "hidden God." We are bound to say "no" to the absolute — by affirming atheism, or remaking God as more palatable, or buying God off with our purported goodness. As noted earlier, this God cannot be explained away. With absolution, however, we as "controllers" die — the old being is no longer in charge of his or her life. Forde thus urges pastors to be more courageous with the office of the keys. One should not be afraid to deliver the unconditional absolution even to those who have not seemingly "changed" or improved their moral lives. Only the unconditional absolution can kill sin — nothing within a person can do that.

Called to Freedom

The third set of essays concerns the Christian life as a call to freedom. Forde is arguing that a forensic, non-transformative doctrine of justification is the irreplaceable center and criterion of any discussion of Christian life, and just so he counters the current self-indulgent libertinism of American culture. Human sanctification is in God's hands, not ours. Forde's is neither a "pro-nomian" nor an antinomian stance for giving shape to a Christian life as if grace were meant to perfect human nature. Instead, grace allows humans to be liberated from their curved-in life so they can in fact live as God intended them to live — honoring and loving him above all things and serving their neighbors and creation.

"Lutheran Faith and American Freedom" was Forde's way to explore the meaning this teaching has for distinguishing church and state. In America this distinction is too often a separation that functions as a divorce between church and state. "Freedom" in our nation often becomes a sham self-expressive license that is really nothing but bondage to greed and lust. Americans feel they are entitled to all that life has to offer, instead of receiving God's good things as gifts. Consequently, when their insatiable desires as self-centered competitor-citizens are not met, many Americans see themselves as scapegoats or victims. Even the "theology of the cross" is misrepresented in this situation, as a kind of glorification of the victim — the illusion that Jesus identifies with us in our frustrations — rather than as the accusation that we are the ones who have victimized Jesus. It becomes a "negative theology of glory": even if you can't prove yourself through your efforts, you can at least suffer! Such claims of victimization, so prevalent now in the church, produce either self-righteous hypocrites who identify with the alleged victim, or despair of systems beyond the power of any one individual or group to transform. We clearly need a resurrection! Genuine Christian freedom is not commensurate to or even compatible with "American" permissivism. Free *from* the law, we are free *for* others. Free *from* self-centeredness and its clamor of entitlement, we can be free *to* uphold our neighbor.

In "Fake Theology: Reflections on Antinomianism Past and Present" (*dialog*, 1983), Forde addresses the antinomianism of current American culture, which as a result of its affluence has for nearly four decades encouraged an ethos of "do your own thing." We might say that Thomas Jefferson's rational self-centered "pursuit of happiness" has degraded into irrational self-pleasuring. Neither of these self-centered positions harmonizes with the new life of the gospel. Ironically, such antinomianism always has a hidden *nomian* agenda embedded somewhere within it. Even the licentious American is bound to "be all that he or she can be" — and therefore hardly free. Forde's point is that you cannot end the law simply by attempting to remove its offense or making it do-able. Christ alone will be the end of the law. Forde distinguishes three views: nomism, overt antinomianism, and covert antinomianism. Nomism is the refusal to allow the eschatological gospel to have its way in our lives. While some Christians will think this route preferable to antinomianism, it finally is a denial of Christ's efficacy in human life. Overt antinomianism affirms that since Christ is the end of the law, then it is no longer relevant for Christian life. This view seeks to realize the eschaton by a theological *tour de force*. It fails to recognize the simultaneity in the believer of saintliness, one free from law, and sinfulness, one still held under law. Forde's response to this view is that Christ is the end of the law to faith — the law cannot be shouted down, it can only be nailed to the cross. The hope of antinomianism is not wrong, but it is premature — only the eschaton will fully end the incurvated self. Covert antinomianism seeks to change the law, make it more adaptable, perhaps add a "third use of the law." Forde notes that this view merely accommodates to sin; in the guise of ethics the law is "watered down" in the attempt to make it do-able. When Christ is experienced as the end of the law for faith, then we are drawn into the world of the neighbor for whom we spontaneously live.

In this same vein, a specific ethical issue is addressed in "Human Sexuality and Romans, Chapter One," a lecture given at Luther Seminary as part of that school's discussion about the way the church would address current issues concerning sexual behavior. Forde takes up the claim of victimization of a specific social group, those who do homosexual practices. He brings the law/gospel hermeneutic to bear on this potentially church-dividing issue. His point is that all humans stand under God's judgment and thus are in no position to condemn others. Nevertheless, specifically with regard to homosexual practices, Paul indicates that this is itself an expression of divine wrath. It cannot be legitimated for the sake of securing self-expressive homosexual "pleasure." Indeed, the answer is not to find loopholes for this sin, but to offer absolution. Forde points out that our hermeneutics — unlike all contemporary approaches to hermeneutics — must enable us to be rendered passive before God. Are we being exegeted by the Scriptures — do we allow them to scrutinize our lives and give us God's promise? The authority of Scripture lies in its power to find, expose, and establish the being of its hearer. From the perspective of the gospel, no law can be imposed on believers — even if it is commanded by God! For faith, Christ is the end of the law — and nothing else. Indeed, the law "hounds" us until we are in Christ. If the law were endless, one would inevitably believe that one must fashion an end of it for one's self. Nevertheless, a Christian may affirm that the Mosaic law is still useful — it may agree with "natural law," for instance. In other words, the gospel permits one to become more natural, to be fully human, living by faith and not driven by a quest for security or self-legitimization. Forde is absolutely convinced of the effectual power of this word — and it alone — to radically transform the world, including sexual practices. Our culture tends to idolize sex — exploit it and not receive it as a gift to be enjoyed and given within divinely established limits. As such, sex too can be a vehicle of God's "wrath," our very practices creating a system and climate ruled by death and not life. God's word alone creates the pathos of new life, allowing human sexuality to be more natural.

"The Lutheran View of Sanctification" was published in a text entitled *Christian Spirituality* in 1988. It came as a request from teachers at the Bethel Seminary in New Brighton for Professor Forde to lay out the Lutheran teaching and have responses from various traditions in light of his remarkable claims. In brief, Forde argued that sanctification is not an addition to faith, but is "getting used to" justification. Sanctification is misunderstood if it is assumed to be a process temporally happening in the believer's life after justification. Rather, sanctification is simply "getting used" to our justification. It is primarily a work of the Holy Spirit and not a work that we do or by which we cooperate with God. The moral life is primarily the business of the "old age" — civil righteousness. Sanctification is not our ascent to God, but God's descent as new being to us — rearranging us to become spontaneously a neighbor to those in need. We are

reborn as humans, not gods. This view of sanctification exposes the rot-
tenness of much religion as attempting to map or control the eternal, to
negotiate with God on the basis of moral bargaining chips. Rather, true
sanctification is to be found in the belief that God has taken charge of the
matters of life. God is worshiped when he is listened to, in the external
word that delivers the promise. Our daily life is not a growth in holiness,
but a process of returning to baptism, always beginning again, as Luther
put it. God moves in on us, not we on God.

"Reflections on the Fries-Rahner Proposal: Thesis I" has a technical,
and not very interesting, title. Yet it lays out a crucial ecumenical argument. In the mid-1980s the most talked-about proposal for ecumenical relationships among Christian churches was the Fries-Rahner proposal. Its
main idea was that the basic content of Christian belief and practice could
be described and agreed upon — even with a variety of *ways of understanding* that core teaching. So, for example, they proposed that we all
ought to agree upon the Trinitarian understanding of God, the full humanity and divinity of Christ, the central place of baptism and the Eucharist in the church, along with basic moral obligations for Christians. The
proposal then sought to lay out where this basic teaching is found, and
once agreement on the doctrinal and moral teaching of the church is
reached, we would then be able to declare unity among churches. These
theologians then developed a series of basic theses to test the possibility of
a common agreement and unity among churches. None of the theses were
more basic than the first thesis, which was given to Professor Forde to discuss among the gathered ecumenists: "The Fundamental truths of Christianity, as they are expressed in Holy Scripture, in the Apostles' Creed, and
in that of Nicea and Constantinople, are binding on all partner churches of
the one Church to be."

Professor Forde himself said that upon first glance it did not seem
that there was much to say about such a general thesis — it seemed so pa-
tently agreeable. But, on second glance this very general statement provided the opportunity for Forde to present what has been the repeated
problem in ecumenical discussions. Ecumenical discussions have always
had two levels, even if not consciously addressed. The first level could be
called "dogmatic." On that level the first thesis of the Fries-Rahner proposal was true to the confession that all Lutherans publicly make. But there
is another level that Forde calls "hermeneutical," which, when not ac-
knowledged and addressed, always leads to the same result: a kind of

agreement on the doctrinal content of statements, but then two very different kinds of "readings" of the same statement. This kind of problem of "reception," as it is often called, has occurred every time a purported agreement is made, whether the *Called to Common Mission* between the Episcopal Church in the USA and the Evangelical Lutheran Church in America, or the Joint Declaration on the Doctrine of Justification signed by Vatican authorities and the Lutheran World Federation representatives.

Forde describes these two kinds of readings as two radically different presuppositions about what faith is and how it is made: either "the move one makes in becoming Christian is from bondage to freedom," or it is "from freedom to bondage." Another way of saying the same thing is that there is a notable difference in meaning for dogmatic statements when one "reads" them from the point of view of the preaching of the gospel, or the distinguishing of law and gospel. When one distinguishes law and gospel, then the highest form of authority is always the proclamation of the gospel itself as the act of liberating sinners — even and especially from the law and death. Once that assertion is made, the church and all its laws and structure must serve this one deed of proclamation, or such laws and structure are subordinate to the gospel itself. In that way of working, dogma and ecumenical agreements on dogma become "rules for proclamation." But rules for proclamation function only in the sense that true authority always liberates for true proclamation rather than binds sinners back to the law. In other words, when the specific way that faith is made is by *preaching,* and when that presupposition is front and center, then church order and especially the particular shape of the office of ministry itself is put in the second place of service to the gospel. The shape of the ministry and church order, including the forms of ordination, are not part of the good news itself. Once that distinction is made, this immediately clears the way for a real ecumenism by setting the shaping of the office of ministry by means of human traditions in a lower place that cannot be required for the true unity of the church — even whatever true church "is to be," as the Fries-Rahner proposal put it.

Forde's contribution to ecumenism in his long service on the American Roman Catholic/Lutheran dialog is well documented. In this essay on Fries-Rahner, Professor Forde offers this important theological contribution to ecumenical work, and one of his most extended comments on the work of the other foremost Lutheran ecumenical theologian of the past generation, George Lindbeck. All ecumenical discussion will always be functioning, knowingly or not, on the two levels of dogma and hermeneutics. The Lutheran proposal for ecumenical work remains the very fruitful notion that the proclamation of the gospel is the highest authority, indeed the only necessary and sufficient authority, that creates true unity of churches. The way faith is made is through word and sacrament. The way unity among churches or communions of churches is made is the same. But of course all of this assumes that becoming Christian as individuals or whole communities or the universal church itself is God's work of moving us from bondage to sin into freedom even from the law. As Forde says, "the purpose of rules, even for preaching, is to drive to the proclamation of the gospel. But the gospel is the 'end,' the goal, the *telos* and *finis* of the law to faith." This ecumenical openness has always been feared by Lutherans and others alike, but is the key to a truly ecumenical future for all. The office of ministry is God's institution for the proclamation of the gospel, but its shaping by human traditions cannot determine who is in communion with whom in the one, holy, catholic, and apostolic church. The proclamation of the gospel as the act of true liberation alone does that. Such freedom opens the ecumenical door so wide that most have sought to shut it lest the wrong sorts get in.

The final essay in this volume was Forde's Presidential Address to the Luther Congress that met at Luther Seminary in St. Paul in 1993, published in the *Lutherjahrbuch* in 1995. In it Professor Forde asserted that freedom has always been the great pursuit of all intellectual study, but even among Christians becomes a defensive doctrine. That is, freedom always seems to be put in the service of some presumed higher goal or value like preserving the place of the law in salvation. Yet for Luther, at least, freedom was the highest goal, and so his teaching made of freedom what Forde calls "an offensive" doctrine. It is untamed. It identifies a historical limit to the law in Christ himself (and alone). Forde asks his poignant question: "Can humans really handle such freedom?" Apparently not, that is, except in the form of the vision given by the gospel to humans in the form of their sure and certain hope. We will one day be free. But this is not only waiting for what will come, it is a hope based in a belief in creation right now. That is, humans are precisely created for the kind of freedom that lives outside the law and is utterly free of sin. They are meant, then, to do "what they want." But that has always been the very fear of all good-minded moralists and the thing that must be avoided, Christian or not, at all cost.

Reading Forde here leads in the only possible direction for this theology — to the preaching of the law and gospel itself. Of course, there is nothing like reading Forde himself on these matters. If you read closely, who knows? Perhaps there really will be an improvement in preaching. We, like many before and after us, have often been moved to say, following such lectures that you will read here: "If what you say is true, then what is to keep us from doing this now?" What indeed! So, we conclude these lectures and essays with a collection of sermons preached by Gerhard Forde over the course of his teaching at Luther Seminary, from the 1960s to the 1990s. These sermons are examples of "doing of the text," as Forde himself taught it. Thus, with thankfulness for his faithful teaching and with hope that it will produce more good preaching, we present this second collection of writings from this most important of American Lutheran teachers, Gerhard Olaf Forde.

MARK C. MATTES
STEVEN D. PAULSON

GOD PREACHED AND NOT PREACHED

Whatever Happened to God?
God Not Preached

Some years ago one would now and again see signs and bumper stickers announcing: "Jesus Is the Answer." The smart-aleck comeback was, of course, "If Jesus is the answer, what is the question?" Usually that was enough to shut down the whole discussion right away; no one could agree what the question was. The question, however, has gradually become more clear to me: *Whatever happened to God?* It is this question that I will answer in this essay, affirming: *Jesus is the answer.* Jesus is what happened to God.

There is a weightier concern here than what one might find on bumper stickers — a matter vital to both theology and preaching: *the vital and overlooked distinction that Luther makes between God-not-preached and God-preached.* People with even a cursory knowledge of Luther know about his distinction between God *hidden* and God *revealed.* God is *hidden* apart from his deeds in Old and New Testaments and *revealed* in them for the salvation of sinners. In a crucial passage in the *Bondage of the Will,* however, Luther links the distinction to preaching. In our everyday discourse we can speak quite differently about God than when we preach. If we do not observe this distinction, Luther insists, the consequences are devastating for theology, ministry, and particularly the proclamation of the church.

Whatever Happened to God?

God has been explained to death. When I sit through a synod convention with its tedious debates and predictable resolutions, or when I read synodical reports in *The Lutheran,* and much current material reputed to be theology in books or journals, the question arises for me: *Whatever happened to God?* Why does God never enter the discussion as a deciding factor?

In these discussions there is much obligatory and (mostly) innocuous talk about God — often pious platitudes about the fact that God is love. But since God is just love, love, love, God fails to enter the conversation in any decisive way. One particular ELCA synod, for example, while debating a controversial resolution, said that they should be "guided by the liberating gospel of Jesus Christ." Someone had the audacity to suggest an amendment to the effect that they should be guided *both* by the restraining law of God and also the liberating gospel. The amendment was defeated, making the synod *officially* antinomian!

I have spent most of my career insisting on the doctrine of justification by faith alone, particularly that Christ is the end of the law to everyone who has faith. But today it seems as though there is a kind of gospel *Schwärmerei* among us. It is not the *proclamation* of Christ alone as the end of the law that drives us, but rather an *explanation* of the gospel that ends up putting the law out of commission. When explanation is substituted for the proclamation of Christ, the result is antinomianism. The end of the law and source of our freedom is no longer *Christ,* but *theology.* This is a terrible and fatal mistake. The theologian, the board, or the committee can report its findings and assure us that God is no longer miffed or wrathful at us! (But think: Have you ever been absolved by a board? Is there any comfort in that?)

What would St. Paul say? "Explanation and committee action are the end of the law to all those who heed it"? But, after all, what should we expect? If God is love, how could God be against anything at all? We seem to have gotten the idea that a loving God cannot be against anything (except, perhaps, being unloving). If God is love, and we are his loving people, the reality of God simply drops out of our reckoning, no matter how much God-talk there is. The wrath of God has become relic of a by-gone era. The upshot is: "God" is more or less a meaningless cipher.

Decadent Pietism

We suffer today from what might be called decadent pietism. It can be called a pietism because it is very sincere, religious, and heartfelt. Its decadence appears, however, when the question is asked: "Whatever happened to God?" Traditional pietism thought it important, first and foremost, to "get right with God" — to experience conversion and feel at peace with the ultimate judge. Furthermore, after getting right with God, one sought to live a morally upright life, guided by the law of God. But in a world where God is just a harmless cipher — just love, love, love — no one needs to worry about getting right or coming to peace with *God*. Our decadent pietists are chiefly interested in getting right with *themselves*. The language is all too familiar: accept or affirm one's self-esteem, own one's feelings. This "getting right with oneself" includes learning how to affirm others in their "self-chosen lifestyle" — becoming "inclusive," "liberated," "open," and "tolerant." We now have what Ludwig Feuerbach said long ago: God is just a projection of the self. This — as Karl Marx already saw — is just pietism gone decadent.

Whatever happened to God? God has been taken to the theological and psychological cleaners. A dominant obsession of most theologies in modernity has been to domesticate God, to explain away everything offensive about God, to absolve God of blame. In terms of Luther's distinction, instead of the preached-God, many theologians today give us all manner of opinions and explanations of the God-not-preached. They give us theodicies, apologies, exonerations, theories, whitewashings, and excuses for God. They even attempt to change God's name! God has been cut down to *our* size: tamed, sanitized, and turned into a harmless pet.

God, the Wild One

I have always liked the scene in C. S. Lewis's *The Lion, the Witch and the Wardrobe,* where Mr. and Mrs. Beaver prepare the children to meet Aslan, Narnia's God-figure:

> "Is — is he a man?" asked Lucy.
>
> "Aslan a man!" said Mr. Beaver sternly. "Certainly not. I tell you he is the King of the wood and the son of the great Emperor-Beyond-the-

Sea. Don't you know who is the King of Beasts? Aslan is a lion — *the* Lion, the great Lion."

"Ooh!" said Susan, "I'd thought he was a man. Is he — quite safe? I shall feel rather nervous about meeting a lion."

"That you will, dearie, and no mistake," said Mrs. Beaver. "If there's anyone who can appear before Aslan without their knees knocking, they're either braver than most or else just silly."

"Then he isn't safe?" said Lucy.

"Safe?" said Mr. Beaver. "Don't you hear what Mrs. Beaver tells you? Who said anything about safe? 'Course he isn't safe. But he's good. He's the King, I tell you."[1]

Later on, when they are being pursued by those whom they perceive to be their enemies, there is Aslan, leading the pack.

Whatever happened to this God, the wild one? Whatever happened to the God who spoke to Job out of the whirlwind?

> Where were you when I laid the foundations of the earth?
> Tell me if you have understanding?
> . . . when the morning stars sang together,
> and all the heavenly beings shouted for joy?
> . . . Or who shut in the sea with doors. . . .?
> . . . Have you commanded the morning since your days began?
> and caused the dawn to know its place?
> . . . Have you entered the springs of the sea?
> . . . Can you bind the chains of the Pleiades?
>
> (Job 38:4, 7-8, 12, 16, 31)

In other words, God asks, "Who do you think you are?" Job is confronted with the riddle of the tremendous variety of life in all its forms, that incredible and puzzling menagerie — from the aardvark to the zebra, the elephant, the ostrich, leviathan. He meets all their strange habits, seeing the near-human and the far-from-human, and is forced to ask their staring faces: Who are you? Why are you here? What in the world did God have in mind?

---

1. C. S. Lewis, *The Lion, the Witch and the Wardrobe* (New York: Macmillan, 1981), p. 74.

Whatever happened to God, the God of the Psalm 8?

O, Lord, our Sovereign,
    how majestic is your name in all the earth!
You have set your glory above the heavens.
    Out of the mouths of babes and infants . . .
    You have founded a bulwark because of your foes . . .
When I look at your heavens, the work of your fingers,
    the moon and the stars that you have established;
what are human beings that you are mindful of them,
    and mortals that you care for them?

The God of Psalm 19?

The heavens are telling the glory of God;
    and the firmament proclaims his handiwork.
Day to day pours forth speech
    and night to night declares knowledge.
There is no speech, nor are there words;
    their voice is not heard;
yet their voice goes out through all the earth,
    and their words to the end of the world.

Whatever happened to the God of Isaiah 45?

I am the Lord, and there is no other,
    besides me there is no god;
    I arm you, though you do not know me,
so that they may know, from the rising of the sun
    and from the west, that there is no one besides me;
    I am the Lord and there is no other.
I form light and create darkness,
    I make weal and create woe,
    I the Lord do all these things.

Langdon Gilkey speaks of nature as an image of God: the infinite vastness, riddles, and ordered turmoil of the heavens; the vast beauty and power of the big bang; the puzzle of the black holes — the variety and certainly the terror of it all. But what about the world's catastrophes and tragedies? Could they be a part of God's natural image too? Would not famine and flood be enough to make us shake our fist in the face of God, or indeed, lose faith, or even disbelieve?

Whatever happened to the God of Psalm 139?

> Even before a word is on my tongue,
>   O LORD, you know it completely.
> You hem me in, behind and before,
>   and lay your hand upon me.
> Such knowledge is too wonderful for me;
>   it is so high that I cannot attain it.
> Where can I go from your spirit?
>   Or where can I flee from your presence?
> If I ascend to heaven, you are there;
>   If I make my bed in Sheol, you are there.
> If I take the wings of the morning
>   and settle at the farthest limits of the sea,
> even there your hand shall lead me,
>   and your right hand shall hold me fast.
> If I say, "Surely the darkness shall cover me,
>   and the light around me become night,"
> even the darkness is not dark to you;
>   the night is as bright as the day,
> for darkness is as light to you.

Modern theologies have made us so used to the idea that we are created in the image of God that we have, in effect, turned the original idea all around and imagined that God is made in our image. This is perhaps the biggest, most common, and most foolish theological error of our time.

Whatever happened to God? God has fallen victim to explanations, to theology itself — theology *about* God-not-preached. Explanation replaces proclamation. Lectures about God are substituted for preaching God. Our personal difficulties with God are assuaged with a little theological tinkering — perhaps a new name, a new image, a new theology more to our liking. Americans, George Steiner says, seek to democratize eternity.

The Suffering *God?*

A recent cartoon depicted people sitting around in hell with the flames licking up around them. One person was complaining to another, "What I am in here for is no longer a sin!" Instead of absolution, we break out our erasers to do battle with sin — like Lady Macbeth, trying to wash the blood off her hands. The problem for poor souls like the one in the cartoon is that theology is important to douse the flames of hell.

A theological revolution has taken place in our day, without a shot being fired! Admittedly, the idea that God suffers directly is heresy: patripassionism. However, this heresy has become a virtue, even a "new orthodoxy."[2] Ronald Goetz's list of theologians who espouse this "new orthodoxy" reads like a who's who of contemporary theology: Barth, Berdaev, Bonhoeffer, Brunner, Cobb, Cone (and other liberation theologians), Küng, Moltmann, Reinhold Niebuhr, Pannenberg, Ruether (and feminist theologians generally), Temple, Teilhard, Unamuno, etc. It is unquestioned that we should be grateful for God's suffering with us, that God is somehow "enriched" by our suffering.[3]

If God suffers, then what is the use of Jesus? The distinction between God-preached and God-not-preached is simply abandoned. God-not-preached is *explained* as being so nice that there really is no need for God-preached. More accurately, the distinction between the Father and the Son is lost. God, as such, simply drops out of the picture, and all those magnificent passages from the Psalms, Job, and Isaiah become an embarrassment.

Can we, as Luther put it, unmask the face of the hidden God? There is a fundamental fact which theologians — especially those who preach — have to learn again and again: the hidden God, the *Deus ipse in sua*

---

2. See Ronald Goetz, "The Suffering God: The Rise of a New Orthodoxy," *The Christian Century* 103, no. 13 (April 16, 1986): 385-89.

3. Goetz, "The Suffering God," p. 388. This is, of course, a very subtle and tricky theological question. We still want to maintain that God is involved in the suffering of Jesus for us, that God is for us in the suffering, dying, and risen Jesus — in the sacrament where he allows himself to be mishandled, spilt, dropped on the floor, and shamefully treated a thousand times over. All of this suffering can indeed be attributed to God-preached, and leads us into the doctrine of the Trinity. With its general ignorance of Trinitarian doctrine, however, the modern tendency is to collapse Jesus and God together. In other words, we have the unity of *essence*, but have forgotten the difference in *hypostasis*. In Trinitarian thinking, one should not unqualifiedly say that God "suffers" or is somehow "enriched by our suffering" any more than one should simply identify God incarnate with God transcendent.

majestate (God himself in his majesty), will not be tampered with. By taming the hidden God with our explanations, we also destroy the only real defense we have, the preaching of Jesus as reconciliation. It is not what we think about God that matters, but what God thinks about us and has to say to us, and has so authorized us to speak. The only solution to this problem of the absolute is absolution! God, you see, is not mocked. The wrath of God does not cease when theologians try to explain it away. "He that sitteth in the heavens shall laugh them to scorn; the LORD shall have them in derision!" (Psalm 2:4).

What happens when we try to alleviate our God-pain by saying that God suffers or is enriched by our suffering? As Goetz remarks, this is not much better than the idea of a sentimental butcher who weeps after every slaughter. (Even more egregious, might God even be enriched by humans suffering the torments of Hell?) Can such a God actually redeem the world? If God is enriched by our suffering, why not have more of it? Accompanying the idea that God suffers is the idea that God is limited, or that God is self-limiting. How then can his love be almighty and immutable? Goetz again notes:

> The doctrine that God is limited in power solves the problem [of evil] by sacrificing God's omnipotence. However, to my mind, any concept of a limited deity finally entails a denial of the capacity of God to redeem the world and thus, ironically, raises the question of whether God is in the last analysis love, at least love in the Christian sense of the term.[4]

In his argument with Erasmus, Luther said: "You say God is love, but not immutable." Calling God changeable does not still his wrath; it comes back in a different, more threatening form. As Goetz incisively puts it, "If the purpose of our life and death is finally that we contribute to the 'self-creation of God,' how, an outraged critic of God might demand, does God's love differ from the love of a famished diner for his meat course?"[5] If we are somehow necessary for God's self-realization, if God "needs us," we are just God-fodder. The immutable, sovereign, unsuffering, transcendent, omni-everything, theistic God — the God-not-preached — is terrifying enough, but at least he has not eaten us for lunch!

4. Goetz, "The Suffering God," p. 388.
5. Goetz, "The Suffering God," p. 388.

The Offensive God

The God-not-preached will not be so tamed. In the nineteenth century the offense of Jesus' divinity caused a Christological reformulation of Jesus as an ethicist, advocating the Fatherhood of God, the brotherhood of man, the immortality of the soul, and other such platitudes. However, the Fatherhood of God or brotherhood of man fails to thrill many today. Once Jesus is separated from the Trinity and God is explained in human notions of Fatherhood, matters just get worse. Instead of a God who can be named "Father" only within the Trinitarian relations and thus preached only as the Father of Jesus Christ, we infer our ideas from the tarnished images of human masculinity and Fatherhood. A paradigm shift that emphasizes the Motherhood of God is likewise no lasting remedy. That too will turn on us. When we shuffle the masks, wrath takes another form.

We need to reclaim the distinction between God-not-preached and God-preached, lest we lose hold of who God is, what God means for us, and why it matters to preach God in Jesus Christ. We have to stop *explaining* God. Words and opinions *about* God do not help anyone. Only the Word of God, a word *from* God can help. If we "let God be God," perhaps then we will understand what it means to say that "The fear of the LORD is the beginning of wisdom" (Proverbs 1:7). God created us because he is, always has been, and always will be love, not because he needs us to become it. God created us out of freedom, out of nothing, not so that we would need him, but for the sheer enjoyment — perhaps we could even say for fun, that we might glorify him, get a "charge" out of him, enjoy him forever.

A "Systematic" Concern

I have approached the task of Christian proclamation as a systematic theologian. My guiding question has been, "How do proclamation and systematic theology relate?" What does systematic theology have to contribute to proclamation? Is there a necessary relationship between the two? What happens if and when there is no systematic reflection on proclamation? Ultimately, what is systematic theology good for? My answer has been that, when done right, it is good for the preaching task of the church. In that light, are systematic theology and systematic theologians in fact doing any good? Are systematicians actually doing more harm than good? Has the task of theology become so conceived that it actually undercuts proclamation rather than serves it? Will systematicians become lecturers delivering learned, sometimes boring, sometimes interesting, discourses on God? Or will they foster a theology that upholds proclaiming the gospel?

Jesus Is the Answer: The Divine Risk

In the attempt to *explain* God, proclamation loses out. God becomes such a patsy that he no longer really matters; preaching, then, has no point. There is one truthful answer to the question, "Whatever happened to God?" It is: *Jesus!* Because Jesus happened to God, we are authorized, and commissioned, to speak for God, to preach God — not to explain or offer opinions about God. Wonder of wonders, we can actually deliver what God wants said!

What does it mean to proclaim, rather than explain, God? Specifically, what is the difference between theology — particularly systematics — and preaching? To be sure, they are necessarily related. But when they are not carefully distinguished, systematic theology — mostly a very bad systematic theology — shuts out the proclamation. The purpose of systematic theology is not to subvert proclamation but to drive to effective proclamation. When systematic theology is done properly, it will not be possible to cheat people with a mere lecture, or even a clever bit of exegesis. Instead, the gospel *must be* proclaimed. What is it, after all, that we are supposed to do if it pleased God by the folly of preaching to save those who believe? And just what is it we are supposed to be about as Christians when we bear witness to the faith that is in us, or especially, for pastors, when we get up into the pulpit on a Sunday morning?

Woody Allen: Armchair Theologian

A seminarian once reported how on internship she had some rather extensive and interesting conversations with Woody Allen, who had leased an old house that the church owned as a set for his next movie. When their conversation got around to theology, it turned out that Allen was a fairly astute theologian. (He could even recommend various books and biblical commentaries!) One day, he said to the young intern, "You know, I would like to believe, but I don't have the gift of faith." "Aha!" I said, "and what did you say then?" She reported honestly, "I didn't know what to say. He knew as much theology as I did. What was I to say?"

After thinking about it I responded, "Well, suppose you could have said something like this: 'Is this for real and not just idle chit-chat? Is this a confession? You would like to believe but you don't have the gift of faith? Well, hang on to your socks because I am about to give it to you!' And then you put your hand on his head and say, 'I declare unto you the gracious forgiveness of all your sins in the name of the Father, the Son, and the Holy Spirit. There! Now I gave it to you! Just as sure as you sensed my extended hand it is yours. Repent and believe it. And if you ever wonder about it or forget it come back and I'll do it again. Or, come to church. We do it there every Sunday. I'll wash you in it.'" "But oh," the student said, "that would take a lot of guts." To which I replied, "Of course, but in the church we call it Spirit! Why not, after all, take some chances, give it your best shot? Perhaps the man does not need any more explanations. He has heard them all. What it takes, finally, is proclamation. What can you lose?"

When faced with doubt — "I don't have the gift of faith" — shall we explain about God, his love, about how it is a free gift? Shall we piously conclude our encounter by saying, "Well, let's pray about it, and maybe one fine day, somewhere, somehow, you will get lucky, God will finally have mercy on you and swoop down out of the blue sky and you will get it"?

All that is pure Schwärmerei. It leaves the poor man on his own to make peace with an explanation. It is the dirtiest trick in the theological arsenal to be everlastingly explaining that justification, faith, and grace are free gifts, but never getting around to giving them: never, that is, moving from explanation to proclamation, never taking the risk of actually preaching! The gift is explained but never given. Proclamation means finally to stop talking about it, and actually to give it. It means not talking *about* God, but speaking *for* God.

But now the usual reaction I get to the advice I gave to the intern is one of anger and shock — even, or perhaps especially, from theologians and pastors. A thousand reservations can and usually are thrown up against the divine risk. Would it not be dangerous to say that to such an obvious sinner — a Jewish one to boot? Couldn't he get the wrong idea? What if he believed his sins actually were unconditionally forgiven? What if it became an occasion for license?

We can always think of many reasons why explaining would be safer. But perhaps the most prevalent response has to do with the proclaimer. You would tell the man you have the authority to give the gift of faith? Who do you think you are anyway? We could spend a lot of time, of course, working out a full and adequate theological answer to that objection, but for our purposes we can go directly to it.

Who do I think I am? Nobody special. Just a Christian. Just an "ambassador" for Christ. You do not even have to be ordained, believe it or not, to do it! (To be ordained just means ordered by the church to do it publicly; it means being entrusted with the public office.)

In and through Jesus, the crucified and risen one, a peculiar band has been unleashed on the world, commissioned and authorized to speak, not merely about, but for God. "The Lord gave the Word, and great was the company of the preachers," a "nation of priests," not just rabbis or theologians or philosophers of religion, a "priesthood of believers" who are sent to say it (not to themselves, but to those within earshot). Finally the great silence of eternity is to be broken; a voice comes through the mask. "You are mine! And don't you forget it!" Of course there is shock. When Jesus just up and forgave the paralytic, the crowds were amazed and offended. "Who can forgive sins but God alone?" they said. "Who do you think you are?" But eventually they glorified God who had given such authority to mortals.

Now if that example about the intern and the actor introduces us to the problem, we have a couple of things left to examine. First, we need to be more precise about what proclamation is, what kind of risk God has decided to take with proclamation. And second, we need to go back to the question about how this relates to the question of God, and our distinction between God-not-preached and God-preached.

Proclamation and Systematic Theology

What essentially is proclamation? We need to be quite careful and analytical here, narrowing the matter down to the bare bones, the basics, the "essence," to know what we are talking about. To get technical, I like to use the word "proclamation" for what we need to get at rather than "preaching." Proclamation is both more pointed and simultaneously covers a broader spectrum than preaching. Preaching tends to be limited to oral communication, pulpit speech, a specific act in worship or sometimes beyond it. And preaching can take a variety of forms that are not necessarily proclamation. There can be a kind of homiletical apology for Christian faith and life; there can be didactic preaching, there can be preaching as ethical discourse, and so on, any number of forms of oratory in and out of the pulpit. "Do not preach to me," children might say if a parent gets on their case about something. And all of those different forms can be legitimate forms of discourse in the church or among Christians at a given time. But we need to get at the heart of what is meant by proclamation, *evangelizesthai*, *Verkündigung*. A preacher has eventually to get around to and aim at proclamation. Not every sermon, certainly not even the entire sermon, will or must be proclamation. But it is what the theologian, the preacher, must eventually be aiming at. Finally you must stop talking about and around the matter and do it. Proclamation is both more specific and covers a wider spectrum than preaching. It is more specific in that it means the direct announcing of the will and deed of God for the hearer, the "I declare unto you . . ." or the "I baptize you in the name . . .", the moment of the actual giving of the gift. It covers a wider spectrum because it takes place elsewhere than in oral preaching, notably, in the sacraments and in the liturgy in general, the absolution, the benediction, blessings, and so on.

To delineate precisely what is meant by proclamation, it is necessary and helpful, at the outset, to distinguish between two different types of discourse employed in the church. We have already been doing that roughly by articulating the difference between explaining and proclaiming. This difference can be maintained as a difference between secondary and primary discourse. Explaining, talking, and writing about God and things theological is secondary discourse. It is the language of theology in general, the language of teaching, and particularly, for our purposes here, of scholarship or systematic theology. Secondary discourse is generally third-person, past-tense discourse. Proclamation, on the other hand, belongs to the primary discourse of the church. Proclamation in its paradigmatic or ideal form is first- to second-person, present-tense, unconditional address. The most obvious example (paradigmatic form) of such address is in the absolution: I declare unto you the gracious forgiveness of all your sins, in the name of the triune God. (When it comes right down to it, that is about all we have to say in a nutshell.) It is first- to second-person: I declare it to you. It is present-tense: here and now I do it. Not tomorrow, not next week, not on judgment day, but here and now in the living present. The deed is done. I give it to you. It is unconditional: I do not say, "God will forgive you if certain conditions are fulfilled, if you properly repent." Nor do I say that we will pray and hope that God will forgive you. I do not say, "May the Lord have mercy on you." No, I say it flat out: "I declare unto you the forgiveness of all your sins." It is proclamation. As such, it belongs to the primary discourse of the church, the chief way the church and the Christian address the world.

It is perhaps obvious from this that there are other kinds of communication that also belong to this primary discourse. The liturgy, for instance, belongs to such primary discourse, as well as the sacraments. Moreover the response to the proclamation, the language of repentance, confession, prayer, and praise also belongs to the primary discourse. Primary discourse as direct, present-tense, first- to second-person address demands the same kind of language in response. If I proclaim: I declare unto you the gracious forgiveness of all your sins, the corresponding response is likewise first-person, present-tense: I repent, I confess, I believe, I praise and thank you, O Lord, or perhaps even, I do not, I will not, I cannot. In any case it is primary. When the proclamation comes, "I declare to you the forgiveness of all your sins," the appropriate response is not, "Well, that's your opinion!" It is not my opinion. If I were to give my opinion of you, it could be something quite different! The proclamation is instead the divine address, speaking not my words but the word God has commissioned me to speak, not what I think, but what God has ordered me to say. The only possible response has to be primary discourse, discourse that is ultimately self-disclosure, revealing who you are. You can only say, I repent, I believe, or I do not.

The most helpful analogy to this difference between primary and secondary discourse is that of the difference between the language *of* love and language *about* love. One might compare it to the difference between writing a book about love, or giving a lecture on the essence of love, or the art of loving or some such, and actually saying "I love you" to one's beloved. It ought to be obvious that one should make a proper distinction between these two types of discourse. There is a place for both. Books about love, like books about God (systematic theology), can be helpful if they are wisely written. But books or lectures about love should never be substituted for the language of love, the word or the promise of the lover itself. Imagine the lover and the beloved arriving at the crucial moment where the word has to be spoken, where the beloved probably asks, "Do you love me?" And instead of an answer, a self-disclosure, a revelation, gets a lecture on the essence of love! Or even a song: "Love is a many-splendored thing."

Perhaps the beloved persists, "That's all very nice, and I suppose it's true, but that is not what I want to know. Do you love me?" The lover then takes another tack and tries to explain things about himself or herself: "Of course, I love everybody." The lover is, you see, a universalist! But of course it is all beside the point. Explanation, talk about love, has been confused with the word of the lover, the direct, first- to second-person address. Only one kind of talk will do in that situation: "I love you." Or at least, "I'm sorry, but I just do not love you." There is an indispensable place for both primary and secondary discourses, but they must not be confused. And it seems to me that one of the biggest temptations in theology today is to do precisely that: to confuse the lecture, the explanation, the remodeling, the attempting to penetrate the mask, with the proclamation, the primary discourse, the "I declare unto you." When that confusion is made, what happens is that the proclamation invariably gets lost and is ultimately silenced. We are left with a lecture — sometimes a second-rate one at that — instead of the commissioned promise. They must be distinguished.

But now we need to take one more step to complete the picture before we return to the question of how this relates to the question of God. If primary and secondary discourses, the word of God and words about God, or, for our purposes, proclamation and systematic theology, are to be carefully distinguished, they must also be properly related. As already established, you cannot have one without the other. The kinds of discourse, systematic theology and proclamation, are genuinely co-related. That is to say, without systematic theology, chances are there will be no proclamation. You might give entertaining lectures, dazzle people with your opinions about lofty matters; you might do insightful exegesis, and persuasive apologetics, but you will not proclaim. Without systematic theology — without, if I may be so bold, doing the sort of thing I am trying to do in these essays — the distinctions tend to get lost, and we forget what it means to proclaim, what our authorization is, what form it is to take, what we are supposed to be doing, and so on. Without systematic theology, we will not proclaim.

But likewise without proclamation, there will be no systematic theology — at least not proper systematic theology. If systematic theology does not understand the place of proclamation, and realize that its purpose is to drive to proclamation, then it will overstep its bounds and try to usurp proclamation. As we have noted, this is one of the major problems today: the explanation takes the place of the proclamation. Both systematic theology and proclamation then are losers. What results from this mess is that second-rate systematics takes the place of proclamation and second-rate proclamation is substituted for systematics.

Systematic theology has to recognize that its purpose is to drive to and foster the proclamation. It has to realize that there is no solution to the problem of God other than the proclamation. Systematic theology, that is, has to recognize that there are definite limits to the enterprise, boundaries to our explanations. It has to realize that proclamation is not the practical application or popularizing of systematic theories, but that it is itself the last move in the theological operation, the last step in the argument. If done properly, systematic theology leads one to the point where the only move left is to leave the lectern and enter the pulpit. That is what is meant, finally, by that example about the intern and the actor. The explanation is done properly only if one arrives at the point where the only thing left is to proclaim — there is literally no other way out. The only point, finally, in saying so loudly and persistently as we do in our systematics that grace, faith, and all those things are free and unconditional gifts is precisely to give them, to do it, to say it, to declare it unconditionally, no holds barred, to take the risk of proclamation. That is what God is up to in this world, because what happened to God is Jesus.

The Preached God

Now, if we have done our spadework, this brings us back once again to the problem of God. Whatever happened to God? God has fallen prey to bad systematics, to a messy soup of sentimental explanation and *ersatz* proclamation. Matters have not gotten better, however, but rather worse. Instead of the old, majestic, transcendent, immutable, almighty creator God, we get a God who supposedly needs us and so eats us for lunch. What we have forgotten is that the only real solution to the problem, the threat, the wrath of the *deus ipse* (God himself), the *deus absconditus* (the hidden God), is the proclamation authorized by the crucified and risen Jesus. The only solution to the terrifying God of election and predestination is not to explain him away, but to go ahead and do the electing. God, the almighty one, does not call off his election. God sends someone — an ambassador equipped with the credentials granted in Jesus, the preacher, the proclaimer — to go and do it. We have forgotten that we cannot do anything to tame or domesticate God, but that God can and has decided to do something about us. God has broken the silence of eternity to claim us in Jesus. And so we also must speak.

But when we undertake to speak for the God who has spoken to us in Jesus we must take careful account of the nature of such speaking and what we are authorized to say. Speaking for God is quite a different matter from speaking *about* God. When we speak for God we are not dealing in universals or abstract generalities or making inferences from them, like talking *about* love or the essence of love. Speaking for God means being authorized to say something concrete and specific now, "I love," or, in worship, "I absolve you." And one cannot draw universal conclusions from that as such about God. One cannot infer, for instance, that because I say "I love you" to someone, I love everyone. One cannot, that is, move simply from the concrete to the abstract universal without further ado. One must make a careful distinction between what can be said in preaching and what might be said in theology or secondary discourse.

This is a crucial lesson for theologians and preachers to learn today. Proclamation is quite a different matter from theology. The classic instance where just such a distinction was made was, as you might guess, by Luther in his battle with Erasmus over the bondage of the will. But most have fled from the distinction as though they had seen a ghost. Just about everyone, including very prominent Lutheran theologians like Paul Althaus and Wolfhart Pannenberg, has blown it when it comes to this vital distinction. Luther insisted we must speak about God-not-preached in a manner quite differently from God-preached. Proclamation (of God's Word) is of a quite different order from theorizing about God. The failure to observe this difference in theology and proclamation is one reason for the theological and practical chaos in which we find ourselves today. Let us look at it a bit more closely.

The particular instance in which the distinction between God-not-preached and God-preached was invoked by Luther was in the context of the discussion of a passage from Ezekiel (18:23) where God instructs the prophet to say to the people, "I desire not the death of the sinner, but rather that he should turn and live." Erasmus wants to treat the passage as an abstract theological statement, a statement about God in general, a premise from which one might draw general conclusions *about* God. Thus Erasmus reasons: If God does not desire the death of the sinner, the death of sinners must be due to the wrong exercise of free will.

Hence the following set-up results: God in general, in the abstract, in majesty, does not desire the death of the sinner. The only way to account for such death, therefore, must be free will. But if that is the case, what would be the message of the passage as far as the preacher is concerned? It could only be something like this: if you want to escape death, exercise free will, stop sinning, and turn to God.

Now what happens when Erasmus does that? First of all, as Luther was quick to assert, instead of being taken as proclamation and turned into a sweet word of gospel promise to the people, the text has been turned into a terrifying statement of law. If the text is about God not desiring death, then it was not a general statement about God but instruction to the prophet on what to preach to the suffering people. That is what always happens when the distinction between God-not-preached and God-preached is not observed. Instead of issuing in a concrete, particular declaration of the gospel, the unconditional gospel proclamation "for you," it gets turned into a conditional statement of the law: "If you want to escape death, stop sinning, exercise your free will! Turn to God." But how shall we do that? How shall we stop sinning? One may as well exhort us to stop dying! The proclamation gets turned into a death-denying project supposedly to be accomplished by us (even if with the help of grace) rather than a word that gives new life out of death.

What we must realize is that such theological reasoning, in general, does not and cannot get us off the hook with God. Only the proclamation can do that. Only if we make a clear and conscious distinction between God-not-preached and God-preached that drives to proclamation will we ever get the hidden God, the God of wrath, off our backs. Theology — systematic, biblical, apologetic, or what have you — does not finally deliver anything but law. Indeed, the purpose of theology, and especially systematic theology, is to drive us to preaching, proclamation. When it is done properly, it should leave us in the spot where we have no other way out than to proclaim, to come out and actually say it: "Here it is! It's for you!" To do theology properly is to come to the realization that there is absolutely no other solution to the problem of God.

Let us look more closely at the classic passage. I expect it is the single most controversial and offensive passage in all of Luther, and probably in all subsequent theology, the one on which just about everyone has choked. Luther argued that Erasmus' mistake in their debate over Scripture was to fail to make the proper distinction between law and gospel, and thus to turn gospel passages into terrifying law. But of course, then the next question would be about law and gospel. Even if one does make the proper distinction, why is it that some are touched by the preaching of the law so as to hear the gospel and others not? This is the 64-million-dollar question — of course it was Luther who put it, not Erasmus. (Generally, in cases of really tough arguments, those who know what they are talking about have to take over the argument from the opponent and put forward really tough questions themselves — see Paul in Romans!) Why are some converted by the preaching and others not? Here, Luther says, theology has reached the end of the line. We have come up against the question of the *deus absconditus,* the hidden God, the God-not-preached. There is, Luther says, *nothing* you can do about this God. Indeed, you must leave him alone. God in hidden majesty will just eat you for lunch and enjoy it if you try to take him on. *This God wills not to be known.* Knowledge of this God is of the sort that is "high — too wonderful for us!" This God wills not to be known, and so will not be known. The classic passage reads:

> God must therefore be left to himself in his own majesty, for in this regard we have nothing to do with him, nor has he willed that we should have anything to do with him. But we have something to do with him insofar as he is clothed and set forth in his Word, through which he offers himself to us and which is the beauty and glory with which the psalmist celebrates him as being clothed (the clothed God!). In this regard we say, the good God does not deplore the death of his people which he works in them, but he deplores the death which he finds in his people and desires to remove from them. For it is this that God as he is preached is concerned with, namely, that sin and death should be taken away and we should be saved. For "he sent his word and healed them" [Ps. 107:20]. But God hidden in his majesty neither deplores nor takes away death, but works life, death, and all in all. For there he has not bound himself by his word, but has kept himself free over all things.[6]

6. LW 33: 140.

The really shocking and offensive statement for theology, ever since, has been the last sentence: God in his hidden majesty has not bound himself by his word, but has kept himself free over all things. The shock and the offense that sets everyone howling is in the objection that if God in hidden majesty, the *deus ipse,* the *deus nudus,* the *deus absconditus,* had not bound himself by his word, how then can we be sure that he will stick to his revealed word? How do we know that he will not just arbitrarily change his mind and reject us, or as he once did in the flood, just wipe us all out? Here, it is thought, we have at last found a place where Luther made a serious theological mistake — one which if allowed to stand would undercut his entire theology of the word. In a real sense, just about every modern theology from orthodoxy through pietism to liberalism and finally contemporary theology like that of Karl Barth has hidden in its innermost recesses the attempt to tie the hidden God to the revealed word — to make sure that God is not, so to speak, unbounded, unlike Aslan, wild and on the loose. Theology, that is, tries to bring God to heel, to domesticate him, pull his fangs, and make him a theological house pet. Instead of getting bitten, you just get gummed to death!

But the point in the passage is that Luther refused to do that. Why? Was it just an oversight, a fatal mistake? Not at all. Luther realized that theology as such is unable to bring God to heel. Luther realized that there was exactly nothing we can do in our theology about God hidden in majesty, God-not-preached. The reason Luther said that God hidden in majesty has not bound himself to the word was the same as the reason for much that appears offensive to us in his theology: because it is simply a matter of the truth, the facts of the case. God has not left himself at our disposal. We do not own God just because he has given us his word. There is nothing we can do about God hidden in majesty, God in the abstract, God-not-preached. The only solution to the problem of God-not-preached is God-preached. The only answer to the question of what the hidden God is up to is the concrete, present-tense, here-and-now proclamation: God sent his word and healed them — for Luther, that means the living word, it means that God arranged not to send something so abstract even as "the revealed word," not even to send a book; but God arranged and authorized to send a preacher to say, "I declare unto you . . ." in the name of God. Luther realized that nothing, absolutely nothing else would help. That is why it is absolutely essential for Luther to make the distinction between God-not-preached and God-preached and to be clear about how speaking relates to both.

Think for a moment. What would it mean if you were to say that Luther was wrong here and that you have to make sure that the hidden God is theologically tied down to and identified with an abstraction, even in something so theologically beyond suspicion as "the revealed word"? What would that mean? (In trying to understand Luther at his most difficult points it is always useful to think of the consequences of the opposite case.) With reference to the question of God, in the passage they were arguing about that would mean — just as Erasmus held — that "I desire not the death of the sinner" would be taken as a statement of general truth about God. But now what are the facts of the case? Look around. The fact is that sinners are dying like flies! If one is to take that at face value it must mean that the hidden God, the *deus ipse,* who supposedly desires not the death of the sinner nevertheless apparently cannot do anything about it! So once again we find ourselves in the same mess we noted before. In trying to improve God's public image by our theological remodeling we succeed only in making matters worse. We end up with a God who would like to stop the death of sinners, but apparently cannot do anything about it. We end up with a God who is no help and, finally, no comfort.

With reference to us, the very nature and freedom of faith is endangered. Since theology has tried to penetrate the mask of the hidden God by peddling some general metaphysical "truths," faith becomes not trust in the proclamation but strives toward sight, to become a kind of *gnosis.* The very freedom of faith, ironically, gets lost. Instead of driving to proclamation as the only possible way to relate to God, theology becomes an intellectual *tour de force,* an attempt subtly to force belief in the God it has made up. Faith is a matter of being set free to believe and trust, not a matter of being coerced into something. Faith is the spirit-fired free flight from God-not-preached, to God-preached.

What Luther realized supremely is that no one, no theology, nothing, can save us from the terror of the *deus ipse,* except the proclaimed word of God-preached. What Luther realized was the absolute necessity for and supreme importance of preaching. Not even God, God-not-preached, that is, the hidden God, can do anything about sin except to come and say, "I forgive you." That is the only remedy. The law is not a remedy. God could not come and say, "Come on folks, stop your sinning now and be nice." Even if we did, we would only become so proud of our effort that we would think we could get along without God. So the law only makes sin worse. The only theological remedy for sin is to forgive it, actually to absolve it, to take the risk of doing it. The *idea* that God is forgiving, you see, does not do any good. God must send someone to do it here and now. Even the idea that God so loved the world that he gave his only begotten Son — the idea, true as it is, and the basis for everything — is not enough. It is past tense: God so loved, that he gave. But what does he do today, for you? The scriptural word *must*, through proper theological reflection — the purpose of systematic theology! — be used to drive to the preaching, the proclamation: Yes it is true, God so loved that he gave. But now, therefore, I today, here and now give it: This is my body given for you; my blood shed for you. Eat it! Drink it!

What Luther knew and what the theological world seems to have forgotten is that unless we distinguish between our talk of God-not-preached and of God-preached, what results will simply be the loss of preaching itself. We just will not venture the risk of proclamation. A kind of bad systematic (or unsystematic?) theology gets substituted for proclamation, and no one will really do it. The only result then is that we do not avail ourselves of the only plan God has for human salvation. God-not-preached, the hidden God, goes his majestic way. Nothing can alter that. That God can do nothing as such about sin and death. God knows, if we can so phrase it, that he cannot help us by theological adjustment. As Luther rather frighteningly expressed it: God hidden in majesty neither deplores nor takes away death, but works life, death, and all in all. There is nothing God can do for us on that level. The only solution is God's coming in Jesus and the proclamation authorized thereby: therein it is seen that God-preached deplores the death he finds in his people and desires to remove from them. The only solution, that is, to the problem of God, to the problem of life and death, is the proclamation, the present-tense "I love you," I forgive you, I baptize you, I give you my body and blood of the New Testament.

What we must admit is that there just is not any other way. Nothing solves the problem for the lover wondering what the beloved thinks except the "I love you." Certainly a lecture on the essence of love does no good. Even a lecture on how nice a person the beloved is does no real good. The general idea that the beloved is a kind and loving person does no good. The silence has to be broken. There has to be a living word, a present-tense, I-to-you declaration. Somebody, that is, must take the risk of proclamation. God did. And so our only commission is to follow and do it. God was in Christ, not in theology, not in the mind of the clever theologian or philosopher, but reconciling the world unto himself. But of course, even that is past-tense: he was in Christ. So there is one more move: God has entrusted us with the ministry of reconciliation. Everything has been done. The risk only needs taking.

When the Old Gods Fail:
Martin Luther's Critique of Mysticism

Everyone knows that Luther is once supposed to have thrown an inkwell at the devil. It is not so well known, however, that his reaction to an appearance or vision of Christ was of the same sort! Since this reaction indicates Luther's attitude toward what might be called "mystical" phenomena or experiences — or at least some types of such — it might be well for us to begin by looking at it. In his *Table Talk* Luther is reported to have said:

> Christ once appeared visible here on earth, and showed his glory, and according to the divine purpose of God finished the work of redemption and the deliverance of mankind. I do not desire he should come once more in the same manner, neither would I he should send an angel unto me. Nay, though an angel should come and appear before mine eyes from heaven, yet it would not add to my belief; for I have of my Saviour Christ Jesus bond and seal; I have his Word, Spirit, and sacrament; thereon I depend, and desire no new revelations. And the more steadfastly to confirm me in this resolution, to hold solely by God's Word, and not to give credit to any visions or revelations, I shall relate the following circumstance: — On Good Friday last, I being in my chamber in fervent prayer, contemplating with myself, how Christ my Saviour on the cross suffered and died for our sins, there suddenly appeared upon the wall a bright vision of our Saviour Christ, with the five wounds, steadfastly looking upon me, as if it had been Christ himself corporally. At first sight, I thought it had been some celestial reve-

lation, but I reflected that it must needs be an illusion and juggling of the devil, for Christ appeared to us in his Word, and in a meaner and more humble form; therefore I spake to the vision thus: Avoid thee, confounded devil: I know no other Christ than he who was crucified, and who in his Word is pictured and presented unto me. Whereupon the image vanished, clearly showing of whom it came.[1]

The significant thing about this account is that it shows us two things that indicate something of the ambiguity of Luther's attitude toward mysticism. On the one hand, Luther was doing the sort of thing that mystics do. He was in his chamber in fervent prayer, contemplating with himself how Christ the savior suffered and died on the cross for our sins. He was practicing what might be called mystical exercises. On the other hand, when a vision is granted which no doubt would have delighted any good mystic and would perhaps be designated as an ecstatic experience, he vehemently rejects it and dismisses it as "an illusion and juggling of the devil." He wants to know "no other Christ than he who was crucified, and who in his Word is pictured and presented" to humans. One should note that Luther does not question the possibility or the "fact" of the "visionary experience," but he does not believe it to be from God. Rather he thinks it comes from the devil, the adversary of God.

So the passage indicates the complexity encountered by anyone attempting to assess Luther's attitude toward what has come to be termed mysticism. Luther seems to have much in common with the mystics. He praises some of them — notably John Tauler — and his own faith-language is liberally sprinkled with terminology borrowed from the mystics. When he wants to describe the experience of faith, Luther seems to find mystical language most congenial and accurate, often resorting to such terms as "rapture" *(raptus)*, mystical "translation" *(translatio)*, and using the imagery of the heavenly marriage.[2] Yet Luther has sharp words for most mystics and rejects what many of them hold most dear. At the decisive point he breaks off and refuses to go the mystics' way.

Our purpose is to attempt an assessment of Luther's ambivalence to-

1. H. T. Kerr, ed., *A Compend of Luther's Theology* (Philadelphia: Westminster Press, 1943), p. 57. Cf. WATR 1, 287, 8-27.

2. Cf. Erwin Iserloh, "Luther und die Mystik," in I. Asheim, ed., *Kirche, Mystik, Heiligung und das Natürliche bei Luther* (Göttingen: Vandenhoeck & Ruprecht, 1967), pp. 60-83, 68ff.

ward mysticism. Why does he seem to like and prefer such mystical terminology and yet reject what might be termed the classical mystical experience, if, indeed, there is such? The major thesis of my argument will be that
the answer is relatively simple: mysticism like every other "ism" is just not,
for Luther, good news; it is not a gospel. Hence, even though it may say a
lot of helpful things and provide a useful terminology it does not, in the
end, help the anguished soul where help is most needed, but only adds to
the burden.

The Place of Mysticism: The Failure of the Gods

An assessment of Luther's — or anyone's — critique of mysticism immediately encounters a notorious difficulty: how to define mysticism. Mysticism is so diffuse a phenomenon that virtually any definition ventured can
be countered by instances or examples that refute it. Consequently it might
appear futile to speak of *a* critique of mysticism on Luther's part, especially
when one might so choose to define the matter as to *include* Luther among
the mystics. Yet Luther's repeated objection to claims made by mystics indicates that for him something vital was at stake and it is incumbent upon
us to try, at least, to ferret out just what that was.

A useful way around the roadblock set by the impossibility or futility
of defining mysticism can be found by asking not for a definition but
rather about the place of mysticism, the historical situation, the conditions
under which mysticism arises. If Luther and certain types of mysticism
arise at the same place this will give us the possibility of assessing both
what they have in common and, hopefully, the precise points at which they
differ.

L. Richter maintains that mysticism always appears under certain
conditions in the development of a historical religion or philosophy and is
thus bound to a particular situation in the religious consciousness and can
enter only at such a point.[3] This fact, he believes, is decisive for an assessment of the nature of mysticism. Mysticism appears when the original and
immediate unity of subject and object in the mythical stage of religion has
been lost and the abyss, the distance, between God and humans has be-

3. L. Richter, "Mystik," in *Die Religion in Geschichte und Gegenwart,* 3rd ed., vol. 4
(Tübingen: Mohr, 1960), pp. 1237-38.

come apparent. The mystic seeks to overcome the consciousness of this distance on a different and perhaps higher level and to reestablish the original unity of subject and object in the "ground" of the soul. Thus the task of the mystic can be seen as the attempt to find the way of the soul out of the abyss of separation to the immediate experience of the divine reality as the original unity of all things. This is usually done by an internalizing religious appropriation of the ancient religious tradition, sometimes even to the point of the dissolution of that tradition in a philosophical pantheism.

Mysticism appears, perhaps we can say, when the old gods of the myth or the prophetic revelation or the sacramental priestly system have failed. The mystic, however, in no way wants to deny or alter or downgrade the tradition. The mystic seeks a new relationship to the *text*, the "letter," the historical deposit. Whereas once, perhaps, the text accurately or truthfully signified or mediated what could be believed about the gods in unbroken manner, it does so no longer. Either the myth is "broken," to use Tillich's word, or the text has been translated into a dogmatic or scholastic language that no longer edifies or feeds the soul. So the mystic seeks a new way in which to appropriate the text. Usually this is done by means of what Thomas Aquinas called *cognitio Dei experimentalis,* the fundamental experience of immediate contact with God or the metaphysical "first cause."[4] The "letter" of the text is internalized by being translated into the language of the *cognitio Dei experimentalis,* the language of the soul and its experience of God. Without for a moment denying the "letter" of the revelation, the mystic nevertheless tends to dissolve its tie to the once-for-all historical and prophetic referent and turn it into the eternal language of the individual soul and its inner life. Thus what in the Holy Scripture was *exoterically* intended acquires an *esoteric* meaning for the initiated mystical soul. The mystic is therefore never divorced from the historical revelation, but the mystic transcends its sense individually even though the "letter" is never altered. The consequence of this internalization is on the one hand that the mystic generally tends to border on and to flirt with heresy and on the other hand that mysticism cannot in the long run maintain itself in separation from its historical religious background.

---

4. Such *cognitio Dei experimentalis* (experiential knowledge of God) is St. Thomas's definition of mysticism.

Luther and the "Failure" of the Old Gods

This type of analysis of the conditions under which mysticism arises affords a vantage point from which to assess Luther's relationship to mysticism, both positively and negatively. For Luther too the old gods had failed. The historical text as it had been interpreted by the scholastic dogmatic tradition no longer rang true. His positive relation to mysticism can be seen in that like the mystics, Luther too sought a new and more direct relationship to the text, the historical revelation. He too, as a good Augustinian, sought a *cognitio Dei experimentalis,* an experienced knowledge of God. On this account he could approve of many of the things that mystics said and use much of the language of the mystics in his own theology. On this account he could — with certain caution — be called a mystic and his theology be dubbed as mystical. Yet that would be at best only a half truth, for Luther has also earned the reputation, historically at least, of being the enemy of mysticism — whether justly or unjustly we can leave undecided for the moment.[5] This negative relation is rooted in the fact that for Luther the mystic's god, the mystic's way of relating to the text also had failed. His anguished question, "Where do I get a *gracious* God?" indicates that even the mystic's answer was no longer adequate. The mystical *way* was not good news.

Without going into all the intricacies of Luther's search for a gracious God it will be most fruitful to stick with the question of the relationship between the text and the *cognitio Dei experimentalis,* the text and experience, since that is what is chiefly at issue in Luther's relationship to mysticism and marks the point of both qualified agreement and disagreement. What was the problem? The difficulty lay in what Gerhard Ebeling has termed the problem of *signification:* what the text, the "letter," *signifies* and how it conveys religiously or spiritually important "meaning."[6] If words are signs, what do they signify that is religiously significant? In the Judeo-Christian scriptures, of course, the religiously significant constellations of words refer mostly to historical events: the "mighty acts of God," the exodus, captivity and return, the cross and resurrection of Christ, etc.

5. Cf. E. J. Tinsley, "Mysticism," in Alan Richardson, ed., *A Dictionary of Christian Theology* (Philadelphia: Westminster, 1969), p. 225, where Luther is credited with being the probable source of basic misgivings issuing in "hostility" to mysticism.

6. Cf. Gerhard Ebeling, "The New Hermeneutics and the Young Luther," *Theology Today* 21, no. 1 (April 1964): 34-46.

So the question was, how can historical events that happened "way back there" be significant for the religious seeker *today?* How can the time gap between then and now be bridged? It is the question that Lessing was later to ask with such poignancy: How can accidental truths of history be the point of departure for eternal truths of reason?

Without going into all the complexities of medieval exegesis we can oversimplify by saying that the non-mystical scholastic (if there was such a thing!) or the traditionalist could meet the problem by *translating* the text, the "letter," in "open-eyed" fashion into the language of doctrine and dogma, the spiritual truth, which is to be believed and is eternally valid. The "letter" that signified historical events had to be interpreted by means of an allegorical system of signification to connote spiritual or eternal truth. What occurs in the sensible world is translated into the language of the intelligible world — something akin to ideas having to do with doctrine, morals, or things hoped for (according to the fourfold method of exegesis). Thus the time-gap could be bridged by means of the system of signification. The historically particular could be translated into the language of doctrine valid "for all time" and appropriated by the believer's act of faith. For the non-mystic this means that the text can be seen to signify something supposedly objective, something out there in the intelligible world (or perhaps in heaven?) that was mediated and presided over by the priestly-sacramental authorities.

Now, if the analysis of the place of mysticism we have given above is at all accurate, it can be seen to appear as a protest against the heteronomy of this system of signification — either because the system lost its force or because it became trapped in its own excesses, arid intellectualism and scholastic hair-splitting. In Tillich's words, mysticism appears as a protest against the demonic distortions of the priestly-sacramental element of universal revelation, the tendency to make the medium and its excellencies into the content, to elevate the conditional into something of unconditional significance.[7]

But now how does mysticism meet this problem of signification? Here again we encounter the diffuse character of mysticism in attempting to formulate a precise and accurate description. Perhaps we can say, however, that whereas for the non-mystic the signification tends to be exoteric,

---

7. Paul Tillich, *Systematic Theology,* vol. 1 (Chicago: University of Chicago Press, 1951), p. 140.

for the mystic, the signification is predominantly esoteric. For the mystic, the text, the "letter," signifies something within, some sort of more immediate relationship to God within, in the ground of the soul. The Greek root for the word *mysticism* indicates this: *myo*, meaning to *close* the lips and/or the eyes. The initiate closes the lips and the eyes to find what the text signifies *within:*

> Mysticism has criticized the demonically distorted sacramental priestly substance by devaluating every medium of revelation and by trying to unite the soul directly with the ground of being, to make it enter the mystery of existence without the help of a finite medium. Revelation occurs in the depth of the soul; the objective side is accidental.[8]

For many mystics, therefore, the text is more or less accidental. It speaks a kind of sign language about the inner life and experience of the soul to which the initiate (perhaps by proper exercises) becomes privy. Whereas non-mystical signification proceeds mostly by way of the *via positiva*, positive and exoteric affirmations about the deity, or by way of analogy, the mystical way is modeled mostly after the *via negativa*, the negation of all affirmations to arrive at union in "the cloud of unknowing," or the "dark night of the soul."

The accidental character of the text or sign is not necessarily true of course for all who have been called mystics. E. J. Tinsley is concerned to insist that the early Christian use of the term *mystical* always associated the mystical experience with something concrete and factual. The written words of Scripture or the action of the liturgy were themselves the mystery. One who was mystery-minded would see in them not only the sign but also the thing symbolized; the sign, the concrete event or situation, or piece of Scripture, and the thing signified were taken as inseparable. Such mysticism, he would maintain, is a genuine mysticism and at the same time completely compatible with Christian belief in a historical incarnation. Yet even when the sign and the thing signified are as closely identified as possible, the relationship between text and believer remains of a certain mystical sort. The true believer is an initiate into this mystery-mindedness, which remains more esoteric than exoteric.

8. Tillich, *Systematic Theology*, p. 140.

Even in more modern forms of mysticism, the pattern tends to remain more or less the same. The text (*à la* Schleiermacher, for instance) is an account of the historical modifications of the pious God-consciousness replicated in the individual. Or the text may be a fund of erotic imagery that touches off such eroticism in the individual. Or if one wishes to classify current Pentecostal and neo-Pentecostal experience as mystical, the text could be seen as signifying certain things about the mysterious ways of the Spirit and the experience of the Spirit repeatable for those properly initiated. The text tends to remain a sign of mystical experience of a more or less esoteric sort. The "letter" signifies what goes on in the esoteric realm of "the spirit," leaving one with the question of how one gets there or how one gets the spirit.

For Luther all such systems of signification, whether non-mystical and exoteric or mystical and esoteric, had failed. The God of mercy and grace of the historical Scriptures was not to be found in them. Through his struggles with the historical text as an exegete and teacher he came to discover a radically different relationship to and experience of that text. To make a long story short, we can say he discovered the *cognitio Dei experimentalis* not in the system of signification of the text's exoteric or esoteric meanings but rather in what the text actually *did* to him and for him. What he came to see and experience was that it was not what the text *signified* according to someone's system of meaning — either mystical or non-mystical — that bridged the gap, but what the historical text as living Word of God actually did *to* him. For Luther, we might say, the text actually *did* what others — both mystic and non-mystic — had said it only *signified.*

The storm center around which the question of signification had raged from the earliest days in the church was the problem of letter and spirit. The problem in concentrated form came to expression in the interpretation of the Pauline passage (2 Cor. 2:6): "The letter kills, but the Spirit gives life." Those steeped in the long traditions and systems of signification took that to mean that the letter was somehow weak or inadequate or insufficient. As a mere sign in the sensible world it could only *point* to or symbolize true realities in the realm of the spirit, the intelligible world. If one remained on the level of the mere letter one would at best be a kind of second-class citizen, a believer stuck on the level of the simple faith of mythological piety, and at worst one might simply perish in this world of appearances, holding onto mere signs, mere letter. One must get beyond the mere letter to the spirit, for the letter kills and the spirit gives life. The transition from letter to spirit thus involves a movement on the part of the initiate from the sensible to the intelligible world, from mere signs to reality. Luther, however, finally came to take that kind of passage to mean *just what it says*. The passage maintains that the letter and the spirit do something, not that they signify something. The letter *kills* and the spirit *gives life*. Luther took this at face value as a description of what God *does* through the word. The letter kills and *through that* the spirit gives life. The letter, therefore, is not weak or insufficient. If it has power to kill it must be taken with utmost seriousness. The spirit, moreover, is not some "spirit world" beyond or above the letter or even within in the "ground of the soul." The spirit comes through the letter when the letter kills, puts to death the sinner who thinks to escape the crisis of the actual history by flights into the intelligible realm of pure spirit.

Thus Luther will insist upon a relationship between letter and spirit in terms of the deed of God through the Word. The spirit does not exist or come apart from the letter, the historical text, but is hidden *in* it and comes *through* it. The spirit is declared ". . . from the letter. The spirit is concealed in the letter, which is a word which is not good, because it is the law of wrath. But the spirit is a good word, because it is a word of grace."[9] God, therefore, does his work through the word as killing letter and life-giving spirit. The text, the literal word, is therefore by no means to be belittled or spoken of as a mere "signifier" or as weak and insufficient. It is no mere allegory of the secrets of a distant or even internal spirit world. It is God's deed that spells death and life. "God's works are his words; he speaks and it is done: because the speaking and the doing of God are the same."[10]

So for Luther the biblical text comes alive as that which does what it says. The literal, historical text is the true initiator, mediator, and mirror of experience — the fountain of all *cognitio Dei experimentalis*. Through the text itself what the mystics talked *about* was actually *done*. The "rapture" and the "ecstasy," even the "union" and the "marriage of the soul with the bridegroom," which the mystic would speak of as the end of a long process, or perhaps, of mystical exercises — all that was done and given through the action of God in his Word. The God of grace himself comes to find the lost in the word of death and life, the cross and resurrection of Jesus

9. LW 10: 212.
10. WA 3, 152, 7.

Christ. The old seeker, whether non-mystic or mystic, is put to death and the new person of faith is created by the divine word.

In this movement from what the text signifies to what the text actually does, Luther's relationship to mysticism is more clearly specified. Therein one can see both his affinity to mysticism and his distance from it. This is spelled out by saying that for Luther the text *actually does* what the mystic says it only *signifies*. This explains why on the one hand Luther can and does use mystical language with approval to describe the experiential knowledge of God, while on the other hand he is radically critical of mystical accounts of how such knowledge is obtained. Perhaps one can say that the goal is affirmed as given by God and his Word; the quest, however, is false and illusory since it only leads in the wrong direction. With that, the basis for Luther's critique of mysticism is established. Any mysticism that regards the text, the external word, as more or less accidental would be rejected. Furthermore, any type of mysticism that regards the text as only significative or an experience that has its ground somewhere else than in an encounter with the text, whether in the metaphysical realm of ideas or in the perennial philosophy of the soul's immediate contact with the deity, would be radically questioned — at least in the sense that such natural knowledge or experience delivers one into the hands of the gracious God. At best, all such knowledge always delivers one into the hands of the God of wrath. In and through the text God "does himself" to the hearer as a God of grace and mercy.

Thus, for instance, all forms of mysticism influenced by a Christianized neo-Platonism such as that of Pseudo-Dionysius would have to be radically transformed. Such mysticism tends to be modeled after the so-called *via negativa:* the negation of all positive affirmations to arrive at unity in the dark night of the soul's ground. The ecstasy would be arrived at by mystical self-negation. Luther would not deny that a negation is indeed involved but that it is the text, through the story of the crucified Christ, that actually *does* such negation, and through which one experiences what negative theology is all about. Indicative of this is a text such as the following, where Luther discusses the thoughts of blasphemy that arise from the experience of rejection:

> Therefore such thoughts of blasphemy are indeed terrifying. But they are nevertheless good, provided that one controls them and uses them to advantage. They include those "sighs too deep for words" (Rom.

8:26) which "pierce the clouds" (Ecclus. 35:21) and, as it were, compel the Divine Majesty to forgive and to save.

These thoughts can be felt, like all other spiritual thoughts. But they cannot be expressed in words, and they can be learned only through experience. Therefore Dionysius, who wrote about "negative theology" and "affirmative theology" deserves to be ridiculed. In the latter part of his work he defines "affirmative theology" as "God is being." "Negative theology" he defines as "God is nonbeing."

But if we wish to give a *true definition* of "negative theology," we should say that *it is the holy cross and the afflictions* in which we do not, it is true, discern God, but in which nevertheless those sighs are present of which I have already spoken.[11]

For Luther, the attempt on the part of the Dionysian mystic to translate experience into the terms of an abstract negative theology is only misleading and ridiculous. It is the text itself, the actual history, the holy cross, that does the negation and interprets the experience. The text becomes the true mediator and mirror of the *cognitio Dei experimentalis.*

Thus Luther, through his own experience with the text, became the uncompromising champion of the literal, external text. The text as living Word mediates and delivers one into the hands of the gracious God, the God who died and is raised for us. All attempts to translate the text into some other story — say, the soul's journey to the One or whatever — or even to treat the text as though it were the mere indication of spiritual experiences or visitations of the spirit to be realized elsewhere or independently of the text and its story would be rejected as of the devil — that is, they would dispatch one on a quest that would lead either to presumption or despair. On this account Luther also became the implacable foe of later Reformation "enthusiasts" who championed a view of the spirit's work or visitations more or less independent of the text, a view somewhat akin to contemporary neo-Pentecostalism. If such were to be termed mysticism he was highly critical, to say the least, of it as well. Excerpts from a passage in Luther's Smalcald Articles indicate this clearly:

In these matters, which concern the external, spoken Word, we must hold firmly to the conviction that God gives no one his Spirit or grace

11. LW 13: 110-11. Emphasis mine.

except through or with the external Word which comes before. Thus we shall be protected from the enthusiasts, that is, from spiritualists who boast that they possess the Spirit without and before the Word and who therefore judge, interpret, and twist the Scriptures or spoken Word according to their pleasure. Münzer did this, and many still do it in our day who wish to distinguish sharply between the letter and the spirit without knowing what they say or teach.

All this is the old devil and the old serpent who made enthusiasts of Adam and Eve. He led them from the external Word of God to spiritualizing and to their own imaginations, and he did this through other external words. Even so, the enthusiasts of our day condemn the external word, yet they do not remain silent but fill the world with their chattering and scribbling, as if the Spirit could not come through the Scriptures or the spoken word of the apostles but must come through their own writings and words. Why do they not stop preaching and writing until the Spirit himself comes to the people without and before their writings since they boast that the Spirit came upon them without the testimony of the Scriptures?

In short, enthusiasm clings to Adam and his descendants from the beginning to the end of the world. It is a poison implanted and inoculated in men by the old dragon, and it is the source, strength, and power of all heresy, including that of the papacy and Mohammedanism. Accordingly, we should and must constantly maintain that God will not deal with us except through his external Word and sacrament. Whatever is attributed to the Spirit apart from such Word and sacrament is of the Devil.[12]

Sharp, uncompromising words, which are no doubt offensive to modern ears! One should note, however, what is being said. What we humans call "the spirit" is in any case *always mediated by words*. The spiritualist or the mystic is fully as dependent upon words — external words — as anyone else. There is, and can be, no such thing as a wordless spiritualism or mysticism. The spiritualists and the mystics fill the sound waves and books with their own chattering and scribbling as well. Thus the only question is: What words shall they be? Shall they be words that describe esoteric experiences or shall they be the Word of God who suffered and died and yet rose for us?

12. BC 322; BC-T 312-13.

All this is coupled, for Luther, with the belief that humans are all, since the fall, *born* enthusiasts. Enthusiasm here does not mean — as it does for moderns — simply being enthusiastic or excited or highly motivated. It is taken according to its root meaning: believing in the god within, or god-within-ism. Humans have succumbed to the serpent's temptation: "You shall not die, you shall be as gods." Thus for Luther the perennial philosophy of god-within-ism is the devil's delusion which places one under the wrath of God, ultimate despair and death. One cannot be saved from such delusion by words that only foster and feed it. One can be saved — and receive the Spirit of life — only through the Word which is truly from without, the ultimate negation, the death of the old and the resurrection of the new: the Word of the cross and resurrection. Only such a Word would be *true* and — ultimately — the only *true* "mysticism."

So perhaps we can begin to understand the words of Luther with which we began this essay. He will steadfastly refuse to credit or transmit any interpretation that translates the text, the literal story, into *some other* esoteric story. Had he credited the vision as a genuine celestial revelation, as the apex of the mystical experience to be replicated by the true initiate, Luther's communication to the world would have been a fundamentally different word, a different "story." It would then, no doubt, have been a communication about *how* one comes to get a vision of the savior or some such thing. The questions to be answered would be fundamentally altered. *How* does one do it? What kind of meditation was it that was so rewarded? What kind of mystical exercises should one practice if one wants to get visions? A fundamentally different relationship to the text would then have to be proposed. One would be dispatched on a quest that for Luther could only be of the devil. All the questions so put would be the *wrong* questions. Therefore he steadfastly rejected the vision in favor of the Christ of the text, the Christ who appears in his Word, "in a meaner and more humble form." For Luther only such a Christ could be the savior and true liberator of fallen human beings. Only such a Christ could be *good* news.

Karl Barth on the Consequences
of Lutheran Christology

Karl Barth did not like Lutheran Christology. That of course is not strange for a Reformed theologian. But it is at least remarkable for a Reformed theologian who had drunk as deeply at Luther's well as Barth had. So it is useful for us, I think, especially considering the Christological starting point of his dogmatics, to look a bit at Barth's problems with Lutheran Christology and what it might mean for the proclamation of Jesus Christ today.

Barth thought Lutheran Christology led to unfortunate consequences, contributing to or at least not being able to counter disastrous developments in the nineteenth century, particularly those ending in the cul-de-sac prepared by one who was brash enough to call himself Luther II, Ludwig Feuerbach. Barth could not resist twitting Lutherans about that. But the matter goes beyond teasing, of course. Barth saw in Feuerbach the realization of an apparent possibility left open by Lutheran Christology: the transformation of theology completely into anthropology, the final absorption of theology's object (namely, God) by the human subject. Feuerbach was one of those who, in Barth's estimation, grasped the rudder of the ship of theology and steered it steadfastly onto the rocks. And Lutheran Christology left the door open to such misadventure. Was Barth right about this? Scholars disagree as to whether such gross theological sins can be laid to Lutheran accounts. Indeed, most think it a rather hasty bit of *Konsequenzmacherei*. However, an age that owes a greater theological debt to Feuerbach than to either Luther or Barth could well afford to pause a bit by this argument to look, as into a mirror, to see whose face is reflected there. My purpose in this paper will be to look at two particular doctrinal issues in the argument between Barth and the Lutherans as a kind of exercise in the consequences of Christology, with the aim of developing a constructive proposal.

There are two particular targets in Lutheran Christology at which Barth shoots. First, he attacks the Lutheran understanding of the *communicatio idiomatum* (communication of attributes), particularly the *genus maiestaticum,* the doctrine that the risen Christ is everywhere present in his human nature, because the personal union between the divine and the human in Christ is such that Christ's humanity shares in the attributes of divine omnipresence. The problem for Barth here is that this so-called abstraction detracts from history.

The second and subsequent of Barth's complaints was that the communication of divine attributes to the human nature of the exalted Christ seems to leave the door open to the idea that all humans could become divine. If it could happen to Christ's human nature, then why not to every human nature? This reinforced Barth's suspicion that *Luther's theological stance was too subjective,* laying itself open to Feuerbach's inversion, that is, turning theology into anthropology. It was this fear of subjectivism, apparently, that finally led Barth symbolically to place an Indonesian screen in front of the Weimar Edition of Luther's works in his study!

It is significant that with this complaint Barth joins a celebrated chorus of Luther's Roman Catholic critics. Indeed, in a letter to Helmut Gollwitzer (commenting on a book by the Roman Catholic Paul Hacker) Barth remarked that this book "hits exactly the reason why . . . the Weimar Edition in my study is hidden behind an Indonesian screen."[1] It is perhaps worth noting, given current ecclesiastical politics, that the same book received commendation, even if somewhat qualified, in an introduction by one Joseph — now Cardinal — Ratzinger!

---

1. October 20, 1966, *Karl Barth Gesamtausgabe. Briefe, 1961-1968.* The Hacker text in question (in my estimation a rather unenlightened, if not intemperate, complaint about Luther's supposed subjectivism) is *Das Ich im Glauben bei Martin Luther* (Cologne: Verlag Styria, 1966); *The Ego in Faith: Martin Luther and the Origin of Anthropocentric Religion* (Chicago: Franciscan Herald Press, 1970).

Barth's Critique of the *communicatio idiomatum,* *genus maiestaticum*

First, let us take a closer look at the problem of ubiquity (omnipresence) and the communication of the attributes of divine majesty to Christ's human nature. Barth takes up the question in *Church Dogmatics* IV/2 (the Doctrine of Reconciliation), where he develops his understanding of the humanity of Christ under the rubric of the exaltation of the Son of Man. There, also, significantly, he attacked the Lutheran doctrine. Barth's objection to the Lutheran view of the communication of divine attributes to the human nature of Christ here has two aspects, reflecting both of his complaints against Lutheran Christology. The first is that the idea of a communication of divine attributes to the human nature of Christ *is much too abstract and, because it is so, violates the actual history of what occurs in Jesus Christ.* Barth avers that he has no objection to what he considers to be the real meaning and intention of "this remarkable train of thought" with "its curious and alien features."[2] The intention, he believes, is that "the reality of the high grace of the reconciliation of the world with God, the perfection of the fellowship established between God and man, and the presence and efficacy of God in our human sphere, are all taken with a final and total seriousness." It is an attempt "to think out to the very last the fact and extent that all this did and does take place in Jesus Christ. . ."[3] Barth cannot fault this intention, but nevertheless, it cannot be executed along the lines proposed by Lutheran Christology.[4] What could it mean to say that something so abstract as "attributes" or characteristics could be packaged up, so to speak, and transferred from one so-called "nature" to another? Is the personal union some sort of metaphysical swap-shop? "You give me your goodies, and I'll give you mine"? True to his Reformed lineage, Barth is concerned, in the first instance, about what such talk could possibly mean.

> What is really meant by the humanity of Jesus Christ as it is appropriated and illuminated and inter-penetrated by His deity — loaded, as it were, with His deity, because participant in all its attributes? The objection can obviously be brought at once against this view that it is a

2. Karl Barth, CD IV/2, p. 78.
3. CD IV/2, pp. 78-79.
4. CD IV/2, p. 79.

strange deity which can suddenly become the predicate of human essence, and a strange humanity to which all the divine predicates can suddenly be ascribed as subject. Does not this compromise both the true deity and the true humanity of Jesus Christ? Does it not involve either a deification of the creature, or humanization of the Creator, or both?[5]

The Lutherans, Barth thinks, have never succeeded in offering a convincing answer to these objections. At the same time, Barth admits, the Reformed never succeeded in convincing the Lutherans of their error and were much too negative in their reaction. Barth wants to transcend the terms of the old debate by pressing the question of abstraction.

> . . . These objections *acquire their full weight* only when they are set in the context of the wider question whether the humanity of Jesus Christ as conceived in this way is not one long abstraction: abstracted, that is, from the history to which we cannot even for a moment cease to cling if we are to see and think and confess "Jesus Christ"; abstracted from the one true Son of God and Son of Man in whom the divine and human are genuinely united, without admixture or separation. On this view are they not both admixed and separated: admixed, to the extent that the human is deified, as is expressly stated, in this union with Godhead; and separated, to the extent that this deification can be ascribed to it only as it is considered statically in and for itself, isolated from the dynamic of history in which it was and is one with the divine? In this isolation on the basis of which it appears an apotheosised humanity, directly filled and furnished with all the majesty of the being of the triune God, is there not committed, in spite of every precaution, the very serious mistake of looking away from the Subject in whom God and man became and are one, from the history in which it took place, and therefore — contrary to the express intention — from the reality of atonement, *the perfection of the new fellowship between God and man,* the real presence and efficacy of God among us, the new element of life which has actually come down into the world of men in Jesus Christ?[6]

5. CD IV/2, pp. 79-80.
6. CD IV/2, p. 80.

Barth's most serious complaint in this regard is that preoccupation with the question of the communication of divine attributes leads one to look away from that history in which the union of the Son of God with the Son of man *actually occurs* to a behind-the-scenes realm where one moves metaphysical furniture about at one's convenience. Salvation occurs as a historical event, not by the shifting about of attributes and the bestowal of a status. "The recognition," Barth continues, "of Jesus Christ as true salvation and saving truth is not really strengthened, as intended, by the theory of a divinisation of his human essence, but weakened and even jeopardised completely."[7] So, Barth concludes, there is no option but to reject it.

The second aspect of Barth's critique has more to do with the question of the consequences of such Christology. It was a consequence not yet perceived in the sixteenth and seventeenth centuries but which, in Barth's view, was fatefully realized in the nineteenth century. The assertion that the divine attributes are communicated to the human in such a way that one can speak of a "divinization" of the human essence and flesh of Jesus as the final goal of the incarnation, Barth warns, leaves a door wide open to the idea that the essence of all humanity is, as such, capable of divinization. For Barth, the problem of abstraction comes home to roost here. It flips over into its opposite, from the objectivity of the abstract to subjectivity. If the divinization (or, as Barth would say, the exaltation) of the Son of Man is claimed without reference to the actual history of Jesus, but of the abstraction, the human essence or nature of Jesus, why cannot such divinization be claimed for every human essence? Once you start down (or up!) the road to abstraction, Barth worries, where do you stop?

It is rather difficult, however, historically to draw a line from the orthodox doctrine to the misadventures of the nineteenth century without further ado. Sensing, no doubt, that he is on thin historical ice here, Barth does not argue the case directly with actual historical evidence. Rather, he insinuates the matter with a battery of rhetorical questions. If the door is left wide open for anyone to wander away from Christology, who is to prevent such wandering? How are we to guard against this deduction? Where does the way through this open door lead?[8] His series of rhetorical questions can, of course, have only one answer:

7. CD IV/2, p. 80.
8. CD IV/2, pp. 80-81.

It obviously leads smoothly and directly to anthropology, and not to a dull naturalistic and moralistic anthropology, but to a 'high-pitched' anthropology; to the doctrine of a humanity which is not only capable of deification, but already deified, or at any rate on the point of apotheosis or deification. If the supreme achievement of Christology, its final word, is the apotheosised flesh of Jesus Christ, omnipotent, omnipresent and omniscient, deserving of our worship, is it not merely a hard shell which conceals the sweet kernel of the divinity of humanity as a whole and as such, a shell which we can confidently discard and throw away once it has performed this service?[9]

So, in Barth's view, the consequences of the Lutheran idea of the *communicatio idiomatum, genus maiestaticum,* are not only that the abstraction obscures the history, but also that in so doing it leads to or at least leaves the door open for the inversion of Christology into anthropology — right, that is, into the arms of Feuerbach and the triumph of subjectivity. Luther's subjective turn bears this bitter fruit, according to Barth. In his essays on Feuerbach, once again, the case is not so much argued historically as assumed and insinuated with batteries of rhetorical questions:

With ingenious overemphasis Luther himself urged us to seek deity not in heaven but on earth, in man, man, the man Jesus; and for him the bread of the Lord's Supper had to *be* the glorified body of the Exalted One. . . . With great elation people triumphantly turned away (and are still turning away) from the Reformed *finitum non capax infiniti* [the finite is not capable of the infinite]. All this clearly suggests the possibility of an inversion of above and below, of heaven and earth, of God and man — the possibility of forgetting the eschatological limit. Indeed, Hegel (by his own confession) showed himself perhaps only too good a Lutheran in his exploitation of this possibility. It is certain that Luther and the old-Lutherans *with their heaven-storming Christology* have left their followers in a somewhat exposed and defenseless situation, in face of the *speculative anthropological consequences that have irresistibly developed.*[10]

9. CD IV/2, p. 80, emphasis mine.
10. "Introductory Essay" to Ludwig Feuerbach, *The Essence of Christianity* (New York: Harper, 1957), p. xxiii, emphasis mine. Hereafter cited as "Essay."

Can we deny that Feuerbach himself, like a not very cunning but slightly keen-eyed spy, lets out the esoteric secret of this whole priesthood, as the saying goes, *"urbi et orbi,"* "to the city and the world"? "Theology has long since become anthropology.". . .

> How does it happen that they seem to have been blind to the obvious possibility of continuing on their own line of thought until they reached Feuerbach's trivial conclusion? Why were they incapable of guarding themselves against this outcome? Why did they not speak at some decisive place in such a way that Feuerbach's question could not concern them in the least; so that the slander could not have arisen at all? If the eyes of that generation were closed, would we find the same blindness in the generation of their disciples, in those who continue their work. . . ? Or will that generation of theologians, in whose midst this spy lived, at least become aware of the threatening danger; will they therefore take pains to work in a direction that would not expose them to that mean insinuation? And if Feuerbach and his question were hidden from his contemporaries, or remained without effect — as certainly can happen — what will the following generation do, whose leading or most characteristic figure will be Albrecht Ritschl?[11]

And so on. The questions, mostly rhetorical, roll out and give the appearance of building something of a case. That Hegel and Feuerbach happened, and perpetrated various theological misfortunes, no one, of course, disputes. That they are in some direct or even indirect fashion the outcome of the doctrine of the *genus maiestaticum,* however, is rather fanciful and is not so much established as insinuated by Barth.

The Limit of Dogmatics

I think we have now heard enough of this argument to know what it is about. But what shall we say of it? And what does it have to say about the consequences of Christology? One could challenge Barth's reading of the consequences of the *genus maiestaticum* in the history of theology (which does seem here to be rather dubious). One could also defend Lutheran

11. "Essay," pp. xxi-xxii.

Christology by showing inadequacies in Barth's analysis or shortcomings in his attempt to understand Luther. But this has already been done magisterially by Regin Prenter[12] and Gerhard Ebeling.[13] Anyone interested in pursuing the many facets of the relationship between Barth and Lutheran theology should at least begin with those essays.[14] These critics find it quite possible to defend Lutheran Christology from Barth's charges precisely because Barth's attempt to lay the Christological sins that he wants to attack at the door of Lutheranism is not very convincing.

But if we are concerned with the consequences of Christology, it is more important for us to look at the problems Barth was addressing from a more systematic point of view. Quite apart from the historical arguments about where to lay the blame for the Christological sins Barth attacks (whether at the door of Luther or even orthodox Lutheran theology), the fact is that the sins have been and are still being committed — indeed deliberately and with gusto and impunity — today. Even by Lutherans! With even a cursory glance at church and theology one can hardly be blind to the fact that the spirit of Feuerbach hangs over us like a marsh gas. Americans, George Steiner once remarked, think they can democratize eternity: if you do not like what you hear of God, such as God's gender or name, just vote him out. Barth was defiantly opposed to that spirit and tried theologically to exorcise it. Surely we must agree with Barth's aim in that. However, we cannot overlook the fact that Barth seems to have failed. Indeed, it seems as if the unclean spirit, finding the house clean, has gone and gotten seven more, even more evil than himself, so that our latter state is worse than the first. In any case, we should look to this argument not as a partisan cause, so as to give aid and comfort to the enemy, but as a genuine problem in Christology, to see what help it might afford us in the battle.

We would do best to look to the two major targets of Barth's attack in his argument with Lutheran Christology: abstraction and subjectivism. The doctrine of the communication of divine attributes to a human nature is an abstraction, Barth insists, which, if it happens once, leaves the door open to the idea that it could happen again, or to every human na-

12. "Karl Barths Umbildung der traditionellen Zweinaturlehre in lutherischer Beleuchtung," *Studia Theologica* 11 (1958): 1-88.

13. "Karl Barths Ringen mit Luther," *Lutherstudien* III (Tübingen: J. C. B. Mohr [Paul Siebeck] 1985), pp. 428-573.

14. See also George Hunsinger, "What Karl Barth Learned from Martin Luther," *Lutheran Quarterly* 13 (1999): 125-55.

ture. Thus the way is open for subjectivism, the idea of a divinized humanity; theology becomes anthropology. *But now the Christological question is, how to guard against such errors?* Barth asked, how could it happen? *Can dogmatics, that is, secure the field against such abstraction on the one hand and subjectivism on the other?* Since a short essay is not amenable to prolonged and careful development of a thesis, I will declare my thesis bluntly now, and then look at and ask questions about how Barth tries to solve the problem in light of my thesis.

How can dogmatic Christology secure the field against the twin problems of abstraction and subjectivism? It cannot — at least not in and of itself. Because dogmatics *is* abstraction and abstraction is always the subject's activity — or even its way of salvation if one is not careful! My thesis is that only proclamation, the actual doing of the divine deed in the living present through preaching and the sacraments, can do that. What theology has to do is to recognize the dogmatic significance of the move to proclamation and to foster it. It must recognize that the concrete deed of proclamation is itself the solution to its problems.[15]

Proclamation is usually looked upon as having no *dogmatic* import but instead just as a more or less practical application of a theoretical solution already arrived at in dogmatic reasoning, a kind of popularized dogmatics. In this scheme, the preacher is to disguise the awful dogmatic truth in some cute illustrations in order to sell it to an unsuspecting congregation. This is a disastrous mistake. What has to be realized in the task of dogmatics is that proclamation is not one more *theory* about presence, it *is* the presence. Proclamation itself *is* the solution, indeed, the *only* ultimate solution to the dogmatic problem. What dogmatics should do, therefore, is to realize this truth and to construct itself so as to drive to and foster proper proclamation. In terms of our theme, the consequences of Christology as an "ology" — a dogmatic exercise — should be proper proclamation. Theology has no business other than to foster that and make it unavoidable. If God was in Christ reconciling the world to himself, such reconciliation does not exhaust itself in dogmatics. God does not vanish into our dogmatic texts, not even if they purport to be about the living God. It is not the case that God was in the mind of the theologian, such as Hegel, Schleiermacher, Whitehead, or even Forde!, reconciling the world

---

15. For a fuller development of this thesis, see my *Theology Is for Proclamation!* (Minneapolis: Fortress, 1990).

unto himself. Were that so, there would be no need for Jesus — except, perhaps, to reconcile you to the theologian! Since, however, God was *in Christ* reconciling the world unto himself, then properly considered, the only consistent move, the proper outcome of Christology, is the move to proclamation. Wonder of wonders, God has entrusted us with this ministry of reconciliation. This is so that the *was* can become *is.* Hence, we are ambassadors for Christ, God making his appeal *through us.*

The Cure for Limited Dogmatics

Having said this, let us return to our argument. It is certainly indisputable that Barth, in attacking the twin errors of abstraction and subjectivism, has aimed at some real enemies. As with many contemporary theologians, the diagnosis of the disease is more or less on the money. Contemporary theologians are good diagnosticians. But the question is then whether the prescribed cure will actually do the job. If one does not see — for the sake of dogmatics — that the move to proclamation itself is the cure, the disease just gets worse. Then we are like the woman with the issue of blood: the doctors only make matters worse. Or as Luther said to Erasmus, "The gouty foot laughs at your doctoring!" It takes a divine deed, a miracle, a Word from God.

The difficulty with Barth's theology arises just at this point. When I read Barth, I find myself so often saying "yea and amen." But then I always find myself waiting, waiting, for him to make the move to the dogmatic significance and the specific nature of the proclamation. Now and again he seems to teeter on the brink, but it never seems assured or secured. He never says too emphatically that dogmatics is not the solution, that the problems he is dealing with can be solved only in the move to proclamation and sacrament. To be sure, Barth is modest enough about his magisterial *Church Dogmatics,* and he is well aware that the job is never finished. But what I miss is a clear and consistent dogmatic recognition that proclamation, as an activity distinct from dogmatics, is the end, the goal, and limit of dogmatics. He does not seem to recognize clearly enough that dogmatics is not proclamation — although he seems to want to make it that. The payoff comes in his weak (for this Lutheran) view of sacrament.

It is no doubt fitting, if not inevitable for Lutherans that discussion with Barth on this matter should come down to an argument about the notorious *genus maiestaticum*. Barth objects to it as an abstraction, something conceived as occurring *in abstracto*, without reference to actual history, the story of Jesus Christ. In so doing, he joins the company of many of my old teachers. Those Pietists who became "Heilsgeschichtlers" always liked to take potshots at the *communicatio idiomatum*, and especially the *genus maiestaticum*. They had learned from the likes of Otto Piper that it was one of the most outlandish examples of dogmatic nit-picking indulged in by the seventeenth-century orthodox dogmaticians, those curators of useless abstractions! And what was the cure to the problem of abstraction, the dogmatic sins of the fathers? History! *Heilsgeschichte!* God, it was loudly announced, is a *living God*, who reveals himself in history, not in dogmatic schemas. We were all brought up on that. At least at the outset we shared this with Barth. The solution to the problem of the abstraction is to conceive and explicate all of dogmatics in terms of the concrete history of Jesus Christ. Dogmatics are a matter of revelation, which radically excludes natural theology.

So Barth proceeds in a fascinating and ingenious fashion to redo all the dogmatic abstractions in terms of the history of Christ. This is particularly evident in his Christology, the massive, unfinished fourth volume of the *Church Dogmatics*, on the Doctrine of Reconciliation. The humiliation of the Son of God and the exaltation of the Son of Man must not be understood abstractly as successive stages, but rather as two sides of one common history. Viewed historically, the humiliation of the Son of God (the way of the Son of God into the far country) is at the same time the exaltation of the Son of Man (the homecoming of the Son of Man). The old doctrine of the offices of Christ is fitted in turn to this picture: his humiliation is the priestly office, his exaltation the kingly, and the self-disclosure in this history is his prophetic office, and so on. We cannot rehearse all the details here. My point is that all the dogmatic abstractions are shifted about and redefined with dazzling and amazing dexterity so as (ostensibly, at least) to be aligned with the actual history of Jesus Christ. To use a chemical analogy, history is the great solvent for dogmatic abstractions.

But, of course, Barth is no "Heilsgeschichtler." He is fully aware of the failures of *Heilsgeschichte* as a dogmatic solution to our problems. Perhaps we can make a long leap here and say that at heart, the problem with *Heilsgeschichte* is precisely our other nemesis: subjectivism. *Heilsgeschichte* is, ostensibly, a history of *our* salvation, our *Heil*. How are we to escape the suspicion that what we are dealing with in this so-called history of salvation is not just our interpretation of history, the history or fulfillment of our subjective longings, the creation of *our* "faith"? How are we to avoid the *cul de sac* of subjectivism once again? In other words, there is a remarkable irony and, no doubt, a theological lesson here. If abstraction opens the door to subjectivism, does not the attempt to overcome it with history lead to the same end? Is not "history" as such also just another abstraction? We should take note of this, but nevertheless move on.

Barth once again seeks to overcome the subjectivism of a *Heilsgeschichte* by reasoning into the event of revelation *(fides quaerens intellectum)* in order to find in it the true and objective *Gottesgeschichte:* not our history, but God's history, the history of God's self-determination, God's election to be a God for his covenant partner in and through Jesus Christ. In other words, instead of moving in the direction of a proclamation that establishes its "objectivity," its absolute "from-withoutness," by virtue of the fact that it *puts the old subject to death in order to call the new being to life,* Barth moves dogmatically to attempt to establish objectivity by finding the eternal *Gottesgeschichte* behind (or in or above) the temporal event. Dogmatics, presented as *fides quaerens intellectum,* attempts to provide the solution to its own problem. But can faith escape the subjectivist trap by seeking its *intellectum?*

But now, when dogmatics moves like that to provide (theoretical) solutions to its own problems, matters just get worse. And this is what happens also to Barth. For what is engendered by this move is a theological split vision. On the one hand we have human history culminating in Jesus and, on the other, the eternal *Gottesgeschichte.* To which history are we to look? How are they to be related? Since we cannot avail ourselves of abstractions, such as substances or essences, we cannot really say that the divine history substantively unites with the human but rather, if I understand Barth aright, that the human story of Jesus is the perfect *analogy* (and only an analogy) in the expression of the eternal self-determination of God.

The Christological problem with that kind of split vision is that it conjures up the ghost of Nestorianism — the view that there are really two sons, the Son of God and the Son of Man, who operate in perfect personal and moral conjunction with one another. In fact, it is hard to avoid this suspicion when one looks carefully at Barth's language. His own substitute for the language of the communication of attributes, for instance, is to pick up the language of the *communicatio gratiarum,* the communication of grace, the "total and exclusive determination of the human nature of Jesus Christ by the grace of God."[16] Barth recognizes that Lutherans never found such talk sufficient since it did not distinguish qualitatively enough between Christ's humanity and ours. Barth disputes this, asking whether it is necessary to deify Christ's human nature so as to make it a real "temple" of the divine. (Incidentally, this shows that the Lutherans used the *communicatio idiomatum,* and *genus maiestaticum,* to *distinguish* between Christ's human nature and ours, not, as Barth fears, to conflate them.) So Barth says of Jesus:

> He is totally unlike even the most saintly among us in the fact that His human essence alone is fully, because from the very outset, determined by the grace of God. This is the *qualitatively* different determination of His human essence, and of His alone as that of the One who as the Son of Man is also and primarily the Son of God. But He is like us in the fact that His human essence determined in this way is in fact the same as ours. . . . It does not alter the human essence that it becomes the recipient, the only and exclusive recipient, of the electing grace of God.[17]

One hears in this a brilliant attempt to speak Christologically without resorting to the old abstractions. But it is likewise difficult to avoid hearing Nestorian undertones or overtones. When Barth speaks of the relation between the Son of God and the Son of Man, he speaks of the "address" of the Son of God to the human essence in Jesus, or even more often of the "effective confrontation" between divine and human, but not of identification. "In Jesus Christ there is no direct or indirect identification, but the effective confrontation, not only of the divine with the human, but also of the human with divine essence, and therefore the determination of the relationship of the one to the other which, without altering its essence, takes place in this confrontation."[18]

Proclamation Is the Answer

Now to go for the jugular. This sort of theological split vision subverts proper proclamation of the crucified and risen Jesus. The concrete histori-

16. CD IV/2, p. 88.
17. CD IV/2, p. 89.
18. CD IV/2, pp. 87-88.

cal event and the proclamation of it always threaten to be overshadowed or upstaged by the eternal *Gottesgeschichte*. The human becomes an earthly shadow, an analogy of something that really takes place elsewhere. In other words, the *Gottesgeschichte* functions as another abstraction that overshadows the concrete historical event. This is the reason, I expect, for the constant complaint that Barth's theology seems always too preoccupied with the question of the knowledge of God. Barth's theology, it is averred, takes its stamp from its early preoccupation with the problem of revelation and has difficulty shifting successfully to the problem of reconciliation. Since the eternal self-determination of God is analogously stamped on the human history of Jesus through the "address," the "confrontation," the *communicatio gratiarum,* this in turn is to be stamped on us through our knowledge of it. This knowledge is to shape us just as it shaped Jesus. It is only consequent, then, that every dogmatic locus concludes with ethics. It is not exactly what I would want to call proclamation that takes place as a result of this, but rather the imposition of the divine self-determination.

Even when Barth moves to what he calls the third problem in the doctrine of reconciliation, the prophetic office, the results are disappointing. Since Barth has moved dogmatically to eradicate subjectivism by making reconciliation entirely objective, he has some difficulty reintroducing the subject to be reconciled. Starting as he did from the doctrine of revelation, it is possible, of course, for him to speak of divine self-revelation. But it is difficult to transfer this scheme to the doctrine of reconciliation and to speak of divine self-reconciliation without losing the subject. When, for instance, Barth speaks of reconciliation as God's yes to himself, the subject threatens to drop out of the picture altogether. Barth's treatment of the third problem of the doctrine of reconciliation, the prophetic office of Christ, is rather disappointing for one who is looking for a real move here to proclamation. Rather, Barth is concerned with the self-disclosure of the divine self-determination in the occurrence of reconciliation — the carrying-out of the divine stamp on the creation. Barth knows well, of course, that revelation "in itself and as such" is not reconciliation. But reconciliation, "as it takes place in its perfection, and with no need of supplement, . . . also expresses, discloses, mediates and reveals itself."[19] But the question remains: When does it "take place" if not in the present proclamation?

19. CD IV/3, p. 8.

The Place and Purpose of Theology

One of the most important questions arising from all of this is that of the place and purpose of theology — systematic and/or dogmatic. Should it be the purpose of theology to move to solve its problems within itself? Or should it rather be the purpose of theology to drive to proclamation, recognizing that proclamation and the sacraments alone are the present act of God which convey "the solution"? Barth, it seems to me, is too anxious to solve all theological problems through dogmatics, and so ends with a certain tension, a certain resonance (to use a chemical analogy), a theological vision split between eternity and time. Barth is no doubt right in pointing to the fact that the Lutheran doctrine of the *communicatio idomatum, genus maiestaticum* could be taken abstractly and so produce a metaphysical monstrosity. Whether this Lutheran doctrine is responsible for the inversion of theology into anthropology remains at least an open question. But it is strange, and perhaps telltale, that Barth never clearly, to my knowledge, recognizes that the purpose of the dogmatic enterprise — whether well or ill stated — is to drive to proclamation as a distinct activity, to insist on the "real presence," the present tense, in both Word and sacrament. Its purpose, that is, should be to foster the proclamation of the "is" — this *is* my body, this *is* the Word of God — the present-tense speaking of the gospel.

How shall we escape the problem with which Barth presents us? The only move we can make is to recognize not only practically but also in our dogmatics the necessity of the move to proclamation. Christological formulations, like all dogmatic formulations, lead us inexorably into the world of abstractions. As such, of course, they are impersonal, nonhistorical. They are, after all, constructs to defend us from mortality, our way of escaping the ravages of time, our grasping for something that does not die. No doubt it marks something of an advance to bring the abstractions down to earth once again and incarnate them in time's story as Barth has done. But time cannot, it would seem, carry our hopes. Even the idea that God is living and reveals himself in history is an abstraction. So once again time becomes an analogy of eternity, and our vision flickers, split between eternity's abstraction and time's concretion.

Can we escape this split vision? I think not — not dogmatically, that is. That, I take it, is the reason for Luther's insistence on the distinction between God hidden and God revealed. Or, even more to the point, the distinction between God-not-preached and God-preached cannot be removed by our dogmatic or systematic theorizing. The attempt to do this systematically or dogmatically is apparently very enticing to theologians today. Only this time, they do it not by peering into the hidden majesty of God, but rather more by seeking to banish eternal abstractions from theology and concentrating on God in time, collapsing Jesus into God, or God into Jesus, the immanent into the economic Trinity, sticking strictly to the narrative and so on. Will this work? I expect this would be interesting to discuss. But, it cannot work — not, that is, insofar as it neglects the move to proclamation as the only genuine outcome and solution of history. Abstractions will not submit to mere erasers. Too many theologies that depend, supposedly, on history's narrative end simply by becoming another abstraction. Theology, if it is to have a point, ultimately must honor proclamation and drive relentlessly to it.

For it is proclamation, not theology, that is the end of abstraction and the beginning of concretion. Split vision is "cured" only when the proclamation is compelling enough to captivate our gaze. It is proclamation, sacrament — not dogmatics — that is the end of subjectivism: a proclamation and sacrament that puts the old subject to death and raises up the new in faith. It is the case that we cannot make do, this side of the eschaton, without abstractions. Abstractions are "laws" that are overcome and ended only when that which they describe — indeed imprison — is actually given and turned loose in the proclamation. Christologically stated, "Christ is the end of the law to those who have faith!" (Rom. 10:4). The proclamation of Christ, the sacrament is the end of the law, the abstraction to those who hear and receive it in faith. Christ, *not* theology, is the end, and Christ comes now by what we preach. Abstraction, like the *deus absconditus,* cannot be erased abstractly. One thereby would only manufacture more (potentially frightening) masks. Like the old tales about fighting with the demons, this only produces one more abstraction. The battle can only be ended concretely by the proclamation. The *deus ipse in sua maiestate* (God himself in his majesty), the *deus absconditus* (hidden God), is always present, no matter how we doctor him in our dogmatics. He can be displaced only by the preached God. There *is* no other possibility. Just so it remains true, in spite of Barth's protest, that there is inevitably a subjective referent here, however dangerous and open to Feuerbach's misunderstanding it might be: "As you believe, so you have him." God proclaimed in Jesus as the end of abstraction can only be grasped by the faith that such proclamation creates. The preached God is simply not available other than in the preaching of him. Faith alone makes both God and an idol. So, as Luther insisted, we must believe and not doubt the proclamation. We can rest assured in the hearing, the sensing, and tasting of it. And theology, certainly, must be so constructed as to foster a proclamation that creates such faith.

It is in this light that we might return, *à la* Barth, and recast our abstraction, the *communicatio idiomatum* and *genus maiestaticum.* That the "human nature" of the exalted Christ is ubiquitous by virtue of union with the divine, that the attributes of divine majesty are communicated to Christ's human nature in the personal union does not mean that the human nature is somehow infinitely extended in space and time. Rather, as Luther liked to insist, he has all time and space present to himself, that as human story (unmixed) it does God to us (unseparated) always and everywhere as it is proclaimed. God pours himself out into this story, communicates divine attributes to it, conquers all distance. Jesus does not need "divinity" added, ubiquity added, to be universal; he overcomes all distance in the proclaiming always and everywhere *pro me.* If God is our end, so he does it to us in the proclamation issuing from this story. Its objectivity, its from-withoutness, comes in the fact that as proclaimed word of the cross it puts an end to us both negatively and positively: it ends us as old beings and gives us a new end. In the proclamation, that is, the Jesus story interrupts and transects ours so that we must confess with St. Paul those always fearsome and startling words, "I have been crucified with Christ, and it is no longer I who live, but Christ who lives in me, and the life I now live in the flesh I live by faith in the Son of God who loved me and gave himself for me" (Gal. 2:20). This is about as clear a statement as one can find about the consequences of Christology!

DOING THE WORD

Preaching the Sacraments

The Sacrament of Preaching

Before we can get on to the matter of preaching the sacraments it is necessary to say something about preaching itself. So I have titled this first part *"The Sacrament of Preaching."* I take this title because my thesis is that we would do well to take our cue for preaching from what we do in the sacraments: We *do* something. We *wash* people. We *give* Christ to them. I remember a heated discussion once in which a theological professor was arguing with students who complained that teaching Christian doctrine with the aim of convincing was "brainwashing." The professor replied without flinching, "We do not wash just their brains, we wash their whole bodies!" In the sacraments, that is, we do not just *explain* Christ or the gospel, or *describe* faith, or give instructions about how to get salvation, or whatever (though we may well do all of that), we just give it, do it, flat out, unconditionally. One of the most persistent problems in this regard is that what is said in the sermon is all too often quite at odds with what we do in the sacraments. If we give unconditionally in the sacraments we are likely to take it back or put conditions on it in the sermon and leave our people completely confused. We are likely to imply in our preaching that the gift is not really what it is cracked up to be so now they better get *really* serious. We are tempted to operate like the TV "evangelists" who warn us not to depend on baptism. The upshot of that is that people are cut adrift between Word and sacrament so that their allegiance to one or the other is reduced to a matter of taste or "preference."

89

So something of a split develops in the Christian camp. On the one hand the preaching of the Word undercuts the sacraments. On the other hand there seems to be a growing antipathy to the preached Word (the "excessive wordiness" of our worship) and in some circles at least, a growing appreciation for sacraments. For the most part, preaching gets a bad name. Preaching is equivalent to scolding or haranguing. "Do not preach at me!" we yell, when all else fails. I expect that one reason people are coming more and more to prefer sacraments is that there you have to become a giver, like it or not. You cannot deny your role, the role of ministry. The rubrics direct you to it and will not let you escape. You actually have to work at it to avoid it or louse it up — though I suppose one can manage that too if one tries! Some, alas, actually succeed! But is there not something of a judgment on us in that people on the fringes, for whatever reason, whatever vestigial remains of faith might be there, are still willing, even anxious, to have their babies baptized, but hesitate or even resist allowing us to holler at them? Indeed, we find ourselves in a kind of Catch 22: they do not want to hear the preaching because likely as not it will take away what is given in the sacrament, and at the same time they have such a poor understanding of the sacraments because they never hear them preached. Of late, there seems to be a move afoot to remedy matters by restricting access to or taking the sacraments away from them altogether! A curious way to solve our problems, I should think!

At any rate, preaching on the sacraments is not likely to do much good if the preaching itself is at odds with what goes on in the sacraments. So we need first to talk about preaching itself as a sacrament, an instance in which one does basically the same thing as one does in those other instances which we have come to term "the sacraments," Baptism and the Lord's Supper. It was Regin Prenter, I believe, who always insisted that for Luther the basic reform move over against the medieval tradition was not, as with most of Protestantism, to "spiritualize" the sacraments, to reduce them to handy illustrations or symbolizations of a spiritual communication that supposedly takes place only by words, internally in the mind, from "spirit" to "spirit." Luther's move, we might say, was not to "wordify" the sacrament, but rather to sacramentalize the Word. The preaching of the Word, that is, is to do the same thing as the sacrament — to *give* Christ and all his blessings. Indeed, since the Word is Christ, preaching is "pouring Christ into our ears" just as in the sacraments we are baptized into him, and he is poured into our mouths. We have tended to overlook or forget the fact that the Christ whose body and blood is really present in the supper is also really present in the speaking of the Word. Preaching is to be understood as a sacramental event.

So we can do no better in thinking about preaching than to take our cue from the sacraments. To preach is to give Christ to the hearer, to do the sacrament to them. Now that, of course, is easily said. But the question is, how do we do it? How do we do something with words? What can we do? In the sacraments we can wash them or give them a bit of bread and some wine. We can do something. But what can we do with words?

Now the Lutheran tradition has had a lot to say about what to do with words. Indeed, one could say that theology itself in this tradition is largely instruction on what to do with words in preaching, how to make them come out right, do what they are supposed to do. The much maligned, caricatured, and misunderstood art of distinguishing between law and gospel is simply a matter of learning what to do with the words. That distinction is the outcome of centuries of wrestling with the problem going back all the way to the New Testament, signaled especially by St. Paul's struggles with the matter and his insistence in 2 Corinthians 3:6 that the letter, the written code, kills, but the Spirit gives life. The claim that the letter kills but the Spirit gives life is an assertion in unmistakable terms about what words can actually do. They can kill and make alive, they put to death the old and call the new to life in Christ. The art of distinguishing between law and gospel is simply the attempt to reclaim in the living present this active, sacramental functioning of the words for the preaching of the church. "The letter kills but the Spirit gives life" translates into "the law kills, but the gospel gives life."

This kind of consideration can help us with our questions about how to preach sacramentally, how to give Christ to the hearers, to do something with the words. When I myself try to put all the pieces of the tradition together in a view of preaching that takes its cue from the sacraments, I come up with what I fear is something of a barbarism: Preaching is doing the text to the hearers. *Doing* the text, not merely explaining it (though that will be involved), not merely exegeting the text (though that is presupposed and indispensable), not merely describing or prescribing what Christians are supposed to do (though that will no doubt result). Preaching in a sacramental fashion is *doing* to the hearers what the text authorizes you to do to them.

Before I go on to talk about what such doing the text to the hearers involves, it is important to consider what it does not mean, because that is most often where our problem lies. Just the task of understanding an ancient text of course confronts us with a number of severe difficulties in and of itself. But *preaching* or applying an ancient text raises the ante much higher. How do we bridge the time gap between then and now? Or as the question most often comes down, how do we make the text *relevant* to our time? The overwhelming, well-nigh incurable tendency we have is to run to some sort of translation, to try to make the text relevant by translating it into more viable terms, either of a more "timeless" metaphysical sort (something that is *always* true like eternal ideas or doctrines or laws) or, since such esoterica are in disfavor today, into more contemporary terms and stories. How many sermons do not begin with some anecdote or "experience" from "real life" so as to set the stage for proving its relevance in some fashion or other? Personally, I have just about reached a state of complete despair over this constantly repeated, dreary approach to the matter. You can just bet the preacher spent most of the week looking for some such handle to sneak the text onto the scene — and little time actually exegeting the text itself! So when you come home and ask yourself whether anything was really said about the text, the answer most likely would have to be that the preacher was too preoccupied with being relevant and so never really got around to it!

Always, it seems, the text has to be translated into *our* terms, twisted to fit what we call our "needs." In the old days, before the Reformation put a stop to it, they were at least more open and above-board about it. They had a method for doing it and that afforded at least some restraint on the nonsense that could be perpetrated even if it was not always terribly successful. They called it "spiritual interpretation." Usually it is referred to as the allegorical method. Even though the Reformation tried to shut down this entire enterprise and suggest other ways of interpreting and preaching the text, it seems simply to have gone underground only to emerge unrecognized (because it is now without a name) particularly in our preaching. The historical method has pretty much banished allegory from interpretation and exegesis, but because that method suggests no effective substitute when we come to preaching, the old monkey-business surfaces again in all sorts of nefarious ways.

We tend to become allegorists. The secret of allegory is that it translates the text into "another story," *allo agoreuo.* "Other-speak" would probably be a good translation for "allegory," something like George Orwell's "newspeak." Basically what happens is not that the story of the text invades our lives or changes them but rather that we change the text to fit *our* story. Or we become tropologists. Tropology was also part of the method of spiritual exegesis and had to do with the moral application of the text — what we are to do about it. Often, in our impatience to be relevant we feel the pressure to translate the text into something to do. Little ever comes of it, of course. Confident that they have gotten their expected scolding, people go home to Sunday dinner and watch the game on television. But at least we preachers can supposedly salve our consciences with the comfort that we have once again managed the marvelous feat of translating the text into some handy moralisms and so accomplished the duty everyone expected of us!

The general result of these misadventures is that preaching does not proceed in sacramental fashion. Instead of *doing* the text to the hearers, preachers at best only *explain* it, no doubt with as many clever and appealing illustrations as one can muster. Or one describes the Christian life, or prescribes what we are to do. The text becomes the occasion for us to do something, if, perchance, that something can be demonstrated to be relevant to our "needs." The text does not do anything to us to change us or incorporate us in its story; rather the text is changed to fit our story. The Word becomes mere information or description or instruction. Thus instead of being a sacrament, the Word becomes an occasion for us to exercise our powers; it becomes a law, perhaps inevitably a club with which to beat people.

We have had much fuss in the church about the relationship between preaching and sacrament. We pride ourselves in being a church of the Word and get nervous about stressing the sacraments to the degree that the priority of the Word is threatened. But we have to be cannier about sorting out the problem here. If the Word we preach does not do anything, if it is not sacramental, then it is only meet, right, and salutary that sacraments come to the fore as the only really viable mediators of the grace of God. This actually happened in ancient and medieval times, when the Word became really just doctrinal or moral instruction. The sacraments became the only available and reliable means of grace. But that development brought with it no little distortion in the understanding of grace. When sacraments are not preached they can degenerate into religious automats for dispensing a substantialized grace. Sacraments too, that is, are removed from the story of the text and fall into a different story. But then, of course, we only compound the felony if in righteous zeal for the preached Word we proceed to exalt a preaching that is not sacramental *over* the sacraments. Exalting a non-sacramental Word over the sacraments will only mean the complete bowdlerization of everything. The sacraments too will then degenerate into religious tea parties. That is to say, the sacraments too will eventually succumb to allegory, "other-speak," be translated into our story. The Holy Communion, for instance, will become merely our communion, our "fellowship," our "celebration" of whatever it is we think we have to celebrate. When the passing of the peace is supposed to take place what you get is, "Hi there, my name is George," rather than the Peace of the Lord! It all degenerates, as Luther already scornfully remarked on one occasion, into a parish fair. Word and sacrament will stand or fall together.

By now we have circled around our prey long enough, I think. It is time to pounce and go for the jugular. What is the sacrament of preaching? How does one *do* the text to the hearers? Now we come to the difficult business akin to lecturing on swimming. Eventually the only way out will be to try some concrete examples, look at some texts and develop what doing such texts might mean. That is always tricky, of course. Preaching styles are often highly individualized and differ a great deal. One runs the risk of a certain arrogance by suggesting one's own as an example to be emulated. But there is finally no way out of doing it if I am to convey some idea of what I am harping about. So I shall make some attempts to do just that.

Before we proceed to the examples, however, a couple of general remarks are in order. First, if one is going to preach in sacramental fashion, do the text to the hearer, one has, of course, to pay close attention to the text. That should go without saying, but since it seems seldom to be done, one must keep on saying it. Doing the text, furthermore, involves paying attention to the text in a quite specific manner: looking to see what the text actually *did* and is supposed to do, and therefore what it authorizes you to do. One must see what it did and then re-aim it to do the same thing in the present to the assembled hearers. Usually the text itself gives you the clues. The texts usually involve highly charged dramatic situations in which the Word of God is cutting into people's lives. It will tell you that they were amazed, shocked, incensed, or even took up stones to kill, or marveled, or glorified God, and so on. Jesus got killed for saying those things. Doing the text again should provide a rather interesting agenda!

Second, doing the text involves wielding the text so as to do what is supposed to be done if the letter, or law, *kills* and the Spirit gives life. Doing the text may help us around some of the perpetual problems we seem to have with the business about law and gospel. We seem always to get ourselves into a bind where we do not do very well with it. We apply it in too wooden a fashion or turn it into psychological gimmickry where first so much law is applied to frighten and then gospel applied to comfort — and on the other hand we do not do very well without it. Sermons degenerate into exegetical lectures at best, or at worst little talks of a popular religious sort on how to cope with "life's problems." Which is to say that when we do not concern ourselves with the difference between law and gospel all we do is preach the law — usually without any teeth in it, but law nevertheless.

We tend to get all tangled up in arguments about whether to preach the law or not. Are people not already sufficiently burdened by it? Do they not encounter it all the time in the general rot and despair of daily life in contemporary society? So the questions go. Preaching the law effectively is indeed one of the most difficult tasks of all. The idea of doing the text may afford some help. For that means that the law is precisely the cutting edge of the text itself, the way the text cuts into our lives. One does not have to scratch around for some law external to the text to preach, look for some "relevant" story or experience or analysis of the current morass to convince of the text's importance. One should seek to preach the law *of the text.* The law is simply the cutting edge of the gospel and is usually immediately to hand in the text itself in the form of the hard saying, the offensive announcement, the cutting remark, the crucial incident, that sets the whole matter rolling. Doing the text involves taking that and running with it, using it to kill the old and then turning it about so that it can, in the end, be heard as gospel. Doing the text involves using the Word to kill and make alive. Perhaps if we get some idea of what that means we will approach preaching as a sacramental event, doing something, not always and forever trying to turn the text into something to do.

To see what that might mean let us look at a couple of texts. The first is the one about the hidden treasure in Matthew 13:44. I like to use this as an example because it was in a struggle over what to do with this text that the idea of doing the text first struck me. The kingdom of heaven, we are told, is like treasure hidden in a field, which a man found and covers up; then in his joy he goes and sells all that he has and buys that field. As with most gospel texts, it is actually rather difficult to turn this into a law text, turn it into something to do. But I expect we can manage it if we work hard enough at it! In itself, of course, the text hardly proposes something to do to gain the kingdom of heaven and makes no sense at all in such terms. It is just a story about the absolute surprise of stumbling onto hidden treasure, and makes the claim that gaining the kingdom of heaven is like that. But how could that possibly be "relevant" to anything? Law theologians, as we shall call them for short, have to find some way to invest the strange words with a "meaning" we can buy into, some way to translate them into something for us to do. Thus I suppose our law theologian might say something like this: "If you plow your field faithfully, if you really stick to it day after day, if you think positively and really believe in your possibilities and refuse to surrender to negative thoughts, and so on, someday, somewhere, you too might find your treasure." Plowing the field seems the most immediate way you could work in something to do. If you plod along faithfully like a good old workhorse, maybe you too will get yours. Life has its little surprises after all. The kingdom of heaven comes to those who think positively and stick with it. Some day your ship too will come in! You can turn the text into such "Little Engine That Could" theology.

Or there is, of course, that bit about selling all. Now *there* is something to really sink your teeth into, something to do! The price is, alas, a bit higher than I expect we would be prepared to pay! But it is something to *do* at least! If you want to get your treasure, you will have to sell all. You really have to get serious now. Renounce everything, the lusts of the flesh, the pleasures of materialistic society, and so forth. The only trouble is that according to the text it was at his joy at having already found the treasure that the man went and sold all. The action sprang from his joy; it was not a condition for arriving at his joy. In general, it is pretty difficult to make anything but complete hash of such texts by turning them into something to do.

For the disturbing, perhaps even shockingly irresponsible thing about the text is that the man in the first instance did not *do* anything to deserve or earn the treasure. He did not plan for it, he did not strive for it, he did not earn it, nothing. He just stumbled onto it one fine day quite by "accident." You feel about him, perhaps, much like you feel about someone who wins a lottery or a sweepstakes. Lucky stiff! What did he ever do to deserve that? The unspoken resentment is always there: "When, oh when, do I ever in this unfair and cruel world get mine?"

Now it seems to me that the preacher who wants to *do* such a text to the hearers would have to sail right into the storm here and drive home precisely the shocking nature of this surprise. The "law" here, the letter that kills, is precisely the shock, the unfairness of it all. It is the cutting edge of the gospel. There *is* nothing to do. Here God is at work, no one else. Nothing avails. One certainly cannot end the discourse by exhorting the congregation to go out and find some hidden treasure! Hidden treasure just is not that available — as though I could resolve while shaving in the morning that today I am going to find some hidden treasure! In the text we are told that the man covered it up after he found it. It even sounds rather unethical. Apparently it was not even his field! It is truly hidden treasure and it stays that way, hidden even under apparently questionable behavior. I expect the very hiddenness here is related to the fact that Jesus spoke in parables so that those whose ears have become fat shall not hear, and those who think they know shall not know, to exclude completely the notion that here there is anything to do. There is nothing. The treasure belongs to God; it is hidden; it is an absolute surprise. Just imagine how that must have hit in a society where all those parties had their formulas for getting into or realizing the Kingdom! Some said keeping the law would do it. Some said retreating into the desert to practice righteousness and wait was the key. Others said they must revolt against Roman overlords, and so on. But here it is said that the Kingdom is like hidden treasure that a man just stumbled onto. Just think of that!

Now, however, the text has you in a corner. Now what can you do? If the treasure belongs to God, if it is impenetrably hidden, what can you do? Where does the preacher go from here? When I arrived at this point and was struggling with what to say it suddenly dawned on me that that was just the point, there was not anything I could do, no way out, nothing to which I could point. And so there was only one course of action left: I could only give them the treasure! Do it to them! I could only surprise them absolutely by daring to say to the hearers, "You lucky stiffs, you have stumbled onto it here and now because I am here to say that Jesus died and went into the blackness of death and still overcame for you. I am here to say your sins are forgiven! There it is! The hidden treasure! The kingdom of heaven. The preacher has to have the audacity to exercise the office of ministry, the audacity to believe that the very moment of the preaching is itself the sacrament, the audacity to claim that from all eternity God has been preparing for just this very moment and thus to say, "Here it is, it is for you!" The preaching itself is the treasure, the sacramental moment. Now when this is clear, when one is absolutely surprised by that, what is left but to sell all in joy? Sell all your reservations, your false freedom, your investment in your prejudices and paltry goods, your status quo-ism. There is a new day coming! Sell out! When the text is done somehow in this fashion it seems to me the words might actually function as the hidden treasure, be sacramental themselves.

Or take a text like the laborers in the vineyard. Again there is the shocking fact that when it came down to the final reckoning, they all got the same. The preacher would have to uphold the scandal of that. How can one run any kind of business that way? How, for that matter, could such proceedings be held up as a model for justice? We like to do that a lot with Jesus these days! Is there any way one could turn the parable into something to do? One might, I suppose, try to recoup something by saying that at least the last workers did show up to do a little anyway! But that is hardly likely to encourage appropriate behavior! That they all got the same was bad enough, of course, but the reply of the keeper of the vineyard to their indignant questions about justice is the absolute *coup de grace*. (I like that French expression for ending the matter in this case: stroke of grace, i.e., a "mercy killing!") "Can I not do what I want with what is my own?" What can we do about that?

Here we can only sail right into the storm once again, take what the text authorizes us to do and do it to the hearers. More and more I believe we should proceed by just taking the hard saying like that, the key assertion, and put it right up front, leading from that rather than from some cute illustration or story that is supposed to be "relevant" but would just get in the way anyway. We have to face the fact that the gospel is just not relevant to the "old Adam," and nothing we can do can make it so. The old is to be killed in order that the new may arise. Is not that the point of the hard saying? "Can I not do what I want with what is my own?" I would be inclined to start right out with that and drive home, what an awful and frightening thing that is. What can we do about that? How can we possibly get on with such a master? Where does it leave us? That is the law, the letter that kills, the cutting edge of the text. But after doing it as letter that kills, one would have to turn it around so that in the end it would be gospel, be a sacrament. One would have to have the audacity to turn it around and say that our only real hope lies just in the fact that he does do just what he wants with what is his own and that he is doing it here and now in the moment of the absolution, the moment of the preaching itself, the moment of baptism and the supper. The preacher must see the proclamation itself as a sacrament, the moment when what the text authorizes is actually to be done once again in the living present, not just explained or talked about. "Can I not do what I want with what is my own?" That *is* a terrifying thought and *nothing*, absolutely *nothing* can relieve the terror of it unless it is true that right here and now in the sacrament of preaching, of baptism, of the supper he is doing exactly what he wants. Unless the preacher has the guts actually to say that, all is lost and the sermon will degenerate into a more or less hopeless attempt to explain or apologize for such an unjust and unreasonable God. The preacher must simply have the courage to say, "I am here to tell you that you are his own and that you can thank your lucky stars that they all got the same because that is all we can count on in the end. For this God has decided to do something utterly and absolutely wild! He has decided to give you his own here and now. I am sent to tell you that."

In some such fashion as that I would seek to do the text to the hearers, to make the preaching itself a sacrament, the moment when the divine deed is done. Preaching today, it seems to me, lacks nothing so much as simply the vision and the courage to do that. If preaching is not itself a sacrament in this fashion, it degenerates into mere instruction or cheap psychologizing. When this happens the sacraments too gradually degenerate into automats for dispensing a mysterious quantity called "grace" that has lost its relation to the gospel story.

Preaching the Sacraments

A student once told me that he asked his pastor why he never preached on baptism. The pastor replied, "I guess because I do not think I myself could preach a whole sermon about that." I do not know whether the pastor was sincere but the remark does indicate a rather serious state of affairs and probably reflects something of the way things actually are. We indeed *do* the sacraments, thank God, but rarely outside of a few stabs at instruction do we talk about them and, I expect, almost never *preach* them. Preaching them is here to be taken in the sense indicated above: not merely talking *about* them but *preaching* them. In the old days, we are told, only those properly initiated, that is, those who really knew what was going on, could participate in the "Holy Mysteries." Nowadays, it seems, virtually everybody participates readily, but few know what is supposed to be going on. Sacraments seem to be held in high esteem, but they tend to remain "mysteries" in a profane sense, a kind of conundrum. Nobody knows what they are for or about. Perhaps the only reason they are preferred in many circles today is that they are at least better than a good deal of the non-sacramental preaching that goes on.

But if people do not know what sacraments are for or what they are

99

about we must raise some questions about the preaching. How shall they hear without a preacher? No doubt we have overcompensated for the days when participation in the sacraments was contingent upon a rather highly intellectualized grasp of the doctrine *about* the sacraments. The result seems to have been that preaching the sacraments too has been silenced. If people, as we are constantly warned these days, have a poor grasp of the gift given in baptism, for instance, it would seem that the first and most positive move we could make is to preach baptism. It has always seemed at least questionable to me to attempt alleviation of the contemporary difficulty with the so-called indiscriminate practice of infant baptism by restricting the practice. If people do not know what it is, perhaps we ought first to try preaching it more and then see what happens. For centuries there seems to have been a kind of conspiracy of silence in the pulpit about the sacraments. Could it be, perhaps, a covert reflection of the age-old competition between pulpit and font/altar and that this competition plays itself out in the silence of the pulpit about the sacraments? Is the preacher in us jealous, perhaps, about the sacraments? Do we fear that sacraments may undercut what we work so hard to establish with our words? Listening to many so-called "evangelical" preachers who like to remind us that sacraments are not to be depended upon, one could get such an impression. Could the "altar call" for instance, be the culmination of this jealousy, when upon arriving at the altar what you receive is not Christ but a personal encounter with the "evangelist" or his representatives?

In any case, we ought to be forewarned that a battle between Word and sacrament is one the preacher is not likely to win. Increasing preference for sacraments may be just a sign of that. But if it is a battle, it must at all costs be headed off. It can only end in disaster, for both Word and sacrament, preacher and priest. Without a sacramental understanding of the Word, preaching degenerates into mere information; without preaching, sacraments degenerate into "magic."

So let us talk of *preaching* the sacraments. Our talk must be of preaching the sacraments, not merely talking about them. This means in the first instance preaching the sacraments as *gospel*, not as springboards for ethical exhortation (though they may be that too) since that is not where our problem lies. The task is to preach the sacraments as a gospel Word for us, a Word which cuts into our lives, puts the old to death and raises up the new. So preaching the sacraments cannot be just explaining them or even just talking about what they are supposed to do, though some of that may incidentally be involved. If preaching, as I have already tried to suggest, is doing the text to the hearer, then in this case the "text" is the sacramental deed, the visible, tangible Word, and preaching must then be the somewhat exacting and tricky task of doing the visible Word to the recipient in such a way that the audible and visible simply go hand in hand, or better, hand in glove. It must be apparent that there is no competition and that the spoken and the visible Word complement each other perfectly, supporting and reinforcing each other so that together they save us.

Preaching the sacraments involves us in the tricky task of doing a visible word by means of an audible word. No doubt one could get rather tangled up in a linguistic jungle were one to attempt sorting out all the issues involved. But perhaps here we can leave the mental gymnastics behind and approach the matter just by considering the traditional problems that arise in thinking about the relation between the benefits of the preached Word and those of the sacraments. Here we come immediately to the old problem of the inner versus the outer, the "spirit" versus the external "sign," or however one wants to put that.

The basic problem with the preached word is that it goes within and rattles around in the psyche where it can, *ubi et quando visum est deo* (when and where it pleases God), set things right, but also, alas, *ubi et quando visum est diabolo!* (when and where it pleases the devil!) create all kinds of havoc. We have an incurable tendency to collapse inwardly upon ourselves all the time, to feed on our own innards. We are, as the Augustinian tradition that Luther imbibed rightly saw, *curvatus in se*, all turned inward upon ourselves. We have a desperate time getting out at all. I may be coaxed out on occasion but like the nervous groundhog I will be frightened, perhaps by my own shadow, and that is the last you will see of me for some time. All it takes is some little word, some slight mistake, some nuance, glance, gesture. It is like reading books on psychology about some quirk or nasty disorder and constantly reading oneself into the picture.

My internal self constantly defeats or swallows up the word coming from without. The preacher says, "Your sins are forgiven," and tries to explain what a marvelous thing that is. But I say, "It could not really be me that is being talked about." Either I do not find it particularly "relevant" to my "needs," or I can find no guarantee that I am really intended by such words. In particular, I just do not see all those marvelous things happening "within" that the preacher is always blowing about. The preacher says,

"Now if we really believe this, then such and such will result. But then I am driven inside again. Do I *really* believe? Deep down, sincerely, absolutely, truly? What would that even mean, for goodness sake? I get caught in all that adverbial theology. You must learn to think positively, affirmatively, to brighten the corner where you are, to celebrate, be joyful or remorseful, and goodness knows what else. Anything and everything can just drive me relentlessly into myself, no matter how well meaning it may be. "Witnessing" about one's marvelous experiences or preaching about joy and possibility thinking can be the worst of all, something like people who are constantly bragging about their sexual prowess. It just turns everyone inward, wondering if anything like that could ever happen to them. The inner self can be, and most of the time is, a sticky quagmire in which we get hopelessly mired, a bottomless well into which we are forever falling, falling.

In John Bunyan's *Pilgrim's Progress* the first mishap Christian endures on his way to the Celestial City is getting mired in the Slough of Despond. When the man called Help comes to the rescue he asks Christian what he is doing in such a place. "Sir," says Christian, "I was bid go this way by a man called Evangelist, who directed me also to yonder gate, that I might escape the wrath to come; and as I was going thither, I fell in here." When Christian asks why the place was not mended so that poor travelers on the way from the City of Destruction might go with more security, Help gives him a very interesting answer.

> This miry slough is such a place as cannot be mended; it is the descent whither the scum and filth that attends conviction for sin doth continually run, and therefore it is called the Slough of Despond; for still, as the sinner is awakened about his lost condition, there ariseth in his soul many fears, and doubts, and discouraging apprehensions, which all of them get together, and settle in this place. And this is the reason of the badness of the ground.
>
> It is not the pleasure of the King that this place should remain so bad. His labourers also have by the direction of His Majesty's surveyors, been for above these sixteen hundred years employed about this patch of ground, if perhaps it might have been mended: yea, and to my knowledge, said he, here have been swallowed up at least twenty thousand cart-loads, yea, millions of wholesome instructions, that have been brought from all places of the King's dominions. and they that can tell, say they are the best materials to make good ground of the

place, if so be it might have been mended, but it is the Slough of Despond still, and so will be when they have done what they can.[1]

Twenty thousand cartloads, millions of wholesome instructions! Just think of it, all those sermons, all that counseling! But the Slough of Despond remains just the Slough of Despond and cannot really be mended. The inner self remains forever just that sort of quagmire.

This problem of the inner life, of subjectivity, means that we should be aware of the limits of the audible word and that it is just at this point that "Help" must come, something "from the outside," what Luther called the "alien Word," the "alien faith," the "alien justice." The "alien" in this case means it is something that comes entirely from without. The irreducible externality, the givenness of the sacrament, is the seal on the truth of the proclamation. The devil, Luther always maintained, is the master of subjectivity; the heart and the conscience are his playground. He can make a nefarious and poisonous brew out of the finest sermon. I expect anyone who has preached much is well aware of that! As a matter of fact, in the Smalcald Articles, Luther describes the Fall itself as the enticement of the human race in Adam and Eve away from the external Word to subjectivity, "enthusiasm" (God-within-ism).

> All this is the old devil and old serpent who made enthusiasts of Adam and Eve. He led them from the external Word of God to spiritualizing and to their own imaginations . . . In short, enthusiasm clings to Adam and his descendants from the beginning to the end of the world. It is a poison implanted and inoculated in man by the old dragon, and it is the source, strength and power of all heresy, including that of the papacy and Mohamet. Accordingly we should and must constantly maintain that God will not deal with us except through his external Word and Sacrament. Whatever is attributed to the Spirit apart from such Word and Sacrament is of the devil.[2]

The devil, however, is ultimately powerless against the "alien Word," the absolutely from-without word, the visible word. It has happened and even the devil can do nothing about that. And that is precisely what must

---

1. John Bunyan, *Pilgrim's Progress* (New York: Grosset & Dunlap, n.d.), pp. 24-25.
2. BC 322-23; BC-T 312-13.

be insisted upon in preaching in spite of all difficulty and objection. Remember an episode from "All in the Family"? Archie Bunker insists on having the baby baptized and plans to take it secretly if necessary to have it done. His son-in-law Michael protests that he does not want the baby baptized. Archie retorts, "What's the matter, you were baptized, weren't you?" "Yes," Michael says, "but I renounce my baptism." Archie astutely replies, "You cannot do that. You can renounce your belly button, but it's still there!" In spite of all the nonsense, Archie is a better theologian than most of us on that point. It is an alien word. It has happened, and there is nothing we can do about that. No doubt that is one of the things that rankles. That is part of the offense. Just so it also stands against the devil because he can do nothing about it either. In the end that may be our only defense. When Luther was demolished by the devil in his *Anfechtungen,* unable to escape wallowing around in his own subjectivity, he could at last only cry out, "I am baptized!" The word from without, the alien word, at the last may be all we have.

Indeed, there is a strain in Luther's theology at this point that is puzzling and perhaps even disconcerting to us so-called moderns. It sticks out in instances where Luther is even willing to suggest that infants are saved by the faith and prayer of the church. But it does not have to do only with infants because Luther can even say the same about himself. He applies the word, "He saved others, himself he cannot save," to his own situation. "I have saved others, but I cannot save myself," he can say. By that he means that he cannot of his own power free himself from his doubt and *Anfechtungen,* his own self-wrought righteousness seeps through his hands like water, the conscience does not hold its ground. Therefore, Luther says, I can be saved only by another, by the preaching, intercession, sacraments, and communion of the church. In his sermon on Preparation for Communion (1518) Luther could go so far as to say,

> If faith fails you, then grasp the last chance. Let yourself be carried to church like a child and speak without fear to the Lord Christ: I am unworthy, but I cast myself on the faith of the church — or another believer. However it is with me, Oh Lord, I will be obedient to your church, which commands me to go to communion. Even if I have nothing else, I bring you this obedience.[3]

3. WA 1: 333, 13-26.

Then, Luther says, believe truly that you do not go unworthily to the Lord's Table. The faith of the church will carry you, the adult, and not leave you in the lurch any more than the little child who is baptized and saved by virtue of alien faith.

But now this turn of the matter from the inner to the outer, the audible to the visible, from subjectivity to objectivity, a "proper" to an "alien" word, does of course raise another set of problems for preaching the sacraments. The alien word can indeed save from the Slough of Despond, it is not without a certain peril of its own — for the old Adam, at least. It is, after all, an *alien* word, like a strange comet from some other realm. While it helps against the devil because he can do nothing about it, it rankles us as old beings because we can do nothing about it either. The peril is that because we can do nothing about it, we may conclude as old beings that we need do nothing about it. What we encounter is the age-old problem of the objective validity and efficacy of the sacraments, the question of the *ex opere operato,* in popular parlance, the question of sacramental "magic." The problem particularly for preaching the sacraments is that what we say about the alien word, the *ex opere operato,* the "magic" seems to save us from our subjectivity only in turn to be a severe threat to it. It rankles that we, like the devil, can do nothing about its sheer givenness. The "magic," so-called, threatens to overpower, to bypass our subjectivity, our "moral selfhood" altogether.

This was, it is to be recalled, a basic problem at the time of the Reformation. The big objection was to the medieval idea that sacraments "worked" just by being done as long as the individual did not object. Protestants objected that this implied a kind of "magic." Most of Protestantism tried to solve the problem of magic by simply rejecting the objectivity, the externality, of the sacraments in favor of preaching understood as a word addressed to our subjectivity, our inner "decision." The sacraments degenerated into symbols of what goes on within, signs of our dedication and the like. Thus the Word basically disappeared into the inner reaches of the soul, rarely to be heard from again, gradually degenerating into pop psychology and greeting card sentimentality.

The question of how one preaches the sacrament, how one preaches the visible word, what one does about the objectivity, the sign, the elements, becomes an important test case, a crisis for preaching itself. For if, as in most of Protestantism, preaching steps in to *domesticate* the alien, to attempt merely to return sovereignty to our threatened subjectivity so as to leave us in control, then all is lost for both preaching and the sacrament. For then preaching enters into *competition* with the sacrament, and loses its own character as a sacramental word at the same time as it robs the sacrament of its alien power. It is fatal for preaching itself to compete with sacraments, to attempt to domesticate the "magic." By and large this is what has happened in modern Protestantism, if not Christianity in general. And it can happen all too easily in Lutheranism just by default where there is a conspiracy of silence about sacraments from the pulpit.

For the Lutheran Reformation had a quite different kind of solution to the problem of the alienness, the "magic," the *ex opere operato* of the sacraments. The problem for Luther was not the alienness as such, the objectivity, the from-withoutness. The problem, Luther always said, was that the medieval tradition did not give proper place to *faith* as the only possible aim of and receptacle for what sacraments have to give. In the quite correct and laudable zeal to guarantee objectivity and givenness so that the sacrament did not *depend* on faith, the medieval tradition tended to neglect the fact that the very point of the objectivity was to *create* faith, to aim for faith, and that faith was the only possible way a sacrament could be received. Dogmatic assertions are made *about* the sacraments to guarantee their objectivity and efficacy which descriptively may be quite true, but nevertheless do not work at all if there is no delivery system. It is like a gift without either the giving or the card. The problem lies exactly in the question of the preaching of the sacraments. The Word and the sign must go together.

Luther did not complain about the alienness of the sacrament, the objectivity, and not even what moderns call the "magic" of it. I have a colleague who likes to say, "Let's face it, sacraments *are* magic." The real question is whose magic is it? Ours or God's? Luther's objection to the *ex opere operato* was not to the idea that the sacraments work *on us* just by being done, but that they had become means put in our hands whereby we could work on God. Magic, that is, becomes reprehensible if it is understood as a means put in our hands by which we can control or manipulate God. When there is no appropriate delivery system, no preaching, the direction of the "magic" gets reversed. Sacraments are understood not as things God does to change us, but as things *we* do to change God. They become means for priestly manipulation of the gods, and subsequently also of the laity. This can be repaired, not by denying the alienness or removing the objectivity or even the "magic," but only by reversing the direction. This has to be made clear in the teaching, of course, but it can actually be done preeminently in the preaching. The preaching, the Word, has to make unmistakable that it is *for you.*

Preaching the sacrament, that is, if it is to be the doing of the visible word to the hearer, must therefore do that text to the hearer in the same way that the audible word does. The preaching of the sacrament, that is, must not domesticate the alien word, not chicken out on it, but just drive it home. It must in the first instance have the cutting edge of the law, the letter that kills the old Adam in us, cuts into our lives. The very alienness of the sign does that. The water of baptism, after all, is out first to drown the old Adam, not to coddle or be nice to us. The preaching of the sacrament cannot back off from the danger, the offense, involved here. The very thing the old Adam finds reprehensible is what is going to save us in the end. If the sacraments are going to create faith precisely by drawing us out of the quagmire of subjectivity, the Slough of Despond, then they shall have to be preached first of all as just the alien word that sounds the death-knell to the self that always collapses into itself like a black hole. It is just that alien word that draws us out again into the freedom of faith.

Luther found a new way to affirm that sacraments save us. True, they do not save us "automatically," as though that could happen without our knowing it. They do not work like a magic potion or a medicine or a vitamin pill. Such things work with or without our necessarily being involved. But sacraments save us because they work on us to create faith, just as the audible word does. They give us something to believe, as Luther said. The sacrament, that is, works to create the faith that receives it. But this can occur only when it is properly done and preached, called and recalled to mind. Not that they work secret magic without us, carry out some hidden agenda unknown to us, but that their indubitable alienness continues to work on us in the preaching of them to put to death the old inwardly directed being and raise up the new, turned outward to God. That is what it means to say that baptism, for instance, is not just a once-upon-a-time act, but a continuing act, a matter of daily renewal. Preaching baptism is the quite alien act that kills and makes alive in the renewal. It is quite correct to say, of course, that sacraments are not efficacious without faith. But the faith spoken of is precisely faith *in* the sacramental deed itself, the faith created by the sacrament. The case is not, as with most modern Protestantism, that one has to go somewhere else and get something called faith to qualify for participation and so come back to get it. No, the faith that receives the sacrament is faith in the sacrament created by the sacrament itself as Word and sign.

Further, in driving home the very alienness of the sacrament, the troublesome and persistent question of the place of the elements also gets a different theological cast and use for preaching. Where sacraments are understood as a kind of magic potion, the words become incantation that are somehow supposed to "change" the elements, to make them "holy." The words need not be addressed to the hearers at all. Or where sacraments are understood as sacred analogies or symbolic actions, one rummages about trying to conjure up the symbolic significance of the elements and signs. One talks about the "nature" of water, or the crushing of the grape and the grinding of the wheat, the symbolic significance of eating, and so on. One tries to ameliorate the alienness, the stubborn materiality and externality of the elements by explaining them or changing them via the verbal symbol system. One tries, you might say, to have the elements swallowed up by the words, obliterated by or disappear into the words. Perhaps it is the sacramental equivalent of allegorizing: the elements are changed to fit our story, not *vice versa*. But the elements will not disappear into some other story. One is reminded of the old argument about whether the body and blood of Christ are changed by the human digestive system when the bread and wine are devoured. Luther aptly replied, as did the Fathers, by saying that *our* bodies are changed, not Christ's. The elements stay in their own story. Indeed, the stubborn persistence of the outward and material is itself both attack on our incurable inwardness at the same time as it is to be comfort.

Luther always liked to insist, furthermore, that the elements, the outward signs, belong intrinsically to the story. God, he said, never gives Word or Commandment without something outward or material.[4] This precisely is part of the attack on our unfaith, our turning inward upon ourselves. When discussing why it is useful to believe that Christ's body is present in the bread, Luther (though first entering a disclaimer about the place of such "why" questions because the Christian is simply to take God at his Word) says that the first benefit is "that clever, arrogant spirits and reason be blinded and disgraced in order that the proud may stumble and fall and never partake of Christ's supper, and on the other hand, that the humble may be warned and may arise and alone partake of the Supper, as

4. LW 37: 135.

St. Simeon says (Luke 2:34), 'This child is set for the fall and rising of many in Israel.'"[5] The elements themselves participate in the attack on our pride and bring us down to eating "humble pie." Just as the water drowns, so the bread and wine bring down the pride. It is, to sum up, a great and mighty offense that I, great religious being that I am, should be reduced to depending for my eternal salvation on eating a bit of bread and drinking a sip of wine.

Perhaps we have gone about matters in quite the wrong way in the business of relating word and element. We have asked what the words do to the elements, expecting, no doubt, that they raise the elements to some lofty spiritual heights. They change them into heavenly substances or elevate them into lofty symbolic systems. Perhaps we ought rather to ask what the elements do to the words. Perhaps it is just as much the case that the elements help to bring the words down to earth. At any rate, it is obvious that it is vitally important for preaching the sacraments that here the very alienness, the materiality of the outward, finds its place and use in a story quite different from our general inward and upward spiritual flight. It is obvious that for someone like Luther, at least, that story is the story of Jesus, the despised and crucified one who was nevertheless raised, the one who brings eschatological hope. In baptism one is baptized into that story. In the supper one participates in its end and its hope. "As often as you eat this bread and drink this cup you proclaim the Lord's death until he comes." The elements stubbornly refuse to be removed from that story and thus they participate in it and, in fact, do that story to us. I expect that is what it should mean to say that the elements are "consecrated." They find their place in the eschatological story and do it to us in the form of the promise. Indeed, one should say that they find their true place in the story, a place that was lost with the fall. Water no longer washes us clean because we have turned inward upon ourselves where the water can no longer touch us. But here it is true once again, back in its true story, the washing of regeneration. One day it will once again be all we need to be clean. A bit of bread and a sip of wine no longer satisfies us here. It no longer gives life. Bread is what we fight for, defend ourselves for, die and kill for. We call it ours. But here it is taken from us and put back where it belongs. "This bread," says the Lord, "is mine and I mean to have it back. "This is my body." And it is free. And so it shall be in the end.

5. LW 37: 131.

Preaching in such fashion might alleviate current worry about the use of the sacraments in the church. Just as with complaint about the risk of free grace we worry whether practice may not be too liberal. Do we baptize too indiscriminately? Are we too open in communion? No doubt we must take care that practice does not undercut, cheapen, or mock the gift. But we also need to remember that the alien justice of God given unconditionally does throw us into a perpetual crisis. When the *sola gratia* does not seem to work to our satisfaction, the temptation is always to retreat and make it not quite *sola*. When we get nervous about "cheap grace" the remedy seems to be to make it at least a little expensive — bargain basement, maybe, but at least not cheap. But then the battle is lost. When confronted by the perpetual crisis of God's liberality we must simply forge right ahead and become even more radical about the *sola*. Grace is indeed not cheap. It is free! But the radicalization must be carried out precisely in the preaching. Grace full and free must always be preached so that it kills and makes alive. If it is cheapened to coddle the old Adam, that is indeed bad enough. But if one tries subsequently to remedy the cheapness by making it expensive, that is absolute disaster. The only cure for cheap grace is radical grace. And this can be done only in the preaching of it, doing the text to the hearers.

There is cause for alarm, I have come to think, in a church where one wonders whether the gospel is being preached anyway, where nervous pastors and theologians are anxious to take steps to remedy supposed misuse of the sacraments merely by withholding or restricting them — in effect, raising the price. If the remedy for cheap grace is not raising the price, but rather radicalizing it to free grace, then could it not be that a large part of the remedy for misuse and misunderstanding of the sacraments lies also in radicalizing them precisely through the proper preaching of them? I just do not believe it possible today to convey the right message by arbitrary restriction of practice. It will always be interpreted as clerical highhandedness and legalism. I suspect the only weapon we have left in this battle is the preaching itself. So it is imperative that we take steps to use it properly.

But how shall we do it? No doubt sacraments should find their way into a good many sermons if not all of them. When there is a baptism or a baptism Sunday there should be a specific baptismal sermon. Perhaps the best way to close out this essay is to offer again some concrete suggestions and experiments to exemplify what I have been talking about.

I begin with baptism. If baptism is to be preached in accord with what I have been saying, it should be preached as the unrelenting and unconditional divine yes that cuts off our inward flight at every point, lays the old to rest, and calls forth the new. It would probably go something as follows. Baptism regenerates, it works forgiveness of sins, life, and salvation. But how can it do that? Simply by being what it is, a washing with water that cannot be erased together with the speaking of the promise, the creative word, the divine yes spoken over us, spoken *to* us from the outside, from the beginning, the first and the last word about us, the word calling us to life out of our death "in Adam." "You are mine," says the Lord God. "You always have been and always will be." But that, of course, is incredible. Maybe even frightening. Thus all the questions come tumbling out, all of them attempts to take the gift and retreat inside, protests of the old Adam and Eve who know themselves to be under radical attack in their inner bastions.

But in the preaching all the questions must be countered relentlessly by the divine yes. Is baptism enough? Yes! It works forgiveness of sins, life, and salvation. Live in that and hear it again each day. Believe that it is enough and that is certainly enough! Would it have all that significance even if I were only a baby and did not know what was going on? Yes, because it was *God* who spoke that yes over you. God is *God*. What about my response? Are you saying that I do not even have to respond? Now that, of course, is the trickiest question of all in the old Adam's arsenal. It too can only be countered ultimately with what is perhaps an equally tricky yes. Yes, I am saying you do not have to respond. What is the matter, do you not want to? It is the old Adam who can only think in dreary terms of *have* to and ask stupid questions about it. The old is through, drowned in the water. If you think it is a matter of *have* to, forget it! Here we are calling forth the new who simply *wants* to! This is the divine yes calling to our yes in the Spirit. "Awake thou that sleepest and arise from the dead!" Come out of your stinking tomb! But, but, do you mean to say I am not free to reject? Yes. I should hope so! What in the world do you want to do that for? How could you call such rejection freedom? To reject must be only the most horrible form of bondage. It certainly is not "freedom"! Does that not mean that God is taking a great risk? Yes indeed. But he takes it nevertheless, even unto death. Are you saying, "Once saved, always saved"? Yes. What is wrong with that? I am counting on it, aren't you? It is the divine yes, *God's* Word. You do not mean that grace is irresistible, do you? Yes. I find it to be so, do you not? To be sure, grace is not *force*. Grace is just grace and as such it is by definition "irresistible," I expect! Does that not mean it could be grossly misunderstood, misused, and abused? Yes, I expect it does. But God suffered all the abuse to bring it to light. Is that not what it's all about? Should God, as Luther could put it, call off his goodness for the sake of the ungodly? If so, who at all would be saved?

The answer, you see, is yes, yes, yes. It is God's yes, and he will go on saying it until finally you die of it and begin to whisper, "Amen! So be it Lord!" Baptism *does* regenerate. Of course this is dangerous business! So-called evangelicals will howl about sacramentalism and object vociferously to the "magic" of such externalism. And they are quite right to do so if sacraments are only analogies or allegories of our inner life. If sacraments, that is, leave the old subject intact we could not speak like this or put such confidence in sacraments. Either we must preach them so they kill the old Adam and Eve or we'd better forget them. A sacrament that has all the objective validity we want to claim for it and still leaves the old subject intact is only an invitation to disaster.

As short experiments on the Lord's Supper, I offer some sermons preached in our seminary chapel. They give some indication, I hope, of what I have been talking about. Also, I expect, since they were preached in a seminary chapel one presupposes some things one would not for the ordinary parish.

Text: John 6:35. I am the bread of life

When your life and mine come down at last to bread and wine, will it be for us the sacrament of his presence? We had thought, perhaps, that we were destined for grander things. We had thought, no doubt, that we should have been eligible for the food of the gods, some celestial elixir perhaps, or at least something capable of "turning us on" or sending us on a trip somewhere, even if it did not turn out to be very far after all. For everyone knows that religion has to do with grand things, being transported, perhaps, to some Elysian fields, some never-never land, some heaven or other, through the food of the gods? Yet here we are, gathered around a hunk of bread and a bit of wine. Is that not strange? Are there not more relevant sacramental substances on the market?

I suppose that in our disappointment, or even despair, we have been tempted to make something more of the bread and wine than just bread and wine. We have told ourselves that it is mysteriously changed into something else, some heavenly substance, or perhaps that it symbolizes a much more important transaction that goes on elsewhere — maybe even in the "depths" of our souls. We have wanted to make it worthy, to promote it, make it worthy of our exalted religious sensibilities. But here it is, just bread and wine. And there is a kind of stubborn persistence in its being just what it is.

Now it may just be that the point, or at least a large part of it, is just that. It may just be that it is the voice of creation, this earth, calling us back from our excursions elsewhere, and that it is here that we will find our Lord and each other. Luther says in one instance with characteristic bluntness that "God used bread and wine in order that the proud may stumble and fall and never partake of Christ's Supper; and on the other hand that the humble may be warned and may arise and partake." Offensive? Perhaps. And yet perhaps it has to be. Because I expect that for most of us it is a long way down here to just bread and wine. It takes some dying. But our Lord is here calling to us, calling us back to our true home. Calling to us out of his sacrifice unto death to a sacrifice that will meet and unite with his. He gives us bread and wine and says to us, "Take, eat and drink. It is good bread and wine. Your sins are forgiven." And when we heed his call, eat bread and drink wine, taste its indubitable reality, we will get an inkling of what he meant when he said, "I am the bread of life." For down here you will find him. And not only him, but yourself and all your brothers and sisters. Eat and drink, rejoice, for you have come home!

Here is a second experiment, preached some time ago during the Watergate affair. The text was 1 Corinthians 11:23-26.

Text: 1 Corinthians 11:23-26. To Reclaim His Own

We meet here today amid the tangled skein of tapes with sections erased, resignations and firings high and low, lies and deceptions, unkept promises and broken truces, wars, injustices, hunger, and poverty, to see if we can once again clear a little space amid the clutter to partake of the Supper of our Lord. And what should it be for us in the midst of all this turmoil of body, soul, and spirit? Well, it is for us what it has always been. Nothing can upset or erase these words. The context in which they were first spoken is not unlike that in which we find ourselves today. It means that God is for you all the way to the end.

We might, I suppose, be tempted to turn that into cheap and easy comfort. God is for me? So what is new, Reverend? A comfort perhaps, that enables us to make peace with what is happening all about us, or at least just to endure it until it all blows over and we have shuffled off this mortal coil for more pleasant climes. But it is not, of course, that simple. For the fact that God is for us in such a fashion as we have here is in many ways rather uncomfortable. It would have been better if he had not gotten quite so close, if he had stayed in heaven where he could do no more harm. But he did not. He has come to be for you. He has come to claim his own back again, come into this place where bread and wine go to the highest bidder, where people's lives and reputations are peddled for it, where clever ones kill and cheat for it while the less clever and the innocent suffer and starve and die. He has come into *this* world and by his sovereign act taken this bread from us and said, "This is my body, my blood, and it is free." He comes to reclaim his own and to give it to us as a foretaste of the way things are going to be. Here is real bread and wine, real because he has reclaimed it; taken it out of our fallen story back into his own story; in, with, and under it is his body and blood and thus it is without price. Bread and wine are what they were meant to be and will be again one day.

Yes, God is for you, all the way to the end, for you in *his* way, with his goal in mind. That is not cheap comfort but it is ultimate comfort. And does this not speak to us amid the clutter of the day? Does not this ultimate comfort discomfort us about the world we see around us? Can we eat this bread and still look away from those for whom bread is too high priced? Can we eat this bread without price and still tolerate the liars and cheaters who traffic in people's lives? I put the question to you and invite you to come and meet the God who is for you, eat this real bread and drink this real wine. Fear not! For he has great things in store and one day, one day, this Supper alone will be left and all the clutter gone. Amen!

My third and last experiment is on John 6:53, the discourse on eating the flesh and drinking the blood of the Son of Man which shocked many of Jesus' own disciples to the extent that they went away and no longer went with him. It is a classic example of the way the preaching of the sacrament does cut into our lives to kill and give the possibility of life.

Text: John 6:53. Come Out, Come Out Wherever You Are

"Truly I say to you, unless you eat the flesh of the Son of Man and drink His blood, you have no life in you." It is of course preposterous, is it not, that we, great religious and indeed "spiritual" beings, aspiring virtuosi in the realm of beautiful abstractions, experts in the domain of inner feelings, and thus masters at avoiding the issue and stalling off the end, preposterous that we should be bidden to depend for our eternal well-being and salvation on eating a bit of bread and drinking a sip of wine? This is a hard saying. Who can hear it? It is indeed enough to drive a person away. But then where or to whom shall we go? Shall we then, as is our wont, turn inward upon ourselves to that enticing realm of pure ideas and warm feelings for some final assurance and consolation? Ah, but the inner self, however much it is indeed to be cultivated can in this regard be a quagmire, a bottomless pit. Our forebears in the faith have warned us about that. We are, they have said, *curvatus in se,* all turned inward upon ourselves so that we have a desperate time getting out again. We are called out, but like that stiff tapioca pudding we used to get when we were children, we keep snapping back again, disappearing into ourselves.

Do you really — I mean really, deep down, in the "ground of your being" — believe? Are you *really* sincere? Have you got the Spirit? How can you tell? So the questions turn upon the inward self. How shall I answer? Indeed, what is all that supposed to mean, after all? (At this point in the sermon I inserted the section about the Slough of Despond quoted earlier in this essay.) The inner self is a quagmire, a Slough of Despond from which there is no escape. Not without Help. "Lord, to whom shall we go?" Is there anyone? Is there anything "out there" at all to help us? Well, there is this preposterous and astounding word: Whoever eats my flesh and drinks my blood has eternal life, and I will raise them up on the last day. You can count on that. Just think on it! That's all there is to it! Come out, come out, wherever you are. The game is over! Repent and believe it. It will save you!

Conclusion

I do not know how successful these very short experiments are. Some are not so radical as others. But I think you can get a glimpse of what I was trying to do. I was trying to do the visible word to the hearers, to preach the sacraments in such a way that they are not undercut and thus in such a way that they might actually be a means of grace, that we might come to trust them as a sheer gift which actually saves us, calls us out of the darkness of our own inner selves into the glorious light of God's salvation.

Public Ministry and Its Limits

So we are ambassadors for Christ, since God is making his
appeal through us.

2 Corinthians 5:20

I have basically two things to say about "special ministry," by which, I take
it, is intended what has traditionally been called ordained ministry. First,
what distinguishes such ministry from other ministry in the church is simply its public nature: It is a public office to and in which one is "ordered"
by the church. One so ordered is called to exercise the office of ministry
publicly, that is, to prosecute the mission of the church publicly and to care
for and be accountable to the public theology of the church. The second
thing I want to say follows from this: This public exercise of the office is
limited, indeed, self-limited, by what it has to ad-minister, that is, by the
gospel itself. The gospel allows no higher appeal beyond itself. Where it ex-
ceeds that limit and appeals to "higher" or "other" authority, it falsifies itself as ministry of the gospel and succumbs to law. The aim of the office is
to set people free from sin, death, and the devil by the word of the gospel
and to call into being thereby the church which proclaims and waits upon
the coming of the eschatological kingdom of God.

Since we are here concerned with "A Call to Faithfulness," probing
the confessional tradition of Lutheranism for guidance in the confusion of
the day, I take the question to be, how can the confessional heritage be so

brought to bear on the understanding of ministry as to ensure that it be a ministry of the gospel and give it the spirit, authority, power, and structure to meet the challenges confronting the ELCA today?

My conviction is that the answer to this question lies in the confessional understanding of the call to public office, the public exercise of the divinely instituted office of ministry as authorized and ordered by the Word of God. It is my belief and hope that this confessional view should provide at least a starting point for our discussion. I believe the confessional view of a call to and investment with public office mediates between more Protestant tendencies on the one hand and more Roman views on the other and that it can provide a foundation for contemporary reconstruction. To state my own conclusions at the outset relative to the questions that are before us lest there be any doubt, I do not find sufficient warrant either in the confessional tradition or in current pragmatic arguments for a threefold ordained office, if by that one means three ranks of ordained clergy. I am not so concerned about a lower order such as that of deacon — though pragmatically it has rarely worked (as even Karl Rahner admits in *Sacramentum Mundi*) and shows no great promise of working except under rather particular conditions. I shall not say anything further about that in this essay because I am more concerned about the claims made for an ordained episcopal office and what goes under the rubric of "the historic episcopate." In spite of the pragmatic arguments that might be entered for it, I believe that the claims made for this office almost always represent a transgression or obscuring of the eschatological limit and therefore endanger a proper evangelical ecclesiology. I believe we should look more seriously at the confessional view of the public office of ministry to meet the problems confronting us.

Ministry: Doing the Divine Deed

First of all, however, I find it impossible to speak about ministry without saying something about its roots, what it is for.[1] The basic problem in our

1. I take conscious exception here to the kind of hermeneutics of the Augsburg Confession that assumes supposed gaps in the argument are to be filled with pre-Reformation material — as in, for instance, Avery Dulles and George Lindbeck, "Bishops and the Ministry of the Gospel," in *Confessing One Faith*, ed. George Forell and James McCue (Minneapolis: Augsburg, 1982). It is not possible here to avoid entering the debate on the level of the

understanding of ministry is a cancer within, a crisis in the message itself that works out into uncertainty and constant fussing about the doctrine in actual practice.

To put it in most pointed fashion for our purposes here, ministry in the light of Lutheran confessional theology is the actual doing of the divine election in the living present by setting bound sinners free through the Word of the cross. Rightly considered, this sets the Lutheran view of ministry off from both Roman views on the right and Protestant views on the left. To put it most pointedly, a minister is not a priest whose task it is to procure or infuse the grace that prepares you to be elected, nor a teacher who informs you about election (or damnation!) in eternity or (more lately in modern Protestantism) tries to explain what to do now that God does not elect anybody. A minister is rather an ambassador, one who is called, authorized, and sent to do the bidding of the sovereign — in this case, to do the electing as authorized by the crucified and risen Jesus.

The necessity for ministry as a specific activity for Lutheranism roots in just that fact. An electing God does not ultimately need satisfying or explaining. An electing God does not need gurus, priests, shamans, rabbis — what have you — but ministers, ambassadors. Ministry *is* publicizing the "mystery hidden for ages in God who created all things," and now revealed in the church (Eph. 3:7-13). The Word of the minister in the name of Jesus *is* the doing of the divine deed in the present.

But just to mention the doing of election by setting the bound free through the word of the cross *(theologia crucis)* is, alas, at the same time to indicate the reason for our persistent problems. For Lutherans, like other Christians, are nowhere so divided as when it comes to such matters as election, bondage, and a theology of the cross.

It is just here that ministry, both Lutheran and otherwise, stands at the crossroads today. Where the sense of doing the electing deed is lost, ministry falls apart into competing camps. It halts between two possibilities, a more Roman one on the one hand and a more Protestant one on the other. Either the minister becomes an ecclesiastically sanctioned priest or a

---

theology of the Reformers themselves and attempting some constructive effort on that basis. The method proposed by Lindbeck and Dulles seems to be rooted in the kind of contemporary hermeneutics that thinks it possible to disregard the historical background and preceding documents as well as the intentions of the authors and arrive at an interpretation determined simply by the text itself. Whatever the value of such a method, it surely demonstrates its shortcomings in the instance of confessional texts with their historical precedents.

teacher-cum-guru. Where we are not about the business of setting the bound free by doing the election, ministry divides according to the various ways one might seek to influence whatever is left of the free will of fallen beings. It becomes either the task of dispensing the power of grace to assist the will or the task of explaining why the supposed free will ought to choose God or let Jesus into the heart (whatever in the world that could mean!). A curious and desperate irony develops. Being scandalized by the divine election, the minister can seek to serve only by undoing it, like an ambassador who seeks to serve by telling sweet lies about the policies of the sovereign represented to avoid scandal. In sum, ministry becomes the business of misrepresenting or hiding, not revealing the truth of the electing God.

The real crisis in ministry is at bottom a crisis in the proclamation itself. The power and authority have to come from within, in the message itself, the power of the Word to set bound sinners free by the actual doing of the electing deed. When that does not happen, it really matters little what kinds of authority we grasp at to lend ourselves some prestige and dignity. That is all just police work, the authority of the law.

The Call to the Public Office

The commission to actual doing of the election culminates in the public office. This means that the sole difference between the ministry of all the baptized and that of the ordained is the distinction between a more private and a public exercise of the office. In the call to public office, ministry "crosses the line," so to speak, invades the orders of this age to set the captives free. Ordination in that sense is not elevation to a higher "order," a being lifted out of this age, but rather a daring and dangerous movement into the world, into this *publicum*. In the public office, the age to come, the kingdom of God stakes out a claim, sets up an embassy, here in this age. One of the most serious problems today is that we have acquiesced to the modern idea that religion is simply a private matter and so surrendered this public calling. As a result, ordained ministry as a call to public office loses its rationale. It is then difficult to explain why any of the baptized with requisite "skills" could not do as well or better than the ordained. If there is no embassy, no public mission, one has really to scratch to come up with a reason for an ambassador, a public minister. Since the Holy

Communion is about all that is left of the public cult, the only unique thing left to the ordained is that for some forgotten reason, they get to preside at the Supper! Subsequently, one then tries to build a rationale for ministry on that basis, and among Lutherans to look, perhaps, to the confessional documents for support. But, it just is not there. Because the Lutheran confessional view of ministry is centered on the understanding of the call to the public office of ministry.

The Confessional View

When one understands ordained ministry as such a call to the public office of doing the divine election, the articles of the Augsburg Confession on ministry make perfectly good sense and are quite adequate and consequent in and of themselves. As public ministry, it is ordered ministry and that in a double sense: one is ordered to do it, and it is to be done in orderly and accountable fashion.

Articles 5 and 14 set forth the move to the public office tersely, and Article 28 discusses the question of the abuse and the limits of the office. Article 5 is not so much directly an article on ministry as it is an article on the way the Spirit takes in the invasion of this age, this *publicum*. The way is through the external Word and the sacraments. Not, that is, through private visitations that would turn the minister into a guru, but through the external Word and the public proclamation thereof. Thus Article 5 declares that in order for justifying faith (Article 4) to be obtained, "God instituted the office of ministry (German: the office of preaching), that is, provided the gospel and the sacraments. Through these, as through means, he gives the Holy Spirit, who works faith, when and where he pleases, in those who hear the gospel." The Spirit, that is, works publicly through external means, not through occasional and private affairs. That this is the main point of the article is clear both from its predecessor in the Schwabach Articles (VII: "other than this there is no means, mode or way to receive faith"), and from the anathemas that follow. Article 5, of course, does not yet speak explicitly about the public office, but the foundation for it has been laid. At least two points must be noted. (1) Since God has gone public in the gospel and the sacraments, God has instituted the office. It is God's idea. It is an office — like that of law, for instance — that simply awaits exercising. (2) Since God has instituted it, and his Spirit uses it as means, when and where he pleases, the power and authority of the office is intrinsic, it comes from the power of the Word itself. That is to say, it is not an authority *we* have or can possess or confer on one another. We are called to exercise it faithfully and care for it, but it is not ours. It is God's. It can be exercised only in the faithful saying, the preaching, of it.

The move to Article 14 about the public ordering of this office is therefore logical and consequent. "Nobody should publicly teach or preach or administer the sacraments in the church without a regular call." This move must be watched very carefully because it is the occasion for both most of the sense and nonsense in our view of ministry. The problem, or the promise — as the case may be — is in its very leanness. What is meant by "regular call," *"rite vocatus"*? Do we not need a lot more than this spare statement? I believe Wilhelm Maurer is right when he says that it is a mistake either to make too little of this idea of a regular call to public office or to read too much into it. So I would like to make some points that seem to me to be consonant with what the confessors wanted to say.[2]

First, one should connect the *rite vocatus* with the fact of divine institution in Article 5. There is no particular sacramental magic here. That is so because for the confessors all public offices are divinely instituted. As Maurer put it, "In [the office God] stoops to serve us, just as he does elsewhere through temporal government. This parallel shows that the institution of the office of preaching is not a special spiritual and sacramental event: it occurs within the three hierarchies [church, politics, economics] through which God rules his creation."[3] As with other divinely instituted offices, the legal form it takes is not important and can vary according to the particular needs of time and place. The only stipulation is that it be regular, that is, in conformity with the law applicable in the given case.

Second, the call to public office has its own internal rationale. Since it is a public matter, the call comes only through the church, through God's people. All private and individual claims to possess the Spirit are uncertain and cannot be taken as a warrant for the public office. No one can make him or herself a King or Queen, or a magistrate or a President, or for that matter, an ambassador. God does that through regular means, that is, in

2. The section on the call to the office of preaching and public proclamation in Wilhelm Maurer, *Historical Commentary on the Augsburg Confession,* trans. H. George Anderson (Philadelphia: Fortress, 1986), pp. 188-204 (hereafter: Maurer) should be carefully studied in this regard.

3. Maurer, p. 189; LW 46: 219-22; 37: 364.

this case, through the church to whom the Spirit has been given. The call to public office has, therefore, its theological rationale from within, and is not simply a matter of "good order." It has to do precisely with the means through which the Spirit works to make the divine decision public.[4] What makes this office "special" therefore, and gives it its status is not the legal form it takes, but precisely the "office" it is to carry out.[5]

Third is the question of what supposedly is missing. Given the fact that the office is divinely instituted in the giving of the gospel and the sacraments, and that thereby the move to public exercising and ordering of the office is inherent to its own nature, I see no justification for the complaint that there is some glaring or frightful lacuna here which for ecumenical, practical, or church political reasons has to be filled in with borrowings from Rome, Canterbury, or Constantinople. A reading of the history and consideration of the theological roots of the matter simply does not support the contention that the confessors at Augsburg either presupposed Roman canonical ordination or were somehow conscious of or worried about the "irregularity" of their own ordinations. I do not see how it is possible upon reading the sources to maintain, for instance, that "regular call" or *rite vocatus* somehow presupposes Roman canonical ordination. As Maurer would put it, "Later efforts to interpret the 'regular' in a ritualistic sense were just as wrong as the attempt to read into it a conscious effort to be vague for tactical reasons." Indeed, the confessors "adopted Luther's broad view, which linked with openness to future legal developments, guaranteed a basic legitimacy to the evangelical office of the Word so it could unfold without restraint."[6] Furthermore, as Maurer points out, the freedom in regard to legal structure did not mean vagueness or openness with regard to but precisely rejection of the traditional form of ordination. As early as October of 1524 Luther insisted on a new order for ordination for theological and not just practical reasons: because the bishops ordained mass priests and that this in itself involved renuncia-

4. See Maurer, p. 191. We should indeed take much care about what we say of this office. It should not be run down but elevated. But such elevation comes because of the content it is to deliver, indeed, the function it has to perform, not by giving it a legal or ecclesiastical form that borrows authority from elsewhere. It was because of its content, its function, that Luther praised it most highly as the foremost of divine estates — indeed as the one without which the world would long since have perished.

5. LW 46: 220.

6. Maurer, p. 193.

tion of the gospel.[7] The evidence is quite clear. "Regular call" *(rite vocatus)* means a call by the church according to its applicable laws and does not imply or need anything more than that.

Fourth is the ordering and accountability of the office. The concept of the regular call to the public exercise of the office carries within itself, at least potentially, all the ordering and public accountability that we need. One called to public office is to exercise that office according to the public standards and theology of the church. Where we are faltering today, we must take steps to fix things. But we do not need to borrow from authority structures inimical to our understanding of the office. In any case, the main problem is the cancer within, and no amount of grasping at institutional guarantees will fix that. Indeed, it will only hasten our demise.

In sum, we have missed a bet in neglecting the idea of the call to public office and turned instead to haggling about in-house ecclesiastical politics. Instead of asking what it means to exercise the divinely given office publicly, we have argued as though it were a matter of qualifications for getting into a private club. If we could recover and extend the idea of exercising the public office responsibly we would, I think, be well on our way. Maurer indicates that the idea of the public office accorded to the preacher of the gospel was something of a new thing. It was not fully fleshed out in 1530. Article 14 itself played an important role in the history of jurisprudence.[8] I should think that were we to go back and pick up some of that we would find plenty of building blocks with which to reconstruct our view of ministry today. For then we would be building on what promises to be more amenable to the modern world rather than regressing to older monarchical ideas of authority.

---

7. Maurer, p. 194; LW 40: 12-15. The argument from silence often used here is not very convincing. It goes something like this: the Imperial Confutatio accepts Article 14, provided "regular call" be taken to mean Roman canonical ordination. Therefore, it is to be assumed that the confessors themselves presupposed such canonical ordination. Neither the history nor theology of the matter as I read it would support such a view. Even if Melanchthon in reply to the Confutatio in the Apology (Art. 14) expresses the desire to retain the traditional church polity, he cannot but reiterate that such polity is of human and not divine authority, and he continues to insist that it is the bishops themselves that make it impossible not merely because of physical cruelty, but because they force the evangelicals to forsake and condemn the sort of doctrine they had confessed. It would seem strange to take this without further ado as an acceptance of or presupposition in favor of Roman canonical ordination.

8. Maurer, p. 198.

The Public Office: Lapses and Limits

Working from the idea of a call to public office, we can begin to assess more usefully some of the problems we face today. As already suggested, when ministry no longer understands itself as the public exercise of the office of divine election, it loses its rationale. One of two things tends to happen. Either ministry lapses, retreats into the sphere of the private and inner life, or it tries to preserve itself by borrowing authority structures from other (and mostly older!) public offices, most often thereby exceeding its limits. Either, that is, the minister becomes a therapist or a guru, or an ecclesiastical power broker, either a functionalist looking for something useful to do or a politician looking for a throne.

Both of these misadventures, it seems to me, are evident today. Time does not allow us to defend that judgment, so I shall attempt just a brief word about them. The first tendency, the minister as privateer, guru, therapist, or what have you, is certainly evident enough not to need much documentation. It is, moreover, perhaps the most serious practical problem for ministry from the point of view of the public calling. It is a result of succumbing to the privatization of religion in the contemporary state. Since the modern world no longer believes in an electing God, it has retreated to the world of the inner self, the world of pure practical religion, self-consciousness, feeling, or other sorts of *Schwärmerei*. Religion becomes a purely private matter. When the church becomes a private cult it is difficult to say any more why an ordained public minister is needed at all. Furthermore, when those called to public office themselves capitulate and no longer do what could be called public proclamation, no longer do the electing Word, but rather just make public display of private emotions and opinions, what does one need that for? Many if not most of the baptized can do just as well or even better at that. If Christianity is a private matter, what we need is better gurus, not public ministers. And the problem is — let's face it — Lutherans do not make very good gurus. Not even batteries of so-called "practical" courses can perform that miracle!

Now this brings me to the second misadventure, the temptation to overstep the appointed limits of the public office. This is the greatest danger, perhaps, from a theological and ecclesiological point of view.[9] Much of

9. If, as suggested above, the sole remaining mark distinguishing public from private ministry is that the public minister gets to preside at the Supper, then perhaps it is only con-

the argument about bishops and the historic episcopate and such seems to be pragmatic: we need them, supposedly, to shore up our sagging practices. Or perhaps for ecumenical reasons: to become legitimate. We could no doubt argue endlessly about such matters. But what concerns me is the more central theological issue. The basic temptation in all public offices — secular or sacred — is to transgress the eschatological limit, to blur or overstep the line between the power of this age and the power of the age to come, to attempt to bolster one's temporal authority by illegitimate drafts on the divine — to claim, perhaps, that the worldly form exists *de iure divino,* as it was said. Not only is the gospel then endangered, but tyranny is always just around the corner. If kings could claim divine right for their rule and succession, why cannot priests and prelates do the same — only with much more clout because they have to do more directly with God's kingdom? If kings could live in palaces, why not bishops and archbishops?

The situation is particularly precarious for the public office of ministry because its task is to proclaim the eschatological power of God through an earthen vessel. It has to do with the transcendent power of the kingdom of God, the gospel. So it must watch itself very carefully. I expect this is one of the most urgent tasks of genuine *episkopē.* The highest exercise of authority it knows, therefore, the ultimate, the end of the line, is always the gospel. The gospel cannot, by its very nature, appeal to or depend on any authority higher than itself, its own inherent power, the power of the Spirit. The bottom line here for the Reformers was always simply, "My sheep hear my voice." "I am the door of the sheep. If anyone enters by another way, he is a thief and a robber." The eschatological limit runs right through the office itself. It is, paradoxically, an office that declares the end of all offices! Perhaps what is "special" about it is that it will be the last to close! The temptation is always to forget that, always to borrow from or

---

sequent that there be a move to bolster the sagging fortunes and prestige of that office by resorting to more Roman and episcopal understandings of ordination. Then ordination does not mean being called to the public office, but rather bestowal of some special charism. One so endowed, consequently, can be said to be "constitutive of the church," and so forth. But this is surely too grandiose. A public minister, however necessary to publicize the message, does not constitute anything, and certainly not the kingdom to be represented. The minister communicates and carries out the policies of the sovereign, but does not constitute them. Where this is forgotten, the office gets remystified, so to speak. One may, of course, salvage some prestige for the office among some in this fashion, but I fear its essence is frittered away.

lean too heavily upon or overextend worldly patterns of authority and power.

The monarchical episcopate is, of course, the most obvious example of transgressing the eschatological limit. But we must ask whether we do not have before us today more subtle and modest but equally dangerous temptations in the same direction. What shall we say of what is called "the historic episcopate"? Can we expect that the vestigial remains of the ancient authority form will rescue us? History and experience, it seems to me, give little encouragement to either pragmatic or ecumenical arguments. History, ironically, is not kind to the "historic episcopate"! The historic episcopate has neither protected the church from error nor has it united the church. Were we to adopt it — how, I do not know — where would we go to get it among all the claimants to it? The historic episcopate, it would seem, does not of itself guarantee anything.

It is surely the case that the Lutheran confessors are concerned first and foremost to place all institutional forms, particularly ecclesiastical ones, under the eschatological limit. Running through all the confessional writings is the basic distinction between divine and human ordinances. That is what the question of abuses is about. Abuses occur when human ordinances are elevated to the level of the divine. It may well be true, as is often said today, that the old distinctions between divine versus human right or divine institutions versus human ceremonies are no longer so clear or usable as they were in the confessional generation. But if that means simply that divine right and divine institution drop out of the picture altogether, we are left just with human right and ceremonies. But then we are worse off than before! For then human right becomes a matter of might makes right, or vote, or influence. The sanction of history or the spirit or whatever humans fancy is likely to be claimed for human right. Then there is no one to protect us at all anymore! We are at the mercy of whoever grabs the power. Lord protect us from that!

What the Lutheran confessors did, to put it in contemporary jargon, was to reinterpret the question of divine versus human right in eschatological terms. That, surely, is what Article 28 of the CA is about. It is essential to recognize that they did not reject the idea of divine right. But they reinterpreted it in terms of the gospel. The only exercise of divine right allowed is the preaching of and care for the gospel and the administration of the sacraments. The only authority bishops can wield by divine right is identical to that of an evangelical pastor: to preach the gospel, to forgive sins, judge doctrine, condemn doctrine contrary to the gospel, and exclude the ungodly from the Christian community.[10] Everything else is strictly penultimate, exists by human right, and is variable human institution. It is penultimate and has its place this side of the eschatological limit. It is human ordinance. Institutions and legal forms are, of course, necessary in this age, and it may even be that traditional ones are preferable. But that is a question of human right. Furthermore, wherever the office of preaching the gospel is denied, inhibited, or frustrated, by either secular or ecclesiastical claims, the ministers of the gospel will have either to suffer or resist — no doubt both. They cannot, that is, knuckle under to any temporal power that claims to transcend the eschatological limit. That is why Luther always insisted that Christ is the head of the church, not any temporal ruler, be it Pope, Patriarch, Archbishop, Bishop, Council, Assembly, or whatever one might name.

Article 28 of the Augsburg Confession is not, therefore, as many would like to claim, an apology for bishops and their power, but precisely the attempt to bring the authority and power of the office back under proper eschatological limits. It was a setting of the conditions under which the confessors could possibly countenance episcopal jurisdiction at all. In those days, the abuse of this-worldly power to enhance the office was open and flagrant since many bishops were also secular rulers. They could back up ecclesiastical decisions with troops. In our day, the temptation is subtler. One calls on an ancient authority system that has the appearance of being ecclesiastical because that is the only place left in the world where it has survived. Or perhaps one calls on the "voice of history" as we are so wont to do today. Are we somehow protected from the ravages of time by calling an office "historic"? Is that in principle different from those medieval bishops who used more physical armies for support? We do, of course, look to history for continuity, guidance, and help. But surely we must not be romantic about it and must look as much at mistakes and discontinuities to learn from them as well.

An episcopate, that is, cannot claim divine "right" over and above that of a pastor on the basis of its being "historic." The highest exercise of authority in the church is the preaching of the gospel, and if bishops were to serve properly, they would be concerned precisely to insist on that. The complaint at the time of the Reformation, of course, was that the bishops

---

10. (CA 28:21) BC 95; BC-T 84.

did not allow the preaching of the gospel. Sometimes one wonders if things have changed all that much! If the bishops then were too occupied with disposing over ecclesiastical affairs and properties to have any enthusiasm for the gospel, have matters changed all that much? Can a bishop — or even the pastor as local bishop — preach the gospel, given all the desperate cares of oversight? Perhaps we ought to ask that question more seriously once again. The most often mentioned reasons, it seems, for the "historic episcopate" have to do with law and not gospel. Why is that? Indeed, we are threatened increasingly today by borrowings from contemporary forms of authority — those taken from the world of business and government bureaucracy and their "head offices." That, of course, affords new opportunities and closets for all sorts of nefarious business. Over against all of that we have to remember the insistence of the confessors that the office is limited by its own eschatological message. Where that is forgotten the office simply cancels itself out. Whatever continuity there is here is a continuity in the preservation and proclamation of the eschatological Word. It is the continuity of the community that lives in this age by hope.

The office of ministry today is beset by many a foe, within and without. I happen to believe that the main trouble is the cancer within, the worm at the core of things, the basic question of the integrity of our confession, our "identity" as current jargon has it. This cannot be fixed merely by cosmetic institutional moves. For then we just take on the identity of the institutions we imitate. We begin to look like them.

The trouble with our understanding of ministry is its rootlessness. It needs first and foremost to be grafted back onto its roots. Our problems are basically theological. It is not possible to graft a Lutheran tree onto a Roman or Episcopal root. The basic structure of authority in Lutheranism rests on different foundations.[11] My contention is that if we could some-

11. Once the move away from doing the divine election to explaining or dispensing grace is made, further problems become immediately apparent. The problem of authority and power in ministry takes on a radically different shape. Since the authority and power of the Word is not understood to be intrinsic to itself, the power to put to death and the authority to call into being that which is from that which is not, one is left just with arguments about words and their interpretation. Who is to say who is right? The hermeneutic demands an authoritative voice. The buck has to stop someplace. We need a pope or a bishop or a Curia to preside over the wayward and unruly enterprise. For if you really believe in the supposed freedom you teach, Lord only knows what would happen! You cannot then aim to set the bound free, but must rather attempt to bring the free under control. So you have to take

how regain the understanding that ministry has to do with the making public of the divine election in Jesus Christ and that the call to ordained ministry is the call to exercise that office publicly in a faithful and responsible manner, then ministry would draw its strength from within and would not be so tempted to look to institutional power structures for support. What has to be done is to re-form the once proud catechetical traditions of Lutheranism, and certainly to concentrate on the preparing of pastors to be ambassadors for Christ who do the divine deed. We need, of course, strong and efficient institutions. But it is a mistake to look to them as such or alone for salvation. They can only serve the proclamation of the gospel. The gospel is the ultimate source of our authority, the *telos* and limit of the office of ministry.

Postscript

Throughout the contemporary discussions about the ministry of the church I have consistently, I believe, tried to raise what appears to me to be the fundamental *theological* issue, specifically, the question of the eschatological limit and how that relates to questions of authority and office. The question I have wanted to discuss is not just the pragmatic question of whether we need a "historic episcopate" to shore up our discipline or close wounds in the *oikumene*, but rather the question of whether our eschatology does not prohibit the moves proposed in that direction because they transcend the eschatological limit.

Rather than serious theological discussion on such matters, one usually encounters only counterfeit arguments — *ad hominem*, regional and even ecclesiastical slurs, or perhaps appeals to the dire needs of the moment. If one objects to the idea of the "historic episcopate" and what goes with it, one is, supposedly, a "Scandinavian pietist," afflicted with an "upper Midwest virus," or perhaps caught in the prejudices of a particular seminary, ruing its lost hegemony, or one has become — *horribile dictum* — a denominationalist! All this is sheer counterfeit argument. There is no

---

steps ecclesiastically to keep that supposed freedom in line. The freedom you give with one hand, *you have to take back with the other!* Beware whenever a minister grants you a little bit of freedom because that is all you will ever get! Furthermore, even that which you have will be taken away! But the ministry of the gospel, the ministry of making the truth of God public, has to be the truth that sets you free!

serious discussion of the theological issue, just smokescreen. Nothing is gained by it but ill will.

Perhaps the greatest disappointment of contemporary discussions on this issue is the tendency to settle back with the labels — most prominently, it seems, those suggested by George Lindbeck: "movement" Lutherans (evangelical catholics) versus "denominational" Lutherans. Given the pessimism of Lindbeck's view that there is little likelihood that these two "confessional construals" will ever change or come together,[12] it simply becomes an excuse for either desertion or schism. Aside from the fact that it is already something of a slur to be called a denominationalist (who would admit to such in an "ecumenical" age?), it is also specious for people who are not themselves yet ready to accept the papacy and all that goes with it to call others denominationalist. Simply harboring serious theological reservations about Rome does not, it would seem to me, make one a denominationalist. Likewise, refusing to believe, on historical and theological grounds, that CA 28 represents some kind of "offer" to Rome that could or should now be renewed, should not be cause for schism. Unless those who consider themselves "movement" Lutherans are proposing that we can accept union with Rome just as things stand now, they should refrain from calling those who continue to be honest about their reservations denominationalists. It is time, it seems to me, for a little less posturing and more honest conversation.

12. Forde is referring here to a paper that George Lindbeck gave at a 1990 Conference at St. Olaf College, Minnesota, on the "Call to Faithfulness." Its proceedings were published in *dialog* 30 (1991). Lindbeck's contribution is entitled "Ecumenical Directions and Confessional Construals," pp. 118-23. Forde's essay in this present volume can be found in the proceedings, pp. 102-10.

Something to Believe:
A Theological Perspective on Infant Baptism

Our know-it-alls, the new spirits, assert that faith alone saves and that works and external things contribute nothing to this end. We answer: It is true, nothing that is in us does it but faith, as we shall hear later on. But these leaders of the blind are unwilling to see that faith must have something to believe — something to which it may cling and upon which it may stand. Thus faith clings to the water and believes it to be Baptism in which there is sheer salvation and life, not through the water, as we have sufficiently stated, but through its incorporation with God's Word and ordinance and the joining of his name to it. When I believe this, what else is it but believing in God as the one who has implanted his Word in this external ordinance and offered it to us so that we may grasp the treasure it contains?[1]

The editor of our church magazine once remarked that baptism is one of those matters about which earnest churchgoers seem to get the most perturbed. Why should this be? Why should supposedly stalwart believers in the unmerited grace of God get so upset when that unmerited grace is given freely? The "world" has no problem with baptism. So-called marginal Christians have no problem with baptism. Infants have no problem with baptism. Apparently only adult Christians, indeed often the most pious, fear that baptism may be harmful to spiritual health. Is there a kind

1. "The Large Catechism" in BC 460; BC-T, 440.

131

of *charo-phobia* (fear of grace) abroad in the church? If baptism is to he withheld from infants, should the latter not also be removed from other ministrations of grace? Perhaps the old practice of dismissing the catechumens was more consistent? But even the catechumens were allowed to come under the preaching of the Word!

Such questions bear examination. Each of them hints at fathoms on the theological depth chart that we cannot begin to plumb in this short essay. Suffice it to say for now that baptism, particularly infant baptism, remains something of a permanent offense, especially, it seems, to the more ardent of adult Christians. This fact provides a kind of backdrop as we proceed to our task: an inquiry into the theological basis for the practice of infant baptism. Here at the outset, we should like to stipulate two clarifying strictures: First, "infant" in this essay shall be taken to mean children of Christian parents, parents who have at least enough relationship to the church to request baptism for their children; and second, the intent is to attend as strictly as possible to the theological argument, leaving aside arguments of a more pragmatic, historical, sociological, or psychological sort that might also be brought to bear on the question.

Setting the Question

First, it is important to frame the theological question properly so that we might hope to arrive at an appropriate answer. Karl Barth looms over the contemporary discussion with an eminence that cannot be ignored, so we shall begin with him. Barth insisted, in essence, that to be valid, the practice of infant baptism must be proved to be part and parcel of the doctrine of baptism itself, grounded and anchored in baptism's very nature. Baptism, that is to say, "ought to be implicitly and explicitly, inclusively if not exclusively, the doctrine of infant baptism."[2]

The case for infant baptism therefore can be made only if it can be demonstrated that we are commanded and permitted to baptize young children, *and that it is necessary to do so,*[3] because they are the children of Christian parents. Furthermore, this is to take place at a time when, according to human judgment, it is impossible for these children to have any

2. CD IV/4, trans. G. W. Bromiley (Edinburgh: T. & T. Clark, 1969), p. 169.
3. CD IV/4, p. 175. Emphasis mine.

knowledge about what is to be decided: The doctrine must prove that such practice is a faithful discharge of the divine commission in conformity with the general dealings of God with humans established in Jesus Christ.[4]

If we were to set the question the way Barth did, it would seem to be this: Can it be proved from the nature of baptism that the baptism of infants is necessary? If not, we must conclude, given all the debits, that infant baptism is at best a "profoundly irregular" practice.[5] To be sure, Barth was no Anabaptist. Even though infant baptism is, as he saw it, "highly doubtful and questionable," one cannot say that it is invalid.[6] Nevertheless, dogmatics cannot any longer support the practice and must call the church to account.

A comprehensive treatment of Barth's (in many ways splendid) doctrine of baptism cannot be our purpose in this essay. Of primary concern for us is the setting of the question. Surely it is too stringent to set the question as though it were a matter of proving the necessity of the practice. Acts of grace, if they are truly grace, simply do not admit of such proof or necessity. A gift loses its character as sheer gift if it comes with the force of necessity. It becomes law. To be sure, the church in the past has often said that baptism is "necessary" to salvation, that it is the only remedy for original sin, and so forth. So it was argued that infants, too, must be baptized lest they be lost.

Arguments about necessity demonstrate, however, that it is imperative to distinguish between legal necessity and what might be called evangelical necessity. If baptism is considered a legal necessity, it becomes a requirement that must be fulfilled lest damnation ensue. The gospel becomes a law. Barth's argument seems to take on this character. Indeed, one wonders whether his demand for a necessity flowing from the nature of baptism itself is simply the final outcome of his insistence that law follows and flows out of gospel. Where such necessity cannot be proved, the practice must be rejected. One wonders as well whether the argument is not a return to the stipulation that all liturgical practices not biblically provable are to be rejected.

If, however, one operates on the premise that whatever "necessity" there is behind baptism is an evangelical, that is, a purely gospel necessity,

---

4. CD IV/4, p. 175.
5. CD IV/4, p. 194.
6. CD IV/4, p. 189.

the question about infant baptism will likely be put quite differently. The necessity involved in baptism is that of a sheer gift, necessity of the sort that evokes faith, trust, hope, and love. Whatever necessity there is, is carried within itself. To use the analogy of love, one might say that baptism has about the same necessity as that of a lover's kiss. That is certainly not a legal necessity! If it is, love has already flown. But if the lover were asked, "Is this really necessary?" what could the answer possibly be? Most likely one would reply that the question was ridiculous! What sort of necessity is behind an unconditional gift?

Such questions expose the peculiar difficulty of setting questions about acts of grace, and especially about infant baptism, properly. Most of the time, the questions presuppose a legal framework and so turn out to be traps. There is no way to answer them without imperiling the close but subtle relationship between unconditional grace and faith. Is baptism necessary to salvation? Can we simply depend on the fact that we have been baptized? Does baptism work "automatically"? So the questions go. But they are traps. If, in the attempt to protect individual choice, one hurries to say, "No," one simply negates the grace of it. The pastor saws off the limb on which he or she is to stand. If, in the zeal to protect grace, one hurries without further ado to say, "Yes," one will likely be accused of ignoring or belittling the place of faith. Then the aim of baptism will be shorted out. The questions must be put more carefully. Perhaps the best immediate response to questions about the necessity of baptism would be: "Speak for yourself. But beware, the answer will be a confession!" Questions that are traps are best turned back to expose the questioner. In other words, one has to make it clear that the answer itself is already a faith statement.

Barth's demand for proof of necessity asks for something an evangelical argument cannot really give. When Luther was asked about necessity with regard to the sacraments, he generally refused to give a legal answer. In the quote from the Large Catechism with which we began, the reasons given for baptism as an external sign are just that faith may have something on which to stand, or that we may grasp the treasure it contains. In reply to the question why it should be necessary to eat bread and wine when all the benefits could be gotten in other ways, Luther says, "God means to fill the world and give himself to us in many different ways, to help and strengthen us by his Word and works; shall we be so complacent and bored that we hinder him and tolerate nothing but the way that happens to please us? You are a black, hopeless devil!"[7] The answer is not a legal one. The necessity involved is simply that of a gift, and the gift carries its own necessity within itself. But, of course, as Luther's parting shot indicates, refusal of the gift exposes the intended recipient. The lover's kiss is not legally necessary, but spurning it carries its own kind of peril! No doubt that is why the church has always said that it is not the absence of the sacrament (that is, where it is not available) that condemns, but the despising of it. The gift is not legally but evangelically necessary. It carries its own power within itself, in its own giftedness. To refuse it means that one is exposed as impervious to such giftedness.

It is the task of systematic theology to impel us to speak and act faithfully in the light of what God has done in Jesus Christ and continues to do through the Holy Spirit. If we are to speak faithfully about baptism, particularly with regard to infants, we must set the question so as not to undermine the nature of the gift itself. The question, therefore, should be put more graciously. It cannot be a question about proof or necessity in a legal sense. Given the gracious activity of God in Christ, must we not rather ask whether there are any evident or overriding grounds for excluding infant children of Christian parents from baptism? The question, then, is not whether it can be proved that we must baptize such infants, but whether we may do so, whether it is a faithful and hopeful practice to do so. The question is not whether we can prove theologically that infants must be included, but whether there are unimpeachable theological grounds for excluding them, not whether we must, but whether we *may* baptize infants. To put it most directly, is excluding infants from baptism simply because they are infants a faithful practice? Does it foster proper witness to divine grace?

Baptismal Faith

Now if we have set the question, we must seek to answer it. The biblical texts do not do this. The answer must, by the nature of the case, be grounded in the theology of the matter. Barth was certainly right about

7. LW 37: 141. The view of necessity represented in this essay — and also, I think, in Luther — parallels that of Eberhard Jüngel on the necessity of God. God is not to be understood as a necessary being but rather one who in sheer graciousness is "more than necessary." Baptism, likewise, is not necessary but "more than necessary." *God as Mystery of the World*, trans. Darrell L. Guder (Grand Rapids: Eerdmans, 1983), pp. 14-35.

this. This is not a counsel of despair. The Bible is not a rulebook for liturgical practices. That is to say, the answers must come from the nature of baptism itself. Since the crucial question for us here is that of the relation between baptism and faith, and since Luther constantly warned us that baptism and faith should never be separated, we can best get at what we need by asking about baptismal faith.

What is baptismal faith? Baptismal faith is nothing other than faith in the activity of the triune God. It is the faith that the almighty creator of heaven and earth acts in Jesus Christ through the Holy Spirit in the living present to reclaim his lost creatures. That is to say, baptismal faith is the belief that there is a God "out there" in what Luther calls, in the quotation cited above, the sphere of this "external ordinance" (*das äusserliche Ding*, as the German more pointedly has it), a God who runs the whole show. It is the trust that this "external" event, this washing with water, is the act of the electing God. It is the belief that this happening, at a specific place and time, is the will of God "for me." In Luther's words, baptismal faith is nothing other, quite simply, than believing in God, the God "who has implanted his Word in this external ordinance and offered it to us so that we may grasp the treasure it contains."

Since it is a strictly "external thing" and not my doing, faith, as Luther says, has something to believe. Such an assertion shocks us because it implies that, without a current event such as baptism, faith has nothing to believe and therefore no ground to stand on. And that is, indeed, Luther's point. Faith is precisely the trust called forth by such occurrences of grace in the "external" world as baptism in the confidence that they reveal the will of almighty God "for you" according to his Word and promise.

Whatever the difficulty involved, there is here the belief that all things happen according to the divine will or, as Luther put it, by divine necessity. We have to do, after all, with the triune God. If it were not so, faith could not have any confidence in baptism or, for that matter, any other present advent of grace, even preaching itself.[8] If it were not so, the

---

8. Cf. LW 33: 43, "Christian faith is entirely extinguished, the promises of God and the whole gospel are completely destroyed, if we teach and believe that it is not for us to know the necessary foreknowledge of God and the necessity of the things that are to come to pass. For this is the one supreme consolation of Christians in all adversities, to know that God does not lie, but does all things immutably, and that his will can neither be resisted nor changed nor hindered." Frightening as that may be, it is nevertheless the guarantee that the promises are not lies.

ultimate will behind baptism would be some form of human willing: social custom, ecclesiastical pressure, parental superstition, personal decision, or just Grandma. But if God is triune, if all things happen by divine necessity, then *whatever* the contingencies that appear to us to be operative, even "just Grandma," the ultimate will behind the event is almighty God.

Baptism is therefore never just an "accident," for the works of the Trinity are undivided. Baptism is the revelation of the will of God, something that comes to us from without, an "external" thing. Without the external thing, faith has nothing to believe except, perchance, some ancient religious history. Faith then simply collapses inward upon itself. Its only recourse is somehow or other to muster the effrontery to trust its own fervor and sincerity.

Because of its irreducible externality, baptism is a preeminent sign of the priority and therefore the offense of pure grace. The difficulty in most arguments about baptism is that the very thing objected to is the point and power of baptism. "You do not mean to say that a mere external ceremony can save, do you?" So the question forever goes. But this is the entire point of baptism. The grace is in the very offense of externality. The grace is in the fact that the triune God has intervened now "for you." The intervention from without is the declaration that the God who runs the whole show is indeed *for* you. Baptismal faith is precisely to believe this. It is simply to believe in God.

The standard worry about this seems to be that such a view will lead to a species of "cheap grace," the current pop defense against all forms of free and unconditional grace. If it is somehow mysteriously infused just by "going through the motions," does that not render all activity on our part unnecessary? Once again, the way we answer will betray us. Usually, one is tempted to turn back to the self again and set up hedges and conditions of various sorts. "No, of course it will not 'work' unless you 'have enough faith,' or are properly converted, or feel it in your heart, or show it in your life," and so on, and so on. The speech implies that one has to go somewhere and get faith and then come back so baptism can "work." The self is simply set back in the driver's seat. But the point is that the very externality of the event renders the self and its activity not only unnecessary but obsolete, old, indeed dead.

The tragic irony of most discussions about baptismal faith is that the temptation to call on human decision to protect baptism simply undercuts it. The very point of baptism is to save us from having to depend on our own decisions. The very offense of externality is itself the only real defense against cheap grace. It is the announcement that God refuses to pander to us. Grace is not cheap, or expensive; it is free. That is the real problem. The free gift alone destroys the self who wishes to stay in control. If it were not free, the old self would still be in business. Baptism signals the end of old beings incurably turned inward upon themselves, who use even their own religiosity as the last line of defense. The self has to be turned inside out.

Baptism, we have always been told, regenerates. How so? Precisely by intervening in the endless turning of the self in upon itself, thus breaking the self's incurable addiction to itself. This is why baptism as external event is the primary attack on original sin. The church has always sensed that there is a consequent relation between baptism and original sin, but has perhaps not defined the matter as aptly as it should have. To be directed outward by baptism spells the beginning of the end for original sin, the "lack of original righteousness," that is, trust in self rather than in God. To say that original sin is "removed," as though it were a quantum rather than a relational matter, would be inaccurate since the old self obviously still persists. But as Protestantism has preferred to say, original sin is now exposed for what it is, its guilt is forgiven and just so its "reign" is over. To be reborn is to be saved from the devil, the world, and the self, to be turned inside out, to be claimed by the baptizing God, the God "from without," who truly transcends us, the triune God. Hence, we are baptized into the name of this God — Father, Son, and Holy Spirit — and no other.

Such is the nature of baptismal faith. The persistent source of difficulty and cause for complaint over against baptism is the failure to get the relationship between baptism and faith right. The most pious Christians in particular seem to be offended by the claim that "baptism saves." Protests are always forthcoming in the name of "really sincere" faith or obedience or whatever. In the name of such protests, it is often asserted that one cannot "count on baptism." But then the preacher simply shoots himself or herself in the foot, leaving faith with nothing to believe. The problem arises because of the failure to see that the claim, "baptism saves," *is* already a faith claim. It is the way faith speaks. Of course it is true, as Luther continually insisted, that faith is the only way baptism can be received. Faith is the only possible "receptacle" for grace, the only possible way to receive a promise. But faith can be faith only when it has a concrete promise to believe. Accordingly, the faith in question has always to be precisely faith in the baptism (Word and sign) itself, not merely belief in ancient religious history — even if it is the history of Jesus.[9] The devils believe the history of Jesus — even that he is the Son of God. But they do not believe that this history is "for them."

Thus we have the systematic insistence on the precedence of the external over the internal. Faith must have something to believe, something that happens in the living present to which it can cling in all adversity. Baptism does not differ in this regard from any of the other concrete occurrences of divine grace. The preaching of the gospel is an "external" event perceived by the senses, as is the Lord's Supper. As Luther asserted, "Whatever God effects in us he does through such external ordinances." The gospel promise "must be external so that it can be perceived and grasped by the senses and thus brought into the heart."[10] The proper order in this sequence is that the promise and sign from without come first, and only then the internal; the faith that receives it comes second. The fire of faith within is always kindled by the flame of the external event. Indeed, the external event comprehended in the divine Word creates the faith that receives it.

Baptism and Time

If we have correctly gauged the nature of baptismal faith, then it should be apparent that the questions about "whom" to baptize and "when" are considerably relativized. Baptism is an eschatological event and so ends all old continuities and sequences. As Edmund Schlink declares:

> In baptizing children the church knows that the temporal sequence of faith and Baptism has been relativized by God's eschatological activity. For in Baptism God encloses the entire past life of the baptized as well as that which is still in the future. The temporal sequence of events in the course of life has been eschatologically nullified in Baptism: The baptized has in Christ already experienced his future death, and the life of the one risen from the dead has already been opened for him. In

9. Cf. LW 40: 213-14. "If now I seek the forgiveness of sins, I do not run to the cross, for I will not find it given there . . . But I will find in the sacrament or gospel the word which distributes, presents, offers and gives to me that forgiveness which was won on the cross."

10. BC 460; BC-T 440, from the Large Catechism in the paragraph just following that is cited at the outset of this essay.

this eschatological bracketing the question whether the faith of the person to be baptized must necessarily precede Baptism fades away, and the temporal sequence of faith and Baptism cannot be made the norm of validity.[11]

Since the appropriate sequence is from the external to the internal, the external event always establishes its priority over its internal reception. There is no essential difference on this score between infant and adult baptism. Indeed, Jesus seemed to think that the adult should become as a child, not vice versa! In baptism the adult, too, is "born again" as a child of God through the external sign and the promise: To be baptized is to be put under the divine priority. To believe this is precisely to let God be God. Whatever one was prior to this event is not to be prolonged but "drowned" in the gracious water. As we have suggested, this is the very root of the offense and the reason why baptism is a persistent target of attack. Old beings always resist the priority of grace.

Included in this view is the understanding that baptism quite obviously can never be a "once upon a time" event. As old beings, we never give up. So baptism continues to work, putting the old being to death, by its very externality, until the end. Whoever is baptized, infant or adult, must be nurtured in this faith until the new self who believes in the God "out there" at last arises. The order is baptism–faith, not faith–baptism. This sequence must maintain itself, whatever the age or maturity of the recipient.

There is, therefore, no overriding theological reason for withholding baptism from infants. Baptismal faith is neither clarified nor promoted thereby. Such practice only invites reversal of the proper theological order with its disastrous consequences. A "faith" based on such reversal may be ever so pious, but Luther's question still remains: Does it have anything to believe but itself? To be sure, the baptism of infants in itself is no guarantee that proper baptismal faith will be forthcoming. And one can, of course, readily recount the failures of the practice.[12] But in infant baptism the sequence is maintained and the possibility of baptismal faith is permanently opened. Since baptism is, in any case, a permanent offense to old beings, what is needed is proper nurture, not belittling, questioning, discrediting,

11. *The Doctrine of Baptism*, trans. Herbert J. A. Bouman (St. Louis: Concordia Publishing House, 1972), p. 160.
12. *The Doctrine of Baptism*, pp. 161-62.

or postponing. An evangelical pastor must not begin by sawing off the limb on which he or she stands. Our speech about baptism must be more faithful than it has been of late. The only cure for the abuses surrounding baptism is to teach and preach it properly, not to withhold it.

As with all ministrations of unconditional grace, the church here stands at a critical crossroad. In the face of all the difficulties and failures in baptismal practice, evangelical preachers must learn to either become more radical about grace or give it up. Of course we all know about the failures. Of course we all know that arousing faith to be grasped by its heritage is the only solution. But the mistake of the past has been to turn to preaching faith, exhorting, describing, cajoling, or threatening. Now we have to consider whether this was not precisely the wrong move. Preaching faith is like trying to make flowers grow by pulling on them. The very thing one wants to promote is killed. So the church is dying. Faith does not grow by preaching faith but rather by proclaiming and nurturing the hearers in the grace given in baptism.

The Great Divide

Now it is obvious in all this that the question of infant baptism entails not just the doctrine of baptism but the broader dogmatic system and its use in its entirety. The ultimate root of difference in our speech is that there is a great divide in the way Christians look upon baptism. It is not just a difference in practice — say, whether to baptize infants or not — but a difference in theology. Edmund Schlink, in his study of baptism, speaks of this difference as an "antithesis," which marks "the most profound difference" in the understanding of baptism. "That antithesis," he maintains, "is the understanding of baptism as God's deed or as man's deed, as the sign given by God or as the sign of human self-obligation before God."[13]

All of which is to say that the root issue is whether in baptism we have to do with divine election or in some way with the self-disposition of the human will. Obviously, where it is assumed that baptism is a sign of human self-obligation before God, infants cannot be baptized. Infants are not capable of such heroics. But the problem is even deeper than this. Wherever it is held that salvation depends in any way or to any degree on

---

13. *The Doctrine of Baptism*, pp. 168-69.

the free choice of the will, infant baptism will always seem a highly questionable practice, even in those churches where it is regularly practiced, for then the self always moves into the center as the real subject of the baptismal act. The faith of the self becomes the primary focus, or perhaps even the faith and sincerity of the parents. The claim that God is actually doing something fades from view, and infant baptism becomes a pious communal custom whose theological rationale has long since been forgotten or surrendered.

This turn to the inner life of the self has, of course, been the sad fate of Christianity since, at least, the Enlightenment. Rejection of infant baptism as a matter of theological principle is but a surface manifestation of this fundamental alteration. Given the presupposition of free choice, traditional definitions of the sacraments themselves contribute to the problem. When it is said, for instance, that a sacrament is a "visible sign of an invisible grace," the implication is that grace is a mysterious something, perhaps in the water, which somehow empowers the weakened but nevertheless free will. All attention is then directed inward. One tries to determine whether it has "worked." If it has not, blame will eventually be unloaded on the self, which is to say that grace becomes a secret agenda. One must search the inner self to discover whether one has it or not.

Yet this leaves sacraments in a precarious position. Given the presuppositions, the house divides itself into those who believe that baptism somehow imparts such "invisible grace" and those who, for fear that the will of the self will be bypassed, reject it. The idea that the sacrament bestows an invisible grace just by being performed is rejected as "magic." The self must then find other ways (for example, conversion or immediate experience) to assure itself of divine favor. The sacraments consequently become mere signs of the supposed success of this venture. That is the end of the road. Everything turns inward upon the self. The self is never set free. The modern self is something like a black hole, endlessly gaining incredible density by sucking everything into itself.

The claim that baptism should be seen as the act of the triune God external to the self and all its continuities, an external deed that itself creates faith, presents us with an alternative to both the traditional view of an infused invisible grace and the modern turning of the self in upon itself. What the church needs today is to be grasped by the audacity of acts of unconditional grace like baptism. God simply breaks into, intervenes, in our lives because God knows what is good for us.

To baptize is to have the confidence that sinners who are bound will be set free. Freedom is not violated if one is set free. So it is that baptism is a "cure" for sin. Sin is addiction to self, no matter how pious its form. An intervention from without is necessary. The dead are not consulted, nor do they play any part in their resurrection. God takes over such matters. We can be saved by divine intervention alone. The external act is as necessary to save the pious from themselves as the impious. So it is never completed in this life and must hit us daily until at last it is done with us, and we finally whisper, "Amen!" Baptism saves us.

If we get an inkling of the audacity of the divine intervention, a consequence even more shocking to the self comes into view. The real question is not whether baptism should be withheld from infants, but whether it can legitimately be withheld from anyone at all! If all we have said here is true, so the question goes, should we not simply go out in the street and "hose 'em down in the name of the triune God"? The question is, once again, a trap, perhaps a last desperate act of self-defense. Answer with a shocked, "No," and the battle for grace is lost. The smile is lost and pessimism sets in. Answer with an unqualified, "Yes," and the grace–faith relation could be lost. In such instances the best reply is a question that might expose the questioner. One might simply ask, "Would that not be fun? Would it not be marvelous if we were in a position to do that?" Mass baptisms of that sort have been done before, even in Scripture, and in some instances are still being done.[14] Most of us, after all, would probably not be Christian today if it were not for some such wild event far back in our history.

Certainly it should be the first desire of the evangelical preacher not to restrict but to spread abroad the grace of God as widely as possible. The fact that we have to refrain from doing so does not follow from the theology of the matter but from the sobering fact that we are not in a position to follow the action with the nurture that is needed. But the fault is then neither in the theology of baptism nor in the candidates for baptism but rather in us. Restricting baptism, that is to say, should never be a matter of theological principle and certainly not a cause for rejoicing. Rather it can only be cause for regret. We have to ask whether it is not really a sign of loss of confidence in both the truth claim of the Christian message and the fu-

---

14. I understand from our church officials that some five thousand Masai are to be baptized en masse this summer in Tanzania!

ture of the church's mission. In one of his more audacious statements, Luther could put the matter this way:

> Since God has made a covenant with all the heathen through the gospel and ordained baptism as a sign thereof, who can exclude the children? If the old covenant and the sign of circumcision made the children of Abraham believe that they were, and were called the people of God, according to the promise, I will be the God of thy descendants [Gen. 17:7], then this new covenant and sign must he much more effectual and make those a people of God who receive it. Now he commands that all the world shall receive it. On the strength of that command (since none is excluded) we confidently and freely baptize everyone, excluding no one except those who oppose it and refuse to receive this covenant. If we follow his command and baptize everyone, we leave it to him to be concerned about the faith of those baptized.[15]

Think of that! A covenant with all the heathen! To be sure, we are not obligated necessarily to baptize everyone, no one can be forced, and we must do everything we can to nurture the baptized. There must be proper prebaptismal counsel and proper baptismal addresses and sermons. But the church must look first to itself in these matters. No good is accomplished by complaining about lack of sincerity or discipline in parents. If what we have said here is true, it is likely that there is more of the vestigial remains of baptismal faith in the "superstition" and "magic" that impel some to the font than there is in all the posturing about self-obligation. What are we to say to the fact that most people are still willing, even eager, to have their infants baptized, but are reluctant to let the church have any more to do with them? Should we not wonder, at least occasionally, whether that is more a judgment on the church than on them? Could it be, perhaps, that baptism is about the only gospel left in the church, the only place left where the church is more or less forced by its own agenda to do what it ought? At any rate, the church would do well first of all to look to itself in these matters before it settles the blame for the sorry state of affairs in baptismal theology and practice on someone else. For a church that has largely neglected or failed in the nurturing task now to think to remedy people's ignorance of the sacraments by taking them away would certainly be rather cynical.

15. LW 40: 257-58.

Grace is not a hidden agenda. The grace of baptism calls us to turn from the endless preoccupation with self and the pessimism that has virtually destroyed the sacrament to the glorious action of the triune God "out there" in his world. The grace is in the very externality of it. It is to be announced and spread abroad, not withheld. None of the abuses attributed to a "too liberal" practice of infant baptism will be corrected by withdrawing it. That is like withholding food from the starving until they have a proper concept of nourishment. We do not need to protect the Lord from the Lord's own generosity! In the current "post-Constantinian" age, withholding baptism does not end but only fosters a more legalistic preoccupation with the self. To be sure, there is wholesale confusion and misunderstanding about the sacraments, just as there is about Christian theology in general. But we do not plan to stop preaching just because it is poorly done or misunderstood. The only real weapon left to the church is the proper teaching and preaching of baptism as the gracious and saving action of the triune God. And that, certainly, is about as it should be.

The Lord's Supper as the
Testament of Jesus

The Foundation

The claim that godless sinners are justified by faith alone without the deeds of the law entails also the claim that the Lord's Supper is properly understood and used only when it is administered and received as gospel — as sheer, unmerited gift. It is a *beneficium* not a *sacrificium*. What happens in the supper, that is, is simply, *the gospel*. What our Lord did at supper "on the night in which he was betrayed" must therefore be conceptualized, taught, and claimed as pure gospel if we are to approach what might be called a "Lutheran" understanding of that supper. The absolute basis for such understanding and practice is first, last, and always, that it is gospel promise.

The Context

From time immemorial theologians have argued about the context by which to extract keys to interpret the supper. Is it or is it not a Passover meal? Is it the last of the eschatologically charged meals of Jesus with his disciples? Is it a covenant meal of some sort? A Torah thank offering? All such contexts are no doubt important. But it appears that something very obvious has usually been missed. Missing is the simple fact that the texts of the supper themselves set forth the essential context within which it is to be understood. That is the fact that it took place *on the night in which he was betrayed.* Any reading of the texts demonstrates that the accounts are laced through and through with the fact of the betrayal. Argument about whether or not it occurred on the night of the Passover meal is rendered more or less irrelevant. What occurred is indelibly stamped by the fact that it took place in the context of the betrayal.

What occurred in the supper is therefore first and foremost encompassed and comprehended within its own concrete and particular story. Jesus was not symbolically or ritually previewing or acting out something that would "really" happen at some other place or time. Disregard for what the texts actually say is largely responsible for the fruitless searches for a context that will supply the supper with some "sacramental" meaning not immediately apparent. All of that is far overshadowed, if not simply canceled, by the fact that it took place in the context of his betrayal. Think on it! He, just when his very body and blood are being "handed over," "surrendered up," to the "authorities" of this age, both religious and civil, takes bread and cup and in contradiction and defiance of the betrayal says, "This is my body given *for you, this cup is the New Testament in my blood shed* for you *for the forgiveness of sins."* And along with it the eschatological promise: I shall not drink of this cup again until I drink it new with you in the kingdom. It is a new testament.

In other words, his body is handed over and his blood shed by the authorities of this age, but he remains sovereign and with the bread and the wine as his testament bequeaths his body and blood to his disciples. One calls to mind Jesus' words from the Gospel of John: "No one takes my life from me, I lay it down of my own accord." On the night in which he was betrayed Jesus gives his body and blood to his own.

The Conceptuality

As Luther rightly perceived, the conceptuality at work here is that of testament, as in "last will and testament."[1] The conceptuality of testament

---

1. Reinhard Schwarz has demonstrated how Luther saw this conceptuality as exegetically necessary from the very beginning of his career. See Reinhard Schwarz, "The Last Supper: The Testament of Jesus," trans. Gerhard O. Forde, *Lutheran Quarterly* 9 (1995): 391-403. Also Reinhard Schwarz, "Der hermeneutische Angelpunkt in Luthers Messreform," *Zeitschrift für Theologie und Kirche* 89 (1992): 340-64.

clearly sets forth and insists upon the gospel character of what occurred. Jesus, in the face of his betrayal, makes his last will and testament and designates his heirs. "This cup is the New Testament in my blood shed for you and for many for the remission of sins." The point here is that what happens on the night of the betrayal is not simply to be conflated with and interpreted by what happens on the day of crucifixion. When that is done, what happened in the upper room necessarily gets subsumed under one's interpretation of Golgotha. It becomes a symbolic anticipation of what happened on the cross.

To be sure, the testament is inextricably related to what happened at Golgotha. Most obviously, of course, the testament does not go into effect until the death of the testator. But the conceptuality of testament should not be subsumed under one's theory about the atoning significance of the death. In the history of the tradition that has meant overwhelmingly that the supper is understood in sacrificial terms: a sacramental and ritual reenactment, representation, or remembrance of the vicarious satisfaction by Jesus of what humans owe God. The "sacrifice of the mass" in Roman Catholicism and the sacrificial character of the eucharistic prayers in Lutheran and Protestant rites are the liturgical offspring of this (mis-)understanding. Reinhard Schwarz puts the matter quite clearly.

> The underlying test for every conception of the Supper is that of the manner in which it can align itself with the situation of Jesus "in the night in which he was betrayed" . . . In the late medieval doctrine of the Supper, the act of consecration, the central part of the sacrifice of the mass, was expressly connected with the last meal of Jesus with his disciples. In that meal celebration, therefore, Jesus had ostensibly acted out a sacramental rite of sacrifice, in a sense a previewing of his own sacrificial death. He was thereby supposed to have transferred to his disciples themselves the priestly duty of redoing retrospectively a sacramental representation of his sacrificial death. In a sense, the sacrificial rite at the Last Supper of Jesus with his disciples therefore relates to the church's sacrifice of the mass in mirror-image-like fashion. The symmetrical axis lies, so viewed, in the sacrificial death of Christ whose sacramental representation once previewed by Jesus is now again retrospectively celebrated. The sacramental activity of Jesus among his disciples therefore finds its meaning in the supposition

that Jesus intended to institute the churchly celebration of the sacrifice of the mass.[2]

But this draws the supper into an entirely different hermeneutical scheme.[3] It becomes a symbolic event, a ritual repetition of something that happened long ago, or a liturgical "re-presentation" or "memorial" of the "sacrifice" on Golgotha. The result is that direction is reversed. The body and blood are offered first and foremost to God and returned to the people only in the form of "sacramental grace" — with all its attendant problems. One is no longer justified by faith alone in the promise and testament, but by *"gratia gratum faciens"* ("grace that makes one graceful") or other appropriate internal motions and modifications. The effect of the sacrament becomes internalized in a way that can do real damage. The gospel character of the supper is lost.

Systematic Considerations

We cannot here engage in an exhaustive treatment of the advantages of the conceptuality of testament for the more systematic problems always attending reflection on the supper. They are many. I shall only allude to some of them here. First and foremost, of course, the supper as testament firmly establishes the proper direction. The testament grants the inheritance from the testator Jesus to the heirs. This also should be insisted upon over against the covenantal language that has become so prevalent today.[4] If covenantal language is used it should be understood as a testament, not vice versa. As Luther observed, a testament differs from a covenant in that it goes into effect upon the death of the testator whereas a covenant depends upon the continued existence of the covenantor. Since, however, in this case Jesus is raised and lives forever, testament and covenant can be taken as equivalent.[5] That means that testament provides the interpreta-

2. Schwarz, "The Last Supper," p. 396.

3. See the article by James S. Preus, "Neglected Problems in the Eucharistic Dialogue," *Currents in Theology and Mission* 3 (1976): 279-87, for an enlightening account of the hermeneutical problems involved.

4. The substitution of "covenant" for "testament" in recent liturgies of the supper (as in "This cup is the new covenant") was *not* a happy development.

5. Schwarz, "The Last Supper," p. 394.

tive key. The new testament is the new covenant, not vice versa. This guards against lapsing once again into sacrificial language.

Second, the language of testament does much better in what we might call the "reality check." Lutheranism has always insisted on the reality of what transpires in the doing of the supper. It is not a representation, not a repetition, not a mere symbolic proceeding, but real. If it is not real it is not gospel. How can this reality be perceived? Where the supper is interpreted in terms of the sacrifice one always runs afoul of the time question. How can the present celebration be a real reoccurrence of an event that happened so long ago? An event, indeed, that was said to be "once for all"? If it is truly once for all why does it have to be made present again, and how is that possible? Various devices have to be constructed for the time gap between the ancient sacrifice and the present to be transcended. One must somehow be initiated, so to speak, into a special time warp so as to become contemporary with a sacrifice buried in the sands of time. How can this be done? The ritual is the answer. The sacrifice must be ritually "repeated," or "remembered," or in the preferred liturgical jargon of today, "re-presented" (made present again) by exact observation of prescribed ritual action, usually by priests who have the proper ontological qualification to do it. Such interpretations, of course, only pile more difficulties upon already existing ones.

No such difficulties arise if the supper is understood as Jesus' last will and testament. What happens when Jesus' followers meet to "do this in remembrance of me" is simply the same thing that happened in the night in which he was betrayed: the last will and testament is distributed to his heirs. What is "repeated" is not Golgotha but exactly the same thing that was done at the Last Supper. "Repeated" is even here a bad word. Rather, the will of Jesus is carried out, the supper *extended now through time* to include all Jesus' heirs in accordance with the will itself. It is not a symbol wrapped up in a ritual time warp, not a repetition, not a re-presentation, not merely a memory, but rather a real event in our time. It is what it says it is: the New Testament.

To conclude here, thirdly, just a word is in order about the question of "real presence" that has so plagued the understanding of the supper. This question too can be more adequately handled through the conceptuality of testament. Jan Lindhart has attempted this in intriguing fashion.[6]

6. See the important discussion by Jan Lindhart, in *Martin Luther: Knowledge and Mediation in the Renaissance* (Lewiston, N.Y.: Edwin Mellen, 1986), pp. 193-203.

Briefly, the bread and the wine hold a place equivalent to the piece of paper called a person's "last will and testament." The piece of paper "really" is the last will and testament, just as are the bread and wine. They are not mere symbols, just as the piece of paper establishing the testament is not merely symbolic. Yet the piece of paper as such is not the entire inheritance, the estate and all its goods. Still, without the piece of paper, the inheritance would not be an inheritance. It would not exist as such. So it is with the last will and testament of Jesus. The bread and the wine really are the testament and they mediate the body and blood because without them there would be no body and blood. Thus the body and blood are given "in, with, and under" the bread and the wine. In Luther's terms, the literary figure at work here is *synechdoche:* the part in reality "stands in" for the whole, not merely in a symbolic or representational sense — in which case the body and blood would "really" exist somewhere else. The presence of our Lord's body and blood "in, with, and under" the bread and the wine is real because it is given to us as the inheritance he has bequeathed to us. It is the New Testament.

Such is what a Lutheran understanding of the Lord's Supper ought to look like. In a time when the pressure is on in ecumenical circles to adopt views of the supper, the liturgy, the ministry, ordination, and the church which quite obviously rest on presuppositions of an entirely different sort, we would do well to pay some heed to these roots.

Absolution: Systematic Considerations

There is a rather delightful story about a bothersome pious Roman Catholic lady who kept claiming to her priest that she had regular visions of Jesus. The priest was doubtful of the genuineness of such visions and was hard pressed to get her off his back. So he devised what he thought was a sure test to put her off. "The next time you have a vision," he said, "you ask Jesus what sins I confessed in my last confession." So some time later she returned and claimed another vision. "Did you ask him what sins I confessed?" the priest inquired. "Yes, I did," said the lady. "What did he say, then?" said the priest. She replied, "He said he forgot!" I do not know that that has anything particular to say about the theme of my lecture but I do think it one of the nicer stories I have heard about absolution. And perhaps it does introduce the subject at least and some of its problems. The priest was not helped in his curiosity about the delivery system but he was reminded of the unshakeable theological truth behind absolution: Remember not, O Lord, our sins.

Our theme is absolution, the actual concrete act of forgiving sin, the exercise of the office of the keys, as it was called, the actual turning of the key in the lock, so to speak. I take it to be my task to introduce the theme by considering some of the systematic presuppositions and questions appropriate to it. To that end, I begin by absolving myself from all responsibility for or guilt toward it. To do this I would like to begin with a kind of play on words that shall serve as a thesis for my deliberations: *The only solution to the problem of the absolute is actual absolution.* Or, otherwise put,

152

absolution, the concrete act of forgiving sin, from me to you in the name of the crucified and risen Jesus Christ here in the living present, is the *only* solution to the systematic problem of the absoluteness of God. What I want to claim here therefore in these systematic considerations is that absolution is not only the solution to the "subjective" problems of guilt, but also and perhaps above all the solution to the systematic problems arising from God's absoluteness.

So I shall begin my deliberations with a discussion of absolution and the absolute, and then turn secondly to absolution and the absolved (the believer) and then try to conclude with some observations about the scope and relevance of such absolution.

Absolution and the Absolute

God, to use Robert Jenson's *bon mot,* is by platitudinous definition absolute. And of course, that is just the problem. To return to our play on words, it is interesting and significant for us to note that this name of God, the absolute, is actually derived from *absolve.* Its Latin cognate and predecessor, *absolutus,* is simply the past participle of *absolvere,* to loose from, to set free, to be disengaged. God, so to speak, as the absolute, is the preeminently "absolved" one. Nothing can be laid to God's charge. The list of meanings for absolute that one can find in Webster's large dictionary is imposing: 1) freed, disengaged; 2) free from imperfection; 3) free from mixture, simple, pure; 4) free from limit, restriction, qualification; 5) determined in itself, not relational, independent; 6) Logic: not relative; 7) Philosophy: not dependent on anything else, not affected by anything outside itself, fundamental, intrinsic, unqualified, self-contained and self-sufficient, free from error natural to human perception, and so on. Just to go down the list is to realize that when we deal with the absolute and with absolution we are dealing with theological dynamite. No doubt that is why there has been such fear of these things in the history of the church.

God is absolute, free. That is the systematic problem. We cannot get on with such a God, with an absolute who is "absolved" from all charge, free, disengaged, independent, and all such. An absolute God is the "end" of us. Such a God leaves us no room, no freedom, destroys us. We see this particularly, I suppose, when we come up against the concepts of divine, that is, absolute, predestination and election. If the absolutely free, disengaged, unlimited one predestines and elects, what room, what freedom does that leave us? As long as we try to tangle with the absolute directly, to wrestle with God in the abstract, or, as Luther put it, try to peer into the things of the *deus absconditus,* it leaves us with *absolutely* nothing, no freedom, apparently, nowhere to move. If God is absolute, that is, determined in himself, then we are, it would seem, likewise simply determined. To the degree that God is free, we are unfree. So we tell ourselves. And so we must turn against the absolute God. We simply cannot take such a God. We *will* not take such a God. This turning against the absolute is something we must and will do. The fact that we must and will do this describes exactly, I believe, what Luther meant by the bondage of the will.

There is a very subtle problem here that is often missed, I think. It is not the absoluteness of God *as such* that *really* binds us, but rather our *reaction* to the idea, the mask, the threat that hangs over us expressed in the concept of absoluteness: the superiority, the priority, the very godness of God. In the day-to-day world in which we live and move, the absoluteness of God does not directly appear to restrict anyone's freedom in actuality. We do pretty much as we please within natural limits. As Luther put it, if we must talk about free choice, we can say we are free in those things "beneath us." Whatever you may think or believe about the absoluteness of God, it does not necessarily make all that much difference in your day-to-day choices. You may be a determinist and I a libertarian, but we both decide to go to lunch and choose what to eat, and God at least apparently does not interfere. Which is to say, I suppose, that as long as I do not think or worry about the absoluteness of God, I get along quite swimmingly — in the realm of things below me. The absoluteness of God does not *actually* restrict me. *Quod supra nos nihil ad nos.* "What is above us is nothing to us." The problem, however, comes when I do think and worry about God, about the absolute — as I expect I inevitably will and must. Death enters the picture. I am not absolute. I begin to worry about whether the absolute is actually pulling the strings secretly, or has actually pre-set my destiny. "We are not puppets, are we?" So the agonized protest goes. The problem comes, that is, when we turn from those things beneath us to those things above us. Since we do not comprehend the ways of God, the ways of "the absolute," since it appears to us that we could only be determined by such a God, we can only turn away from such a God in one way or another. This turning away, this reaction, the fact that we must and will do this, that is our bondage. We are bound to say no to the absolute. We can and will do no other. That is to say, we are bound to say no to the hidden God, the abstract God, who is, of course, the only God we know apart from Christ. In other words, we flee a theoretical loss of freedom into a real one. We flee the threat of the absolute, an apparent determinism, say, into a real one. We flee the threat of the absolute, an apparent determinism, say, into a real bondage under the law. The sting of death is sin and the strength of sin is the law. Since we claim the freedom to determine our destiny over against the absolute, we are left to save ourselves. Then we must see to it ourselves. There is no absolution. We go out of the frying pan into the fire.

The problem of the absolute simply drives us into bondage. To go out of the frying pan into the fire is not an *option,* not a choice. It is something we must and will do. We are bound to do it. We are not forced to do it. It is a matter of the bondage of the will, not the forcing of the will, or the determinism of the will. It is not, you see, a matter of what we can or cannot do in the abstract. We often get caught playing that game of hide-and-seek with the absolute, arguing about whether or not we have or do not have something called "free choice of the will," or discussing what we can or cannot do. That is not the question. The question is what we *will* actually do when we come up against "the absolute." Will is originally a future-tense verb, not a noun. When we go abstract and theoretical we try to make a substantive out of it and talk about it as though it were a thing we *have* and can push this way or that. So we indulge, as Luther said, in a lot of fictitious talk. The question, however, is what we will do when the crunch comes. "Before the cock crows, you *will* deny me thrice." "No," Peter said, "I *will* not." Uh-huh. What *will* we, when we come up against the absolute? That is the question. The natural will will not will God to be God. Rather, he wills himself to be God, and God not to be.

The only solution to the problem of the absolute is absolution. That is my thesis. That is to say that the only solution to this systematic problem is the *pastoral* one, the move from the abstract to the concrete, from the hidden to the revealed God, from, we might say, the lectern to the pulpit, font, and altar. Only if the absolute actually absolves here and now can our bondage be broken and we be *saved.* However, in this regard it seems that since Luther, in general, and certainly more particularly in recent times, the theological world has been gun-shy if not downright skeptical of this fact. In the absolution controversy it was considered Popish nonsense and error. Instead of seeing absolution as the solution to the absolute, theology seems rather to have stuck more to the lecterns, to the old, old fantasy that theology itself could solve the problem. Theology then only becomes the further enactment of our bondage. That is, instead of seeing that the only solution is to move to the pulpit, font, and altar, theologians (and indeed the pastors they taught as well) thought the problem could be solved in the study, the classroom, at the lectern, or pious folk, in the heart. Thus instead of moving from the absolute to absolution, theology undertook the dissolution of the absolute. The problem of the absolute is to be solved by dissolving, dismantling, cutting down, reducing the absolute to manageable proportions. If the absolute is bothersome just remodel him, cut him down to size, make him more or less just one of the boys or girls. This move has today reached almost epidemic proportions. Everyone proposes to "do something" about the absoluteness of God. As Ronald Goetz pointed out in a *Christian Century* article,[1] the idea of the suffering and limited God has become virtually a new orthodoxy in our day — and the battle has been won virtually, without a shot being fired. Everyone seems obliged to fall all over themselves to explain away the absolute, the timelessness, the wrath, the impassibility, the aseity of God. Process theologians seem to say that God is not absolute yet, but is, apparently, working on it. Perhaps this only means that where absolution is denied the absolute has to be as well. Do we believe in *God* anymore?

Where absolution is effectually denied, sin, too, must also be denied. Sin will, of course, have to be explained away or treated with therapy rather than absolved. If it were not so tragic, it would be comical to follow the way our church bureaucracies and management committees crank out papers assuring us that this or that tragedy, disease, or addiction, or consequences of a lifestyle are not really evidence of the wrath of God. Just think, is it not comforting to be told by a specially appointed task force that the AIDS tragedy that hangs over society is not an indication of the wrath of God? Perhaps it is too bad that the people of Sodom and Gomorrah did not have the *Lutheran Standard* to comfort them! Imagine the prophets announcing that the Babylonian captivity was not a manifestation of the wrath and judgment of God but just an unfortunate and inconvenient instance where the balance of political powers was temporarily displaced and was working itself back to a new and different equilibrium! If one gets unduly upset about it, what one needs is a little therapy! A stu-

1. Ronald Goetz, "The Suffering God: The Rise of a New Orthodoxy," *Christian Century* (April 16, 1986), pp. 385-89.

dent prefaced his paper on sin this last term with a cartoon depicting people sitting around in hell with the flames licking about, where one person was saying to the other, "What I am in here for is no longer a sin!" Since we have apparently taken the road of explaining sin away or changing the list rather than absolving it, perhaps we should at least have the good grace to declare it retroactive! Consider the Baptist convention that decided infant baptism was not a sin and moved to make it retroactive.

The refusal to realize that absolution is the only solution to the problem of the absolute has meant that theology has stayed more or less in the classroom and become an increasingly "abstract" and "academic," theoretical business of watering down the absolute and dissolving it. A curious and confusing situation arises where academic theologies try to be pastoral by undercutting the need for or practice of absolution. The modern split between theory and practice relates to this, certainly. God is reconciled to us in the *theory,* and the practice is just a matter of "applying" the theory in cute and popularized ways. If you do not get it, you are wrongheaded. Pastoral practice is then predominantly therapy, not absolution. The absolute has been dissolved and sin explained away. If you still labor under the illusion that you are a sinner, what you need is therapy, counseling, a new self-image, a new sense of self-worth, and so forth; but not absolution. Thus the people wander like sheep without a shepherd.

The only solution to the problem of the absolute is actual absolution, the concrete act of forgiving, through the external word. If the post-Reformation church had realized this, the story and shape of modern theology would have been vastly different. But the way of absolution is a costly and dangerous business. The bare-bones systematic logic is to absolve the other, to set the other free unconditionally; the absolute can only die. And, on the other hand, to be absolved, to be set free, the one bound to its own rejection of the absolute must die in order to be made new. The way of absolution, that is, for both God and the sinner, goes through death. It is costly and dangerous, costly to God and dangerous for the sinner. I expect the reason why modern theology has been so skittish about the way of absolution is just this cost and this danger. Let us look at it a bit more in detail.

For absolution to take place the abstract absolute can only and must die, and get out of the way. The point is that God cannot forgive in the abstract. God cannot be merciful in the abstract. God is "in general" merciful. Why? Precisely, I expect, because of God's absoluteness. The *idea* that

God, as absolute, is one who will have mercy on whom he will have mercy, is of course, most threatening of all. For then we are left wondering who it is upon whom he will have mercy — left with the threat of the absolute as predestining, electing one. The *idea* that the absolute *is* forgiving in general is hardly of help to anyone and is usually just frightening. It recoils on us: God is forgiving, what is the matter with you? You have to learn how to claim the promise. It leads to a sentimentalizing view of God, or to the threat of "universalism." God, the absolute, cannot be merciful, or more accurately, cannot actually *have mercy on you* in the abstract. Thus Luther: apart from Christ God is wrathful, hidden, not distinguishable from Satan. For the absolute is simply absolute and as such free, disengaged. The absolute, that is, is removed, absent from us. The only solution for the problem of absence is, of course, presence, the external word coming to us. To have mercy, he must actually come and be present among us. To absolve he must be here. He must say it, do it, "to you." The only solution to the question of predestination, to the question of upon whom he will have mercy, is if he comes to say it: "You are the one." "Your sins are forgiven."

But this "solution" to the problem of the absolute is, of course, preposterous. How can anyone who comes among us, anyone here, actually forgive sins, actually absolve? As we read in the Gospels, Jesus was deemed blasphemous. His listeners protested, "Who can forgive sins but God (the absolute) alone?" The problem with Jesus was that he freely forgave really wicked people! In other words, it is far safer if forgiveness is reserved for the realm of the absolute, if it remains an idea, an abstraction. Perhaps God, who is free, who has nothing to lose, God in his heaven can forgive, but certainly not here. Forgiveness cannot work here. Certainly not if it is free, a setting loose, an *ab-solvere*. Forgiveness simply cannot work here. It is too disruptive of the way we must run things. How can you run a business, or a country, or even a temple or a church on forgiveness? The appearance, the actual presence of the absolute as absolver among us is just too explosive and dangerous a business. We cannot have it. For the absolute, even an absolver is the end.

What then can God do? He could, I suppose, draw back, compromise his determination to have mercy on whom he will have mercy by placing conditions on his forgiving. He could say, "Come on now folks, be nice, will you not please change your ways and accept my forgiveness?" "Will you not please exercise your free choice and decide for me?" Ah, but then he would surrender to us. His absoluteness would be dissolved in conditionalism. Thus, precisely in order to retain his absoluteness as presence, to be the absolute as absolver, he goes to his death. He knows that we as bound sinners will not be absolved, and he will not be anything other than the absolver. So he dies for us. He refuses to give in to our conditionalism, refuses *absolutely* to be the abstract God of wrath for us. He dies, crying "Father forgive them," and the resurrection is his vindication, the vindication of his determination, his absolute self-determination to be the absolver. Thus God in Christ solves the problem of his own absoluteness by insisting on *being* the absolver, concrete, here and now unto death, and vindicates this by the resurrection. He insists on being the absolver, not an idea, but an actual presence, a person who comes to say it, to do it in the concrete: to say, *you* are the one, *you* are forgiven, flat-out, unconditional, startling, new. "I will have mercy on whom I will have mercy." Absolution is the solution to the absolute! There is the systematic of Christology for preaching — God (the absolute, the end) is repeated in the absolution.

But of course, that was all a long time ago. It lapses into the past. Perhaps where once it was said "Who can forgive sins but God alone?" we now might be tempted to say, "Who can forgive sins like that but Jesus?" After all, he knew the hearts of people, and all that comes with that. But how can we forgive? So it all might lapse, once again, into past history. Once upon a time there was absolution, but now no longer. But if we let it so lapse, we forget the Spirit. The risen Lord in John's Gospel breathes on his disciples and commands them to go and do it, to carry the presence forward in the absolution. Since Jesus has been raised, since the unconditional absolver has been vindicated, the absolution is to go on. Absolution remains the only solution to the question of the absolute. The followers of Jesus are to be absolvers. Why can we not ever get that through our heads? Pastors, particularly, are to exercise the office *publicly*, ordered to do it right out there in the open, make public argument for it and do it. They are primarily absolvers. We always seem to think we have a thousand better ways to reconcile the absolute to ways of mortals. Students and pastors often ask about that other part about binding people's sins — are not we supposed to do that too? Yes, we need to consider that too — but not here. That is not my assignment, I think. Here it might be appropriate to remark that we seem naturally to be pretty good at that! Ironically that is what we mostly do anyway and unwittingly when we think we have better ways to solve the problem of the absolute than actual absolution!

Absolution and the Absolved: The Question of the Believer

Now we cannot conclude this exercise without turning to the question of the absolved, the believer, the workings of absolution on the "you" to whom it is addressed. Here we deal with the danger to the sinner. Actual absolution has, of course, always been considered a dangerous business. When Jesus absolved the paralytic, we are told, the crowds "were afraid, and glorified God who had given such power to men." It has always seemed presumptuous for humans to claim such power, and dangerous to use it, and certainly to use it too indiscriminately. So it would seem, the church has always found it necessary to bring the danger under control. To use an image from atomic physics, they have always tried to put rods in the reactor to get some kind of controlled energy flow, one that they could control, that is, rather than have it blow all at once. If it were to do that, it might just make all things new.

Before the Reformation, the practice was developed of doling out absolution to approved candidates only after private and carefully monitored confession and assignment of appropriate penance. The church was only a closet absolver! Luther's Reformation did not reject the idea of private confession and absolution, but tried to excise the ecclesiastical monitoring and control, the conditionalism to which it had fallen prey. What was helpful about it was the one-to-one doing of the absolution. Thus, Luther said that private confession was to be retained *because* of the *absolution*, not because of the confession as such, or its compulsory nature, or the need to demonstrate proper penance. What is to be loosed from its Babylonian captivity is the absolution. Doing it one-to-one, privately, is thus a beautiful and primary paradigm of just what absolution essentially is: the concrete I-to-you, setting the bound will free, unconditionally. But basically, Luther's move was even more daring than that. He took the absolution and "went public" with it in the preaching of the gospel. He came out of the closet, so to speak. The liturgy, sermon, and the sacrament are basically a public absolution. That is its heart and soul.

But somehow after the Reformation this confident assertion of absolution was always considered too dangerous. Surely, it was thought, the sinner will take advantage of it. If things go wrong, if sinners step up the fever of their sinning, if liberty becomes the excuse for license, if antinomianism threatens, and so on, all the way down to the present day with the complaint about the lack of concern for social justice, surely it must be unconditional, open absolution that is at fault. Curiously the gospel and absolution are the first candidates for blame when things go wrong! As Luther already put it in the argument with Erasmus: Was not the world always full of war, deceit, violence, quarreling, and iniquity? "Yet now that the gospel has come, men start blaming the world's wickedness onto it — when the truth is, rather, that the good gospel brings the world's wickedness to light; for without the gospel the world dwelt in its own darkness. So do the uneducated blame education for the fact that as education spreads, their own ignorance becomes apparent. Such are the thanks we return for the word of life and salvation."[2]

Unfortunately the charge seems to stick. Absolution is too dangerous in a world of sinners. So steps are invariably taken to bring the danger under control. At least proper penance must be demanded before absolution can be granted. Absolution is made conditional, at least on demonstration of proper penance, and the deep fog begins to roll in once again. Conditional absolution is, of course, just the practical counterpart to the dissolution of the absolute by theoretical manipulation. Somehow it seems awfully difficult to get that unconditional absolution out into the open. As Luther wrote, "They fled this morning star as though their lives depended on it." So we have had, especially among Norwegian-Americans, arguments about whether public and unconditional absolution is appropriate. The pietistically inclined always suspected it was popish chicanery and that it simply ran roughshod over the need for personal conversion and repentance.

Of course, those who feared that unconditional absolution was dangerous were quite right in spite of themselves. The problem was that they did not see that if the right to absolve unconditionally costs the absolute a death, it also spells death for the sinner. All the problems with and fears about unconditional absolution are rooted in the fact that after the Reformation the prevalent tendency was to work with the wrong anthropological paradigm. They thought of the sinner as a continuously existing subject who was only *altered* by sin for the worse, as well as for the better by grace. The human was a substance whose qualities were changed. They thought in terms of *change*, not in terms of death and resurrection. Absolution is "dangerous" if it is just granted flat out to a sinner who has not "changed" in any noticeable way. So it could be granted only conditionally. The only other alternative in such a system would be to say that absolution

2. BW 94; LW 33: 55.

freely granted, publicly, unconditionally, must mean the blanket absolution of the whole world, changed or not. Some of the Norwegians who wanted to counter conditional absolution thus found themselves willy-nilly espousing "the justification of the world," the next step to universalism. In other words, absolution simply relapses once again into a universal, an idea. It disappears again into the absolutist heaven.

The problem was and still is that we work with the wrong paradigm, the wrong theological anthropology. The sinner is not just changed. Rather, the sinner must die to be made new. The paradigm is death and resurrection, not just changing the qualities of a continuously existing subject. Unconditional absolution is indeed dangerous for the sinner. It means the death of the sinner one way or another. Either the sinner will try to appropriate it on his or her own conditions as a sop to the self, and go to that death which is eternal, or the unconditional absolution will itself put to death the old and raise up the new in faith to new life.

Yes, it is a dangerous business for sinners. It spells death, and it gives new life. But what we need is precisely to see that. What we need to do, I believe, is not to chicken out, not to compromise, and fiddle away while the City of God burns (this time!), but precisely to forge ahead in uncompromising fashion. The only solution to the problem of the absolute is absolution. It is, of course, quite consequently and necessarily therefore, also the only salvation for the sinner. The absolute dies to become the absolver; to be absolved is therefore to be saved, to die to the old and be raised to the newness of life. It is the purpose of theology, therefore, to lead us to see that and to drive us to do the absolution authorized by the crucified and risen one, actually to break the silence of eternity and say it: Your sins are forgiven for Jesus' sake.

CALLED TO FREEDOM

Speaking the Gospel Today

**Assessing the world to which we are to preach,
or, running after the train that has just left (the Catch 22)**

It was Karl Barth, I believe, who said that trying to make the gospel relevant to the contemporary age was like running after the train that has just left. "The World" that we are supposed to address with the gospel, that is, is a moving target. By the time we think we are finally getting to understand it, it is too late. It has moved on. Or as Hegel put it, the Owl of Minerva takes flight only in the gathering dusk. When a historical, tragic accident occurs we investigate the causes. We search the wreckage for the "black box." We understand, if at all, when it is too late. So I guess you could say this first section will, alas, take on the character of a run after the train that is leaving. I do not relish such sprinting; I think I am getting too old for that. So if you detect a lot of puffing and wheezing you will probably be right in thinking I will not make it. (The question for relevance is one of the more depressing in the theological enterprise. Recitation of what is wrong too often gets to be a hopeless and pessimistic kind of jeremiad.) When I was young and foolish, I used to think I could say something relevant about relevance, and then tune my message accordingly. Such exercises, it should be said, are often enlightening and useful. They give us something of the flavor of the times in which we live. But, alas, I often discovered that all too often the problems I groveled about in were of a sort I either had no solution for or were relatively impervious to my proposals. I usually dug myself into a hole so deep I could no longer get out! Back in those days we rattled on about and railed against "The Age of Anxiety," and "The Lonely Crowd," "The Hidden Persuaders" and Madison Avenue, "The Establishment," and so on. But, of course, all those things did not go away. They have just changed their names, I think. Now it is "Leadership Development," "Contextualization," "Self-Care," "Diversity," and "The Search for Meaning."

My reservations arise not so much from the fact that the holes I dug were entrapping but perhaps, you might say, because they were quite the wrong holes to begin with. To use Lutheran grammar, they were most often problems having to do with the Kingdom on the Left and were, potentially at least, better handled by the devices of that Kingdom than by pious phrases from the pulpit. As Paul Tillich told us, conditioned problems and anxieties are best treated by conditioned remedies. If you have a broken leg, you would likely be better served by a medical doctor than a preacher. If your anxieties arise from conditional causes, you are better served by a therapist than a theologian. The fact that many churches — even of our own — do not seem to have learned that simple but apparently hard lesson is no doubt the reason for the transformation of many churches into service organizations, social reform clubs, and support groups, rather than proclaimers of the coming reign of Our Lord Jesus Christ. Seeking to be relevant to the age, they just succumbed to it. Claiming to be wise, as St. Paul put it, they became fools. The most serious mistake of theological attempts to understand the age is the assumption that the gospel could somehow be made to appear relevant to old beings. "The unspiritual" (I have always liked the old translation better, "the natural man"!), Paul tells us, "do not receive the gifts of the Spirit of God, for they are folly to them, and they do not understand because they [the gifts] are spiritually discerned" (1 Cor. 2:14) — always a favorite passage used to caution against being overly optimistic about appeals to relevance.

The difficulty in this kind of venture is that we face something of a Catch 22. On the one hand, one is not likely to hear the gospel as good news unless one is aware that something is wrong. But on the other hand, it is not possible to accurately know what is wrong unless you have been grasped by the gospel. This Catch 22 ought to be taken with considerable seriousness when we set out to assess the problems of the age. Especially the second half of it — that we do not know really what is wrong unless we are grasped by the gospel — needs particular emphasis just because it is so universally neglected. The reason why we dig ourselves into the wrong holes is most likely because we do not take the measure of our problems from the viewpoint of being grasped by the gospel itself. So I always fight with myself over whether it is not better to start from the gospel and then reflect on the troubles of the age. But that is, I guess, a reflection of the Catch 22 again. Do we begin with the gospel or with the malaise of the current age? In any case I always find it useful to begin with some preliminary words about being grasped by the gospel, which will be amplified later.

I say being grasped by the gospel in order to convey the fact that the action here lies on the side of the gospel. It is not we who grasp the gospel, but the gospel of Jesus Christ, crucified and risen, that grasps us. More accurately: we are put to death and raised in faith. It is a deed done to us in which we are simply rendered — as Luther repeatedly said — completely passive. The mode of reception peculiar to the gospel is that most passive mode of all, hearing. Faith comes by hearing. The gospel is the Word of God spoken to us here and now in the present: "I declare unto you the forgiveness of all your sins in the name of the Father, the Son, and the Holy Spirit." "I baptize you . . ." "This is my body and blood given for you." From the point of view of the hearing of the gospel one can say that the problem of this, and every age, is basically that we do not hear well. To be sure, most of us hear physically or mechanically well enough. Our eardrums are rattled properly, but the message does not get through. We are even deceived, often, by the fact that we hear well enough physically. We think that picking up the noise and deciphering it is all there is to it. But the situation is such that — as we find it in Isaiah and in Mark's Gospel — "hearing they do not hear, seeing they do not see." Luther, of course, tried to spell all this out in his classic battle with Erasmus over the *bondage of the will.* The problem, put in terms of will, is that we do not hear or see because we do not want to. "Scripture," he says, "sets before us a man who is not only bound, wretched, captive, sick and dead, but who, through the operation of Satan his lord, adds to his other miseries that of blindness, so that he *believes* himself to be free, happy, possessed of liberty and ability, whole and alive."[1] He is bound but does not see it. Left to ourselves, we are simply bound to say no to the gospel's story of the crucified and risen one. Indeed, the very things most glorious about the gospel are the most offensive to us. The statement that we are rendered passive by the gospel's Word, for instance, is most distress-

---

1. Martin Luther, *The Bondage of the Will,* trans. J. I. Packer and O. K. Johnston (New York: Fleming H. Revell, 1957), p. 162.

ing. We are not about to take that. The declaration that God is an electing God who disposes over all persons and things is horrendous. The idea that I should have to depend for my eternal salvation on being taken in hand and washed with water or on eating a bit of bread and taking a sip of wine is just preposterous. The sheer and simple "from-withoutness" appears as a mighty attack on our self-esteem. The gospel turns us "inside out" so to speak, addresses us from without in the proclaimed story of Jesus.

So if we are to attempt an assessment of the current predicament we shall have to keep in mind the Catch 22. Along with an attempt to cast an eye on the world to which we must preach, we must also keep our eye on the gospel.

The End of the Theology of Glory?

Keeping an eye on the gospel while looking at the world, I have come more and more of late to think that one way we might describe the situation to-day is as the agonizing and lingering death-throes of the theology of glory. To make a long story short, the theology of glory is one that rests and oper-ates on the conviction that we know the way, that there is an ascertainable realm of glory for us, and that there is a way to get there. The theologian of glory, Luther said, thinks it is possible to see through the world to God from the things and happenings of the world. The world, so to speak, is transparent. That means, of course, that the realm of glory is simply the extension of the way this world runs. In terms of the Reformation, that means a theology of works, merit, and rewards. But we should make no mistake here. The theology of glory is an attempt to discover the good news. It believes, however, that "the glory road" is the good news. The the-ology of glory is, you might say, the theology of *The Little Engine That Could.* Or in more sophisticated terms it is the religion of the Enlighten-ment. One recalls the words of Gotthold Lessing, for instance, when he said, "If God held all truth in his right hand and in his left the everlasting striving after truth, so that I should always and everlastingly be mistaken, and said to me, 'Choose,' with humility I would pick on the left hand and say, 'Father grant me that. Absolute truth is for thee alone.'"[2] A nicely

2. Lessing, Introduction, *Theological Writings* (Stanford: Stanford University Press, 1967), p. 43.

turned-modest statement. At least so it seems. But it is a subtly disguised theology of glory. The striving is the way. Sheer reception of the gift is too cheap. This is not to say, of course, that a theology of glory rejects divine aid. Generally, but not always, it is willing to admit that we cannot get to glory entirely on our own and that we stand in need of help. Even a Lessing was willing to admit that it would have taken a lot longer to arrive at the truth if it had not been for progressive revelation. In the Christian form of such theology the divine aid would be called grace. Grace is a helping hand that makes up for our failures and weaknesses.

The point is that the theology of glory presupposes and provides a certain framework, an overarching story, the "big picture" into which all our little scenes will somehow fit. Even the story of Jesus is made to fit the big picture. He "comes from glory" and makes up for our shortcomings. We can "make sense" of it all. Not entirely, perhaps, but enough to go on. I believe it can safely be said that in spite of all attempts to insist on the *sola gratia* at the time of the Reformation, the theology of glory survived as the presupposition of all subsequent systems. So the little engine that could chugged along, "I think I can, I think I can, I think . . ." I can, can't I?

What we are witnessing today, it seems to me, is the death spasms of our theology of glory. Perhaps death spasms is too strong a characterization, since the theology of glory never really goes away. But perhaps we can say that it is in a severe crisis; it is running off into sand. And it is not just that the little engine has come to the astute conclusion that it cannot, but more seriously it has discovered that it does not want to, that the price is too high, or it has been told that it does not even have to try because the King of Glory is not judgmental or choosy anyway. The "big picture" is questioned. It no longer orders the scene. There is no universal story into which our stories can fit. "Life is but a walking shadow; a poor player that struts and frets his hour upon the stage and then is heard no more. 'Tis a tale told by an idiot, full of sound and fury, signifying nothing." So said Shakespeare's Macbeth long ago when his world was collapsing around him. The words seem to fit our day as well or better than his. Or was he prophetic? In any case, his "signifying nothing" is, as I understand it, what some would mean by "postmodernism." Or what Robert Jenson has referred to as the world's loss of its story. But I do not want to get too distracted by arguments about just what postmodernism might be. I am interested in what this situation spells theologically. For our purposes we can say it spells, if not the end, at least a severe crisis for the theology of glory.

For then the once-assumed frame of meaning, the structure, the assured way to glory, has lost its hold. The track for the Little Engine That Could has, so to speak, been torn up and melted down for scrap. The engine sits on a siding, a decaying curiosity.

What Went Wrong

So now that the gloom is descending, it is perhaps time once again to see if we cannot prod or spook the Owl of Minerva into flight. To get our bearings in these perilous times we shall have to be up to our old game, trying to get a handle on what went wrong, poking around in the wreckage for the black box. Now there are many attempts to assess what has gone wrong. In general, it is held in some way or another, that the "acids of modernity" are responsible: modern science, modern philosophy, modern politics, and general secularism, have eaten away at the story and eroded the framework so that it no longer can carry the burden of our longings. Such assessments carry truth and are often enlightening, helpful for preachers in knowing their audience for the sake of communicating. Without discounting the importance of such studies, I contend that if we look at what has happened from the vantage point of the gospel (that means looking at it as a theologian of the cross — more about this later) we will likely come up with an assessment quite different. It is crucial for the church to assess its history in terms of its own internal problematics rather than simply to accept judgments from without. Talk of the "acids of modernity" lends itself too easily to putting the blame on someone or something outside. It carries the implication that all of what has happened is somehow just accidental. But surely that is just fanciful and hardly very helpful. We in the church must first look to ourselves and ask where we might have failed and/or continue to do so.

When we do this we can begin to detect that the theology of glory dominant in the church is itself responsible for most of the difficulty. A careful reading of the history of theology shows that quite clearly. It is not just coincidence that so many of the thinkers responsible for the "modern" age were educated in theology and came out of the church — and "came out" is the right word. If we are to come to some positive assessment of our history since the Reformation, we need to understand that our predecessors were searching for something. They were trying to escape the oppressive weight of the law inherent in a theology of glory. They were searching for a gospel.[3] But the tragedy in the whole affair is that they did not know where to find it. In essence, they rejected the very gospel for which they were searching, the salvific Word of the Cross from without, and sought to remove what they thought offensive so as to arrive at what was truly glorious in the theology of glory. But the problem is that there is no glory in the theology of glory. In Reformation terms: there is no gospel in it. Unmasked, the glory road turns out to be just the way of the law. As time goes on, what Melanchthon said repeatedly in the Apology to the CA becomes more and more apparent: *lex semper accusat!* No way out! "The law always accuses." They, indeed we as well, seem never really to learn that. They kept looking for the gospel but they could never seem to find it. They kept trying to arrive at it by making law into gospel. But that does not work. Matters just get worse and worse.

In this short essay, I can only cursorily suggest how this happens. It is a history that still needs to be written: the failed search for gospel. Since there is no real grasp of, or being grasped by, the gospel, the basic method of modernity has to be one of accommodation. Heteronomy, the offensive and authoritarian legal character of the church's theology and most particularly the offense of a once-for-all divine intrusion in history, must give way to autonomy, the law built into and enhancing the self. Theology takes a subtle but dangerous antinomian turn, the theologian's most constant temptation. The assumption of antinomianism is that one can take care of the law and heteronomy by theological accommodation of some sort, either by just erasing it (always the most honest kind of antinomianism) or by pulling its teeth in some way. What once appeared to come via arbitrary divine revelation and ecclesiastical fiat must be seen as "natural" to the self, an *auto-nomos,* a law that speaks from within the self. Whatever does not so seem must be discarded. The tiger is to be turned into a domestic house pet, its teeth pulled and its claws trimmed at the theological grooming clinic. So now you do not get bitten anymore, you just get gummed to death! Recall William Blake's poem about the Tiger: "Did he who made the Lamb make thee?"

That, of course, is the question. Did he who made the lamb also

---

3. Recall Lessing's cry in "The Education of the Human Race," in *Theological Writings,* p. 96. "It will assuredly come! The time of a new eternal gospel, which is promised us in the primers of the New Covenant itself." Compare Revelation 14:6.

make the tiger? This is taken to be inconceivable, so God must be cut down to size. An Almighty God is usually the first casualty of the antinomian procedure. God has to be made nice. (Some time ago J. B. Phillips wrote a book entitled *Your God Is Too Small*. Perhaps there should be another now, entitled *Your God Is Too Nice!*) Of course, the electing God of the Scriptures was simply out of the question for a theology of glory to begin with. A theology of glory can ultimately have nothing to do with such a God. The underlying anthropological presupposition for the theology of glory has to be that of free choice. We do not need a "new creation," we just need a little help, perhaps a jump-start. As Erasmus already insisted in his argument with Luther, the law and all the admonitions of Scripture make no sense if there is no free choice. The idea of an electing God is not only a horror but rational suicide. Kant says so literally in a passage from *Religion Within the Limits of Reason Alone* that I have always taken as a key to the hermeneutics of modernity. Speaking of the idea of faith in historical revelation, he says:

> ... Were this faith to be portrayed as having so peculiar a power and so mystical or magical an influence, that although merely historical, so far as we can see, it is yet competent to better the whole man from the ground up (to make a new man of him) if he yields himself to it and to the feelings bound up with it, such a faith would have to be regarded as imparted and inspired directly by heaven (together with, and in, the historical faith), and everything connected even with the moral constitution of man would resolve itself into an unconditional decree of God: "He hath mercy on whom he will, and whom he will he hardeneth," which, taken according to the letter, is the *salto mortale* [the death leap] of human reason.[4]

So passes the belief in God, the living God, who comes from without to work his will in our time. So passes, in actuality, the God of the gospel! The general rejection of the electing God is the first move of a theology of glory and the first step on the way to disbelief. (To be sure, not everyone takes the further steps. But what usually happens then is that some form of authoritarianism becomes a check or becomes a surrogate for God — eccle-

4. Immanuel Kant, *Religion Within the Limits of Reason Alone* (New York: Harper, 1960), p. 111.

siastical, biblical, or such.) In any case one can detect the beginning of the decline and fall of most denominations from the time they rejected belief in the electing God. I often wonder these days whether our root problem is not that there is no belief in God — Almighty God, that is, the assumption, the belief that there is someone "out there," transcendent to us, who actually runs the show. For the project of an autonomous self, if Kant is right, that is simply out of the question. But the problem is that one does not arrive at the gospel by dispensing with the electing God, the God who does something. For then all that is left is just the God of the Law alone, who only receives and judges. For a time, perhaps, as long as people could believe that this God condescended at least to be a help to them by entering into their history, God was relatively safe on his throne. But soon even that belief became onerous or perhaps even they began to wonder if they needed all that much help. A God who dispenses punishments and rewards according to law and demands belief in the one-time historical payoff through the death of his Son is not really good news to an autonomous self. God appears as "a touchy eastern potentate, who demands that we make an appropriate bow when we pass before his apparently empty throne," to use a phrase from John Hick. The implication, of course, is that "our image of God," as folks call it today, comes from ancient mid-eastern politics rather than from the supposedly gentler vision of the New Testament. It is not reasonable for modern people. Not natural, as they like to say.

So the next move theologically has to be to dismantle the God "out there" altogether. Whatever is left of a gospel as word from without is largely rejected as heteronomous. If retained at all, it is only as a bearer of symbolic meaning, or perhaps as myth or parable. Law is natural and reasonable and therefore what really matters. It must be seen as something built-in to the human self and its reason. Law is taken from the threatening hands of God and put within the pious heart. Perhaps we might say, "In the beginning was the law, and the law was with God and the law was God. . . and law became flesh and dwelt in our hearts, and we beheld its majesty, full of fire and smoke!" "Two things," Immanuel Kant said, "fill the mind with . . . awe. . . . The starry heavens above and the moral law within."[5] The law within is now supposed as the good news. The universal laws of reason, the guarantee of those "inalienable rights" with which we

5. Immanuel Kant, *Critique of Practical Reason* (Indianapolis: Bobbs-Merrill, 1956), p. 166.

have been endowed by nature and "nature's God," are the ground beneath our feet.

Ah, but is it? The trouble is the idea of a universal law built into the human psyche turns out to be even more difficult to put up with than an objective divine law. Those who followed Kant — Hegel, Schleiermacher, Feuerbach, Marx, etc. — all saw that in one way or another. Once, God was safely enthroned in heaven where he only occasionally bothered folks. Now, as Emil Fackenheim put it, he has left his throne and taken up residence bag and baggage in the pious Protestant heart where he can really do some damage. For now the self is really trapped. The sought-for good news has been virtually identified with the universal moral law. Any sort of help, any word from outside fades from sight. And that means that there is no way out for the self except some kind of revolt. Against what? Against law, basically, and that means now everyone and everything, ultimately, that imposes or reminds of that law from which we cannot seem to escape. Against the church, surely, since with no gospel to preach the church has nothing much to say but law. Against the government and the police, against corporate economics, against capitalism, against the bourgeois, against the establishment . . . We could go on and on; you all know the list. We can wind it up just by saying it is a revolt against anyone and anything who proposes to set a law over us that can in any way be construed to violate the rights of the self. Robert Hughes, art critic of *Time* magazine, wrote a book some time ago called *The Culture of Complaint,* subtitled "The Fraying of America." I have not read it all, but the title itself pretty well captures the stance of the self. The self is a vortex of complaint. The cry of intolerance is heard whenever criticism of any sort arises. Language falls out of place. It has to be trimmed so as not to step on anyone's toes. A paragraph picked at random:

> Just as language grotesquely inflates in attack, so it timidly shrinks in approbation, seeking words that cannot possibly give any offense, however notional. We do not fail, we underachieve. We are not junkies, but substance abusers; not handicapped, but differently abled. And we are mealy mouthed unto death: a corpse, *The New England Journal of Medicine* urged in 1988 [page 20], should be referred to as a "nonliving person." By extension, a fat corpse is a differently sized non-living person.[6]

6. Robert Hughes, *The Culture of Complaint* (New York: Oxford University Press, 1993), p. 25.

Language itself slips and falls out of place. One must always think, act, and speak "positively" — something promoted, alas, and probably introduced into popular parlance by some of the church's well-known clergy. These clergy go about conducting seminars, I understand, for a fat fee, of course, on the glories of positive thinking for business. Think of it! This is what has come of the gospel. But some are beginning to smell a rat. As Donald Smith put it recently in a *Wall Street Journal* column, "A Positive Attitude? Bah, Humbug!"

In business parlance positive means that people are not supposed to object — ever.

> It is one of the most manipulative phrases ever conceived, and it is more often used to club heads than to extract excellence. To object is to be negative, the all-purpose no-no of the century.[7]

He concludes by saying:

> I believe that the greatest contribution anyone can make is to kill a bad idea. When this power is curtailed, everyone loses because stupidity and inefficiency are allowed to grow and flourish. I realize that business is not a democracy, nor should it be. But a leader who will not allow "negativism" is on the road to destruction.

But when the law of reason is gone and the language itself no longer speaks the truth, we have no ground beneath our feet. To use the analogy of Allan Bloom's *The Closing of the American Mind*, we have fallen into the basement of the human house. The house used to be a three-story one. There was the upstairs of transcendent truth. That was dismantled when the house was "modernized." So for a time we found ourselves in a one-story bungalow. We thought there was a floor under our feet, the universal laws of reason and "nature" on which we could rely to keep society in shape. Even then there was not complete confidence in human nature. There was a healthy suspicion of the motives of the self and so we needed some checks and balances: duty, patriotism, concern for human rights, and so forth. But now the floor has rotted away and we have fallen into the basement, the dank darkness of the self groping to find itself. The older

---

7. Donald Smith, *Wall Street Journal*, December 12, 1994.

suspicions about human nature are deemed too negative. They produce a bad self-image. Psychologists complain that social restraint promotes repression and repression drives to neuroses and all sorts of bad things. So there is nothing left now but the self and its so-called "needs." All truth is relative, relative to the self's own demand to develop itself. Everything solid has melted in the polluted air. The self is the center and measure of all things. All of this has been duly observed, diagnosed, dissected, rued, and regretted accurately and appropriately by studies like Robert Bellah et al., *Habits of the Heart,* and so forth, so we do not need to grovel about in that too long. The self becomes a whirlpool of need, always trying to draw everyone into the vortex of its own pain. Pity is substituted for justice. And pastors who like to look upon themselves as "need-fulfillers" are of course gobbled up, often without a trace. Or, perhaps, a better analogy is that the self is a black hole, endlessly sucking everything into itself and eventually crushing it, all the while gaining incredible density. (You see it all explode every once in a while when someone finally collapses entirely in upon himself and tragically shoots up a McDonald's or some such and then kills himself, saying that when he goes he will take as many as he can with him. Like an exploding star, this is the only way he has left to call attention to the fact that he ever lived at all.)

Now then, what is the upshot to all of this? We have said that it is crucial for the church to look at this development from the vantage point of the gospel, in the sense of a *theologia crucis.* When we do that we see more clearly that the major impetus behind modern intellectual history has been the search for a gospel, the attempt to get rid of the oppressive weight of a *heteros nomos.* And it is surely a legitimate quest to throw off childhood tutelage. There is something right about enlightenment! But the quest was doomed because it was attempted under the presuppositions of the theology of glory, presuppositions rooted in law. And one cannot make a gospel out of the law. Like medieval alchemists trying to turn lead into gold, theologians have from time immemorial tried to make gospel out of law. Many of them still are. It cannot work. But the outcome of the attempt has been fatal, nevertheless. You might say they did succeed in turning gold into lead. The overarching problem for the church is that the gospel itself has been contaminated and corrupted. The gospel has willy-nilly become identified with the great quest to domesticate or even erase the law. It has become the gospel of antinomianism, a kind of gospel *Schwärmerei* that possesses us. Now, even antinomianism is not all mistaken — just premature!

Indeed, there ought to be a streak of antinomianism in every Pauline and certainly Lutheran soul. But the point, of course, is that the preached Christ, *Christ crucified and risen,* is the end of the law, not theology. Christ is the only key to that "undiscovered country from whose bourne no traveler returns." In Christ alone we are at last safe from the law. It is ultimately an eschatological hope held by faith in the tension between the now and the not yet. So, alas, in this age, the theology of glory will persist in some form or other. It is the religion of *homo naturalis.* And, of course, it has some political utility in the Kingdom on the Left. But that is a different story, one that will not be straightened out until we are straight on the gospel. The question for us in the church now is whether it will be possible for us to somehow seize the day and understand the malaise of the theology of glory as opportunity rather than simply defeat.

To do that it will be necessary for those who seek to preach the gospel to spend more time looking at the state of the message within the church itself. We must look to ourselves. The real enemy is not what is going on "out there" somewhere, it is what is going on within. The gospel, we have said, willy-nilly has become identified with the attempt to get rid of the law by theological manipulation. It has become the gospel of antinomianism, 'anti-law-ism,' not the gospel of Christ. What does that mean? I propose that we understand that in a broad sense. The "nomianism" that has been the target of modernism is, of course, not just or even primarily law in a moral or ethical sense (although it is that) but rather law in a doctrinal and intellectual sense. It is law in the old sense of the letter, the offense of the narrative itself, what we have called once-for-all historical revelation itself, that comes under attack. The antinomianism I have in mind is a basic stance, a tacitly and almost universally assumed method that thinks it is possible to remove the offense by theological and linguistic manipulation. It assumes, as did Feuerbach, that theology is like metaphysics, that it can construct "the other world" out of its own genius. It operates under the delusion that theology can make the gospel acceptable to this age by reshaping the language to lessen, blunt, or remove the offense of what has happened. Although Marxism is politically dead, we still operate intellectually and theologically with Marxist presuppositions. Language is a function of ideology. If you do not like what you hear, just change it, erase it, rewrite it, build a dream world more to your liking. If you do not like an almighty God, vote him out. We are like theological students who think they can escape the wrath of God just by changing professors. And we actually believe that accomplishes something! The real enemy here is the enemy within, the desperate attempt to escape, the desire on the part of theologian and clergy to make the message likeable to old beings and the presumption that it is possible or, for that matter, even strategically practical.

The profile of the enemy within has already been sketched for us in books like James Turner's *Without God, Without Creed*. Turner, an intellectual historian, set out to answer the question of the root of unbelief in American society. After his investigation of recent American theological history he came to the startling conclusion that it was not the godless, the Robert Ingersolls and their like, but really the theologians and the preachers who opened the road to unbelief. And what they forgot was precisely that God could not be cut down to size and still remain worthy of belief. They forgot the radical otherness of God.

> Unbelief emerged because church leaders too often forgot the transcendence essential to any worthwhile God. This committed religion *functionally* to making the world better in human terms and *intellectually* to modes of knowing God fitted only for understanding this world. They did this because, trying to meet the challenge of modernity, they virtually surrendered to it.[8]

Studies like Turner's indicate that gospel preachers today must be very careful of what they are about. The real enemy is within. Decades ago Dean Kelly (*Why Conservative Churches Are Growing*) raised questions not only about the theological futility of the all-pervading quest for relevance but also about its practical viability. The very moment in which mainline churches committed themselves to the search for relevance was the moment in which they began to decline. There may be more than one reason for such decline of course, and if what we have been saying here is true, it is questionable whether remaining conservative just to gain members succeeds in escaping the theology of glory. Still we have to seek out the enemy within.

So where does all this leave us in the Evangelical Lutheran Church today? The ELCA is a rather disparate body so it is risky to pretend to

---

8. James Turner, *Without God, Without Creed* (Baltimore: Johns Hopkins University Press, 1985), p. 267.

speak with assurance about the church in general. There is, for better or for worse, quite a difference between the piety and practice of the average congregation and officialdom. But I shall speak out of my experience as a professor of some thirty-five to forty years now and of my observations gathered as I've gone about the church. As far as I can gather, the enemy within is taking a heavy toll on our theological reserves. On official levels, judging from the "Social Statements" and other position papers we are to respond to, theological and ethical antinomianism seems to determine the method and the outcome. On the congregational level sermons and practices seem likewise more and more to take the same tack. Tune the language so as not to hurt anyone's feelings. Pity rather than justice or righteousness, sin and forgiveness, is the guiding principle. As Allen Jones, Episcopal Bishop of San Francisco, aptly put it, "We live in an age in which everything is permitted and nothing is forgiven." God and lately even Christ is less and less the subject of the sermon. (A notice in the paper for an Advent service at a Lutheran Church announced that they were going to have an address about pets and the Humane Society. I do not know what brought that on. I suppose it was inspired by the donkeys and cattle and sheep in the manger scene!)

What is the result of all this? To sum it up — I call it decadent pietism. All Lutherans in this country are descendants of pietism in one way or another. But under the pressure of theological antinomianism it decays. And as my colleague Gracia Grindal — a pietist herself — likes to say, when orthodoxy goes bad it gets hard and cold and dead like stone, but when pietism goes bad it decays, it goes rotten and soft, and begins to smell bad. In the old pietism first and foremost came the call to get right with God. It was a matter of law and justice and one had to come to some personal experience of divine grace else one was just lost. But when God is just a projection of the desires of the self, what sense does it make to demand that one get right with such a God? How could one possibly be wrong with such a God? God, that is, becomes just a cipher. God is love, love, love, not to say luv, all over the place. That is about the sum and substance of what we have to say about God. Of course, the occasional tragedy may provoke us to ask where God has been, but usually we assure ourselves that he probably had nothing to do with it anyway. God, for all practical purposes, simply drops out of the picture. If God is love and pity, who needs to worry? God does not speak because he has nothing to say. He just sits around being love. The great silence. Like the Buddha. The idea that God could be wrathful is an outrageous proposition and does not register on our computer screen at all. Have you noticed, by the way, that almost all references to wrath have been omitted from the pericopes for the church year? (I have a word processor that beeps every time I write Jesus. Jesus is not in the auto-spell vocabulary. Something like that is true theologically with God.) Nor do we take God's adversary the devil seriously. We have a kind of blink when we stumble onto him in our texts. Meaningless. It does not register. The heights, the depths, the dimensions of the spiritual world of the old pietism are all gone.

So pietism just becomes decadent. Perhaps some of the religious fervor is still there; that is why it is still a pietism. But the fear of God is gone. Since it is no longer necessary to get right with God the only thing left is first of all to get right with ourselves. That is only consequent since God is a projection of the self anyway. If we have "God problems" what we need is a better image of God, which is about the same as a better self-image. Coming to our own feelings, to love and affirm ourselves as "something special," finding our self-worth, and so on and so on is the fundamental religious move. The therapeutic model takes over. Therapy has its place in this age. It deals with our conditioned anxieties, as Tillich used to say. But it cannot be allowed as the solution to unconditioned anxieties. Imported into pastoral practice and the preaching of the church it simply promotes decay. The idea that you cannot love another unless you first love yourself becomes the universal and unquestioned dogma heard from lectern and pulpit. So self-love, getting right with the self, becomes the gospel. That would have been an abomination to the old pietists, just as it was to Luther and the Reformers, not to say Jesus. What shall we do, for instance, with Jesus' words in the Gospel of John spoken just when "the hour has come": "Those who love their life will lose it, and those who hate their life in this world will keep it for eternal life" (John 12:25)? I expect our silence on passages like that is just the mark of our decadence.

In the old pietism the second order of importance after getting right with God was to live the godly life, the life commanded and approved by God. But now decadence has set in. Since we can expect no affirmation from a silent God, we must become God-surrogates for one another. Now the task is to learn how to affirm one another in our chosen lifestyles, whatever they may be. The church becomes your local support group. Since God does not disapprove of anyone or anything, so also we must not. Disapproval, negative thinking, is a no-no. If there is such it must come from some character flaw. "They" are the cause of all discomfort, the head-shakers and finger-wavers, always trying to put a guilt trip on us and damage our self-esteem. If you disapprove of some practice or other you are the problem. You are trapped in some phobia or other, old-fashioned, out of touch, judgmental, and so on. The "leadership" of the church seems to operate on the premise that church people are particularly prone to these ills, that they are fundamentally behind the times. The missives from the head offices propose to lead us to more up-to-date views. If you think something is wrong what you need is therapy or sensitivity training.

Sin, consequently, if it remains part of the picture at all, comes to be thought of primarily in a passive mode. Sin is not really our doing. It is something that happens to us because of "them." So we are victims. We are oppressed, alienated, put upon, trashed, harassed, and so on. Now one cannot ignore the fact that such things do happen with alarming frequency in this godless world. But the point here is to note the decadence that sets in when we confuse the conditional with the unconditional. Christology does not concern itself with the fact that Jesus comes to deal with sin and save us from the wrath of God but rather becomes mostly the idea that in Jesus God "identifies with us" or "enters into solidarity with us" in our misery, a kind of "misery loves company" Christology. When God disappears and we seek our solace and comfort in one another, looking desperately for affirmation, not only do we become rather pathetic and pitiable creatures, but matters usually become worse. Why is there so much oppression, alienation, harassment? If God is a meaningless cipher, do we really think we shall find mercy from our fellow creatures? If there is no God, why should I bother to affirm you? "I'm goin' for the gold, and anything I can do to ruin your confidence is to my advantage, right?"

In a decadent pietism, the gospel becomes the gospel of acceptance, affirmation, permissiveness, and toleration. Pity, not mercy or grace or justification, becomes the central motif. There is no bite in the message anymore. The word is not, with Jeremiah, like a hammer, breaking the rock in pieces, or with Hebrews like a two-edged sword piercing to bone and marrow. Quite naturally so, because the hidden motive behind the development of modern theology is antinomianism, the attempt to pull the teeth of the tiger, to isolate and promulgate a sweet-Jesus gospel without regard to the law or its function. So what is heard in the church is a good deal of gospel *Schwärmerei*. Most students, I find, and most pastors in the Lutheran Church, sincerely want to preach the gospel and intend and bend every effort to do so. But the tragedy is that it does not seem to work. The most common complaint from hearers is that what they hear turns out to be law. Something is seriously amiss. But given the history of the matter it is not so strange, I think. Because antinomianism is the one heresy that is actually impossible to pull off. Law does not erase. As Luther insisted, if you want to get rid of law you have to get rid of sin and death. But we are not up to that. At best all we can do is change its mask. That may be temporarily seductive, but it always comes back, most of the time worse than before. It simply cannot work. It is a drama played in an empty theater. Now I have finished my jeremiad. What this might mean for us in our preaching and practice shall be the topic of the next section. I hope that will be a little more pleasant.

Preaching the Gospel Today: The Killing Letter and the Life-Giving Spirit

The Futility of Antinomianism

In the first section I proposed that if we look at what has happened to the preaching of the gospel from within rather than from without we will begin to realize that everything has gone soft and mushy. Our real problems are within. A decadent pietism has set in. There is no "bite" anymore to the Word. The hammer does not break the rock in pieces. The salt has lost its savor. An insipid gospel of sympathy has to do double duty for the law. Church documents aver that they are going to settle the social and ethical controversies confronting us "according to the principles of the gospel." Whatever happened to the law? (One synod actually voted down a motion to the effect that they should be guided by both law and gospel. So a synod of the ELCA is actually on record espousing Antinomianism!) Sympathy and intimacy — good things become substitutes for pastoral ministry. All this can be laid, I proposed, at the door of the basic antinomian presupposition and method of modern theology and practice, the assumption that theology can, so to speak, overpower eternity, that it can make a gospel that will be attractive to the world by accommodation, by erasing or ameliorating the offense. So what one hears from the pulpit all too often is gospel *Schwärmerei*, just "sweet Jesus" schlock of one sort or another, or perhaps lately the kind of thing leaking out of the Jesus Seminar, "Jesus as

Sage," and so forth. As someone has quipped, we shall have to rename our churches "Our Sage's Lutheran Church"! But the trouble with that seems to be that we cannot be sure that he said any of the things attributed to him after all. Perhaps we shall have to rename the churches "Our Silent Sage's Lutheran Church"!

Now the difficulty with antinomianism is that it just does not work. On the objective level the law or the offense does not go away, it just changes its "mask" and becomes more subtle. On the subjective level as well it does not finally help people. It is supposed to emancipate from childhood tutelage (Kant: enlightenment) and build self-esteem. But when it becomes apparent that it is only superficial word-playing, self-esteem can soon turn to self-loathing. Luther was certainly already aware of this in his own battles. Writing against the antinomians he says,

> The devil knows very well that it is impossible to remove the law from the heart. . . . But the devil devotes himself to making men secure, teaching them to heed neither law nor sin, so that if [it actually happens] sometime that they are suddenly overtaken by death or by a bad conscience, they have grown so accustomed to nothing but sweet security that they sink helplessly into hell. For they have learned to perceive nothing in Christ but sweet security. Therefore [when such real terror comes] it is taken as a sure sign that Christ (whom they understand as sheer sweetness) has rejected and forsaken them. That is what the devil strives for, and that is what he would like to see.[9]

When it begins to appear that the Little Engine That Could actually cannot, we have double trouble. On the one hand, the gospel itself is discredited and useless. It becomes just "sweet security," to use Luther's term (that is, false security). It cannot stand when the going gets rough, when death, tragedy, or bad conscience really hit. Optimism is no cure. We are constantly being exhorted and/or exhort ourselves. We tell ourselves, "you can quit, just do it." That optimism is supposed to build our self-esteem and so forth. But when we cannot quit we must find some way to escape the voice of the law, some way to hide what we are up to. And the supposed optimism only leads to deeper self-loathing and despair. Only an "intervention," "bottoming out," can save us. Current television culture gives an in-

9. LW 47: 111.

teresting picture of this. The advertisements are full of sweetness and light, promising simple and easy roads to success, the right deodorant, the right coffee, the flashy car, the fast life, and so on. But the dramas have all the signs reversed: drugs, addiction, abuse, crime, battered wives, battered children, tragic disruptions of one sort and another. The dramas take place in emergency rooms, police stations, back alleys, among the poor, the homeless, the helpless, the lost. This is socio-drama substituted for tragedy. It is an appeal for sympathy. But even such drama seems more and more to be disappearing from the screen. I suppose we no longer want to see it on TV. We see it every day in the newspapers if not in actuality. So the sitcoms take the stage to cover it all over with canned laughter. We become anesthetized with the trivial.

The Word Lost Its Bite?

Here is my question: If the Word has lost its bite how shall that be remedied? If the salt has lost its savor, wherewith shall it be salted? In the old days there used to be an answer for that. It had to do with the proper preaching and distinction between law and gospel. The gospel, it was insisted, must never be preached unless the law is preached first. First must come the conviction of sin before there could be the promise and assurance of grace. Pastors were supposed to master the use of that method in both preaching and the cure of souls. But it is not too big a stretch to see that it is just that method that has been a target of the attack of the antinomianism we have been outlining. Both law and gospel were an attack on the citadel of the self. The law exposed the sin and the gospel granted divine forgiveness — neither of which was particularly welcome to the autonomous self. Of course as time went on the method could lead to many abuses, the chief being that it could easily be turned into a kind of theological scare tactic, as if one could frighten people into heaven by literally scaring hell out of them. But such abuse did not circumvent but finally only reinforced the autonomous self. It appealed to the self to save itself by making the proper choices.

The outcome of the antinomian movement of modern theology has been to call the old law/gospel method into question. The outcome of this questioning is, however, still difficult to assess with complete accuracy. There seem to be two contradictory judgments. On the one hand is the persistent claim that people today no longer suffer under the burden of a guilty conscience as they did in Luther's day. We can no longer assume that people live in a world under the sacred canopy of a shared moral law. In Allan Bloom's words, there is no floor beneath our feet. We have fallen into the dark basement of the self. How can we preach forgiveness to people who do not and will not recognize guilt? We have this marvelous cure (called grace and forgiveness) but no one has the disease. So, it is thought we have to find other topologies to make what we say relevant: meaninglessness, shame, identity, self-worth or esteem, and so on. But on the other hand there is the fact that psychiatrists' offices are crowded with people plagued by guilt. So there are many who will tell us that people who come to church are already hurting and crushed, so much so that they do not need to hear more law. They have had enough of it already. All they need to hear is gospel.

So we have seemingly opposing judgments when we try to gauge the viability of the law/gospel method today. One says it will not work because no one feels guilty. The other says that people are already crushed and hurting. The reason, I suspect, is due exactly to the confusion that antinomianism breeds in theology. The aim of antinomianism is to get rid of law. But law cannot be gotten rid of. What gets eliminated then is invariably the offense of the gospel. So the attempt to erase the law only makes matters worse. The addict who cannot quit only doubles despair. And if the preacher only spouts sweet security there is probably no other place to go than to the psychiatrist's couch. Either that or the pastor, in order to have something to do, becomes a therapist.

In any case, what seems to have happened is that the preaching of the law in an effective manner has more or less dropped out. There is, of course, plenty of law. Attempts to preach gospel often end as covert law, but the *effective* preaching of law has thereby evaporated. Given the development we have been tracing, the effective preaching of law today is one of the most difficult things a pastor has to do. If we are to get the bite back in the preaching of the Word it seems to me that we need to do some serious thinking about this. The whole trend of modern theology has been to take the bite out, to pull the teeth and thus to make it just a kind of *Schwärmerei.* Antinomianism has taken its toll. What is to be done?

Doing the Word: Getting the Bite Back in the Word

How shall we think about getting the bite back in the preaching of the Word? I would like to propose a number of considerations that I have found useful in approaching the matter of preaching today. Each of them could be the subject of a lecture or a book or two in themselves, so what we do here is just a sketch. I have attempted to sum up the outcome of all these points in what I have called *"Doing the Word to the hearers, or Doing the Text to the hearers."* That is to say, preaching can be viewed not merely as exegeting the text, or explaining it, or even just expounding it, or updating it; all such exercises are necessary and useful but are preliminary. The final task of preaching is *doing* it, attempting to do again in the living present what it once did to its ancient hearers. The aim: that the text is a living word that will make its own way, that it packs its own punch. Doing the text involves several considerations.

First Consideration:
The Hermeneutics of Letter and Spirit

The first consideration is that if we are to get the bite back in the Word today it will be quite necessary to broaden and deepen what the tradition meant by rightly dividing and preaching law and gospel. To do this it is necessary to go back to what lies behind the law/gospel method, the hermeneutics (as we would say today) of letter and spirit, particularly as one can find it in studies on the early exegetical work and theology of Luther. When we do that we will see that the concept of law is rooted in the understanding of letter, and gospel in the functioning of spirit. Law, that is to say, is not only laws, but letter, the literal deposit, the whole of Scripture, the very text itself in its first instance as it strikes us bound sinners. Indeed, Luther could expand the letter even beyond the text of Scripture and speak of creation itself and all that happens therein as the *opera literalia dei*, the literal works of God. He apparently had great fondness for that passage in Leviticus about how the sound of a driven leaf shall terrify a whole army and set them to rout, so that they flee for their lives when no one pursues. There is nothing more lowly and despised, he liked to say, than a dead dry leaf. Worms crawl around on it and it is quite innocent and useless. But when its "moment" comes it terrifies horse, rider, soldier, entire army. Are we not fine people, he remarks, driven in panic by a little leaf, when we otherwise so proudly pooh-pooh the wrath of God whenever we get the chance? Law is broadened to letter, to the way the text — the entire history of God with his people — works, even the way the creation itself impinges on the lost sinner. And what the law/letter does in the first instance is clearly specified in the passage that was always taken as the key, 2 Corinthians 3:6, "the letter kills." It is only in the second instance that we come to the function of what was called "gospel": the Spirit gives life. We will say more of this later.

But the question through the centuries has been just how, in what sense, does the letter kill and the spirit give life? Most, if not all, of the tradition, following the philosophers, held that the letter killed because it was dead, belonging to the world of appearances, change, decay, and death. So if you remain stuck just with the literal history you will perish. What is necessary is to find what the letter signifies above and beyond this world and death; one must get beyond dead letter to life-giving spirit, where spirit means a transcendent realm of truth, that which endures beyond all change, decay, and death — the transparent world. But this would mean that the text would have to be translated into what is basically a different story, the story, say, of the exit of the many from the one and its return — allegory. The letter would be a secret code, so to speak, an allegory whose true "meaning" containing the ultimate solution to decay and death (every hermeneutic is a covert soteriology!), lay elsewhere. Our first question, as it almost invariably is because we are inveterate metaphysicians — (I expect this is part of our fallenness) — would always be about meaning, the secret meaning and final promise of the text. We would use it as a mine from whose rough ore we could refine our doctrine and ethics. The text is always just a point of departure for some "spiritual" enterprise or other. So the text becomes just a clue, the occasion, for constructing "another world" which is supposed to be the real one. (It would be worthwhile to follow out the problem of what the letter signifies into the modern and postmodern periods. In the ancient world it signified a transcendent metaphysical realm of truth. In the modern world that realm collapsed into the interior world of the self and the psyche. In the postmodern world that too has collapsed, and the letter, it seems, "signifies nothing." But if it is not a matter merely of what the word signifies, but what it does immediately in and of itself — if it is a text that "makes its own way," so to speak, if it kills the old and calls the new into being, what then?)

But Luther, as was his wont, simply took the passage about the letter killing and the spirit giving life literally. That has as a consequence that the letter is not simply dead, but deadly. That is to say that the history of God and his people leads finally to the cross. It spells but one thing for old beings. It spells death. Only then can there be life, new life in the spirit. This is what lies behind the old method of rightly dividing and preaching law and gospel. It is not merely a matter of a guilty conscience set in the context of a fixed moral universe, it is more broadly a matter of the old self under attack by the letter, the text, the very story itself. Luther saw quite clearly what had strangely been overlooked, that the text of 2 Corinthians was actually not about interpretation as such, but about ministry — that we claim nothing for ourselves, for our sufficiency is from God who has qualified us to be ministers of a new covenant, not according to the letter but the Spirit, for the letter kills, but the spirit gives life.

When the law-gospel method of preaching is seen against the background of the letter/spirit dichotomy there is a possibility of recovering something of the bite of the Word. The Word is not intended to open up possibilities for old beings to exercise their spiritual muscles. The Word comes not to coddle but to kill old beings, to put them out of their misery, to make way for the life-giving spirit.

A Functional Understanding of the Word

The second consideration flows quite naturally from the first. The Word, and that means Word as law and gospel, should be understood and used much more consistently in its *functional sense*. Where it is understood that letter kills and spirit gives life then it will be seen that, at least for the purposes of preaching, law and gospel do not designate sets of differing or even opposed propositions but *functions*. That which offends, accuses, attacks, and ultimately kills does the "law function." That which comforts, forgives, and ultimately gives life exercises the "gospel function."

Even though this functional understanding can seem at first glance to introduce some confusion — after all, how are we to control how our words function? — it does help us to deal with some of the questions we have raised about our preaching today. In the first place it can help us to identify more accurately the target that the antinomianism we have spoken of was aiming at but could never quite hit. It can help us define the nature of the *nomos* that virtually the entire modern world has been *anti*. It was never so entirely clear just what they were against, whether law or gospel. But if we proceed functionally it is clear that it was not really the law that they were against since that was generally rehabilitated in one way or another, but it was the gospel in its function as killing letter, the gospel as a "heteronomy," a *heteros nomos,* the very idea that God has entered into history, taken time (literally) to deal with us, to carry out his election. It was and still is, I expect, the unconditional mercy of God that is finally most offensive to the oldness of being. I can quit! The oldness in us is incensed because it senses that its kingdom is under radical attack and might lose control. One does not have to look to Enlightenment rebels to see that. It is readily apparent even in the church itself. The attitude toward the sacraments, particularly baptism, even and sometimes especially of the most pious, is a good indication. One of the most controversial issues in the church is always baptism. People are always so desperately afraid that we will "take baptism for granted" and so forth. There seems to be tremendous fear that God is going to go and spoil everything by giving it all away. Of course such procedure is dangerous. It does actually lead to death one way or another. It is quite possible for the Old Adam or Eve to twist baptism into an excuse for faithlessness and license. If so, it leads to a different kind of death, one from which there is no resurrection. But shall God, as Luther could put it, call off his goodness for the sake of the ungodly?

In the second place, more importantly, the functional understanding can help us to answer the difficult question of preaching law effectively today. If it is the case that people no longer suffer from a guilty conscience under the moral law, or if it is the case that some are already hurting and crushed, then we would do well to see that it is the very goodness of the gospel itself, the unconditional givenness that must carry out the "law function." The word of the gospel itself is in the first instance the killing letter. It is the cutting edge of the gospel that is the final crescendo of the law. The gospel in this sense is a sword that cuts both ways. It is not just a cure looking for a disease. It is not merely comfort to the hurting. As Ernst Käsemann liked to say, the gospel of the justification of the ungodly is a polemical doctrine. To be sure, the gospel exalts them of low degree. But what we seem most consistently to have forgotten is that it puts down the mighty from their seats. It is the final attack on the old self in its *securitas.* And it is the completeness, the fullness of the gift that puts the old being out of its misery. This is to pick up on what has remained an apparently

unresolved question in Reformation theology. What brings about true repentance, the preaching of the law or the preaching of the gospel? This old
debate can be resolved more usefully when we understand the matter in a
functional sense. It is the very unconditionality of the gospel that functions as law to put old beings finally to death, whether high and mighty or
of low degree. To be put to death in this sense is to be put in the position
where there is nothing to do, to be rendered entirely "passive" as Luther
liked to say. It is to be made a creature of grace, or better, to be regenerated,
made new, to be remade a creature by the grace of God. Baptism, we teach,
drowns the old Adam and Eve. A new being is pulled out of the water. We
are killed, so to speak, with goodness, the very givenness, the unqualified
goodness of the deed. It is the very offensiveness of this, the very thing
about which we complain the most that is of the essence. Now since it is
this offensive that has been the target of modern theology then I think we
must sail right into the storm. Preachers must realize that precisely what
upsets us the most is where the question of law and gospel is to be settled,
rightly divided, and preached today. Preaching must not, in the first instance, seek to apologize the offense away but must rather use it to kill and
make alive; it must seek to do the deed.

Third Consideration: Bondage of the Will

The third consideration is the question of the hearer. What shall we presuppose about those to whom we are to speak the gospel? If what we have
been saying is true, if the word comes to kill and make alive then we do not
come to make an appeal to the religious sensibilities, or even the guilt feelings, the good will, the supposed freedom, of old beings. We do not have to
do with the Little Engine That Could or could not. Rather the presupposition for preaching, as Luther insisted, is the bondage of the will. That is to
say that our problems as prospective hearers of the Word of God are rather
more serious than we might have thought from the various analyses of the
contemporary scene. Our fundamental difficulty is not merely that something more or less accidental has happened in our time to frustrate our desire to believe. If that were the case then a little apologetics could probably
fix things. No, the problem is one that is exposed only from the inside. It
begins to show up precisely when we come up against the very unconditionality of grace itself, when we come up against the sheer givenness of

the sacraments, the nature of the word as killing letter and life-giving spirit. What begins to appear is that here God alone is at work. And we cannot have that.

Our fundamental problem is that we cannot get on with God. And we cannot because we will not. Our wills are bound. Now to clarify such an assertion would take considerably more time and space than we have here. Basically I think we can take it to mean not that our power to choose is somehow interfered with but rather that we do more or less what we please. And that is just the problem. We do what we are bound to do. When we come to God and the things of God we are bound to say no. "Man by nature," Luther could say, "is unable to want God to be God. Indeed, he himself wants to be God, and does not want God to be . . ."[10] This bondage becomes most apparent when we come up against the godness of God. It comes to expression in those impenetrable masks usually called the divine attributes, or especially when we hear tell of such matters as divine election and predestination. When all is said and done we cannot give in to such a God. We cannot trust our eternal destiny to one who decides the matter alone. We must bargain for some leverage in the matter, even if it is just a little bit. In actuality we have no choice in the matter, not because we are coerced by outside force, jerked around like puppets, but because we just cannot.

This consideration of the bondage of the will as presupposition for preaching sets us clean contrary to what I have called the antinomian method of modern theology. The basic anthropological presupposition of that method is the freedom of the will. The method proceeds on the assumption that it is the business of theology to make the message attractive enough for old beings to choose. Thus talk of an electing, predestinating God must either be removed or quietly rendered functionally inoperative. So God becomes at best the one who waits upon our choices. Inevitably that means that God becomes the God of Law and Wrath. Even if we say, as we are wont, that God is Love, Love, Love, it turns on us. God, apparently, is obligated to love everyone and so would violate his very being if he actually got around to saying "I love you" to anyone in particular. Furthermore, a God who only *is* love and never *does* anything about it always turns on us. If God is love, then what is the matter with you, unloving slobs? One of the most fatal miscalculations of theology, I expect, has been to think that the

10. LW 31: 10.

message could ever be made acceptable to old beings. All that has been accomplished thereby has been to render the message trivial and dead. Here, it seems to me, lies hidden the real reason for talk about the death of God. Theologians have killed him. He is kept "alive" now, if at all, only by the artificial respiration of linguistic manipulation. As in the movie *El Cid*, the dead hero is propped up in the saddle and sent charging out of the fortress in hope that just the memory of what he once was might frighten the enemy into flight.

If preaching is to regain some vitality today it must have a clearer vision of the predicament of the hearers to whom it is addressed. The problem, plain and simple, is that we just cannot get on with God. In biblical language, it is just that we are not reconciled to God because we cannot or will not manage it. When it comes to the Living God, we are bound to say no. And it is the triune God alone who has undertaken to do something about this. God was in Christ reconciling the world unto himself and nowhere else. We are not informed that God was in the mind of the philosopher or the theologian reconciling himself, but in Christ. This is the second move of the triune God. The third move, that of Spirit, is in the fact that he has entrusted us with this ministry of reconciliation. Much more needs to be said about this, of course, but that last bit — that God has entrusted us with the ministry of reconciliation — bids us to move on to our fourth and final consideration.

A Sense for the Present

That God was in Christ reconciling the world unto himself and that he has, *mirabile dictu*, entrusted us with this ministry of reconciliation is God's "solution" to the problem that God is for us. It is quite simple really. If God is the living, electing God, then what God has done is to find a way to go ahead and do it. There is no theoretical solution to the problem of the electing God. It is killing letter. When students clamor for solutions I usually tell them there are none, not in the abstract, at least. If you try to come up with one you just go out of the frying pan into the fire. If you want a solution to your problems with God you have come to the wrong place. You have to go to church and pray that the preacher knows what he or she is supposed to be doing. The solution, that is, is precisely in the move of God the Spirit into the present. If the electing God is the problem then the solution is not to explain that God away, but to do what that God authorizes us to do — to go ahead and do the electing deed. What preaching needs is a sense for the present. Too often preaching never recovers from the classroom. Preaching goes on as though the mighty acts of God have long since ceased. God *was* in Christ reconciling. What is he up to now? God so loved the world that he *gave* . . . All those things are true, of course, but they are past, or at least we treat them as such. Preaching, however, is to move into the present, to speak "in the Spirit" of the living God. It is to assume that what I have to do now in the living present is the present edition of the mighty acts of God. There ought, it seems to me, be much more speaking in the present tense, the declaration here and now, the attempt to make it plain that this is the moment now in which the text comes true, doing what the text talks about. After all, this is what happens in the sacraments. We are authorized and instructed *to do* what is usually only *talked about*. For some reason or another the move to the present seems one of the most difficult to make. Often, it seems to me, sermons can be excellently done and one sits waiting for the final move to the present, but it never comes. Actually, of course, that just means that free choice remains the controlling presupposition. So the hearers are left to make the last move somehow for themselves. Or muttering, perhaps, "Well, that is all very nice, Reverend, but when will it happen to me?" One of the dirtiest tricks in the "evangelical" bag is to be endlessly talking about grace and justification as a free gift, and then never actually giving it. Preachers need to be much more sensitive about the move to the present.

Conclusion: Doing the Text

When I try to put all this together I come up with the idea that we might look on preaching as doing the text to the hearers, doing the text as a word that ends the old and calls the new into being. The letter kills. The bite of the gospel is restored in that the law function is done. The Word does not present possibilities upon which free choice may exercise itself. It brings all that to an end so that the spirit can give life. Now in order to make this a little more concrete I always like to look at some texts to illustrate how I try to put this into practice. I realize that preaching styles differ and that there are a variety of literary devices one might use to get the job done. The selection of sermons in the last section of this volume serve not as a model for the way one must preach, but rather as an indication of how I try to practice what I have been preaching in the hope that it might be helpful to others as well.

We need simply to acknowledge that the word we preach as God's word is powerful, as law and gospel. It is a word that does what it says and says what it does. It kills and makes alive. It sets free men and women who are otherwise bound to sin, to death, and to the tyranny of the law. There is no greater privilege or joy for a preacher than to share this word, one that will raise us from our decadence and bring new life to the world. May we be so empowered to preach this word with courage, faithfulness, and integrity.

Lutheran Faith and American Freedom

To get right to the point, when we confront the question of American freedom from a theological point of view, we are immediately in trouble. There are several dimensions to that trouble, but perhaps we can get at it most quickly by saying that what most Americans call freedom today is what theology — particularly Lutheran theology — would call bondage. Freedom to do as we please usually ends in bondage to the lusts of the day. Freedom to do as we please equals bondage to self. Perhaps it was not always so. Originally, I suppose, freedom for Americans had to do with shaking off the tyrannies that had plagued them in Europe. Freedom was political liberty. Originally the founding fathers claimed the right to life, liberty, and the pursuit of happiness over against tyrannical forces. But they knew well, in the early days, that freedom could not be only freedom from such tyranny. If it were so, freedom would be license, and likely just run amok. If freedom were to work, there would have to be some way to restrain it to keep it from running amok. And if it were to remain freedom, it would have to be a voluntary restraint. That meant, as Terry Eastland[1] and others have pointed out, that American freedom could work only if it had a religious base.

It was religion that preached and inculcated the virtues and the sense of duty that gave freedom something worthwhile to do. Thus that perennially quoted and sharp-eyed observer from France, Alexis de Tocqueville,

---

1. Terry Eastland, "In Defense of Religious America," *Commentary* (June 1981).

observed that whereas freedom allowed the American people to do just about anything, there were things their religion prevented them from imagining, and forbade them to dare. Religion, he said, was America's "foremost political institution." Religion provided what a Constitution based on commercialism and self-interest could not provide. Religion provided a check on the freedom guaranteed by political institutions. Freedom depended upon the old religious warning against license. But now, as we all well know, religion is no longer a "political institution." Indeed, religion, since about the 1920s, according to Eastland, has slipped into rapid decline. Politically, in recent decades, given the impression left by court decisions and the general tenor of the times, the voice of religion seems to be about the only voice that cannot be heard on important political and moral issues — particularly, it seems, the voice of the Christian religion. Indeed, one can say that we seem to have slipped over into a more or less anti-religious mood. "Religion is a cruel joke," announced a placard in an abortion rights parade. The separation of church and state, intended originally to give the differing denominations equal voice, has become a divorce, an antagonism.

People use the principle of separation as a defense against religion. If the original intent of the Constitution guaranteeing the free exercise of religion is to mean anything more than trivialities, then surely it should mean that religion should have a voice equal to that which is not religious. But that seems no longer to be the case. Since there is separation, people seem to think, religion has no right to speak publicly at all. Freedom of religion has become freedom from religion. Now the result of this, of course, is that American freedom has lost its religious moorings and threatens to run amok and destroy itself. Americans rarely today have the original modesty to think they have the right to pursue happiness, but rather that they have the absolute right to possess it — no matter at whose expense. Rights we talk about gladly, but not duties or responsibilities or character. Since we will not police ourselves voluntarily, from the highest CEO down to the lowest drug pusher, our police force is less able to cope, the jails are filling, the justice system is clogged, and people are suing each other for any violations of their rights imaginable.

From a Lutheran standpoint, one might say that the American marriage between freedom and religious restraint was doomed to failure from the start. However, we need not attack that question here. Once freedom loses its moorings in religion and becomes the unbridled pursuit of whatever rights turn one on, it modulates rather rapidly into just what Lutherans would call bondage. Unencumbered by any call to virtue or responsibility, freedom becomes fertile soil for addiction. Freedom, that is, sells itself to greed and lust. Now, what does this mean for Lutheranism? Mark Noll rightly says, I think, that Lutheranism stands at a crossroads. Lutheranism has always been a champion of freedom, as we all know. But now the danger is that Lutheranism will just sell out to the idols of current American culture. The freedom of the Christian that Luther championed will just get melted together with the freedom of the American. But that would mean the surrender of whatever distinctiveness we have to contribute. As Noll put it, "The infusion of European migration has been over for two generations. Assimilation to American cultural patterns proceeds rapidly. Lutherans now cannot avoid choices about how to relate more generally to other American churches and to the American environment itself." But Noll, even though believing that Lutherans have much to contribute, is not optimistic about the way things are going. "The choices that have been made so far seem to throw into doubt either the ability to communicate an authentically Lutheran word in America or the capacity to maintain such an authentic word."[2] That is, we have to make choices, but the choices already made are not good ones. If the LCMS has retreated into parochial dogmatism, the churches that formed the ELCA appear to be drifting toward the common fate of the old, large, Americanized, and increasingly endangered denominations. "The dominating concern [of the ELCA] seems to be less the offering of Lutheranism to America than the promotion of social engagement and bureaucratic efficiency."[3]

This estimate parallels, I think, what I have said on other occasions about the dangers of slipping into a kind of decadence. If, in our attempts to become American, we simply allow the freedom of the Christian to be dissolved into and assimilated to the freedom of the contemporary American, we are in danger of losing our unique voice. The peculiar danger of Lutheranism is evident precisely because of its passion for the gospel. We all intend and wish to preach the gospel. We do not want to fall into the trap of the law. But given the current slide toward accommodation with the idols of American culture, the result of the intent to preach the gospel can all too often result in a kind of gospel *Schwärmerei* — an attempt just to preach the

---

2. Mark Noll, "An Evangelical Protestant Perspective," *Word and World* 11 (1991): 314.
3. Noll, "An Evangelical Protestant Perspective," p. 315.

gospel without law. The result is just a slip into the swamp of permissiveness. We repeat theologically the error of antinomianism — the idle dream that we can escape the clutches of the law just by ignoring it or avoiding it, by refusing to preach it. It is, as Luther said, as though you could rid yourself of the law just by going through your theological books and erasing the letters L-A-W wherever they appeared, or taking your sermon and erasing everything that appeared to you to smack of law. But that is a drama played in an empty theater. One cannot get rid of the law by theological erasure, just as one cannot similarly get rid of wrath. The law *is a power* that remains even when all the words are gone. Indeed, as with most such matters, it becomes more destructive precisely because we have lost the name for it. And when we no longer know how to name the law or its power, the gospel becomes aimless, or perhaps rather something like a scatter gun that shoots at anything and everything in sight that seems to threaten. The enemy turns out to be an amorphous "they," who are against me, perhaps just because they inhibit or make claims on me. In the end, everyone becomes the enemy. The gospel gets reduced, willy-nilly, to sentimentality, to being affirming of anything and everything, just saying gospel, gospel, gospel, all over the place. Preaching, as Luther once said, becomes a mater of spreading "sweet security" all around. But then matters only get worse. Then we do not know how to handle our terrors. If the gospel brings sweet security, how come we are so insecurely situated in this world? One of the reasons we have so much trouble with the question of evil today might be because we have been brought up on sweet security and so do not know how to respond when things go wrong. As Luther put it,

> The devil knows very well . . . that it is impossible to remove the law from the heart. . . . But the devil devotes himself to making men secure, teaching them to heed neither law nor sin, so that if sometime they are suddenly overtaken by death or by a bad conscience, they have grown so accustomed to nothing but sweet security that they sink helplessly into hell. For they have learned to perceive nothing in Christ but sweet security. Therefore such terror [they think] must be taken as a sure sign that Christ (whom they understand as sheer sweetness) has rejected and forsaken them. That is what the devil strives for, and that is what he would like to see.[4]

4. LW 47: 11.

Even the theology of the cross, one of our rock-bottom theologoumena, tends to get swallowed up in the soup of sentimentalization. The theology of the cross becomes merely the idea that "Jesus identifies with us in our suffering," and isn't that nice. Now for those who are suffering, there is, of course, some comfort in that. But without the resurrection, it becomes just what one might call a "misery loves company" theology. It becomes a negative theology of glory. If we could not make it by good works, perhaps we can gain some purchase on the Kingdom if we suffer enough. And so you can see immediately how the theology of the cross, too, loses its gospel character and becomes law.

There is, of course, just enough truth in the fact that suffering is a mark of the Kingdom to make all that plausible. But we tend to forget a couple of matters. First of all, even though Jesus did in a real sense identify with us, we did not identify with him. Nobody identified with him. "He was despised and rejected of men, he had no form or comeliness that we should desire him. He was as one from whom we hid our faces, despised, and we esteemed him not" (Isaiah 53). We tend to forget that we did not identify with him, but did him in. He was wasted for — at the hands of — our sins. We should at least hesitate a bit before we move so quickly to talk all this identification language. We did not identify with him, we killed him. Not "they" . . .

Secondly, much of the theology of the cross today seems to lack or at least ignore the resurrection. It is impossible to have a true theology of the cross without the resurrection. For without the resurrection, we cannot face up to the awful truth of the cross. We cannot face up to the fact that in the end no one identified with Jesus, but everyone joined the crowd to cry "crucify him." Even the disciples forsook him and fled. And, as Paul could put it, to the extent that we still try to avoid such facts, we do it again. For the point of the theology of the cross is that even though we did not identify with Jesus, God did. God raised the crucified Jesus from the dead and so turned the table exactly around. Had Jesus remained in the tomb, then, of course he would have been just one more unfortunate victim of "them." And we might try to use him, identify with him, against "them" in our suffering. The suffering Jesus would be our "Lord." And our sin would still be masked from us. But the point of it all is that Jesus did not remain in the tomb, that God has made him Lord and Christ by raising him from the dead — not just by sending him to suffer. So now the tables are turned. Now it becomes apparent that there is none righteous, no not one. Now it comes to light that had Jesus remained in the tomb then we would be right, and he wrong. But since he is raised, then we are wrong and he is right. Or as Paul could put it, since he is alive, we, as old beings, as sinners, are dead, but nevertheless alive in Christ. In brief, we can take the truth about the cross only in the light of the resurrection. We do not need God just to be miserable with us, but rather finally — as the saying goes, to put us out of our misery.

But now enough of this jeremiad. If it is true that the danger once again is precisely the confusion of Christian freedom with American freedom, that the temptation is to slip into the idea that freedom means the right to do whatever we fancy, what is to be done about it? What is the road we should be taking? How, that is, are we to stem the tide, the slip into decadence, permissiveness, sweet security, sentimentality — the ills that beset American Christianity?

Perhaps it is well to begin by noting that the problem we face is not a new one. It is, in effect, the chronic problem of Protestantism, the chronic problem of the attempt to preach the gospel of justification by faith alone. What is to be done if such a gospel is taken advantage of? What do we do when faith is on the wane? What do we do when it seems as though the gospel just leads to laxity and accommodation, when freedom is taken as license? Anyone who undertakes to preach the gospel of salvation by faith alone knows this problem. Paul knew it. Luther knew it. You all no doubt know it. I am constantly being harried by those who suspect such a thing because I am weak on sanctification!

If we are to make any progress on the question we are addressing here, I think we need to look back over the way Protestantism has tended to handle this chronic problem. We are justified by faith alone without the deeds of the law. It is all God's doing, not ours. And in classical Protestantism, this was backed up with the doctrine of election. God decides the whole matter. So, briefly, the position is stated. But then, of course, as my students always show every year with infallible inevitability, the immediate question is: But do we not have to have faith? And isn't that somehow, at least a little bit, our doing? Now, it has not been sufficiently recognized, I think, that the entire fate of Protestantism hangs on the way that question is answered. Overwhelmingly what happens is that we are trapped (for the question is a trap) into answering, "Yes, of course, you have to have faith. Faith is the only proper response." True enough, of course; then we are off and running. A host of questions spill out like water over a broken dam. "But does that not mean we decide?" One may try to forestall disaster for a moment by calling on the all-around anti-Pelagian handy-person, the Holy Spirit, and say no, it is the Spirit's doing. But then we only get farther and farther into the woods. "But how do I get the Spirit, know I have the Spirit?" "Well, you can feel the Spirit." "You have to have the proper experience." "You have to get converted." The normal way to become a Christian, to get faith, is through the experience of conversion. If you are converted you can lay claim to a true faith. So goes virtually all of Protestant revivalism.

It is crucial to note what happens in this kind of move. The major effort of theology and preaching comes to be invested in describing faith. We are justified by faith alone. Indeed. But then all the attention shifts to the subject, to the question of faith. What does it mean to have faith? It is not enough to have just plain ordinary faith, we are told, but we must be possessed of "real," "true," "sincere," "heartfelt," "experienced" faith. Theology becomes descriptive and adjectival or adverbial. And as the adjectives and adverbs pile up, the confidence of believers goes down. It may, of course, be salutary and even necessary for theology to describe faith. However, when, as inevitably happens, one resorts to preaching the description we are in big trouble. Preaching descriptions is deadly. We think we are preaching gospel, but actually it is one of the worst forms of law. Preaching a description is like reciting the characteristics of "true" love to your spouse during a quarrel, and complaining, "The trouble with you is that you just do not know what love is and you do not love me enough." Even if it is true, it is not likely to be very salutary!

Yet I think we can say that this has been the basic method for Protestantism, particularly in America, for curing its ills. To cure a flagging faith, one preaches faith. Something, I say, like trying to make flowers grow by pulling on them! You only kill them.

The result has been to introduce a fundamental split in the body ecclesiastic, a split between those who think they can lay claim to all the adjectives and those who cannot, between the real Christians and the ordinary or lukewarm Christians, the ins and the outs. This was evident in this country already in the distinction between the real full-covenant Christians and the halfway covenant, or perhaps between what William James called the "once born" and the "twice born," or today between "evangelical" and — what? Non-evangelical? Whatever that is? And in general, this has simply meant that the "ordinary" Christians have gradually slipped away into their various forms of secularization, whereas the "real" Christians continue their business of converting folks in their various ways. The split, I think, has been rather disastrous. Perhaps our real question in America is, "Is there a true gospel for 'ordinary Christians' who do not think it necessary to get overheated and blow a gasket?"

So, whither away? Whither Lutheranism? What shall be the road ahead for us? How shall we recover and speak an authentic message to America without slipping into the swamp of secularization on the one hand, or reverting just to hollering at people about faith on the other? How shall we preach the Christian message in the face of an American freedom that has lost its religious moorings? As you are all aware, there are various suggestions being made, various parties forming. Some maintain that what we need is to reappropriate some of the hierarchical machinery that was jettisoned at the time of the Reformation, that the answer to the slide into the swamp is to establish a stronger teaching office and shore up our discipline, restore a historic episcopate. Some suggest that we try to recapture the rigor of the authentic pietism of our past, that we press for a reawakening of the pietist spirit. Some would suggest, or rather insist, on more serious ethical effort over against the injustices of contemporary culture.

Without going into the pros and cons of such suggestions it seems to me that there is still an underlying question to which we have first to attend. It is still a matter of law and gospel for Lutherans. Do we think that the way ahead, the fundamental solution to our problems, lies in the law or the gospel? It seems to me that the various suggestions made all revert too hastily to the law. Episcopal succession, pietist revivalism, ethical exertion: the way to revival is via the law. If we live in an antinomian culture, what is the solution to that? Once again, the question is an old one. It was really the first basic problem of the reform of the sixteenth century. When they discovered in the Saxon visitations the sorry state of affairs and feared that the gospel of justification by faith was just leading to laxity, they faced the question of what to do — similar to ours. A great debate ensued, the "antinomian" controversies, which stretched over several decades and took various shapes. It is one of the most salutary questions for us to investigate. At the outset there was the question: how to counter the moral laxity and the misperception of the gospel as "sweet security"? Melanchthon, and those who followed him, thought that rigorous proclamation of the law first was the remedy. If folks are abusing the gospel and Christian freedom, they must be brought to true and heartfelt contrition and repentance by preaching the law in all its rigor. If they were apprised of the seriousness and consequences of sin, they could be brought to repentance and proper living. This standard "evangelical" approach evolved into "fire and brimstone" in some instances.

On the other hand, there were those (starting with Johann Agricola) who smelled a rat in this method. They held that you cannot really scare people into faith. Repentance that comes from fear of consequences is merely *legalistic* repentance based on the self's own desire to preserve itself. True evangelical repentance, Agricola held, comes from preaching the gospel. And because he insisted that the law should be banished from the church and the pulpit he earned the title *Antinomian*. The law, he said, does not belong in the pulpit. It belongs in the courthouse and the sheriff's office. From the pulpit we preach the gospel alone, and the gospel brings true and heartfelt evangelical repentance.

Now in those days, when all was said and done, the general outcome tended in Melanchthon's direction. One is to preach the law first in all its rigor to produce repentance, and then come with the comfort of the gospel. This position in one form or another became the staple of evangelical preaching about Luther himself — Luther's hermeneutic and the attempt to shore up a sagging enterprise by various applications of law, institutional, moral, or otherwise. In these days, to the contrary, we have to go with the gospel. However, we should consider a proclamation of the gospel that actually outdoes the law — a gospel with a cutting edge that does not coddle old beings, but goes on the attack to end them, that has the aim of making new beings.

And to return at last to the question of freedom, I expect the difficulty in the American view of freedom is that it can be a dangerous thing to set old beings free. When religious restraint fails, when even the law has problems coping, where are we to turn? The role of the Lutheran Church in this venture has certainly not been very prominent to date. But it would seem to me that if somehow the original restraint could be replaced or at least augmented by the spontaneity that Luther envisaged, American freedom would also stand on firmer ground. If American freedom has turned out to be bondage, then what is needed is liberation at the deepest level, and that is what the gospel is for.

Human Sexuality and Romans, Chapter One

Since Romans, Chapter One, is the focus of our discussion it would seem that the most appropriate way to honor it for starters would be to read it. It may just be that hearing it will go a long way toward answering our question, just as Paul intended so long ago.[1]

> For I am not ashamed of the gospel; it is the power of God for salvation to everyone who has faith, to the Jew first and also to the Greek. For in it the righteousness of God is revealed through faith for faith; as it is written, "The one who is righteous will live by faith." For the wrath of God is revealed from heaven against all ungodliness and wickedness of those who by their wickedness suppress the truth. For what can be known about God is plain to them, because God has shown it to them. Ever since the creation of the world his eternal power and divine nature, invisible though they are, have been understood and seen through the things he has made. So they are without excuse, for though they knew God, they did not honor him as God or give thanks to him, but they became futile in their thinking, and their senseless

1. What J. L. Martyn says about Galatians holds also, I would expect, for Romans: "Paul wrote Galatians in the confidence that God intended to cause a certain event to *occur* in the Galatian congregations when Paul's messenger read the letter aloud to them. . . . The author we see in the course of reading Galatians is a man who *does* theology by writing in such a way as *to anticipate* a theological event." See "Events in Galatia," *Pauline Theology,* vol. 1, ed. Jouette M. Bassler (Minneapolis: Fortress, 1991), p. 161.

minds were darkened. Claiming to be wise, they became fools; and they exchanged the glory of the immortal God for images resembling a mortal human being or birds or four-footed animals or reptiles. (Rom. 1:16-32)

Do we really need to ask about the "normative character" of those words? If we have heard them at all, should we not rather ask, "Who shall deliver us?" And this is only the first leg of Paul's law sermon in which he is going to end in the mighty crescendo, "There is none righteous, no not one." I would think, therefore, that the first question is really not whether we shall presume to honor the normative character of Scripture. The primary question is rather just who is exegeting whom? Are we exegeting the Scriptures first and foremost, or are we being exegeted by the Scriptures? Who is the acting subject in this matter? We? Or the Spirit who speaks through the Scriptures? Perhaps the question for this session ought to be rephrased. Will Scripture exercise or be allowed to exercise its normative character among us in the midst of our conflicts?

Two Models for Interpretation

Broadly speaking, there are two fundamentally different models operative in the interpretation of Scripture. In the first and perhaps most universally assumed model, the exegete as "subject" stands over against the text as the "object" to be interpreted. The interpreter occupies the space between the text and the reader or hearer. The immediate problem with such a model is subjectivism or potential arbitrariness. How can we be sure the interpretation is correct, that is, not distorted by the biases of the interpreter? At this point one usually appeals to authorities beyond or above the individual, to the tradition perhaps, and ultimately, as in Roman Catholicism, to a teaching office or finally a pope. The model seems to drive inexorably toward some place "where the buck stops." Where there is no such place, the model founders. Protestants, as we are all aware, have tried to make Scripture itself the place where the buck stops by appealing to doctrines of scriptural inerrancy. But exegesis itself soon undermines such claims. So in the end we are left only to hope in some more collective instance of authority, perhaps in scholarly consensus — hardly a likely or even a pleasant prospect! — or of late, perhaps even the pronouncements of a task force, an attempt on the part of the church, it would seem, to reclaim its lost teaching office. But such attempts meet with little success. While this model has been useful in answering questions about the basic "what" of the text, it leaves us in the lurch when we come to disputed issues, the "so what?" Where the exegete stands as interpreting subject over against the text as object to be interpreted, the threat of subjectivism is never really overcome. Pluralism appears as our only recourse. Then either the conflict rages on with no prospect for resolution or it grinds to a halt under the weight of repressive tolerance or just plain ennui.

The second model is much more subtle and perhaps difficult to operate with. It is the model proposed by the Reformation understanding that sacred Scripture interprets itself *(Scriptura sacra sui ipsius interpres)*.[2] To make a long story short this means that the roles of the text and the interpreter are essentially reversed. The Spirit speaking through the Scriptures effects this reversal by the weight of the scriptural claim itself. Upon the hearing of Scripture, the interpreter cannot remain standing simply as subject over against the text as object to be interpreted. Rather, in the engagement with Scripture, the Scripture comes to interpret the exegete. The scriptural word, that is, finds, exposes, and establishes the very being of the hearer, that is, as creature, as guilty sinner, as justified, obligated, called to serve, etc. It is the task of the exegete to "get out of the way," so to speak, and allow the Spirit who authored the Scriptures to speak. That means that the subjective stance, the *sensus proprius* of the interpreter is set aside so that Scripture can have its way with us. The interpreter is to be the mouthpiece, so to speak, for the text. The interpreter, that is, is finally to become a preacher of the text.

Here too it is recognized that the greatest difficulty for interpretation is the subjectivism of the interpreter. But in this view it is recognized that subjectivism cannot be overcome simply by formal or juridical appeals to institutions over and above the individual. Appeals to tradition, teaching office, or scholarly consensus, or purely formal declarations about biblical

2. A helpful recent study on the matter is Walter Mostert, "Scriptura sacra sui ipsius interpres," *Lutherjahrbuch* 46, ed. Helmar Junghans (1979): 60-96. The claim that Scripture interprets itself is not to be confused with the concept of the perspicuity of Scripture. That simply means that Scripture does not disagree with itself, or perhaps that where one passage is unclear, another can be found to clear up the difficulty. That Scripture interprets itself means much more — that Scripture as divine word is active in establishing itself over against the interpreter.

inerrancy are attempts merely to substitute collective for individual subjectivism. Even the claim that possession of the Spirit gives one special advantage is a power play that attempts to elevate the individual above the storms of conflict.[3] The claim that Scripture be heard as interpreting itself means that the problem of conflicting interpretations can be handled only when one allows the Spirit speaking through the Scriptures actually to speak and end the matter — which is to say, to end the claims and needs of the old dying subject and call to life a new one who hears and heeds the Word. That Scripture interprets itself is simply the hermeneutical correlate of justification by faith alone. The Word finds us, finds us out, and gives us life. Therein lies its authority. From this perspective claims made for extrascriptural authority structures and/or merely formal declarations about biblical authority are constructs that in one way or another are simply a reflex of the needs of the old subject.

The Place of the Law

What might this have to say about the problem at hand? We are concerned here in Romans One, and other passages concerning sexuality, with the law and its uses in the light of the gospel. As we indicated at the outset, if we hear Romans One with any sensitivity at all, perhaps we begin to grasp what the Reformers meant by Scripture exegeting us, not vice versa. The question that arises is not so much "What do these words mean?" That is painfully obvious, I should think. The question is rather, "Who shall deliver us?" "How can the voice of the law be stilled?" And the only answer to that, if one is to honor the normative claim of Scripture, is Christ. Christ is the end of the law that those who have faith may be justified. That being the case, the Christian understanding of the normative character of Scripture as law "resonates," to use an image from chemistry, between two poles. The first pole is the announcement that "Christ is the end of the law so that there may be righteousness for everyone who believes" (Rom. 10:4). But the second is a question put to us, "Do we then overthrow the law by this faith?" To which Paul replies with his emphatic *me genoito*, "By no means! On the contrary, we uphold the law" (Rom. 3:31).

---

3. Thus Luther always insisted that the claim to authority based on possession of the spirit in the "enthusiasts" was basically the same as that of the papacy.

"Christ is the end of the law so that there may be righteousness for everyone who believes." That is the first pole. It is the announcement of the gospel and that, I take it, is the deepest reason why we are here. Acknowledging that gospel announcement is the necessary first step in honoring the normative character of Scripture in the matter before us. If we do not take that first step, we will get no farther together. We must be clear above all that the law is not the way of salvation. Christ alone is that. We must be clear that the issue before us is not immediately one of salvation. It is rather a matter of the law and how we shall honor what Scripture has to say on that score. If Christ is the end of the law, what does that mean for our deliberations? Two points should be made. One, since Christ is the end, and I take that to mean both *telos* and *finis*, both goal and cessation, no law of any sort can be imposed upon us simply on the ground that it is biblical, or even that it is commanded by God. Christ is the end. Legalism is over. But two, that means exactly what it says: *Christ* and Christ alone is the end, nothing else, no one else, not theology, not exegesis, not ecclesiastical authority, not the pope, surely, not human progress, not some assurance that "things have changed," not developments in genetics, not even a task force, can bring the law to an end for us. If we hear the voice of the law in Romans One and are troubled by it, there is only one remedy for that: Christ. Only as we are in Christ, indeed, only to the degree that we are in Christ, does the law end. If we are not in Christ we are under the law. Indeed, to put it most strongly, the law hounds us until we are in Christ. And I suppose, truth to tell, that is also the reason why we are here, on whatever side of the issue we find ourselves. The law is after us. We should make no mistake about that. To recognize that is to begin to see what it means to say that the Scripture interprets itself, i.e., it is doing it right now. It exposes who we are and just what is going on. And Christ alone is the goal of it all. God does have a goal for us and will not give up on us until it is reached. If we do not realize that, we have no inkling whatsoever of what the normative character of Scripture is all about.

But now that brings us to the second pole. If Christ is the end of the law to those of faith, do we by that faith render the law useless? "Absolutely not," says Paul. "On the contrary, we set the law in place, we establish its rightful place and it true authority." No doubt this is the subtlest aspect to the doctrine of the law. How is it established by a faith that believes its end? That is precisely the point. Only a faith that knows of its true end, both its goal and its cessation, will be able to let it stand just as it is and begin, at least, to gain some insight into the way God the Spirit puts the law to proper use. Without that faith, I have no hope, I do not know or can no longer trust the end, and then must take steps to defend myself. Then I proceed in a faithless manner. If the law is endless I must fashion an end of my own. I must take steps to explain it away, tone it down to manageable proportions, pronounce it obsolete, or perhaps erase it altogether. This can have only one result. If I do not believe in the end, then willy-nilly I become a defense attorney against the text. And such a move, it seems superfluous to say, can only spell the ultimate denial of any normative character for Scripture. It is because Christ and Christ alone is the end that I can let the law stand *just as it is.* The law is established in that it stands until the goal to which it points is reached in Christ. Indeed, I think Paul can be read in these early chapters of Romans to be saying that now that Christ has come we all have no excuse for not heeding the law, whoever we are. It is not just coincidental that these words follow immediately upon a classic statement of justification by faith. It is not just coincidental that the unrelenting champion of the gospel could be the one to write these words. Because we are justified by faith, there is now neither any need for nor point to changing it, toning it down, indulging in casuistry, or erasing it. But such activity is, of course, futile. We cannot really do much about a text like Romans One. "It is written." It is "inspired" Scripture. It is canon. It cannot be changed. It will always be there waiting for us. Unless, of course, we plan to expunge it altogether. In that case, this entire discussion would be pointless.

So, if our discussion is to honor the normative character of Scripture, it will "resonate" between the two poles. Christ is the end of the law to faith on the one hand, but on the other, such faith does not render the law useless but rather establishes it. What might this mean for us in the discussion of the difficult questions of sexuality? First of all, since Christ ends the law, no direct or literal legalistic appeals to isolated passages of Scripture can be taken as decisive. As Luther could say, Moses is dead.[4] We do not want to hear Moses. At the same time, however, if the end establishes the law, it cannot be ignored or treated as simply irrelevant. It is now put to its proper use. We may want to ask about some passages. Do they apply to us? Some passages obviously hit us harder or more directly than others. Yet we must ask whether something is not to be retrieved from even the most ob-

---

4. Luther, "How Christians Should Regard Moses," LW 35: 165.

scure passages. In any case, it would seem that if we are to honor Scripture we can only proceed on the premise that at least within the perspective of Scripture there is a reason for things and we cannot rest until we are satisfied we have done our best to see it. Thus Luther could say, for instance, that even though Moses is dead, there is much in Moses that is useful for us because it is reasonable in the daily tasks of shaping and caring for life. Or to put it in another way, it is in agreement with the "natural law." Mention of natural law, of course, conjures up all sorts of ghosts out of the ethical abyss which we need not contend with at the moment. By natural law Luther just meant that which nature and common sense enjoin to care for human community.

Outcomes

What might this mean for recognizing the normative character of Scripture? We have tried to set the stage hermeneutically. Where do we go with it? First, since we do not wish to proceed in absolutist or legalistic fashion, careful arguments will have to be made. But they must be arguments that seriously strive to honor the biblical perspective. That means that it will not do, surely, simply to isolate and dispute for or against certain passages that speak of homosexual acts. The problems we face are deeper than that. And we will begin to sound those depths, I expect, only if we read with some of the fear and trembling that arise from the realization that Scripture interprets itself, that ultimately it is we who are being exegeted, not vice versa.

Is it not obvious, for instance, that our fixation with "having sex," as it is called, is itself an idolatry akin to those of which Paul speaks in Romans One, a fixation that vacillates between obsession on the one hand and trivialization on the other? We seem to think that everyone has a right to life, liberty, and the pursuit of a satisfying orgasm whenever and wherever it may be found. Once that is assumed, any honoring of the scriptural word on either homosexual acts or heterosexual relations is already undercut and it is just arbitrary to raise questions about preferring one over the other. Consequently a text like Romans One will become a threat to all "holding down the truth in unrighteousness." Could it even be that the almost universal objection to Paul's words about homosexual acts roots simply in the suspicion that were we to credit them, our own "preferences" are next to go?

A text like Romans One calls upon us to concern ourselves in our argumentation with much broader biblical perspectives, no matter how difficult that may be. Questions of sexuality can be considered only within the horizons of biblical anthropology, the understanding of creation, law, sin, redemption, marriage, and family. And, we dare not neglect the tradition of the church. The tradition, after all, is simply a record of how the faithful have read and sought to honor the Scriptures in the past. Even though we are not legalistically bound to it, it deserves to be honored and ought not be changed without compelling argument.

Second, honoring the normative character of Scripture means something of paramount importance for the approach to interpretation. It simply will not do for interpreters of texts like Romans One simply to take up the role of defense attorney for the hearer against the text. This is not about wearing hats in church. The argument is as terrifying as it is massive. Paul is not immediately or even ultimately concerned with homosexual practices. He has something much more serious and frightening in mind. It is the wrath of God. It is idolatry and subsequent abandonment by God. The abandonment by God spawns all manner of wickedness. Homosexual practices are a prime example for Paul, but one among a whole catalog of ungodliness and wickedness. Since they did not honor God as God or give thanks to him, they became futile in their thinking and their senseless minds were darkened. Because of that, Paul says, "God gave them up in the lusts of their hearts to impurity, to the dishonoring of their bodies among themselves." Or, "God gave them up in the lusts of their hearts to impurity, to the degrading of their bodies among themselves . . . They were filled with every kind of wickedness, evil, covetousness, malice. Full of envy, murder, strife, deceit, craftiness . . ." (Rom. 1:24, 29).

What shall we say? Who is being exegeted here? Have you listened to the news lately? According to Paul, all of this is not finally due to biology or to willful choice, but rather to God's giving up. A rather frightening thought, is it not? And what shall we do about it as interpreters? Just here is where we are tempted always to become defense attorneys for our hearers. The usual move seems to be to defend ourselves with our modernity. Surely we cannot not be so gauche, so gothic, as to believe that there is actually a God who might do such things! Is Paul then wrong, or out of date? Can we comfort ourselves with that? Or perhaps he had been reading the

Old Testament too much? If I assume that I am somehow the interpreting and acting subject here, then of course, my biggest temptation will be to act out of sympathy and try to protect you from the text. For, to steal a line from Luther, "My heart is not made of stone. I am no child of the Marpesian crags." Do you think I do not feel any sympathy? Do you think I enjoy doing this?

But you see I cannot come away from a reading of Romans 1–3 without the realization that I too am on the line. I too am being exegeted. Who, after all, is the "they" of whom Paul is speaking? Is it not all those against whom the wrath of God is being revealed from heaven for holding down the truth in unrighteousness, not only those who do the things cataloged but also those who condone them? How shall we honor a text like that unless we realize that it intends to catch us all in its web and end with the crushing word that there is none righteous, no not one? Can I step between you and the text to assure you that this curious business about the wrath of God is *passé* now? What good would that do you? Can my sympathy or cleverness protect you from the wrath of God? It would be rather dangerous to think so, to say the least![5]

Finally, if Scripture exegetes us rather than vice versa, we will likely ask a somewhat different set of questions in these matters. What is it that we are up to here? Why this incessant knocking on the door of the church for approval or blessing? Can even church pronouncements help us? A task force is not the end of the law! Why are we constantly looking for loopholes in Paul's argument? Paul's point in Romans 1–3 surely is exactly that there is no way out. Shall we come away from this exercise with the hollow consolation that this text holds only for some long forgotten Romans, perhaps, who knew no better than to worship snakes and birds? Can we really

5. The point here is that you do not need me to protect you from the accusing voice of the law. You have Christ for that. You do not need to be comforted by all the statistics of change and so forth (dangerous comfort anyway!). Christ will free you from the curse of the law. Indeed, if I am doing my duty, I should be hammering away even more relentlessly until you at last give up and cry "I repent, have mercy, Lord!" You should really be on your guard if I try to comfort you by toning down or defending you from the law, because before you know it, I will take Christ from you too and make you a present of "my theology," my "opinions" about God. You do not need me for that. I can at best preach Christ to you for that. The question for you now is the second one: Shall we continue in sin that grace may abound? Now the question is how my life is to be shaped for care of the neighbor and the world.

rest comfortably with the claim that Paul did not even consider or know of the possibility of loving and committed relationships between persons of the same sex?[6] Could one really expect Scripture to support the idea that loving and committed relationships justify just about any sort of sexual activity? Or is it possible that had Paul known that sexual preference is an orientation rather than a conscious choice he would not have said the things he did?[7] From the biblical perspective, and certainly from Paul's, this would seem hardly persuasive. Sin in the biblical view is never simply a willful act. The tradition has always held that sin was "original," some would even say "inherited," and not at its root just the result of a conscious and deliberate act of will. But that does not make it any less a sin. It only makes it more tragic.

No, I fear Paul's point is that there are no loopholes, there is no way out but the one God has set: "Jesus Christ my sure defense," as the hymn writer put it. Jesus Christ alone is the end of the law, and the law will sound until we arrive there at last. We would be less than sympathetic if we did not direct our hearers to that end. For when it comes down to it, if we are to honor Scripture all we have to offer finally is not loopholes but absolution. If that is not the end of our conversation, I fear it has no end at all.

6. The argument that Paul was speaking of heterosexuals involved in homosexual acts, and that it would have been alright had it been homosexuals doing such acts seems to me to be quite preposterous — an extreme case of the exegete trying to defend the hearer against the text.

7. The attempt to marshal so-called scientific evidence to prove that homosexuality is an orientation and not a choice and to call Paul's indictment into question on this score, is, it seems to me, not a proper or careful way to argue. In the first place, the evidence is still eminently doubtable. There is still no agreement in the scientific community, and even if there were, most true scientists would be more modest. But in the second place it hardly seems appropriate for those who seek to honor the normative character of Scripture to call it into question on such a slim basis.

Fake Theology: Reflections on Antinomianism Past and Present

Antinomianism is a prevailing modern heresy. It comes in many shapes. Just about everybody "wants out" and thus seems to be some kind of antinomian. We have all learned to complain loudly and long about legalism, about heteronomy, about absolutism, about fixed and inflexible norms and standards of any and every sort. That everyone should have the right to "do their own thing" seems virtually to be the dogma of the age. If laws and norms get in the way, they can be discredited as relics of an outmoded "lifestyle" and changed to fit what we call contemporary-lived experience. Antinomianism is the spiritual air we breathe.

The trouble is that hardly anyone seems aware of the heresy, or perhaps cares. We do not seem to know what it is, what causes it, or what to do about it. The purpose of this essay is to reflect a bit on the essence and root causes of antinomianism in its various forms, ancient and modern, so as by implication, at least, to afford some insight into what might be done about it. We are well used to the Martin Luther who fought, like St. Paul, for freedom from the law. We are not very well apprised of the Luther who attacked antinomianism, or of the precise and careful way in which he fought that battle. We need to know more about it. This essay makes no claim to fill the need by way of historical analysis. It attempts only to reflect a bit on the issues involved from perspectives gained by looking at the historical debates.

The "Essence" of Antinomianism

Antinomianism is fake theology. In Luther's picturesque way of putting it, it is a drama played in an empty theater.[1] It is a theological playing with words: the attempt to get rid of, to change, to water down "the law" — that which makes demands, attacks, accuses, or threatens us — by a theological *tour de force*, by changing words. One tries to end the law by erasing the offensive words or finding more accommodating ones, by changing definitions and usages, or more lately by shifting or just multiplying metaphors and symbols until the matter is obscured beyond recognition. One creates the illusion of escape from "the law" by a verbal sleight of hand. That is where the problem arises, of course. The illusion of escape only imprisons all the more. Nothing is accomplished. The theater for the wordplay is empty.

The root cause of antinomianism is failure to apprehend the gospel in its full eschatological sense. The point of the gospel is that "Christ is the end of the law so that there may be righteousness for everyone who believes" (Rom. 10:4). *Christ*, not theology, is the end of the law to *faith*, experienced as new life from death, the breaking in of the eschaton. Where Christ is not grasped by faith as the end of the law, then we with our theology must take steps to *put* an end to law. We must attempt to banish law from the church or its preaching perhaps, by relegating it to the courthouse. Or we go through our theological books and erase law wherever it appears, thinking to accomplish something thereby. We think to give the gospel a boost by refusing to preach or talk about the law. But all that is simply a failure to understand what the gospel is and what it does.

As the name indicates, antinomianism arises in religion generally and particularly in the Christian church, as a reaction, an "anti-" movement. It arises in reaction to *nomism*, to a prior refusal to allow the eschatological gospel to have its way. What happens more often than not in the church is that the eschatological outlook and hope are displaced by law as an eternal order, and nothing is allowed to break its hold or disrupt its continuity. Eschatology is banished from the church and from the Christian life. Law is always the bottom line. Antinomianism is usually a desperate last-ditch reaction to the strangle hold of nomism in a church that has given up on eschatology and settled down to being "practical" and "relevant" to this age.

---

1. WA 39/I: 355 (Fifth Disputation Against Antinomianism, Thesis 32).

As such, antinomianism is a complex and interesting phenomenon theologically, because it is the attempt to correct one mistake by another. It attempts to correct the mistake of nomism just by becoming theologically antinomian, to remedy the loss of eschatology by constructing a theologically "realized" eschatology. Its mistake is to assume that the law ends or changes (the Kingdom comes) just because our theological books and assertions say so. It assumes that it *is* possible to end or banish law, somehow, this side of the eschaton.

At the same time, a theology seduced by nomism (all too often the case in the church) is ill equipped to do battle with antinomianism. Since it has already compromised the eschatological gospel, it can fight only from the position of law and charge its opponents with the "terrible heresy" of being anti-law. Thus the term "antinomian." One gets the impression that whereas other heresies are relatively mild, being antinomian is about the worst thing one could be! At any rate, to defend itself, nomism appeals to already given anti-gospel sentiments, compounding the confusion. So the general victory of nomism over antinomianism in the church is hardly cause for celebration. Nothing is solved. No insight into the nature of the problem is gained. The war of words is only inflated and the issues become more and more obscured. Worst of all, antinomianism just goes underground to reappear covertly among those who thought to banish it. Then it becomes really insidious. More of that a bit later.

Overt Antinomianism

Since the root cause of antinomianism is failure to grasp the gospel's eschatological impact and its relation to faith, it is to be expected that antinomianism can take different forms — as many, perhaps, as the different failures to grasp the gospel. Indeed, one of the reasons for the prevalence of the heresy is that ignorance of the cause produces blindness to the effects. We do not usually know it when we see it. To get at the problem it is helpful, I think, to begin by making a distinction between overt and covert antinomianism.

Overt antinomianism is a direct and frontal attack on the law. It is open and honest. This is what is usually understood by the term "antinomian." Overt antinomianism simply asserts that since Christ is the end of the law, law is no longer of theological import and should be removed from the preaching of the church. Law has come to a temporal (Christ's death and resurrection) and perhaps also spatial (banished from the church to the courthouse) end. As John Agricola put it in Luther's day, true repentance is not produced by preaching the law, but rather from the sweet comfort of the gospel. Law is not a theological matter now that Christ has triumphed. All things are new.

Even though overt antinomianism has through history attracted most of the attention, arousing the ire of nomist sentiment and consequently being vilified as a most heinous heresy, it is actually the most benign form of antinomianism. Covert antinomianism, as we shall see, is infinitely more dangerous because it arises basically out of underestimation of or despair over the gospel. The problem with overt antinomianism, however, is a kind of impatience, an "enthusiasm" about the gospel that tries to transcend the limits of faith. It is an attempt to realize the eschaton by a theological *tour de force*. Because one is so powerfully grasped by the gospel one is impatient to be rid of the law, and so takes steps to banish it by *theological* means. One erases it from theology and preaching and banishes it from the church. While this is a mistake, it is usually not of very serious consequence, since it *is* rooted in an understanding of the powerful impact of the gospel. As long as one is grasped by that, the heresy is relatively benign. Abuses can arise, of course, when the impact of the gospel fades to mere sentimentality and becomes the occasion for self-indulgence. The usual ploy then is to return to legalism to avert disaster. Then we are back to square one.

The error of overt antinomianism is to forget that Christ is the end of the law *to faith*. In *Christ* apprehended by *faith* the end has come, but not yet otherwise. The *theology* of overt antinomianism outruns faith and attempts to realize the eschaton in purely verbal fashion by just shouting the law down. What is to be done about antinomianism must therefore be very carefully calculated. If, as is usually the case, one undertakes to argue flatly that the law or part of it (the moral law, for instance) does not end in Christ but just goes on in some fashion or other, the jig is up for the gospel as well. Antinomianism is countered merely by "pro-nomianism" and the battle is lost. One may save society from the consequences of antinomianism that way but saving faith will be lost.

Luther, in his day, confronted mostly overt antinomianism, in the form advocated by Agricola. It is crucial to note the careful way in which Luther nuances his arguments so as not to destroy the eschatological nature of the gospel, which he had fought so hard to establish. His basic argument is not that antinomianism is just wrong, but rather that it is *impossible*. Theologically considered, that is, antinomianism is an impossible heresy! One simply cannot get rid of the law by theological wordplay this side of the eschaton. One only makes matters worse. Thus Luther in his sermon "Against the Anti-nomians" says that they ". . . do nothing more than throw out the poor letters: 'L-A-W,' but only reinforce the wrath of God thereby, which is interpreted and understood by these letters."[2] Antinomianism is fake theology.

Luther's argument is eschatologically tuned throughout. It is not, that is, a "pro-nomian" argument. His contention is not that the *hope* or the *aim* of antinomianism is wrong, but that it fails because it is premature, not up to the task, not good enough. Only Christ is the end of the law. And Christ can be apprehended now only by faith. Therefore, while we still live "in the flesh" this side of the eschaton, the law continues to sound. The repeated theme of Luther's disputes with the antinomians is that law correlates with sin and death:

14. Necessarily, therefore, in as far as they are under death, they are still also under the law and sin.
15. They are altogether ignorant and deceivers of souls who endeavor to abolish the law from the Church.
16. For that is not only stupid and impious, but *absolutely impossible.*
17. For if you want to remove the law, it is necessary at the same time to remove sin and death.[3]

As long as sin and death remain, law remains, and it is impossible for humans to stop it by any means whatsoever. The end can only be eschatological, anticipated and participated in only by faith. Only to the extent that one is in Christ, that is, is it "safe" to be "antinomian":

10. Indeed, in Christ the law is fulfilled, sin abolished and death destroyed.
11. That is, when through faith we are crucified and have died in Christ, such things are also true in us.

2. WA 50: 474, 34ff. Cf. LW 47: 115.
3. WA 39/I: 354.

40. Now, in so far as Christ is raised in us, in so far are we without law, sin and death.[4]

The hope is not wrong. As is so often the case, however, theology preempts the place of Christ and thus becomes a fake. Antinomianism fails because it substitutes theology for Christ.

"Do we then overthrow the law by this faith?" That of course is the question vis-à-vis antinomianism. St. Paul answered it as all true preachers of the gospel will answer: "By no means! On the contrary, we uphold the law" (Rom. 3:31). Precisely because faith sees that Christ alone is the end of the law, that law correlates with sin and death and cannot be removed by our theologies, law is established this side of the eschaton. Precisely because the gospel is an unconditional promise, justification an unconditional gift, faith sees law in its absolute clarity, stringency, and strength. Precisely because Christ (and Christ alone!) gives perfectly that to which the law points, there can be no reason for or attempt to tamper with the law. When the end is given, the law is established. All theological fakery is over.

The eschatological nature of the argument against overt antinomianism is crucial because it will govern the manner in which one deals with other forms of antinomianism. If one fails to see it is not the *hope* that is wrong but the theological attempt to realize it prematurely, one ends by arguing against the hope as well. Then the argument against antinomianism becomes an argument against the gospel and eschatological salvation.

Covert Antinomianism

When Christ and the gospel are not apprehended as the end of the law, when the eschatological hope fades or is obscured, when preachers lose their courage or get nervous about how the unconditional promise will affect morality, then means other than the direct frontal attack on law must be resorted to. If there is neither end in sight nor promise of such end, and the overt attempt to manufacture one theologically is manifest failure, one must take steps to change, ameliorate, water down, or blunt the force of the law. Thus is born a rarely detected form of antinomianism. We can call it

4. WA 39/I: 355-56.

covert antinomianism — covert because it is for the most part unperceived and even unwitting. It usually passes for a more genuine form of piety and high ethical and moral seriousness. It resists overt antinomianism with a shocked disavowal, but then unwittingly takes over many of its arguments in a form that makes them infinitely more insidious and dangerous. Instead of a clear *end* to the law, covert antinomianism tries to ameliorate the law's stringency by a *change* of the law, in either content or function.

Covert antinomianism is ultimately much more dangerous and debilitating than the overt sort, because it is the result of an underestimation of or nervousness about the eschatological power of the gospel. Eventually such underestimation and nervousness issue in resignation and despair. The hope is gone; there is no light at the end of the tunnel. The best we can do to comfort ourselves then is to reduce the law to manageable proportions, cut it down to size. As long as such antinomianism remains even remotely attuned to the gospel, it does realize that the gospel is to have some effect on the law. But since the gospel does not end the law it can only change the law in some way. It is again a theological *tour de force*. It is, you might say, a futile attempt to make law *sound* like gospel. Under the guise of regard for the law it pulls the teeth of the law. Instead of really getting bitten we just get gummed to death!

Covert antinomianism, seen in this light, comes in many different forms. Early in Christian history some tried to accommodate to law by altering the law's content, arguing that while ceremonial law came to an end with Christ, the moral law did not. Nervousness about the effectiveness of the gospel in the confessional generation of Protestantism resulted in the positing of an added *function* of the law: a "third use" by the "reborn Christian." The gospel does make a difference, supposedly, but only such as to add to the function of the law. But the function is really a watering down and blunting of the impact of the law. Instead of ordering and attacking, law is supposed to become a rather gentle and innocuous "guide." More recent biblical exegetes do something of the same sort when they try to comfort us with the information that to the ancient Israelite law was really not so bad but as part of *Torah* a blessing.

In ethics we seem readily to take to contextualizing, or rather easily modifying, law to accommodate our preferences. No doubt laws do need to be changed to fit the times. But it would seem that they should be changed to *attack* sin in the new forms it takes, not to accommodate it. Under the guise of concern for ethics, morality, and justice, law is watered down and blunted to accommodate our fancies. When there is no end in sight that is the only way we can make peace with law.

But once again, this is fake theology. If overt antinomianism is impossible, covert antinomianism is even more so. It will not work. The law just changes its tack and becomes, if anything, worse. Is there any comfort in the idea that the ceremonial law ends, but not the moral? And what, finally, is the difference between them? Are the first three commandments ceremonial or moral? Does the law attack any less just because theologians say it is a friendly guide? Or does that only make matters worse? Is the idea that *Torah* was a blessing to ancient Israel of any comfort to a twentieth-century gentile? Have we really escaped from anything by all the contextualizing and interpreting and relativizing? Or have we succeeded only in bringing the voice of despair closer?

When the attempt is made to make law *sound* like gospel by purely verbal change, the gospel also, of course, becomes pointless and simply lapses into a kind of sentimental reassurance for our preferences. The gospel loses its vigor and rigor as a life-giving word, Christ is reduced to the "sweet Jesus" of mass-media piety. Luther was well aware of this, way back there in his battles with the antinomians, and saw it as the work of the devil.

> The devil knows very well . . . that it is impossible to remove the law from the heart. . . . But the devil devotes himself to making men secure, teaching them to heed neither law nor sin, so that if sometime they are suddenly overtaken by death or by a bad conscience, they have grown so accustomed to nothing but sweet security that they sink helplessly into hell. For they have learned to perceive nothing in Christ but sweet security. Therefore such terror must be [taken as] a sure sign that Christ (whom they understand as sheer sweetness) has rejected and forsaken them. That is what the devil strives for, and that is what he would like to see.[5]

Antinomianism of all sorts succeeds only in making matters worse. The law does not go away by theological arrangement. It comes back, though unrecognized, in worse and more devastating form. The fact is that there really *is* no other end to the law than the Christ who died under the law and nevertheless was raised.

5. LW 47: 111.

Linguistic Antinomianism

The argument against antinomianism as fake theology, as mere wordplay that fails because it outruns or falls short of the reality it is attempting to mediate, opens up an interesting perspective on the use in theology of language in general. This is reinforced when we recall that for Luther "law" did not mean merely *laws* but anything and everything that accuses, especially the way language attacks the lost. What do we do when our language — particularly our religious language — turns on us? The most immediate and dominant answer in our day seems to be to erase it, to change it, to blunt its effect by dissolving it in a sea of pluralistic options. The stratagem, that is, is exactly the same as that of the antinomians. So we must complete this essay by raising the question whether the predominant form of antinomianism today is not a kind of pervasive linguistic antinomianism, the idea that whenever we encounter that which threatens and judges and accuses or just generally upsets our preferences, the way to solve our problems is just to play with the words, change them, shift them, erase them, thinking that thereby we have accomplished something.

Current discussion about the problem of "sexist" language and the use of metaphor in theology is an example of the temptation to linguistic antinomianism. It is quite true that the language we use turns on us and attacks in unexpected and even unsuspected ways *(lex semper accusat!).* It is also true that language can be used either intentionally or unintentionally to oppress. But the idea that much of anything is *really* accomplished merely by erasing or changing the language is antinomian folly. We need, of course, to be constantly on guard against the ways in which we use language to accommodate sin and perpetuate injustice. It is the task of language to restrain and attack such perfidy (first and second uses of the law). But merely changing the metaphors or the language when one has no perception of the end only makes matters worse. The law only changes its guise and becomes more devastating because it is supposed to be "gospel."

This is not the place to go into a thorough discussion of the complicated issues involved. From the perspective of the analysis of the antinomian mistake, however, it becomes apparent that mere change from male to female or even neuter gender accomplishes little more than to obscure the issues. If "the Father" is a threat to us, who shall convince us that "the Mother" is not also — in "her" own way? It is quite possible, is it not, when one considers the fact that the gospel *establishes* the law, that one should find "the law" stated in its most uncompromising fashion precisely where the gospel is believed? If "the Father" is the clearest statement of this, then what is accomplished by unreflective and hasty change to "the Mother," except to confuse by a futile attempt to lessen the statement of the law? The on-again, off-again alternation between "he" and "she" falls into the same trap.

The current fashion of talk about the metaphorical nature of theological language would also benefit from a closer look at the antinomianism heresy. Those who push "metaphorical theology" seem to think that recognition of the metaphorical character of theological language will save us from all the ills that beset us: literalism, heteronomy, patriarchalism, religious exclusivism, theological imperialism, and so forth and so on. If we would just realize the parabolic nature (extended metaphor) of communication and take Jesus as a parable of God we would be out of the woods.[6] It is difficult to escape the impression that for a host of thinkers today the solution to all our problems is wordplay. If we get into trouble with a "metaphor" we can just change it. Metaphors seem to be basically interchangeable, and since we can make them or break them or shift them around at will we are in charge of our own destiny. But that is just linguistic antinomianism. It will not work.

"Language is the house of being." So we have been taught today — by Heidegger perhaps. But then it is also true that language is the prison house of being. Unless there is an actual *end* to the law, unless there is one who actually "breaks out," there is no hope. All we do then by changing our language is give the illusion of freedom by offering a choice of cells, or perhaps even a "pluralism" of them. When eschatological hope is lost we think that "gospel" means making the prison as comfortable as possible. But that is fake theology.

Christ the End of the Law

The only cure for antinomianism of all sorts is the proclamation of the unconditional gospel of the crucified and risen Christ. He was destroyed by our language, he was done in by law, sin, and death, and yet raised. And

---

6. See, for instance, Sallie McFague, *Metaphorical Theology* (Philadelphia: Fortress, 1982).

that is the end of it. *Christ*, not theological wordplay, is the end of the law, that those who have faith may be justified. Anything other than that is futile, fake. But we must hold on to the fact that there *is* an end. Antinomianism is right about that, certainly much more right than nomism. But Christ, not denial or change of "the law," is the end, the hope of humanity. If "the Father" has become a burden for us, then I expect it is only Christ who can reconcile us to him. At least that seems to be the claim of the New Testament. Indeed, it is because only Christ is the end that the law is established. Because this one man, this person with his history, is the concrete and actual end of the story, then the history, the story itself is established. The language, that is, has reached its conclusion. There is nothing more to say. Thus it cannot be changed at will. The once-for-all, the offense, has been set. Jesus is not a parable of God. The point of the doctrine of the Trinity is that he *is* God from God. Only when we forget that Christ alone is the end do we resort to our own artifices to make fake endings.

For the most part in this essay I have considered antinomianism from a theological rather than an ethical point of view. The reason for that is that mostly we do not realize or recognize the theological dimensions of the heresy. I hope these reflections have made them a bit clearer. But perhaps we should say something about the ethical dimensions before stopping. After all, it seems to be mostly the ethical consequences of antinomianism that have made people nervous through the ages — even though consistent antinomians are few and far between!

The claim that Christ is the end of the law to faith seems to make people nervous. The idea that the Christian as "new being" "walks by the Spirit" lends itself too easily, it is feared, to self-indulgence. One can, as the Formula of Concord put it, "under the appearance of God's Spirit establish their own service to God on the basis of their own choice without God's Word and command."[7] The new being in Christ takes on too much the aspect of a mystical theologoumenon with no concrete reality. The outcome of such fears is usually pell-mell retreat to some species of nomism — usually covertly attenuated to make it attractive or manageable. The result is loss of the gospel.

Here we simply have to face the fact that there is no cure other than a more radical proclamation of Christ as the end of the law who because he is the end establishes the law prior to the end. When the end is given we no

7. BC 590; BC-T, 567.

longer *need* to be antinomians. This, it seems to me, was Luther's point in all his writings on the matter. Because the end is given we can enter gladly into life under law for the time being, to care for the world, for others, and do battle with sin and the devil. When there is no end we have no time for that. Either we must spend all our time trying to reach the end or creating an end we can (supposedly) reach. We must become either nomists or antinomists. When the end is given in Christ, however, the law is established for its proper uses. The law, Luther always insisted, was not given to make people merely pious, but to draw them into the world of the neighbor where they can be of some use. Where Christ is the end of the law that is what happens. It is the task of Christian preaching to put an end to theological fakery so that can begin to happen.

The Lutheran View of Sanctification

Sanctification, if it is to be spoken of as something other than justification, is perhaps best defined as the art of getting used to the unconditional justification wrought by the grace of God for Jesus' sake. It is what happens when we are grasped by the fact that God alone justifies. It is being made holy, and as such, it is not our work. It is the work of the Spirit who is called Holy. The fact that it is not our work puts the old Adam/Eve (our old self) to death and calls forth a new being in Christ. It is being saved from the sickness unto death and being called to new life.

In German there is a nice play on words that is hard to reproduce in English. Salvation is *das Heil* — which gives the sense both of being healed and of being saved. Sanctification is *die Heiligung* — which would perhaps best be translated as "being salvationed." Sanctification is "being salvationed," the new life arising from the catastrophe suffered by the old upon hearing that God alone saves. It is the pure flower that blossoms in the desert, watered by the unconditional grace of God.

Sanctification is thus simply *the art of getting used to justification*. It is not something added to justification. It is not the final defense against a justification too liberally granted. It *is* the justified life. It is what happens when the old being comes up against the end of its self-justifying and self-gratifying ways, however pious. It is life lived in anticipation of the resurrection.

As such, sanctification is likely not the kind of life that we (old beings!) would wish, much as we might prattle piously about it and protest about how necessary it is. For the most part we make the mistake of equating sanctification with what we might call the moral life. As old beings we get nervous when we hear about justification by grace alone, faith alone, and worry that it will lead to moral laxity. So we say we have to "add" sanctification too, or we have to get on to what is *really* important, living the "sanctified life." And by that we usually mean living morally.

Now, living morally is indeed an important, wise, and good thing. There is no need to knock it. But it should not be equated with sanctification, being made holy. The moral life is the business of the old being in this world. The Reformers called it "civil righteousness." Sanctification is the result of the dying of the old and the rising of the new. The moral life is the result of the old being's struggle to climb to the heights of the law. Sanctification has to do with the descent of the new being into humanity, becoming a neighbor, freely, spontaneously, giving of the self in self-forgetful and uncalculating ways. "But when you give to the needy, do not let your left hand know what your right hand is doing, so that your giving may be in secret. Then your Father, who sees what is done in secret, will reward you" (Matt. 6:3-4). Sanctification is God's secret, hidden (perhaps especially!) even from the "sanctified." The last thing the sanctified would do would be to talk about it or make claims about achieving it. One would be more likely, with Paul, to talk about one's weaknesses.

No, sanctification is not the kind of thing we would seek. I expect we do not really want it, and perhaps rarely know when it is happening to us. It is the work of the Holy Spirit, the Lord and giver of life. It is given to us in the buffeting about, the sorrows, the joys, the sufferings, and the tasks of daily life. As Ernest Becker rightly put it in his classic work (that ought to be read by everyone interested in the question of "salvationing" today) *The Denial of Death*, the hardest thing is not even the death, but the rebirth, because it means that for the first time we shall have to be reborn not as gods but as human beings, shorn of all our defenses, projects, and claims.[1] Can flowers bloom in this desert? Can we survive and get used to justification? Can we live as though it were true? That is the question.

---

1. Ernest Becker, *The Denial of Death* (New York: Free Press, 1973), p. 58.

The Argument

Talk about sanctification is dangerous. It is too seductive for the old being. What seems to have happened in the tradition is that sanctification has been sharply distinguished from justification, and thus separated out as the part of the "salvationing" we are to do. God alone does the justifying simply by declaring the ungodly to be so, for Jesus' sake. Most everyone is willing to concede that, at least in some fashion. But, of course, then comes the question: What happens next? Must not the justified live properly? Must not justification be safeguarded so it will not be abused? So sanctification enters the picture supposedly to rescue the good ship Salvation from shipwreck on the rocks of Grace Alone. Sanctification, it seems, is *our* part of the bargain. But, of course, once it is looked on that way, we must be careful not to undo God's justifying act in Christ. So sanctification must be absolutely separated from justification. God, it seems, does his part, and then we do ours.

The result of this kind of thinking is generally disastrous. We are driven to make an entirely false distinction between justification and sanctification in order to save the investment the old being has in the moral system. Justification is a kind of obligatory religious preliminary that is rendered largely ineffective while we talk about getting on with the truly "serious" business of becoming "sanctified" according to some moral scheme or other. We become the actors in sanctification. This is entirely false. According to Scripture, God is always the acting subject, even in sanctification. The distinction serves only to leave the old being in control of things under the guise of pious talk.

On the level of human understanding, the problem is that we attempt to combine the unconditional grace of God with our notions of continuously existing and acting under the law. In other words, the old being does not come up against its death, but goes on pursuing its projects, perhaps a little more morally or piously, but still on its own. There is no death of the old and thus no hope for a resurrection of the new. The unconditional grace of God is combined with the wrong theological anthropology. That is always disaster. As we shall see a bit later, justification by faith alone demands that we think in terms of the death of the old subject and the resurrection of a new one, not the continuous existence of the old. Unconditional grace calls forth a new being in Christ. But the old being sees such unconditional grace as dangerous and so protects its continuity by "adding sanctification." It seeks to stave off the death involved by becoming "moral."

Sanctification thus becomes merely another part of its self-defense against grace. Justification is rendered more or less harmless. Talk about sanctification can be dangerous in that it misleads and seduces the old being into thinking it is still in control. We may grudgingly admit we cannot justify ourselves, but then we attempt to make up for that by getting serious about sanctification.

Even under the best of conditions, talk about sanctification in any way apart from justification is dangerous. It has a tendency to become a strictly verbal exercise in which one says obligatory things to show one is "serious about it" — but little comes of the discussion. Perhaps one feels sanctified just by talking impressively about it. The result of such talk is what I like to call "the magnificent hot-air balloon syndrome." One talks impressively *about* sanctification, and we all get beguiled by the rhetoric and agree. "Yes, of course, we all ought to do that," and the balloon begins to rise into the religious stratosphere solely on the strength of its own hot air. It is something like bragging about prowess in love and sex. It is mostly hot air and rarely accomplishes anything more for the hearers than arousing anxiety or creating the illusion that they somehow can participate vicariously. We got started in that direction even in the above exercise in this thesis when we talked about how sanctification is "spontaneous," "free," "self-forgetful," "self-giving," "uncalculating," and all those nice things. Dangerous talk. Dangerous because, like love, none of those things can actually be *produced* by us in any way. Theology indeed obligates us to talk about them, to attempt accurate description, but unless we know the dangers and limitations of such descriptions, it leads only to presumption or despair. So let the reader beware!

And so at the very least, we can say that sanctification cannot in any way be separated from justification. It is not merely a logical mistake, but a spiritually devastating one. In fact, the Scriptures rarely, if ever, treat sanctification as a movement distinct from justification. In writing to the Christians at Corinth, for instance, Paul refers to them as "those sanctified in Christ Jesus, called to be saints together with all those who in every place call on the name of our Lord Jesus Christ"; and later, he refers to the God who chooses what is low and despised in the world, even the things that are not, as the source of our life in Christ Jesus, "who became for us wisdom from God, and righteousness and sanctification and redemption," so that whoever boasts should boast in the Lord (1 Cor. 1:2, 28-31).

To the Thessalonians Paul writes that they have been chosen by God from the beginning "for salvation through sanctification through the Spirit and through belief in the truth" (2 Thess. 2:13). Hebrews says that "we have been sanctified through the offering of the body of Jesus Christ once for all" (Heb. 10:10). Sanctification appears in Scripture to be roughly equivalent to other words for the salvation wrought by God in Christ, a phrase that designates another facet or dimension of sanctification, but never calls it something distinct or logically different from justification. J. K. S. Reid is right when he concludes, "It is tempting for the sake of logical neatness to make a clean division between the two [justification and sanctification] but the temptation must be resisted, if in fact the division is absent from Holy Scripture."[2]

It is difficult to escape the suspicion that the distinction between justification and sanctification is strictly a *dogmatic* one made because people got nervous about what would happen when unconditional grace was preached, especially in Reformation times. "Does justification not do away with good works? Who will be good if they hear about justification by faith alone?" So the anxious questions went. Sanctification was "added" as something distinct in order to save the enterprise from supposed disaster. But dogmatic distinctions do not save us from disaster. More likely than not, they only make matters worse.

Justification by Faith Alone

It becomes clear, then, that we cannot talk about sanctification without first saying something about justification. The difficulty we have arises because justification by faith alone, without the deeds of the law, is a mighty breakup of the ordinary scheme of morality and religion; a mighty attack, we should say, on the theology of the old being. The fact that we are justified before God — the eternal Judge, Creator, and Preserver of all life — unconditionally for Jesus' sake and by faith alone, simply shatters the old being's entire system of values and calculations.

As old beings we do not know what to do with an unconditional gift or promise. Virtually our entire existence in this world is shaped, deter-

2. Alan Richardson, ed., *A Theological Wordbook of the Bible* (New York: Macmillan, 1960), p. 218.

mined, and controlled by conditional promises and calculations. We are brought up on conditional promises. We live by them. Our future is determined by them. Conditional promises always have an "if-then" form.[3] *If* you eat your spinach, *then* you get your pudding. *If* you are a good girl, *then* you can go to the movies. *If* you do your schoolwork, *then* you will pass the course. *If* you do your job, *then* you will get your pay. *If* you prove yourself, *then* you will get a promotion. And so on and so on, endlessly until at last we die of it, wondering *if* we had only done this or that differently, perhaps *then*... Though such conditional promises are often burdensome and even oppressive, they are nevertheless enticing and even comforting in their own way because they give life its structure and seem to grant us a measure of control. *If* we fulfill the conditions, *then* we have a claim on what is promised. We have what we call "rights," and we can control our future, at least to a certain extent.

So, as old beings, we hang rather tenaciously onto these conditional promises. As a matter of fact, that is what largely characterizes our *being* in this world as *old*. We hang desperately onto the conditional promises, hoping to control our own destiny. We live "under the law" and cannot get out — because we really do not want to. We prefer to go our own way even up to the last barrier: death. And there we must either hope that the conditionality ends and all account books simply close, or perhaps we make the fatal mistake of thinking that we can extend our control under the conditional promise even into the beyond. We think we have a claim on heaven itself if the proper conditions are met. Religion is most often just the attempt to extend this conditionality into eternity and to gain a certain measure of control even over the eternal itself.

But the saving act of God in Jesus Christ — comprehended in justification by faith alone — is an *unconditional* promise. Unconditional promises have a "because-therefore" form. *Because* Jesus has overcome the world and all enemies by his death and resurrection, *therefore* (and only for that reason) you shall be saved. *Because* Jesus died and rose, *therefore* God here and now declares you just for Jesus' sake (not even for your sake, but for Jesus' sake). *Because* Jesus has borne the sin of the whole world in his body unto death and yet conquered, *therefore* God declares the forgiveness of our sins.

3. Eric Gritsch and Robert Jenson, *Lutheranism: The Theological Movement and Its Confessional Writings* (Philadelphia: Fortress, 1976), pp. 8, 42.

Now, of course, as old beings we have a desperately difficult time with such an unconditional promise. It knocks everything out of kilter. We simply do not know how to cope with it, so we are thrown into confusion. Is it really true? Can one announce it just like that? No strings attached? Do we not have to be more careful about to whom we say such things? It appears wild and dangerous and reckless to us, just as it did to Jesus' contemporaries. The best we can do is to try to draw it back into our conditional understanding — so all the questions and protests come pouring out. But surely we have to do *something*, do we not? Do we not at least have to make our decision to accept? Isn't faith, after all, a condition? Or repentance? Isn't the idea of an unconditional promise terribly dangerous? Who will be good? Won't it lead perhaps to universalism, libertinism, license, and sundry disasters? Do we not need to insist on sanctification to prevent the whole from collapsing into cheap grace? Does the Bible not follow the declaration of grace with certain exhortations and imperatives? So the protestations go, for the most part designed to reimpose at least a minimal conditionality on the promise.

It is crucial to see that here we have arrived at the decisive point which will entirely determine how we look at what we call sanctification. It is true, you see, that as old beings we simply cannot understand or cope with the unconditional promise of justification pronounced in the name of Jesus. What we do not see is that what the unconditional promise is calling forth is a *new being*. The justification of God promised in Jesus is not an "offer" made to us as old beings; it is our end, our death. We are, quite literally, through as old beings. To use the vernacular, we have "had it." All the questions and protests that we raise are really just the death rattle of the old Adam and Eve who sense that their kingdom is under radical and final attack. No doubt that is why the defense is so desperate, and why it even quite innocently takes such pious and well-meaning forms.

But isn't the unconditional promise dangerous? Of course it is! After all, look what happened to Jesus! It is the death of us one way or another. Either we stick in our conditionality and go to that death which is eternal, or we are put to death to be raised to new and eternal life in the one who lives eternally. The point is that when we come up against the danger and radicality of the unconditional promise, the solution is not to fall back on conditionality but simply to be drawn into the death and resurrection of Jesus. The old being cannot survive the promise, the promise that makes new beings out of nothing. God is the one who calls into being that which is from that which is not. The new being finds its center now not in itself, but in Jesus.

One has only to follow out the argument in Romans to see Paul clearly developing this point. The law, the conditional promise, did not stop sin; it only made it worse. As a matter of fact, the law was given to show sin as sinful beyond measure, a bottomless pit, an endless hall of mirrors. But where sin abounded, grace abounded all the more! But is not such argument terribly dangerous? Aren't all the careful barriers built against sin suddenly destroyed? Does one not come perilously close to saying that sin is somehow presupposed by or even necessary for grace? Couldn't one then justly say, "Well then, shall we not sin the more that grace may abound?" It is a serious question and one that has to be raised. As a matter of fact, if the question isn't raised, one probably has not yet grasped the radical *hilaritas,* the joy of grace. No doubt, it is the old being's last question prior to its death. But what is the answer? It does not lie in returning to the law, to conditionality, but rather in the death of the old.

> Should we continue in sin in order that grace may abound? By no means! How can we who died to sin go on living in it? Do you not know that all of us who have been baptized into Christ Jesus were baptized into his death? Therefore we have been buried with him by baptism into death, so that, just as Christ was raised from the dead by the glory of the Father, so we too might walk in newness of life. For if we have been united with him in a death like his, we will certainly be united with him in a resurrection like his. We know that our old self was crucified with him so that the body of sin might be destroyed, and we might no longer be enslaved to sin. For whoever has died is freed from sin. But if we have died with Christ, we believe that we will also live with him. We know that Christ, being raised from the dead, will never die again; death no longer has dominion over him. The death he died, he died to sin once for all; but the life he lives, he lives to God. So you also must consider yourselves dead to sin and alive to God in Christ Jesus. (Rom. 6:1-11)

Actually, all evangelical treatment of sanctification should be little more than comment on this passage. The end to sin is death, not following the law, not moral progress, not even "sanctification" as the old Adam or Eve thinks of it. To sin the more that grace may increase is, of course, absurd and impossible precisely because of the death. To do so would mean to will to return to sin in order to get more grace. That would be like a lover desiring to return to the state of unloving in order to experience falling in love again. Quite impossible! How can one who has died to sin still live in it? The movement is simply irreversible if one catches a glimpse of what the grace is all about.

Furthermore, it is crucial to note that Paul does not tell his readers that they have to get busy now and die. He announces the startling and unconditional fact that we *have* died. It is not a task to be accomplished. All who were baptized into Christ Jesus were baptized into his death, so that out of that death may come newness of life, just like and as sure as the resurrection of Christ. Sin is a slavery from which we escape only through that death. Only one who has died is free from sin. There is no other way. The old self has been crucified so that the sinful body might also be destroyed and we might at last be set free. There is no continuity of the old self to be carried over here. Christ now becomes our life.

Just the sheer and unconditional announcement "You have died!" — the uncompromising insistence that there is nothing to do now, that God has made his last move — just that, and that alone, is what puts the old being to death, precisely because *there is nothing for the old being to do.* The God who says, "I will have mercy on whom I will have mercy," has decided to do just that through the death and resurrection of Jesus. There is no way for the old being to do anything about such grace. The unconditional justification, the grace itself, *slays* the old self and destroys its "body of sin" so as to fashion a new one. It is all over! Christ being raised from the dead will never die again. One cannot go back and repeat it. He died to sin once for all, and now he lives to God. Conclusion? You can now only consider yourself dead to sin and alive to God in Christ Jesus!

So, when we come to the decisive and crucial point about justification and the unconditional promise of grace, it is imperative to see that God is at work making new beings through this (to us) shocking act. The answer to all our questions, to the "death rattle" questions of the old Adam or Eve, lies not in falling back on conditionality, but in learning to cope with death and resurrection. All the questions must therefore be answered with a confident *yes.*

Do you mean to say we do not have to do anything? Yes! Just listen! Do you mean to say that even faith is not a condition, nor is making our decision, nor repentance? Yes! Faith is a gift. It comes by hearing. It is the

Spirit's work. It is a being grasped by the unconditional promise, a being caught by the sheer newness and joy of it, a being carried by the Word of Grace. But is not such unconditional promise dangerous? Yes, I suppose it is in this evil age. After all, Jesus got killed for it! But God has apparently decided to take the risk, and sealed it by raising Jesus from the dead. "Sleeper, awake! Rise from the dead, and Christ will shine on you" (Eph. 5:14).

But do you mean to say we cannot say *no?* That kind of question is, of course, the trickiest of the old Adam or Eve. But in spite of everything, it must be answered with a confident *yes* — from the point of view of the new being. The old Adam or Eve will, of course, only say *no,* can really only say *no.* The old Adam or Eve wants to remain in control of the matter and so says *no* even while wanting to say *yes.*

So saying *no* is not an option? Perhaps the best answer would be, "What do you want to do that for?" It would be like arriving at the altar for the wedding and answering the big question. "Do you take . . ." with, "Do you mean to say I cannot say *no?*" If we see at all what is going on, we would see that even here the answer finally has got to be *yes:* "Yes, I do not see how you can say *no!*" The new being by definition *is* one who says *yes.* One is not *forced* here, one is made new, *saved* — heart, soul, mind. One is *sanctified* in the truth of the unconditional promise of God. The answer to the persistent questions of the old Adam or Eve is therefore always *yes, yes, yes* until at last we die of it and begin to whisper, "Amen! So be it Lord!" Sanctification is a matter of being grasped by the unconditional grace of God and having now to live in that light. It is a matter of getting used to justification.

Simultaneously Just and Sinner

But now we must look a bit closer at how the unconditional promise — justification by faith alone — works in our lives if we are to arrive at an appropriate understanding of what we might call sanctification. The first thing to grasp is, of course, that the unconditional promise works quite differently from a conditional one. The unconditional promise, the divine decree of justification, grants everything all at once to the faith it creates. We are simply declared just for Jesus' sake. But that means simultaneously that we are revealed to ourselves as sinners. The sin revealed is not just a misdeed, but it is precisely our lack of faith and trust over against the incredible goodness of God. The sin to be ultimately expelled is our lack of trust, our unbelief. All our impetuous questions are shown for what they are: unbelief, our reservations over against the God of grace, our fear of being made new.

And still we ask, Do we not have to do something? You see, that is all we really planned to do — just a little something! We hadn't counted on being made new! Just that, you see, is the sin exposed! Nevertheless, God simply declares us to be just for Jesus' sake because that is the only thing that will help. That act of God itself finally exposes us as sinners, desperately in need of saving. So then, for the time being, we are, as Martin Luther said, *simul justus et peccator,* simultaneously just and sinner. It is the unconditional grace of God that makes us so. In that, we see the truth. And it is in the truth that we are sanctified. The first step on the way of sanctification is to realize that.

This is radically different from our usual, conditional thinking. Conditional thinking is wedded to the schemes of law and progress characteristic of this age. Sin is understood primarily as misdeed or transgression of such a scheme. "Sanctification" is the business of making progress in cutting down on sin according to the scheme. Holiness or righteousness could not be said to exist *simultaneously* with sin in the same scheme. Righteousness and sin would simply exclude each other. The more righteousness one gains, the less sin there would be. This would be measured by what one does or does not do. It would be a matter of works. Grace would then have to be understood as the power to do such works, to achieve such righteousness. The logic would then be that with the help of grace one progressively gains more and more righteousness and thus sins less and less. One strives toward perfection until, theoretically, one would need less and less grace or perhaps finally no more grace at all.

But such conditional schemes pose all sorts of problems for one who wants to think and believe "in the fashion of Scripture," as Luther called it.[4] In the first place, it does not fit with the divine act of justification by grace alone, by faith alone. There is no real place for justification in the scheme. If it comes at the beginning of the scheme, it makes the subsequent progress unnecessary. Why work at becoming just if you are already declared to be so? On the other hand, if justification comes at the end of

---

4. Martin Luther, *Lectures on Romans,* trans. and ed. Wilhelm Pauck, The Library of Christian Classics, vol. 15 (Philadelphia: Westminster, 1961), p. 128.

the scheme, it becomes unnecessary. You do not have to be declared just if you have already become so.

The systematic problem is that both justification by faith alone without the deeds of the law and such a scheme of sanctification cannot possibly coexist together. The tradition no doubt recognized this when it insisted on making a sharp and complete distinction between the two, at least in theory. In actual practice, however, one or the other of them generally comes to be regarded as more or less fictional or dispensable. And more likely than not, it will be justification that is so regarded. It comes to be looked upon as a decree contrary to actual fact, a kind of "as if" theology. We are regarded "as if" we were just. Or perhaps it is a kind of "temporary loan" granted until we actually earn our way. Sanctification according to this scheme takes over the center of the stage as the real and practical business of the Christian.

But this leads only to a further, more personal problem in the life of faith if one becomes honest before God. What if the scheme just does not seem to work? This is the much celebrated problem of the "anxious conscience" that bothered Martin Luther. What if one is honest enough to see that one is not actually making the kind of progress the scheme proposes? I am told that grace gives the power to improve, to gain righteousness and overcome sin. I am told, furthermore, that grace is absolutely free. But what if I go to church to "get grace" and then get up the next morning and see the same old sinner, perhaps even a little bit worse, staring back at me through the mirror? What then? I am told that grace is free, and that there is nothing wrong with the "delivery system." Not even a bad priest, minister, or a faulty church can frustrate or limit the grace of God. But I do not seem to get better. If I am in any way serious, I can only become more and more anxious. I am told that grace gives one the power to love God. But as a matter of fact I only become more and more resentful of a God who sets up such systems and makes such demands. I do not seem to grow in love of God. I begin to hate him! The magnificent hot-air balloon bursts.

Now I face the really desperate question: Whose fault is it if the scheme does not work? There are two possibilities. Either I have not properly responded to or cooperated with the free divine grace, or most frightening of all, the God of election who presides over such grace has decided, in my case, not to give it. The scheme leaves me either depending on my own abilities to respond, to remove all obstacles to grace, to "let myself go," and so forth, or it leaves me with the terrors of predestination. Usually, of course, we recoil in horror from the very thought of predestination. We piously would not want to lay the blame on God — and besides, we would then lose all control of the matter!

So all things considered, we would rather take the blame for the breakdown of the scheme on ourselves. If it did not work, it must be because we did not do something right. We did not repent sincerely enough; we did not really and truly seek him; we did not wholly give our hearts to Jesus; and so on. But in that case, the more we talk about "free grace" the worse it gets. When the system does not work, "grace is free" turns out to mean that there is no way we can put the blame on grace. But then no matter how much we *talk* about the grace of God, absolutely everything then depends on us, on our sincerity, our truthfulness, the depth of our feeling, the wholeheartedness of our confession, and so on. The system simply turns against us. While we live as old beings in this age, we simply cannot escape the law.

So it is impossible to put God's unconditional act of justifying sinners for Jesus' sake alone together with our ideas of progress based on conditions. It does not work either logically or in the life of faith. That is why Martin Luther came to see that we must take a radically different approach. In place of all ordinary understandings of progress and sanctification, the true Christian life begins when we see the *simultaneity* of sin and righteousness. God begins with us simply by declaring us to be righteous because of Jesus. We begin to see the truth of the situation when we realize that because God had to do that, we must have been at the same time sinners. God would be wasting his breath declaring people to be righteous if they were not actually and wholly sinners! Indeed, as Paul put it, "if justification comes through the law, then Christ died for nothing" (Gal. 2:21).

And there can be no cheating here. Since the declaration of God is total, and depends totally on what Jesus has accomplished for us, the sin simultaneously exposed is total. All the dreams, schemes, and pretensions of the old Adam or Eve are unmasked in their totality. Sin, as a total state, can only be fought by faith in the total and unconditionally given righteousness. Anything other than that would lead only to hypocrisy or despair. If there is to be anything like true sanctification, it must begin with these considerations.

If our righteousness depends totally on Jesus, and is appropriated only in the relationship of trust (faith), then we can begin to see that God has two problems with us. The relationship can be broken in two ways.

The first would be by our failure, our immorality, our vices. Since we lack faith and hope in God's cause, the relationship is threatened or broken; we go our own way. That problem is usually quite obvious. But the second problem is not so obvious. It is precisely our supposed success, even our "morality," our virtues — the relationship with God is broken to the degree that we think we do not need the unconditional justification, or perhaps even to the degree that we think we are going to use God to achieve our own ideas of sanctity. The relationship is broken precisely because we think it is *our* holiness.

The first problem, our failure and immorality, is usually most easily recognized and generally condemned because it has consequences, both personally and socially. But the second problem, while generally approved in human eyes because it is advantageous and socially useful, is more dangerous before God (*coram deo,* as Luther put it) precisely because it is praised and sought after. It is the kind of hypocrisy Jesus criticized so vehemently in the Gospels: "like whitewashed tombs, which on the outside look beautiful but inside they are full of the bones of the dead and of all kinds of filth" (Matt. 23:27). No matter how good and useful such virtue is in the world (and we must not fail to see that it *is* really so and does have its place), it *cannot* be counted as sanctification. Those who blow their own horns when they give alms so as to be seen and admired by the public do indeed have their reward: the praise of others. But that is all they get. True sanctification is God's secret (Matt. 6:2-4).

So the first step on the way to sanctification is to see that, before the judgment of God as it comes through the crucified and risen Jesus, we are rendered totally just at the same time as we are exposed totally as sinners. Sanctification is thus included in justification as a total state. True sanctification is at the outset simply to believe that God has taken charge of the matter. Where can there be more holiness than where God is revered and worshiped as the only Holy One? But God is revered as the only Holy One where the sinner, the real and total sinner, stands still and listens to God. There the sinner must realize that his or her ways are at an end. The final assault is under way. There the sinner begins to realize that neither virtue nor vice, morality nor immorality, neither circumcision nor uncircumcision counts for anything before God, but what matters is the new creation (Gal. 6:15). Sanctification is not a repair job. God is after something new. He wants his creation back as new as when it came from his hand.

Progress in Sanctification: The Invasion of the New

But is there not such a thing as *growth* in sanctification, progress in the
Christian life? No doubt there is a sense in which we can and even should
speak in such fashion. But when we do, we must take care, if everything we
have been saying up to this point is true. If justification by faith alone rejects all ordinary schemes of progress and renders us simultaneously just
and sinners, we have to look at growth and progress in quite a different
light.

That brings us back to our thesis: sanctification is the art of getting
used to justification. There is a kind of growth and progress, it is to be
hoped, but it is growth in grace — a growth in coming to be captivated
more and more, if we can so speak, by the totality, the unconditionality, of
the grace of God. It is a matter of getting used to the fact that if we are to be
saved it will have to be by grace *alone.* We should make no mistake about
it: sin is to be conquered and expelled. But if we see that sin is the total
state of standing against the unconditional grace and goodness of God, if
sin is our very incredulity, unbelief, mistrust, our insistence on falling back
on our self and maintaining control, then it is only through the total grace
of God that *sin* comes under attack, and only through faith in that total
grace that sin is defeated. To repeat: sin is not defeated by a repair job, but
by dying and being raised *new.*

So it is always as a totality that unconditional grace attacks sin. That
is why total sanctification and justification are in essence the same thing.
The total sinner comes under the attack of the total gift. That is how the
battle begins. How then can we talk about the progress of the battle — the
transition, let us call it — from sin to righteousness, old to new?

There are, I believe, two aspects of this transition we need to talk
about. The first is that since we always are confronted and given grace as a
totality, we find ourselves always starting fresh. As Luther put it, "To progress is always to begin again."[5] In this life, we never quite get over grace, we
never entirely grasp it, we never really learn it. It always takes us by surprise. Again and again we have to be conquered and captivated by its totality. The transition will never be completed this side of the grave. The
Christian can never presume to be on the glory road, nor to reach a stage
that now forms the basis for the next stage, which can be left behind. The

5. Luther, *Lectures on Romans,* p. 370.

Christian who is grasped by the totality of grace always discovers the miracle anew. One is always at a new beginning. Grace is new every day. Like the manna in the wilderness, it can never be bottled or stored. Yesterday's grace turns to poison. By the same token, however, the Christian never has an endless process of sanctification to traverse. Since the totality is given, one knows that one *has* arrived. Christ carries the Christian totally.

Looked at from Luther's point of view of "always beginning again," the transition is therefore not a continuous or steady progress of the sort we could recognize. It is rather more like an oscillation between beginning and end in which both are always equally near. The end, the total gift, is constantly and steadily given. But to grasp that we have constantly to begin again — we never can get over it! It is like lovers who just cannot get over the miracle of the gift of love and so are constantly saying it over and over again as though it were completely new and previously unheard of! And so it constantly begins again.

The second aspect of the transition of the Christian from old to new, death to life, is that all our ordinary views of progress and growth are turned upside down. It is not that we are somehow moving toward the goal, but rather that the goal is moving closer and closer to us. This corresponds to the eschatological nature of the New Testament message. It is the coming of the Kingdom upon us, not our coming closer to or building up the Kingdom. That is why it is a growth *in grace,* not a growth in our own virtue or morality. The progress, if one can call it that, is that we are being shaped more and more by the totality of the grace coming to us. The progress is due to the steady invasion of the new. That means that we are being taken more and more off our own hands, more and more away from self, and getting used to the idea of being saved by the grace of God alone. Our sanctification consists merely in being shaped by, or getting used to, justification.

Getting used to justification means that the old Adam or Eve is being put to death, and thus, as Paul put it, "being freed from sin." How might we conceive of this? Here we must be careful lest in our attempts to describe the matter we once again get seduced into inflating the magnificent hot-air balloon. Being freed from sin by the unconditional promise means that the totality of it begins to overwhelm and destroy our fundamental skepticism and incredulity, our unbelief. "Lord, I believe; help my unbelief!" (Mark 9:24) becomes our prayer. We can see light at the end of the tunnel. We begin to trust God rather than ourselves. When Martin Luther talked about these things, he began to talk more about our actual affections than lists of pious things to do.

Under the pressure of the total gift, we might actually begin to love God as God, *our* God, and to hate sin. Think of it: We might actually begin to *dislike* sin and to hope for its eventual removal. Ordinarily we feel guilty about our sins and fear their consequences, but we are far from *hating* them. I expect we do them, in spite of all fears and anxieties, because we like them. Sanctification under the invasion of the new, however, holds out the possibility of actually coming to hate sin, and to love God and his creation, or at least to make that little beginning. It is not that sin is taken away from us, but rather that we are to be taken away from sin — heart, soul, and mind, as Luther put it.[6] In that manner, the law of God is to be fulfilled in us precisely by the uncompromising totality and unconditionality of the grace given.

Sanctification always comes from the whole, the totality. Whether it takes place in little steps, in isolated actions against particular sins, in those tender beginnings, it is always because of the invasion of the new. Always the totality is intensively there — the total crisis, the entire transition, the dying and becoming new.

What is the result of this? It should lead, I expect, to something of a reversal in our view of the Christian life. Instead of viewing ourselves on some kind of journey upward toward heaven, virtue, and morality, our sanctification would be viewed more in terms of our journey back down to earth, the business of becoming human, the kind of creature God made. Our problem is that we have succumbed to the serpent's temptation, "You shall not die, you shall be as gods." Creation is not good enough for us; we are always on our way somewhere else. So we even look on sanctification in that light — our "progress" toward being "gods" of some sort. If what we have been saying is true, however, our salvation, our sanctification, consists in turning about and going the other way, getting back down to earth. The trouble we have is that it is a long way back for us. To get there we must learn to trust God, to be grasped by the totality of his grace, to become a creature, to become human.

What might that look like? When I think about such sanctification, I think about several things: spontaneity, taking care, vocation, and attaining a certain elusive kind of truthfulness and lucidity about oneself. Perhaps I can end by saying a few words about these things.

6. Luther, *Lectures on Romans*, p. 194.

Spontaneity

What is a truly good work, one that might qualify as the fruit of sanctification? One, I think, that is free, uncalculating, genuine, spontaneous. It would be like a mother who runs to pick up her child when it is hurt. There is no calculation, no wondering about progress, morality, or virtue. There is just the doing of it, and then it is completely forgotten. The right hand does not know what the left is doing. Good works in God's eyes are quite likely to be all those things we have forgotten! True sanctification is God's secret.

Taking Care

If we are turned around to get back down to earth by grace, then it would seem that true sanctification would show itself in taking care of our neighbor and God's creation, not exploiting and destroying either for our own ends, religious or otherwise. It would mean concern for the neighbor and society, caring for the other for the time being. Here one should talk about the place of morality and virtue and such things. Although we do not accept them as the means by which we are sanctified, they *are* the means by which and through which we care for the world and for the other. This is what the Reformers meant when they insisted that good works were to be done, but one was not to depend on them for salvation.

Vocation

How does the one who has died and is being made new, the one who has been taken off his or her own hands, enter into the battle in this world? The answer comes in the concept of carrying out one's vocation as a Christian in the tasks and occupations of daily life. We always get nervous about what we are to do, it seems. The magnificent hot-air balloon syndrome seduces us into thinking our sanctification consists in following lists of pious dos and do nots. That always seems more holy. But it is in the nitty-gritty of daily life and its tasks that our sanctification is hammered out.

Precisely because of the totality of the gift, the new being knows that there is nothing to do to gain heaven. Thus the Christian is called to the tasks of daily life in this world, for the time being. Students, for instance, are sometimes very pious and idealistic about "doing something," and so get caught up in this or that movement "for good." It never seems to dawn on them that perhaps for the time being, at least, their calling is simply to be a good student! It is not particularly in acts of piety that we are sanctified, but in our call to live and act as Christians.

Truthfulness and Lucidity

In many ways, this essay has been an appeal for more truthfulness in our talk about the Christian life and sanctification. I think that should be the mark of sanctification as well. As Paul put it, we are not to think of ourselves more highly than we ought (Rom. 12:3).

The talk of progress and growth we usually indulge in leads us all too often to do just that. But if we are saved and sanctified only by the unconditional grace of God, we ought to be able to become more truthful and lucid about the way things really are with us. Am I making progress? If I am really honest, it seems to me that the question is odd, even a little ridiculous. As I get older and death draws nearer, it does not seem to get any easier. I get a little more impatient, a little more anxious about having perhaps missed what this life has to offer, a little slower, harder to move, a little more sedentary and set in my ways. It seems more and more unjust to me that now that I have spent a good part of my life "getting to the top," and I seem just about to have made it, I am already slowing down, already on the way out. A skiing injury from when I was sixteen years old acts up if I overexert myself. I am too heavy, the doctors tell me, but it is so hard to lose weight! Am I making progress? Well, maybe it *seems* as though I sin less, but that may only be because I'm getting tired! It's just too hard to keep indulging the lusts of youth. Is that sanctification? I would not think so! One should not, I expect, mistake encroaching senility for sanctification!

But can it be, perhaps, that it is precisely the unconditional gift of grace that helps me to see and admit all that? I hope so. The grace of God should lead us to see the truth about ourselves, and to gain a certain lucidity, a certain sense of humor, a certain down-to-earthness. When we come to realize that if we are going to be saved, it shall have to be absolutely by grace alone, then we shall be sanctified. God will have his way with us at last.

Reflections on the Fries-Rahner Proposal: Thesis I

Thesis I: The fundamental truths of Christianity, as they are expressed in Holy Scripture, in the Apostles' Creed, and in that of Nicea and Constantinople are binding on all partner churches of the one Church to be.

I must confess at the outset that I find the invitation to reflect on this thesis to be somewhat challenging and difficult under the conditions of the assignment. I found myself thinking at first that I didn't see how I could write more than a page or two about it. But on further reflection I began to think that one could, or perhaps should, write hundreds of pages.

It seems apparent that taking account of both the Fries-Rahner proposal and the various reactions that have come to my attention, one must discuss the matter on at least two levels, the level of dogma and its content on the one hand, and the level of the hermeneutics of dogma on the other. This is what I propose to do, and then to conclude by offering an attempt at a revised thesis.

On the level of dogma and its content it would seem to me that the thesis under question is simply to be affirmed. The "one Church to be" can only be one if it confesses a common faith and such common faith has definable and agreed-upon content. The commentary to Thesis I spells this out in an accurate and acceptable fashion. Holy Scripture is the normative origin of the faith, the creeds (Apostles', Nicene, and Constantinopolitan) articulate the content of the faith in their "concentrated center," and "present the totality of the fundamental truths of the Christian faith."[1] No later creeds or confessions have superseded the ancient creeds, nor will they. The ancient creeds, to be sure, demand the continuous task of interpretation and reinterpretation to address changing times, but this does not call for new creedal statement.[2] If there are differing interpretations on the part of the various partner churches, they can, at least initially, be grasped as various interpretations of the one faith.[3] Perhaps this last affirmation will cause one to raise an eyebrow, since one wonders just what the limits of such latitude might be. But precisely that sort of question leads us already to the second level of dialogue, the question of the hermeneutics of dogma.

Not only do questions suggested by the commentary internally lead to problems in the hermeneutics of dogma, but also, and most emphatically, the various reactions to the Fries-Rahner proposal impel us in that direction. If we take reactions at what may perhaps be considered opposing ends of the Protestant–Roman Catholic spectrum, for instance, those of Eilert Herms[4] and Daniel Ols,[5] it seems apparent that progress is not likely to be made in ecumenical discussion unless the hermeneutical questions are squarely faced. In the absence of such open discussion a kind of "hermeneutic of suspicion" intrudes, which only impedes true progress. Thus, Herms seems to suspect in the Fries-Rahner proposal a final move toward realization of the Counter-Reformation,[6] while Ols suspects a sellout to unity at any cost. Somewhere in between, Cardinal Ratzinger suspects a skipping-over the quest for truth "with a few political maneuvers."[7] Such suspicions indicate, even if one does not agree with them, that more careful discussion of the hermeneutics of dogma is imperative to further progress. Such discussion may be difficult, and will no doubt lead into areas of even

1. Heinrich Fries and Karl Rahner, *Unity of the Churches: An Actual Possibility* (Philadelphia: Fortress, 1985), p. 15.

2. Fries and Rahner, *Unity of the Churches,* p. 19.

3. Fries and Rahner, *Unity of the Churches,* p. 20.

4. Eilert Herms, "Ökumene im Zeichen der Glaubensfreiheit," *na Sancta* 3 (1984): 178-200.

5. Daniel Ols, "Scorciatoie ecumeniche," *L'Osservatore Romano* (February 25-26, 1985).

6. Herms, "Ökumene im Zeichen der Glaubensfreiheit," p. 193.

7. Joseph Cardinal Ratzinger, "Luther and the Unity of the Churches: An Interview with Joseph Cardinal Ratzinger," *Communio* (January-February 1985): 220.

greater potential disagreement or uncertainty, but it would seem unavoidable. We have long known that in a post-Enlightenment age, dogma must be handled in a different fashion. It might even be that the slowdown or standstill in the ecumenical movement is related to our inability to deal with such fundamental questions.

Speaking from my own, admittedly somewhat limited, experience with ecumenical discussion in the Lutheran–Roman Catholic dialogue in this country, it seems to me that Herms has a point when he argues that the usual method of discussion and comparing different dogmas *seriatum*, and even coming to agreement, often does not get at the essential questions of the *Prinzipienlehre* in order to concede the point. It is perhaps possible to carve out agreements or convergences on individual points and yet remain quite divided on the underlying authority structures of dogma and the purpose and use of dogma thus agreed upon. The recently completed round on justification in this country was so protracted and, no doubt, frustrating for many for just that reason — and one might add, its agreements so limited. It is not without reason that the Institute for Ecumenical Research in Strasbourg is initiating a study to get at some of the more difficult issues in this area: *basic* differences beyond just differences in particular dogmas. Nor is it quite right, I think, easily to discount Herms's discussion about the nature of revelation simply by saying there was no disagreement about this at the time of the Reformation. To be sure, there was no *explicit* discussion of the matter as such, but certainly the matter was there in such profound themes as the hidden and revealed God, the problem of the letter and Spirit, and above all, as Cardinal Ratzinger points out, in the question of law and gospel. Even in the Reformation era, when Melanchthon understood to write his Apology for the Augsburg Confession's statement on justification (CA IV) he could not simply go directly to the dogma as such, but had to get at the issues through a discussion of law and gospel, i.e., through, one might say, the hermeneutical detour. The fact that subsequent theology never understood these matters very clearly does not mean that they were not already implied and sometimes explicitly discussed in Reformation times.

To move to the hermeneutical problem in the first thesis itself, the difficulty begins to appear when one reduces the thesis to its simple elements: "The fundamental truths of Christianity . . . are . . . binding *(Die Grundwahrheiten des Christentums . . . sind . . . verpflichtend)*." It would be helpful, perhaps, to have a more careful investigation of just what that means, since it is around that center that the storm seems to rage. The commentary seems to suggest a somewhat loose sense of "binding." Being "bound" to the fundamental truths does not exclude further interpretation and development, if such is a "faithful exposition" of them. Furthermore, "if it seems conceivable" that the various churches understand different and sometimes contradictory teachings as various interpretations of the one faith, then "a great ecumenical opportunity has been opened up."[8] The difficulty is that such a loose sense of "binding" is not exactly reassuring. It bears too much the mark of a chastened absolutism, which seeks to accommodate itself to a post-Enlightenment age by interpretation and theories of development. The constant threat to such a move is relativism. How are these interpretations and developments to be assessed? In any case, such a move already involves one in a rather massive hermeneutical project.

The principle of the "hierarchy of truths" affirmed in Vatican II is also suggested in the commentary as important, not as a principle of selection but of correct interpretation, in ecumenical discussion as help and guidance. But this, to me at least, has always been a somewhat puzzling concept when dealing with such things as "fundamental truths" or dogma. Does it mean that some dogma is less binding than other dogma? Are there lesser dogmas, perhaps, which can be neglected, practically speaking, or even not believed? To be candid, it strikes me as another attempt to qualify a more absolutist stance that tends to get rather fuzzy in actual application.

Given the hermeneutical question mark that stands over the proposal, the reactions of both Herms and Ols are perhaps understandable. Herms sees in it, so to speak, a hidden absolutism, while Ols sees a sellout to relativism. The task of a hermeneutic of dogma, it would seem, is somehow to get beyond this kind of impasse. What follows will be an attempt to sketch out a way to do this. It will be done from an admittedly "Lutheran" perspective, but I hope it can be taken as a contribution to the discussion along the lines of an "evangelical counter-proposal" suggested by Eberhard Jüngel.[9]

There are no doubt several ways one could go about attacking the problem of the hermeneutics of dogma. One could talk about the nature of language, about the phenomenon of dogma-construction, about myths,

8. Fries and Rahner, *Unity of the Churches,* p. 20.
9. Eberhard Jüngel, "Ein Schritt voran," *Süddeutsche Zeitung* (October 1-2, 1983).

models, and metaphors, and so on, but I would like to do it by talking about bondage and freedom, both because this is the form in which the thesis before us raises the question and also because it is the form in which the post-Enlightenment world encounters the problem of church dogma. Let us go back to our simplified thesis: The fundamental truths of Christianity . . . are binding. There is a sense, as mentioned at the outset, in which that is quite true, especially when one has church dogma as *Lehrgesetz* in mind. Yet one must go on to ask why the fundamental truths must be seen as binding. Surely in the church and its message, dogma and fundamental truth must have something to do with liberation and freedom! Would it not be more correct to say that the fundamental truths of Christianity . . . are freeing or liberating? No doubt one cannot say it quite that directly, since it is the proclaimed gospel of Jesus Christ, indeed, Christ himself that liberates. Yet at the very least must we not say that the fundamental truths, the dogmas, of Christianity protect, foster, indeed drive to, the proclamation of the liberating Word and giving of the sacraments? Must it not be said that the very reason we hold to these fundamental truths is because they do that? Dogma, it seems to me, should have the character of a charter of freedom, perhaps a letter from the highest authority declaring the holder, a former slave, to be free. It has indeed a legal form, the form of a *Lehrgesetz*, one might say, but its function ultimately is to liberate. One holds to the charter; one is "bound" by it precisely because it sets free.

The point I wish to make is that the hermeneutic by which dogma is understood is radically different if one presupposes that the move one makes in becoming Christian is from bondage to freedom rather than from freedom to bondage. This latter has been, I think, the continuing temptation of the church. When one assumes that humans are basically "free" and relatively autonomous, the imposition of dogma can only become a form of bondage. One becomes subject to a heteronomy, subject to the "letter" of the law. One can seek to escape only by some sort of appeal to "spirit" beyond letter. In traditional Christian schemes such appeal will be to the "Holy Spirit" who is supposed to convince of the "truth" of the dogma in some more or less mysterious fashion, and reconcile one to the church. The result of that is that the Holy Spirit either comes to mean a kind of divine hidden agenda that seems to move quite independently from the ministrations of the church, or is institutionalized and regularized by the church. But if one reacts against such heteronomy, as the western world did at the time of the Enlightenment, the appeal will be to "human spirit" and autonomy. One tries to escape the move from freedom to bondage by denying the "binding" character of the "truths" that are imposed from without. One tries to escape from absolutism by throwing up the smokescreen of relativism. To be free one has to become an unbeliever.

Although I have not read the book by Herms, my immediate impression from his article written in response to the Fries-Rahner proposal is that something of the same presupposition (freedom to bondage) is at work. He wants to resist the apparent threat of heteronomy by driving a wedge between the event of revelation and the "traditioning" by which it is carried, claiming that at the most all the church can do is mediate the external Word while the Spirit works the event of revelation within. Such a move seems to me not to be very helpful. One tries to rescue the self and its freedom by making too much of a split between outer and inner, with the result that the Spirit becomes a kind of inner, hidden agenda too detached from the outer Word. One may be saved from churchly heteronomy by this means, but one is delivered into the hands of a chance, hidden agenda. It seems to me that Fries is quite right in asking, therefore, whether the witness is merely the offering of the external word and not rather participation in the *viva vox evangelii,* the living voice of the proclamation.[10]

But the move to the proclamation, the *viva vox evangelii,* simply presses home the question of the hermeneutic of dogma. The question to which we need to attend is that of the relation between dogma (the "fundamental truths of Christianity") and the proclamation. Where it is understood that the *proclamation,* the living voice of the gospel, liberates, and that the fundamental move is from bondage to freedom, the dogma is seen in a quite different light. The purpose of the dogma, the fundamental truths, is to authorize, to drive to, and to foster the appropriate proclamation of the liberating Word. Where that is realized, there will be no move to relativize the dogma in order to accommodate it to human autonomy. Indeed, the tendency would, for the most part, be quite the opposite, to hold fast to the dogma as that which fosters the proper proclamation. To be sure, the move from the dogma to the proclamation involves constant attention, interpretation, and reinterpretation. No doubt one might want to ask whether in all instances the received dogma does support the procla-

10. Heinrich Fries, "Das Rad der Ökumene zurückdrehen?" *Christ in der Gegenwart* 34 (January 1985): 30.

mation as directly as it might. Yet it will be realized that the dogma is a charter for freedom and as such is to be accorded its appropriate place.

This means, no doubt, that dogma will function more as rules for gospel preaching, perhaps somewhat along the lines suggested by George Lindbeck.[11] I say "perhaps somewhat" because even though I find the idea of dogma as rules helpful and suggestive, I do not think that leads necessarily to the "cultural-linguistic" theory Lindbeck employs to support his analysis. Lindbeck's distinctions are useful in finding our way. Dogmas are not usefully understood as "cognitive-propositional" statements of absolute truths to be believed, nor are they merely "experiential-expressive" formulations bringing our experience to expression in many-splendored variety. Rather they are rules for, in this case, Christian proclamation and living. Without entering into a discussion of Lindbeck's "cultural-linguistic" theory of religion, I think it useful to look upon dogma as rules for proper proclamation of the gospel from the point of view of the nature of such proclamation itself.

The difficulty we face is that there has seldom, if ever, been a hermeneutic of dogma developed from the point of view of the preaching of the gospel. The Reformation, one can say, made a proposal to the church about the preaching of the gospel — what Eric Gritsch and Robert Jenson have called a "meta-linguistic proposal of dogma" based on justification by faith alone.[12] The Reformation proposal was essentially one about how to go about preaching the gospel. What is needed, it would seem, is a way to reflect back on the nature of dogma from the hearing of the gospel. Thorough reflection on that would no doubt require those hundreds of pages mentioned at the outset. What follows are some preliminary reflections along those lines.

If dogmas are rules, they partake of the nature of law, indeed, beyond that of the "the letter." The purpose of the rules is to drive to the proclamation of the gospel. But the gospel is the "end," the goal, the *telos*, and *finis* of the law to faith. The gospel, therefore, proposes no attenuation or revision of the law this side of the *eschaton*. For the time being, therefore, faith does not abolish the law but establishes it. Perhaps approaching the question of

11. George Lindbeck, *The Nature of Doctrine* (Philadelphia: Westminster, 1984), pp. 32ff.

12. Eric Gritsch and Robert Jenson, *Lutheranism: The Theological Movement and Its Confessional Writings* (Philadelphia: Fortress, 1976), pp. 42ff.

dogma in this fashion could get us beyond the constant standoff between absolutism and relativism. Just as the gospel limits and establishes the purpose of the law, so also it is the gospel that limits and establishes the purpose of dogma. The ever-present threat of absolutism in dogma cannot be ameliorated by any kind of move in the direction of relativism. Indeed, moves in that direction will probably only mean a loss of the gospel itself, just as relativizing the law makes the gospel pointless by posing pseudo-solutions to human problems. It is the gospel, and only the gospel, that removes the "sting" of absolutism, not relativism. It is the gospel as the "end" that makes it possible to hold to, to guard, to cherish the dogma precisely as a charter for freedom. The church holds to the dogma just for that reason.

To put the matter in another way, dogma is letter. But the letter kills so that the Spirit may give life. Spirit is not a hidden agenda floating somewhere beyond the letter, attainable by authoritative churchly interpretation, or by occasional "spiritual experiences." Spirit comes through the letter. There cannot be, therefore, attempts to relativize or attenuate the letter so as to accommodate it to the situation of bondage. The Spirit gives life when the letter kills, not when the letter is altered to make it more amenable to us.

No doubt this proposes something of a different kind of authority structure for the church and its dogma. The highest instance of the exercise of authority in the church is the proclamation of the gospel, the act of liberation. The church exists to see to it that such exercise of authority is actually carried out. Its disciplining is for that purpose. It cares about its dogma for that reason. Its leaders, teachers, and pastors are there to see to it that the gospel happens. It exists to set people free from bondage. True authority liberates.

The point of this is to suggest that if dogma, "the fundamental truths of Christianity" if you will, is looked at from the point of view of preaching and hearing the gospel, its place beyond absolutism and relativism is more readily established. Such an understanding also provides a basis for critical evaluation of dogma. Dogma is to be critically examined according to whether or not it fosters a liberating proclamation of the gospel. No doubt this will require a quite specific understanding of what a liberating gospel is and how one is to move from dogma to proclamation. No doubt there will not initially at least be widespread agreement about that. But it is precisely that about which the church ought to be concerned and upon which it must focus its theological attention. Again, much more would have to be said about this than a paper of this scope can begin to suggest. But the basic direction in which one might move is, I hope, sufficiently clear.

I trust that these ruminations on the problem of the hermeneutics of dogma will not be taken as simply another attempt to put the brakes on or to stall efforts toward unity. I hope and pray that the church will be one. I have, however, one overriding concern that should be evident from these pages. That is the concern that what is to be preached in the one church be the gospel of Jesus Christ which liberates from sin, death, and the devil. Without that there is little point in unity. It is possible for the church too to gain the whole world and yet lose its own soul.

It is, needless to say, difficult to capture all that has been said in a satisfying thesis that might at the same time lay some claim to being a "real possibility." Nevertheless, since that is what we are here for, I suggest the following for consideration and discussion:

> All partner churches of the one church confess and proclaim the liberating Word of God, the gospel of Jesus Christ, authorized by the Holy Scriptures and regulated by the Apostles' Creed with those of Nicea and Constantinople.

I am not entirely happy with that thesis on several counts. It does not express the sense of being bound by "fundamental truths of Christianity" as it perhaps might. The idea of the proclamation being "regulated by" the creeds has a somewhat foreign ring though it tries to capture the sense of dogma as "rules for proclamation," the ancient concept of *regula fidei*. An alternate might be this:

> All partner churches in the one church acknowledge themselves to be bound by the liberating Word of God, proclaimed in the gospel of Jesus Christ authorized by the Holy Scriptures and regulated by the fundamental truths of Christianity confessed in the Apostles' Creed and those of Nicea and Constantinople.

This statement of the thesis attempts to capture more the sense of a "dialectic" of bondage and freedom, but may tend to be a bit too complex. The idea of being bound by the liberating Word may be somewhat ambiguous. Yet I expect no such thesis will stand without considerable exegesis. At any rate I hope that these suggestions will further the ecumenical discussion.

Called to Freedom

"*Exsurge Domine, et iudica causam tuam!* Arise, O Lord, and judge your cause!.... Arise O Peter ..., Arise thou also, O Paul, we beg thee.... Let every saint arise and the whole remaining universal Church.... Let intercession be made to almighty God, that his sheep may be purged of their errors and every heresy be expelled. ..."

These dramatic opening words from the Bull of Pope Leo X (June 15, 1520), threatening Martin Luther with excommunication, remind us that we have to do here with one who was judged by his church to be a heretic. The dramatic language doubtless bespeaks the fact that His Holiness was at the time exercising his role as vicar of Christ on earth from the vantage point of his hunting lodge. "... Foxes are tearing down the vines.... An especially wild boar out of the woods is snorting about and rooting the vineyard![1] The carefully groomed gardens of civilization and Church are in peril! The hunters must come to the rescue!"

A wild boar indeed! And it can hardly be disputed that the most wild and uprooting of his "heresies" is our subject: Luther's understanding of freedom and liberation. Judging from current complaint, this understanding seems to be as "heretical" today as it was in the sixteenth century and probably for the same reasons. Luther is usually charged with "heresy" on two counts: too much bondage on the one hand and too much freedom on

1. *Bulla Leonis X contra errors Mart. Lutheri et sequacium.* In D. Martini Lutheri, *Opera Latina,* Erlangen ed. vol. 4 (var) 263.

the other! The fact that the charges appear contradictory is no doubt a measure of the world's puzzlement. So it is fitting that we should take some time to consider Luther's vision of freedom. We will concentrate as directly as possible on this vision of freedom, to the virtual exclusion of a host of questions about the law, ethics, social responsibility, politics, etc., that also need to be addressed. I gladly leave that to others! I will concentrate on freedom as a theological rather than as an ethical, social, or political concern. I do so because usually when we set out to talk about Luther's view of freedom we find ample excuse to talk about everything else. There is a reason for that, of course. As I shall try to point out, Luther's idea of freedom is itself radical enough to engender an anxiety that sends us scurrying to do damage control. So it would seem that some attention specifically to the understanding of freedom itself might be the proper place to start.

Freedom! Liberty! Liberation! Just to say the words is to enter into the Holy of Holies of modern society itself. We sing it, preach it (although perhaps only too rarely), march for it, protest about it, fight for it. Our documents claim it; our politicians promise it; we die for it. Everyone wants it desperately and claims it as a right, yet few if any are ever satisfied that they have found it. Do we even know what we are looking for? Can Luther help us? That is what we now are to consider.

What is Luther's contribution to our quest? First of all, I think we must say that it was Luther who initiated the modern discussion of and quest for freedom when he called for a reform of the church's teaching on the matter.[2] He raised the discussion to a level unknown since the days of St. Paul. He understood freedom first of all as an actual liberation, not as a covert enslavement of the self. This uproots everything. Prior and subsequent to Luther, freedom appeared predominantly as a defensive doctrine. In early Christianity it appeared as a defense against Gnostic and Manichaean fatalisms. Freedom had to be postulated to make sense of Christian claims. How can humans be held responsible for their sin on the one hand and redeemable on the other if there is no freedom? So humans had to be accorded at least some freedom in order to shift the blame for sin and evil from God to human beings. God did not cause evil, humans did, by a wrong exercise of freedom. Recent interpreters put their finger on the

2. In this regard it is significant that theological treatises on freedom prior to and even after Luther are rare if not virtually non-existent.

defensive nature of the argument when they dub it "The Free Will Defense."[3] Erasmus used this standard defense in his argument against Luther.[4] If there is no free will, how can we be held responsible for our misdeeds or be rewarded for our good ones? So the argument went and often still goes. We justify God and indict ourselves in the same move.

The effect of the free will defense, however, is not to liberate but to enslave. Human beings are granted just enough freedom to be found guilty for their sin and perhaps to cooperate with divine grace in doing meritorious deeds, but not much more. As a defensive doctrine, freedom of the will does not liberate, but precisely makes certain that one remains enslaved under the law. It is the law that gives freedom its opportunity. The result is that law takes over the conscience and traps the self in its own deeds, whether they are good or evil. We cannot escape.

Luther raised this whole discussion to a new level by insisting that freedom was not a defensive but an offensive doctrine. He rejected the free will defense and saw freedom as the fruit of the gospel, not the law. "Where the Spirit of the Lord is, there is freedom" (2 Cor. 3:17). Like Paul, he proclaimed freedom in the gospel as an offensive doctrine in the double sense of the word, liberation, a setting free of captives, and at the same time and for that very reason something of an offense, a scandal. We have to do with something entirely new, a new creation, a new age. Thus the problem of freedom is a theological problem, first and foremost, a spiritual matter.[5] It is a matter of what we believe in and hope for. Christian freedom, for Luther, means in the first place to be liberated from the pervasive power of the law in the inner life, the conscience.[6] It means to get the law "out of there," to be made a new creature. This is something quite literally fantastic. We stand, as Luther liked to say, like a cow staring at a new gate. What is this freedom? How can it be? Is it not dangerous? Can we really be set free from the law? This is the question before the house.

---

3. See, for instance, Anthony Flew, "Divine Omnipotence and Human Freedom," *New Essays in Philosophical Theology,* ed. Anthony Flew and Alasdair MacIntyre (New York: Macmillan, 1955), pp. 144-69, and John Hick, *Evil and the God of Love* (New York: Harper & Row, 1966), esp. pp. 302-27.

4. See Erasmus, "On the Freedom of the Will," in *Luther and Erasmus: Free Will and Salvation,* Library of Christian Classics 17, trans. and ed. E. Gordon Rupp and A. N. Marlow (Philadelphia: Westminster Press, 1969), esp. pp. 89f.

5. LW 31, 344; WA 7, 50, 13f.

6. LW 27, 4; WA 40 II, 3, 5-8.

We need to examine it more closely. What is the power of the law? It rests in the matter of temptation. The power of the law is not merely its intellectual or moral persuasiveness. Rather it is that as fallen beings we are tempted — by the devil, for Luther — to believe that the law is our salvation, the remedy for sin, our escape hatch over against the sting of death. The result is that we are trapped by temptation, caught in our own projects, be they good, bad, or indifferent.[7] Luther's scandalous claim that in the sight of God *even our best works are mortal sins* indicates the radical nature of the shift that is being proposed. We cannot get out of ourselves because we are under temptation. That means we cannot because we really do not want to. The temptation in this case is to be convinced that freedom is really a dangerous idea. And such a temptation is the devil's art. That freedom from the law is dangerous and impossible seems quite sane to us. What should we do if there were no law? How can we answer? We have no defense.

The problem we face is seduction of the spirit. That is to say, we are quite convinced by the arguments against freedom. But how then shall we escape the seducer? Christ is for Luther the only answer. Christ must simply defeat the tempter and drive the law out of the conscience. Christ is the end, that is, both goal *(telos)* and cessation *(finis)* of the law to those who have faith (Rom. 10:4). The freedom that Luther championed was the freedom of faith, the freedom for which Christ has set us free (Gal. 5:1), liberation of the conscience from the power of the law, sin, and death. We are set free, Luther says, "not from some human slavery or tyrannical authority but from eternal wrath from God." Such freedom "comes to a halt" in the conscience, "it goes no further."[8] Indeed, for Luther, this is the highest reach of freedom: "This is the most genuine [Latin: *verissima*] freedom; it is immeasurable. When other kinds of freedom — political freedom and the freedom of the flesh — are compared with the greatness and the glory of this kind of freedom, they hardly amount to one little drop."[9]

But now it seems that such freedom of the "inner man," freedom of conscience, is as much a heresy for the modern world as it was in the sixteenth century. For the world, modern as well as medieval, does not accept either the value or the power of such inner freedom. The modern

7. LW 27, 8-10; WA 40 II, 8-10.
8. LW 27, 4; WA 40 II, 3, 21f.
9. LW 27, 4; WA 40 II, 3, 24-26.

world especially has complained that since freedom, for Luther, is pure inwardness, it does not get out into the "real world" where it can do some
actual good.[10] Indeed, where it is taken with any seriousness at all, the
most prevalent reaction seems to be a kind of skepticism and anxiety. Can
it really be? Has not Luther gone too far? Is he not too naïve about freedom's possibilities? Does his view not lead to license and antinomianism?
(To be an antinomian is about the worst thing one can be! Almost any
heresy can be permitted these days, but not that!) Is it not subversive to
social order?

What are we to say to such complaints? Ironically, it is appropriate to
note that here as in many cases opposition to Luther's argument does not
refute it but rather endorses, substantiates, and illustrates it. To say that
freedom will never work is precisely to show that one does not have it and
to betray one's unbelief. The skepticism expressed is simply a reenactment
of one's bondage. It is simply to illustrate what has been claimed: we are
under temptation and cannot escape enslavement to the law. Arguments
with Luther usually turn out to be confessions. Unless, Luther said, Christ
dwells in the conscience and drives out all fear, we are captive and there is
no hope. To believe in freedom, one must be liberated.

What conscience under the law's temptation is afraid of is precisely
that freedom is not going to work. Things will get out of hand. So freedom
will be deemed dangerous and must be curtailed. With great fanfare the
law returns as the savior.

But the assertion that anxiety about freedom only causes us to reen-
act our bondage leads us deeper into the subtlety and complexity of the
matter. It is in the nature of the case not strange that the world and even
the church has rarely, and certainly not wholeheartedly, followed what Luther has to say about freedom. The papers for this international Luther
conference — particularly those on the reception of Luther's view in the
years following the Reformation all the way down to the present — certainly indicate that unqualified reception of Luther's view is rare.[11] But Luther was well aware that his view — which he believed to be biblical and
Pauline — had never found much favor in the church or the world. "They

---

10. See, for instance, Eberhard Jüngel, *The Freedom of the Christian,* trans. Roy A.
Harrisville (Minneapolis: Augsburg, 1988), pp. 5of.

11. See especially those by Mark U. Edwards, Walter Altmann, Martin Brecht, and
Marc Lienhard.

fled this morning star," he said, "yes, this sun, as if their lives depended on it; for they were in the grip of their own carnal ideas. . ."[12]

Through the years, therefore, anxiety seems to have dictated that discourses on Luther's view of freedom are always expected finally to reassure us that things are not so bad as they seem. Everyone waits for the other shoe to drop! In one way or another, moralisms reassert themselves, all with the aim of bringing freedom under control and forestalling the damage it might do to our little moralistic kingdoms. We always seek the comfort that along with the *Gabe* there is the *Aufgabe;* that hidden in the indicative is the imperative; that we must not only think of freedom as freedom *from* something, but also freedom *for* something. Freedom is never the last word, the ultimate goal. A vast defensive rhetoric builds on the foundation of anxiety that reduces Luther's vision to the banalities against which he directed his scorn. The offense is leeched out of freedom and it dies a lingering death. It is, we could say, a dangerous thing to have a congress on Luther's contribution to the understanding of freedom because it is all too likely to turn it into one more defense against Luther's view! We could embark once again to domesticate the wild boar!

Theologically, both before and after the Reformation, the most common move toward domesticating freedom has been the attempt to qualify the Pauline claim that Christ is the end of the law to those of faith. "Reason," as Luther would put it, simply cannot entertain such an idea, the conviction that in Christ the law comes to an end, that law is over and freedom begins. As we have seen, freedom as usually conceived needs law as the mediator of possibility. What shall we do if there is no law to tell us what to do? But is Paul then wrong in his claim? Theologians as usual, however, found a way to have their cake and eat it, too. They made a distinction in the content of the law — something Paul never did — between ceremonial or ritual laws on the one hand and moral law on the other. Then they proceeded to say that Christ was the end of ceremonial law but not the moral law. Christ ended the necessity, that is, for sacrifice, circumcision, food and ritual regulations, etc., but not the demands of moral law (e.g., the Decalogue). Christ died, it seems, to save us from the liturgiologists! One might grant, of course, that that is no small accomplishment, but the price does seem a bit high!

Luther categorically rejected all attempts to qualify the claim that

12. LW 33, 270; WA 18, 771, 30-34.

Christ is the end of the law, the whole law. Freedom is not a defensive doctrine. It is "offensive." It is about the new creature, the new creation. Both early and late Luther attacked the idea that Christ is the end of the ritual law but not the whole law. In both the early (1519) and later (1531-36) Galatians lectures he pounded away on this issue whenever he got a chance.[13] In his argument against Erasmus he said that this error has made it impossible to understand Paul and has obscured the knowledge of Christ. Indeed, he claimed that "even if there had never been any other error in the Church, this one alone was pestilent and potent enough to make havoc of the gospel."[14] The presupposition for true freedom, for Luther, is that Christ is the end of the law in its entirety. The freedom of the Christian means just such liberation. "The Christian is a free Lord of all and subject to none." So reads the first of Luther's two theses on freedom from the treatise on "The Freedom of the Christian."[15] It is for Luther, as it was for Paul, a matter of a new creation.

But, to say it again, such pronouncements cannot fail to be rather frightening or even maddening to us. Is it not dangerous so to speak? Can humans really handle such freedom? Surely the other shoe must drop! What usually happens is that we hurry on by that first thesis into the safe haven of the second: "The Christian is a perfectly dutiful servant of all, subject to all."[16] At last we are saved from the specter of freedom! But is not the price a bit high? Servant? Of all? Hold on a minute! You have to be free to say that. But Luther would not bid us to hurry. The second thesis is not a defense against the first, nor its contradiction. It is rather the quite natural outcome of the first. The point of the treatise on Christian freedom, Luther said, is to see how they fit together. Indeed, we will never get to the second thesis unless all our moralistic pretense has been shattered by the first. It is really the first thesis we have the hardest time with. That we should be free lords of all, subject to none, free from the law, is inconceivable for us. It is just not reasonable. Reason can only cast us back to the law.

13. For the 1519 Commentary, see LW 27, 188, 223, 230, 248, 256-57, 264-65, 287, 358; WA 2, 468, 32f; 491, 5f: 496, 30f: 508, 12f; 514, 10f; 519, 18f; 534, 26f; 582, 31f; 596, 9f. For the 1531-36 Commentary, see LW 26, 122, 130, 156-57, 180, 181, 202, 203, 330, 333, 446-47; LW 27, 139, 161; WA 40, 218, 12f; 229, 34; 242, 16f; 268, 24f; 302, 18f; 32, 17f; 510, 32f; 671, 25; 672, 28; WA 40 II, 177, 33f.

14. LW 33, 258; WA 40, 204, 12-18.

15. LW 31, 344; WA 7, 53, 15f.

16. LW 31, 344; WA 7, 53, 15f.

And "as soon as reason and the law are joined," Luther would put it, "faith immediately loses its virginity."[17] There is no way to freedom for the conscience trapped in the law, simply no way. No real argument can be made to dissuade the law from its hold on the conscience. The only way is that Christ and his work simply throw out the law, expel all dependence on our own work, from the conscience. Faith means to *be so grasped by Christ that the demands of reason and law are simply no longer heard.* They are ended, killed, devoured. It is, for Luther, hardly a matter of argument — as though faith could argue reason into freedom. There is no way across the chasm from the law to freedom. For reason is committed to law. There can only be a violent break. "Faith," Luther pronounces, "slaughters reason and kills the beast that the whole world and all creatures cannot kill."[18]

It is in this light that one should consider the images used in *The Freedom of a Christian.* They are explicitly not such as could be drawn from the realm of reason and law. Faith is "intoxicated" by the promises of God. The faith that clings to the promises of God will be so closely united with and altogether absorbed by the promises "that it will not only share in all their power but will be saturated and intoxicated by them."[19] Faith in the promises of God is itself the greatest obedience. Any trust in one's own works is the ultimate in rebellion and idolatry. And finally, of course, there is the celebrated image of the union of the soul with Christ as a bride with her bridegroom. Christ displaces reason and law in the conscience by means of a "marvelous exchange." Because of the wedding ring of faith everything Christ has — all his righteousness and works — become the believer's and everything the believer has — all the sin and death — is taken by Christ.[20]

The point of the violent talk and the move to different images is precisely to move to a different view of freedom. Freedom means actually to be set free, free from the law, free from sin, free from the flesh and its lusts, free to be the creature God intended. To be sure, that is not yet entirely possible in this life. Death, sin, and the law constantly beset us. For the time being we can have it only in the union with Christ through the "wedding ring of faith."

Now I have referred to Luther's view as a vision of the freedom

17. LW 26, 113; WA 40, 204, 12-18.
18. LW 26, 228; WA 40, 362, 15-16.
19. LW 31, 349; WA 7, 52, 34-55, 23.
20. LW 31, 350-52; WA 7, 53, 15f.

granted in Christ that will one day be completed. Luther believed that we would actually one day be free — free from sin, free from law, free from wrath, free from death. Free! To be sure we do not have it yet. We do not even have a very good idea of what that is. But in faith, Luther thought, we can begin to sense it, to catch the vision. And it can, by the grace of God, grow. Not, indeed, the kind of growth one might trace according to our theories of progress — imminent improvement according to some legal or developmental scheme. It is rather to be increasingly possessed, or as Luther put it, intoxicated, by the promise, the vision itself. And it will one day reach its goal. We will be free.

Now this has profound implications for who we are and what life is meant to be, for theological anthropology. We will, one day, be free. That meant for Luther that we will freely, joyously, and spontaneously live in love to God and neighbor and in care of the earth. That will be who we are. We will live, that is to say, as the creatures God had in mind when he first called the cosmos into being. But that means that what stands behind this vision of freedom, ultimately, is a belief in creation. Humans are created precisely for this kind of freedom, free spontaneously and joyously to love and care, quite apart from the law, to be free lords of all, to do with creation as they want. Think of that![21]

21. This understanding of creaturely existence is implicit in Luther's argument with Erasmus about the fall. Erasmus argued the standard free will defense. The tree of knowledge gives free will its opportunity to choose between good and evil. The command mediates the possibility. That wrong choice made is, of course, serious but cannot mean that freedom is entirely lost. Enough must remain to allow the system mediated by the law to survive. So there is, in the end, no real freedom.

Luther argued in quite different fashion. Creatures, he said, were originally left to their own counsel, to take care of the garden. They were, quite simply, free to do as they wanted and were not to worry about "good and evil." The warning not to eat of the tree of such knowledge did not, therefore, give freedom its opportunity, rather *took away* freedom. It took away the freedom to dispose over "that which was above them," to question of life and death. That was God's business. To step over that line, therefore, is not an exercise of freedom, but precisely a succumbing to temptation, a descent into a bondage to death, sin, and law. It is to become obsessed with the question of good and evil, i.e., to be trapped by the law in the game of self-defense. Law does not therefore mediate freedom. It takes it away. Luther then draws the conclusion that makes connection directly with the quest for Christian freedom: "By way of comparison one might say that *the gospel has left us in the hand of our own counsel, to have dominion over things and use them as we wish;* but Moses and the pope have not left us to that counsel, but have coerced us with laws and have subjected us rather to their own choice." To be free, for Luther, seems to mean precisely to be left "in the hand of

Thus in *The Freedom of the Christian* Luther said that the works of those justified by faith in the free mercy of God should be thought of in the same way as the works that Adam and Eve did in Paradise before the fall. They would be the freest works, done spontaneously only to please God. "The works of the believer," Luther said, "are like this. Through his faith he has been restored to Paradise and created anew, has no need of works that he may become righteous. . ."[22] The believer, like Adam and Eve in Paradise, does works out of freedom only to please God, to care for the body and the creation God has given. Of course, Luther is well aware that we are not there yet, not wholly re-created, but that does not alter the vision. Freedom is at the very heart of creation itself. We are created to be free. But this also means that the skepticism so often expressed about Luther's naïveté in matters of freedom and spontaneity is in the last analysis also skepticism about creation itself. The suspicion that freedom will never work is at the same time the suspicion that creation was a bad job! Luther believed in creation. His doctrine of freedom is a measure of that belief. His celebrated statement about faith in his preface to Romans is but one example of what it means to be free.

> Faith . . . is a divine work in us which changes us and makes us to be born anew of God. . . . It kills the old Adam and makes us altogether different [people], in heart and spirit and mind and power; and it brings with it the Holy Spirit. O it is a living, busy, active, mighty thing, this faith. It does not ask whether good works are to be done, but before the question is asked, it has already done them, and is constantly doing them.[23]

---

one's own counsel," not to be placed under constraint, external or internal, of Law, not to worry about good and evil and death. It is just that, no doubt, that frightens us. For we cannot but fear that we will "go wrong." We literally can't trust ourselves. We have lost faith. We don't believe in the creator or in creation, Luther would say. We cannot conceive of a free being — one who naturally out of sheer delight lives to please God without worry about "good and evil." "Reason" cannot believe or understand that. And that is just what Luther's claim is about. Reason believes the Law. It has no entry at all to freedom or salvation. We may sense this new territory, but we cannot fathom it yet. So we really are like a cow looking at a new gate! It is ironic but quite consequent, while Erasmus who argues for freedom of the will ends with enslavement, Luther who argues for the bondage of the will champions the freedom of the Christian. LW 33, 118-19; WA 18, 671, 19–672, 24.

22. LW 31, 360; WA 7, 61, 1-17.

23. LW 35, 370; WA DB 7, 10, 6f. Luther's view of creation should be scrutinized much

Freedom, for Luther and Paul, is therefore not something peripheral or dispensable for the Christian. It belongs to the very fabric of creation; it is that to which human beings are called. It is not incidental or accidental to the Christian life; it is that life itself. In his *Judgment on Monastic Vows* Luther comments on Paul's declaration in Galatians 5:13, "You . . . are called to freedom," by saying:

> You can take it from this that no one may teach or permit anything against evangelical freedom. This freedom comes from divine authority. God ordained it. He will never revoke it. He can neither accept anything that runs counter to it, nor allow anyone to violate it even by the most insignificant ordinance.[24]

One need not ask, for Luther, what such freedom is for. It is as St. Paul pronounced, for freedom itself. "For freedom Christ has set you free" (Gal. 5:1). It is a freedom *in* Christ, not apart from or for something. To retreat from freedom is simply to make Christ of no effect. If it is our purpose to ask what Luther's contribution to the quest for freedom and liberation is, it is simply that Luther unlike virtually everyone believed that what the fallen world really needs first and foremost is more freedom, not less. What is distinctive about Luther's view is the *hilaritas*, a certain fearlessness, even recklessness, in setting forth the claims of freedom.

Whence comes this fearlessness and recklessness? It comes from the fact that Luther also knew the nature of human bondage. The vision of freedom can be understood only over against what he has to say about human bondage. Indeed, as we have contended throughout, the promise of freedom itself exposes and even drives us to enact our bondage. Because Luther knew the nature of that bondage he was not afraid of the gospel

---

more closely in this regard. In his 1527 Preface to Sermons on Genesis he can say, "For without doubt the highest article of faith is that in which we say: I believe in God the Father, almighty creator of heaven and earth, and whoever rightly believes this is already supported and set right and restored to that from which Adam fell. But those who come to the point of fully believing that he is the God who creates and makes all things are few, because such a person must be dead to all things, to good and evil, death and life, hell and heaven, and must confess from the heart that he can do nothing out of his own strength." WA 24, 18, 26-33. The many statements he makes in his Genesis commentary about the created perfections of Adam and Eve indicate his high doctrine of creation.

24. LW 44, 309; WA 8, 613, 9f.

that sets people free. One who has some idea of what bondage is can be trusted with freedom. But still, is this not all too naïve, yes, even optimistic? No doubt, the question will always be with us. What if it does not work? There is always, of course, a backup plan, the rather menacing left-hand rule ready to use all the force of the law to see that we will stay in line whether we like it or not. There is always the judge, the jury, and the hangman. But that is a rather grim business and not the subject of our present inquiry. Our question is about freedom. What do we do if the liberating gospel does not work? Shall we just cease preaching it? Shall we just sign the whole enterprise over to that judge, jury, and hangman? The question can be put to Luther himself, since he was so often depressed in his later years by what he thought was the limited success of the Reformation. The following comment is, I think, typical:

> ... When the rabble hear from the Gospel that righteousness comes by the sheer grace of God and by faith alone, without the Law or works, they draw the same conclusion the Jews drew then: "Then let us not do any works!" And they really live up to this.
>
> What then are we to do? This evil troubles us so severely, but we cannot stop it. When Christ preached, he had to hear that he was a blasphemer and a rebel; that is that His teaching was seducing men and making them seditious against Caesar. The same thing happened to Paul and to all the Apostles. No wonder the world accuses us in a similar way today. All right, let it slander and persecute us! Still we must not keep silence on account of their troubled consciences; but we must speak right out in order to rescue them from the snares of the devil. . . .
>
> Therefore when Paul saw that some were opposing his doctrine . . . he comforted himself with this, that he was an apostle of Jesus Christ for the proclamation of the faith to the elect of God . . . , in the same way we today are doing everything for the sake of the elect to whom we know our doctrine is beneficial. I am so bitterly opposed to the dogs and swine, some of whom persecute our doctrine while others tread our liberty underfoot, that I am not willing to utter a single sound on their behalf in my whole life.[25]

25. LW 26, 305–306; WA 40, 474, 30–475, 29.

What is one to do if the gospel of freedom in Christ does not seem to work? Luther's answer appears at first, no doubt, to be utterly uninspiring. Nothing! One can do nothing about it! One can only go on preaching to liberate the consciences from the snares of the devil. One might be tempted to try the law, but the wicked will most surely not be helped thereby. Yes, we can and no doubt will exhort and admonish, but Luther seems to realize more and more that this only makes matters worse.[26] One can only go on preaching the gospel.

This is the final step in the reconstruction of the doctrine of freedom. Luther recognizes that freedom, if it is truly to be liberation, cannot be forced. There is no way to argue that one ought or must be free. To do so would be to make a law out of it and thereby lose the whole game. Freedom can only be its own apology. Freedom, that is, can be propagated only by setting people free. It is the end of the law. It must not betray itself in its own defense. Luther is supremely aware that the preacher of the gospel of freedom is in a real sense without levers. "Therefore anyone who wants to proclaim Christ," he says, "and to confess that he is our righteousness will immediately be forced to hear that he is a pestilent fellow who is stirring up everything."[27] But there is nothing to do about that but suffer the abuse — which will come from both the righteous and the unrighteous — and go on preaching. And if there is fear that nothing is being done, if the law accuses of laziness and indolence, the only thing to do first and foremost is just to be still and listen. Luther has a marvelously shocking and gutsy comment on Galatians 4:27 ("For it is written, 'Rejoice, O barren one that does not bear; break forth and shout, thou who art not in travail; for the desolate hath more children than she who hath a husband'").

> . . . Sarah, the free woman . . . that is, the true church, seems to be barren; for the Gospel, the Word of the cross, which the church preaches, is not as brilliant as is the teaching about the Law and works, and therefore it has few pupils who cling to it. Besides, it has the reputation of forbidding good works, making men idle and faint, stirring up here-

26. LW 27, 53; WA 40 II, 67, 22f. . . . In our churches, where the true doctrine of good works is set forth with great diligence, it is amazing how much sluggishness and lack of concern prevails. The more we exhort and arouse our people to do good works, to practice love toward one another, and to get rid of their concern for stomach, the more lazy and listless they become for any practice of godliness.

27. LW 26, 451-53; WA 40, 677, 28f.

sies and sedition, and being the cause of every evil. Therefore it does not seem to have any success or prosperity; but everything seems to be filled with barrenness, waste, and despair. Hence the wicked are fully persuaded that the church will soon perish along with its doctrine.[28]

Our temptation is always to resort to the law, to some scheme or other, to some attempt to prove our relevance, some program for church growth or other to preserve ourselves from extinction. But Luther will not go that way. He sticks to his guns. He carries out our argument for us: "But I have not done anything good and am not doing anything now!" Luther's reply:

> Here you neither can nor must do anything. Merely listen to this joyful message, which the Spirit is bringing to you through the prophet: "Rejoice, O barren one that does not bear!" It is as though He were saying: "Why are you so sorrowful when you have not reason to be sorrowful?" "But I am barren and desolate." "Regardless of how much you are that way, since you have no righteousness on the basis of the Law, Christ is still your Righteousness . . . Moreover, you are not barren either, because you have more children than she who has a husband.[29]

Freedom comes from the gospel. It cannot be sold out under any circumstances, lest everything be lost.

But now we must draw this to a close. Much, of course, remains to be said. Some words are called for, no doubt, on the persistent questions about whether this view of freedom actually leads us out into the "real world," as we like to call it, where it might contribute to the struggle for liberation from the ills, political and social, that continue to plague us. I have two comments to make. First of all, Luther's understanding of freedom through the gospel of Jesus Christ in fact gives us an entirely new world, the world of the neighbor. It is a sheer gift. It is what Luther called the world of the "outer man." The world of the neighbor, the "outer world" or the left-hand rule of God, is never just completely "there" like the physical, empirical world. It is a world given back to faith. It is of the essence of sin that we are curved inward upon ourselves. Left to ourselves we can never make it into the "outer" world. We are not content to do our work in the

28. LW 26, 443; WA 40, 667, 10f.
29. LW 26, 447; WA 40, 672, 29f.

left-hand kingdom. That is just our bondage, our enslavement. What we so often call the "real world," a world supposedly something other than the purely "spiritual," is not what Luther meant by the world of the "outer," but mostly just a projection of our own agendas beyond ourselves. We can't get out of ourselves. We have to be freed for that.

The fact that freedom is a spiritual matter, that it occurs "in the conscience," and that there it "comes to a halt" and "goes no further" means precisely that one so liberated is now given a wondrous new world, the world of the neighbor — to take care of. For every possibility that one might turn inward on one's own projects is excluded by the fact that Christ is the end of the law. All the space in the "inner world," the conscience, is occupied by Christ. There is no room for a self that wants to feed only on its own self. One is turned inside out. The law cannot get in there anymore. It can only be turned back to the world where it belongs, to be used to do what it is supposed to: take care of people and not tyrannize them.

The fact that freedom "comes to a halt" and "goes no further" than the conscience is an indication of the eschatological nature of the matter. The kingdom of God comes by faith alone. But that means that for the time being there is a big sign on the eschatological kingdom: KEEP OUT! GOD ALONE AT WORK! COMING SOON — BUT IN THE MEANTIME, MIND YOUR OWN BUSINESS! But the line must be drawn absolutely. Luther's absolute HALT! here is precisely the driving force behind any move of freedom into the outer world. It is the key to how Luther's two theses in *The Freedom of a Christian* fit together. Only the free lord of all can make it to the outer world to be perfectly dutiful servant of all. All genuine movements of liberation have to be movements of freedom.

My second comment flows quite naturally from this. To be a liberator in any sense that could correspond with what Luther was talking about, I believe, one has to be liberated. Surely the collapse of so many movements in our day that pretended to liberate but did not ought to make us acutely aware of that. Too many of these movements turned out to be just the worldly double of the law's invasion of the conscience. And like that law, they end by tyrannizing and killing. Luther's contribution is to try to tell us that before we set out to liberate we had best look to our own liberation lest we submit again to a yoke of bondage and tyrannize others with it.

Ever since Luther raised the discussion about freedom to a new level, there have been repeated attempts to correct, augment, change, revise, and of course, reject his vision. The freedom in Christ he preached has usually been deemed either too dangerous or too fragile to survive on its own. Luther apparently believed that there was a power in freedom itself. It is, after all, the gospel. It may indeed be a tender plant in this age. But one would think that it needs to be nurtured and encouraged, not stifled. Why the terrible shape of the world today? Have we lacked for schemes and programs? Have we lacked for laws? Is the only way to betterment purchased at the cost of freedom? Have we not tried all this? Luther believed that what the world needs is more freedom, not less. It might just be interesting to pay some heed to that belief. For freedom Christ has set you free. So St. Paul said. Luther was one of the few who heard and echoed that. So it comes to us. We are called to freedom.

SERMONS

The Doing of God

No one has ever seen God. The only Son, who is in the
bosom of the Father, he has made him known.

John 1:18

Jesus said to them, "Truly, truly, I say to you, the Son can do
nothing of his own accord, but only what he sees the Father
doing; for whatever he does, that the Son does likewise."

John 5:19

We live in an age that likes to tell itself, apparently, that it is a terribly difficult thing to believe in God. God is so ephemeral and elusive. It's so hard to
see where he could fit into the picture of a "modern" and "enlightened"
world where the human is the maker and master of things. He is so far
away, so "spiritual," so old-fashioned, so many odd and impossible things
that, oh my, it's just too hard to wing believing in him anymore. Judging
from the kind of thing that is dignified by printing these days, a lot of people, even many theologians, are very concerned to let others know just how
hard it is to believe. It is almost as though we are supposed to take a certain
amount of pride in having come this far — so far as actually to manage
unbelief. Or perhaps it is that we have to justify ourselves for not believing
by constructing all these elaborate and windy apologies for unbelief!

Along with this kind of chronological imperialism, this rather specious kind of intellectual superiority complex, goes of course the idea that people in earlier times had a much easier time of it, because they, after all, were so simple, and so primitive. This would apply, of course, especially to the people of New Testament times. They must have been an especially gullible lot. No doubt it was an easy thing for them to believe that God, who was more or less a well-known celebrity, could show up in almost any way he pleased.

It is interesting, now and then, to take a good look at the New Testament in the light of these modern prejudices. When we do that, it soon begins to appear that the writers of the New Testament in a very real sense see a range of difficulties that make the so-called modern ones look relatively like child's play. Certainly Jesus himself was supremely conscious of just how difficult it was, not to say even impossible, for God to be manifest as a human. Indeed, when it comes to that, most of our popular beliefs, including our modern ones, are more of a hindrance than a help to the real manifestation of God.

So the Gospel of John begins with what is an unusual and shocking statement for a supposedly religious document. It says, forthrightly, "No one has ever seen God." No one, past or present, has had any corner on seeing God. No worldview, *Zeitgeist,* or whatever kind of spiritual marsh gas hovering over an age makes that any more or less possible. That, after all, *is* impossibility. But even though such seeing is an impossibility (and this, of course, is the point), the only Son, who is in the bosom of the Father, he has made him known. But such "making known" is no easy thing. We ought to be especially conscious of that during the season of Lent. It took the hiddenness of the suffering, the being spit upon and being beaten; the being "obedient unto death," and the ultimate mystery of the cry, "My God, My God, why hast thou forsaken me?" — it took all that, before there could be a resurrection. This is the "making known" of the Father. It is what the Son does and what happens to him. As Jesus put it: "The Son does only what he sees the Father doing, for whatever he does, that the Son does likewise." He is the doing of God among us. No man has ever seen God. But Jesus is God in the flesh, the perfect translation of God into our terms, into the terms of human flesh. In Trinitarian terms, we might say, he is of the same essence, the same operation, the same doing, albeit a different hypostasis, a different mode of being. He does what he sees the Father doing. He is the doing of God among us, the *only Son* of the Father.

And now we meet today around his table to receive what he has done. For he is doing today what he did of old, doing what he sees the Father doing, giving himself absolutely for you. For he says: Here I am for you. Think on that, and tremble! And, repent and believe!

Until He Comes

As often as you eat this bread and drink this cup you proclaim the Lord's death until he comes.

1 Corinthians 11:26

It wasn't fair, you know, to go away and leave us like that — with just a bit of bread and a sip of wine and this word — that when we eat this bread and drink this cup we proclaim the Lord's death until he comes. For what is that to proclaim — the Lord's death? Should we not rather proclaim the Lord's resurrection, especially now that we have celebrated it once again? Indeed we should, but these words remind us that we cannot have the Lord's resurrection without the death. To be sure, if he be not raised, then our faith is in vain. But if he did not die, then the resurrection too is in vain, an empty charade. Indeed, it is because he is raised that we are called to proclaim his death. And in that, I expect, is the point of this text. *We* don't die, you know. We are much too busy building our defenses against death. Of course, we know that one day it will cease somehow. But we don't die. We just "pass on," or "pass away," or "go to meet our maker," or "leave a legacy," or some such, and because we are so busy staving off death, we don't live either, and so life is just frittered away.

But the *Lord* died. I suppose we can't even do that well. So the Lord died for us. It commenced in the midst of his feast. He was betrayed by one of us who thought to build one last defense against death. The feast was interrupted. The Lord died, and we are called to partake of this feast that was interrupted by death.

Yes, just a bit of bread and a sip of wine. No doubt it is hard on us proud, undying beings to be reduced to this, indeed it is death itself, and to think that our eternal salvation hangs here in the balance. But so it is and so we come together actually to proclaim it. But don't forget that last part of the text: until he comes. For therein lies the real aim of the feast that was interrupted by death, as all things will be. But this feast, we are promised, will be concluded. So come, eat, drink, and proclaim the Lord's death until he comes.

The Interrupted Party

Truly, I say to you, I shall not drink of the fruit of the vine until that day when I drink it new with you in the kingdom of God.

Mark 14:25

Is there anything to wait for? These words from the Last Supper remind us, if it is not too indelicate to say it, that we have to do with an interrupted party. I have always wondered why these words got left out of the communion liturgy. Even more skeptical interpreters than I suspect that the words go right back to Jesus. Yet we don't say them. Why? Are they something of an embarrassment? Did we just get tired of waiting? In one way or another the omission has something to do with religion in the end. Already the early fathers seem to have objected to imagery that was a little too concrete and materialistic. We really shouldn't literally expect to drink new wine with our Lord in the Kingdom, should we? That would be overdoing it! And of course, centuries of temperance piety have served only to reinforce that judgment. At these words even the fiercest literalist is likely to go spiritual on us. We have a hard enough time holding out for just a little sip of wine in the supper, let alone a real party! So the words go begging.

But, of course, and alas, there is some reason for our caution. There is a danger in what Jesus says. We do have a tendency to want too much too soon, to lust too much after this world's nectar like those Corinthians who hogged it all for themselves and didn't discern the body. They were the first to go and spoil it all. Alas, it seems we cannot be trusted with this either, and some of us have even used up our partying and either must cut it out altogether, or in our despair be reduced to grape juice! Put some of that in old wineskins and I guarantee you nothing will happen — it will do no harm at all! Yes, there is a danger here in Christ's words concerning the fruit of the vine, so we have reduced it all to just a taste, a little sip. This side of the *parousia*, wine, I guess, is something like religion — a little goes a long way!

But don't forget it, one day, finally, all that will be past, and the feast — the party — will go on as it was intended and there will be no danger, no harm at all. (You won't even have to worry about driving home! You will just be there at last!) We have a promise about that, believe it or not, and even the most sober and pious might be forced to crack a smile: "I shall not drink of the fruit of the vine again until that day when I drink it new with you in the kingdom of God." Yes, the party was interrupted, but it was interrupted just for you so that you too might be a party to it. So come and taste it. And if it awakens some joy and anticipation in you, just that, I expect, will cover a multitude of sins. Indeed, all the sins you've got.

Abstractions Aside

Truly, I say to you, I shall not drink again of the fruit of the vine until that day when I drink it new in the kingdom of God.

Mark 14:25

"Grace our table with your presence, Lord, and give us a foretaste of the feast to come." So we pray. But it is odd, is it not, that we, great spiritual beings that we are, should look to a feast as our final goal and somehow be dependent on this event for our salvation? It isn't much, you know — just a bit of bread and a sip of wine. One would think we could do better. Are there not more transporting sacramental substances or procedures on the market? Could we not, perhaps, drink the elixir of the gods, or even better, partake spiritually of the great and grand ocean of ideas, the eternal abstractions?

There is a story I remember from somewhere about a man who was told by his doctor that he must go on a diet of fruit lest he die. So he went to the grocer and asked, "Do you have any fruit?" The grocer replied, "We have apples, oranges, peaches, plums, pears, melons, berries of all sorts, you name it, we got it."

"Well, no," said the man, "I need fruit." Not getting any satisfaction, he went to the next grocer where the result, you can guess, was the same. The upshot of the story was that he could find no one who could give him fruit, and so he died. Stupid man, you say. Perhaps. But that is to miss the point. Religiously, all of us tend to seek fruit as an abstraction. I suppose it is because fruit seems to have one big advantage over apples, oranges, peaches, plums, and pears. It never rots, never decays. It is eternal. It doesn't die. If only we could get some of that. We rarely notice, of course, that it doesn't live either. But no matter, we seek it nevertheless, and so we die.

So we need to be saved, cured so we might live. And here it is for you, this bit of bread and a sip of wine. It's reality. To be sure, it won't fill you up, not yet. It won't sustain your life. Like everything else it too decays, it goes sour. And in our fallen world it too has gotten caught in the tangled web of our myths and abstractions so that we think it is ours and we fight and bleed and die for it. But here our Lord comes to claim it back and says, "This is my body, my blood, I mean to have it back, and it's free for you." Now, *there* is a promise, a vow. There will come a time when it will be enough. "I shall not drink again of the fruit of the vine until I drink it new in the Kingdom." So you can forget the abstractions. This is the beginning of your salvation — you can taste it!

Celebrating the Future

> Truly, I say to you, I shall not drink again of the fruit of the vine until that day when I drink it new in the kingdom of God.
>
> *Mark 14:25*

These words from St. Mark's account of the Last Supper of our Lord and his disciples remind us that when we come together, as we have tonight, to break bread and to drink of the cup under the words of promise, we are celebrating the future. In doing so we anticipate something that will one day come to light where all can see. It is the gospel, the good news of that which will be, that we celebrate, the new that comes into our midst.

People today question the validity and the usefulness of sacred rites and "mysteries" or "sacraments" such as this, and I suppose they well might. Perhaps it is even good that they should. For sacred rites and mysteries of the usual sort, we might say of the "pagan" sort, are backward looking. They are attempts to draw us back to reestablish oneness with the nature from which we have come. They are attempts to draw us back to the "paradise," the dreaming innocence of the past, and to merge us with the old.

But not so this sacrament. It tells us to leave the past. It bids us to repent of the past, to accept forgiveness for our yesterdays, and to look to the future, to the new. We do not know entirely, I suppose, what that means.

We have only hints, indications, and promises. We see through a glass darkly. For the moment, the important thing is simply that it brings us together in a way we are never brought together elsewhere. We are called out of our past under the sign of the cross and resurrection, to lay aside that which separates us, and to come together as human beings, as men and women, brothers and sisters, to break bread together, to drink from the same cup. For the moment perhaps that is all we need. It is new. Thereby in hope we drink the new wine of the Kingdom.

Ascension Day: Later!

So when they had come together, they asked him, "Lord, will you at this time restore the kingdom to Israel?" He said to them, "It is not for you to know times or seasons which the Father has fixed by his own authority. But you shall receive power when the Holy Spirit has come upon you; and you shall be my witnesses in Jerusalem and in all Judea and Samaria and to the end of the earth." And when he had said this, as they were looking on he was lifted up, and a cloud took him out of their sight.

Acts 1:6-9

How like him! Just to take off into the blue with a word that amounts to something like kids use these days when you never know what to expect from them next or when: "Later!" So now he is gone. Disappeared. Ascended. Missing. Gone. Or is he? Has he abandoned us to our own devices? Or is it rather that now he is everywhere? Now that story of his, that story of his life among us and his terrible death and his glorious resurrection, is inescapable, it penetrates and searches every corner of our lives. As he once put it, "It is expedient that I go away . . . I will send you another comforter and he will convince the world of righteousness, of sin, and of judgment." Had he stayed, goodness knows what would have happened. Perhaps we would constantly have been running after him, everyone claiming him, pushing and shoving, pinning him down as if we were the Washington press corps trying to get him to say something clever or damaging or new. Or perhaps we would just have tired of it all and crucified him again. Who knows? But now he is gone. We can't do that anymore. But of course, he is not just gone, he is on the loose now. We can't own him. He goes his own way. What is to be said of this? He is on the loose now and so we have no choice but to meet him where he promises to be. So we come to eat this bread and drink this cup for the forgiveness of sin. When we do that, we are reminded, we participate in his story once again, we proclaim his death until he comes. What is to come of that? We shall have to see. As he might well have said: Later!

Moses' Baccalaureate

LUTHER SEMINARY BACCALAUREATE SERMON 1998

At a lodging place on the way the Lord met Moses and
sought to kill him.

Exodus 4:21-26, Psalm 90, and 2 Corinthians 5:14-15

What a strange and terrifying turn of events! The Lord, who had called
Moses, ordered him back to Egypt, argued him out of all his excuses,
equipped him with miraculous powers, gave him all he needed for his
calling, and even revealed his sacred name to him, now meets him along
the way and tries to kill him. Not only a strange text, you might say, but a
weird choice for a baccalaureate service. And yet, I think we might say
that this little incident, tucked away and obscured from sight by its very
strangeness, is Moses' baccalaureate. Here he is, all prepared for his mission with all his objections countered; like some I've heard tell of now and
then, he was not particularly happy about the situation into which he is
being called. But, he is given all the "leadership skills," as we would say today, to meet the challenge. Of course, he modestly claims he is no good at
public speaking (and where have we not heard that before?) so he has to
be fixed up with a "mouthpiece," a smooth-talker like Aaron. Apparently
they didn't have speech therapy in those days, or God was not good at it
or didn't care about it. Moses even has miraculous powers to dazzle and
upstage the Egyptian magicians. He has it all. But God met him and tried
to kill him. What are we to make of that?

The text doesn't really give us any answers. God doesn't say anything, so we have no clue to what God is up to. But I expect we can imagine what was touched off in Moses' heart: "Have I forgotten something, or overlooked something? Am I blind to something? What could it be?" Our text seems to leave us with just one possibility. The problem could only be with God, with his relationship with God. Could it be that Moses forgot God? At any rate it appears that God wasn't through with him yet. We can well imagine that he had become so preoccupied with his anxieties and acquiring his skills and techniques that he became all tangled up in himself and impressed with his qualifications. And he forgot God, the God who could call into being everything that is and yet blow it all away with no apologies, who could flood the whole earth, who drove Abraham to offer up Isaac, the very child of promise, the God who wrestled with Jacob all night at the Jabbok and set his mark on him and sent him limping on his way. He forgot, no doubt, that God was not one who could be cut down to size, and who could be manipulated, not even by magic tricks. He might even have begun to think that the whole exodus affair depended on him. And so God encountered Moses at an inn along the way and tried to kill him.

Tomorrow we will celebrate the graduation of this class. Tomorrow will be a happy day, smiles and sweetness and light, a rite of passage, speaking of degrees earned, achievements accomplished and awards granted. We shall all enjoy it and take pictures and embrace and laugh and celebrate. It will be a joyous day. But today we have other business to attend to. "Baccalaureate" means, according to contemporary wisdom, an address made to those being graduated in the form of a sermon. Today, therefore, we experience someone else who comes through this Word, one in whom all this is rooted — the creator and disposer over all things, who nevertheless met his chosen leader and tried to kill him.

What does this say to us? The trouble with this text is that there is no way through it or around it. It doesn't surrender a "meaning" for us to grab onto. We aren't told the whys or wherefores at all. God trying to kill Moses? Why? There is no recorded conversation. God says nothing. We might be able to imagine what was going on in Moses' soul, but God is another matter. The problem is that it is just opaque, we can't see through it. All it renders to us is what Luther would call the *deus absconditus,* the hidden God. It is an awesome, awful event. What interpreters try to do with a text like this is predictable. They dance on it as though it were a bed of hot coals. Nobody knows what to do with it. Most try to get God off the hook. Surely

God is not responsible for these strange goings-on! Some say it means that Moses got deathly sick. Is that all? But what help is that? Are you comforted by such a thought? Does it help to cut God out of the picture? Some think it has something to do with the business of circumcision — that Moses' failure properly to observe the rite of circumcision either for himself or for his youngest son caused this. But does that help? Is that a "meaning" that makes trying to kill Moses easier to take? Some will say it is a bit of ancient mythology, perhaps used to explain the practice of circumcision. But shall we be protected from the terror by the mythologists? And so it goes.

There is no way through this text. That is just the point. That is the terror of it. We are driven to halt before it — and tremble. The God who meets Moses and tries to kill him brooks no explanation, and neither asks for nor needs any. With Moses we need to realize that this is all God's affair, and that God will do as he pleases and that we had best stand in awe. It would seem that what a text like this has to do with — at the very least — is simply the fear of God. And I expect we should not move too quickly to lessen the gravity of such fear. We are accustomed, you might recall in our teaching, to making a distinction between servile fear — the fear of a slave for an angry master — and filial fear — the fear of a child for a loving parent. Well and good. But the problem is that such neat distinctions desert us when the crunch comes. I don't suppose Moses, confronted with the God who was bent on killing him, would be likely to say, "I know, God, that you don't really mean this, and that at bottom you are going to let me go, so my fear here is really only filial!" No, if the Psalm for our consideration in this service, Psalm 90 (which ancient tradition attributed to Moses), is any indication, Moses learned something through it all. Listen to some of the words again:

> Thou dost sweep men away; they are like a dream,
> like grass which is renewed in the morning:
> in the morning it flourishes and is renewed;
> in the evening it fades and withers. . . .
> Who considers the power of thy anger,
> and thy wrath according to the fear of thee?
> So teach us to number our days
> that we may get a heart of wisdom.

Moses learned something about the fear of the Lord. Moses learned that he would have to go to his calling as one who had escaped death only by the mercy of God. He learned that past is past, over and done with, and that he would have to look to the future, laying his trust on this God who ends the past and makes all things new.

What are we to make of this, as we are brought suddenly to a halt? Surely it is that the fear of the Lord is the beginning of wisdom. Think on that! Our problem is that today God has become something of a cipher, more or less just an empty name. God has been virtually stripped of all that makes him God. He has been reduced to a mere projection of our wants and needs. God has been remodeled, renamed, toned down, and watered down until he is nothing but a patsy. Some years ago J. B. Phillips wrote a book entitled, *Your God Is Too Small.* Perhaps we need a sequel today called something like, *Your God Is Too Nice!* We don't know what to do with a God who would meet Moses and try to kill him. I sometimes wonder whether our perplexity indicates that we don't actually believe in God at all anymore. Do we believe that there is someone "out there," "up there," "in the depths," or wherever we think he might be, running the show, presiding over life and death and all things? In such a strait this text calls us to halt and ponder the fact that such halting before the mystery of the God whom Moses met — which seems so incomprehensible — is, as a matter of fact, the beginning of wisdom. It constrains us to take to heart those words of Hölderlin ("Empedocles")

> Away! I cannot bear the sight of him
> Who follows sacred callings like a trade.
> His face is false and cold and dead
> As are his gods!

So now I say to you, especially to those being graduated, but also to all: You will meet this God, yes, even a God who kills, sooner or later. So number your days that you get a heart of wisdom. But the mystery before which you are to halt only gets deeper and deeper. For the fact is that you have already met this God. He has put his mark on you in baptism. You are sealed with the cross of Christ forever. You are baptized into his death, buried with him, so that, being raised you might walk in newness of life. As our Epistle text proclaims, this God has actually carried through to completion what he, in forbearance, didn't do to Moses: "We are convinced," Paul announces, "that one has died for all; therefore all have died." It's all over. The death is past tense. You have died. As our

Gospel lesson announces, there is a resurrection. Death is not avoided, but defeated.

And are we not allowed, at last, to catch at least a glimpse of an answer to the riddle of our strange and fearsome text, even if we see only "as in a mirror" — the mirror of faith — "dimly"? The God who tried to kill Moses has remained in charge and he has seen it through to completion. Moses is indeed dead. He never got to the Promised Land. God himself buried him, in an unmarked grave. Think on it! The great lawgiver cannot enter the Promised Land! (There is a sermon just in that!) There will be no shrines for Moses. But now you live. Yes, we have tried to give you all the theology we could get into you and equipped you with all the skills. But don't forget Moses' meeting with God. Don't forget that the fear of the Lord is the beginning of wisdom. You have "escaped" only by the mercy of God in the crucified and risen Lord Jesus. Thanks be to God!

Breaking the Conspiracy of Silence

COMMENCEMENT ADDRESS, LUTHER SEMINARY 1985

O Lord, open my lips and my mouth shall declare your praise.

Psalm 51:15

What is to be said now? I suppose that is the question that worries any teacher who has one last chance with a graduating class. Hasn't it all been said? One hopes at least that enough has been said. But there is perhaps one thing more, one last thing, and that is to hand over the saying of it to you graduates. Now it's your turn. Now you must say it. And that is my theme, my one last shot, so to speak, one last thunderbolt from the professorial chair: Say it! For God's sake, say it! Had I the courage I would have used that as the title for these words. But I was advised that it might look a bit irreverent or even frivolous on a printed program among the many serious matters in these ponderous proceedings! So I settled for the more sober and academic-sounding theme of "Breaking the Conspiracy of Silence." The one thing I wish to urge upon you in distinction from all else is that the office to which we are called is to break the conspiracy of silence and say it. The hope and the prayer that undergirds what I have to say is expressed in the verse from Psalm 51 which you have sung over and over again in the Matins service in the seminary chapel: "O Lord, open my lips and my mouth shall declare your praise."

For God's sake, say it! Say what? Say the gospel of Jesus Christ, God's

Son, crucified and risen for us. Yes, say the gospel that God justifies the godless by faith alone. Say the gospel of the unconditional forgiveness of sins for Jesus' sake, the gospel of absolutely free grace. Take up the office of ministry, the ministry of Word and Sacrament — be an absolver. For God's sake, for the sake of him who gave his life to open your lips, say it! In the power of the Spirit who on this day so long ago loosed our tongues, say it!

Why this charge? This perhaps impetuous plea to say it? A funny thing has happened to the church on its way to the modern forum. It seems to have forgotten what it was going to say! There is something of a conspiracy of silence abroad among us that seduces and entices us not to say it, or at least not to say it too confidently. It is not an overt or even self-conscious conspiracy — not that malicious or evil-intentioned persons in some back room plotted to silence the saying of it. It is much more subtle than that. Indeed it comes more from within than without, being made up mostly of good intentions, bits of advice, observations on this or that — which taken by themselves may even be quite justified, but which when put together lead willy-nilly in one direction: you had best not say it, you had perhaps best find something else to do, something else to justify your calling.

You have heard it all, I expect, in the course of your seminary career, the litany of complaints that seem innocent enough, the bits and pieces of counsel, the good advice, the proper observations, the wise commentary on the times. It goes something like this: Is it not presumptuous or even preposterous to think that much can be accomplished just by saying it? Do words count for much after all? Is thinking all that important? You can't just say it, you know, you have to do it. Deeds speak louder than words. Besides, you have to earn the right to be heard, don't you? It's not what you say but what you do that really matters. Just "being there" is probably more important. The ministry of presence is more important than the ministry of preaching. Just put on your collar and show up, be nice, and all will be well. Besides, the relevance of a gospel of absolutely free grace is questionable in an age more concerned about finding a gracious neighbor than a gracious God. Salvation by works is wrong of course, but after all, who is trying these days? Isn't the promise just pie in the sky bye and bye? Isn't free grace dangerous? Or too cheap? Who will tend to the pressing problems of the times like hunger, justice, and peace etc., etc., if they hear of such grace? Is it not too individualistic, too Pauline, too Lutheran, too un-ecumenical, too much the province of so-called evangelicals, and so on? Put the pieces of the litany together and they seem to add up to one thing: a conspiracy of silence. Don't say it. Find something better to do.

What shall we say to all this? "O Lord, open thou my lips, and my mouth shall speak thy praise." Whatever you do, do not let it reduce you to silence. It is the Lord to whom this prayer is addressed, the Lord who is doing an absolutely new and as yet unheard-of thing, the Lord who casts out the spirits who are dumb. The Lord has opened our lips and will do so again and again. It is for *God's sake* we are to say it. God, our confession maintains, has instituted the office and the office is first and foremost to say it, to break the conspiracy of silence and say it!

Yes, of course, saying it is not everything. It is also crucial to do it. But someone does have to say it. Faith comes by hearing, and how shall they hear unless someone says it? Our impatience repeatedly fires the question, "Why do we always just talk? Shouldn't we rather be out there doing it?" An important and agonizing question indeed! But consider your calling. There are, after all, many callings in the one body: apostles, prophets, teachers, healers, helpers, administrators, and so on. If you are more interested in doing it than saying it, there is certainly nothing wrong with that. Consider your calling, even if it seems a little late for that now. Saying it, reflecting on it, is not everything. It may even be a relatively modest thing. The point is that *someone* has, at last, to say it. It is the office of the pastor to say it, to care about the saying of it, to reflect on and work at the saying of it. Salvation, I expect, still comes by hearing, not by hugging — however much good that may do in reducing one's anxiety. There are lots of good huggers about these days, apparently, but someone does have to say it, to break the conspiracy of silence and speak the Word of God.

Is that Word relevant? Indeed the relevance of what we have to say is questionable and disputed in this age, and we must bend every effort to speak so as to be heard. But when has it not been so? We make a rather serious miscalculation if we easily assume there ever was a time or ever will be a time when the gospel of free grace just happens to meet what we like to call "our needs." The gospel is never, strictly speaking, relevant to this age, or any age, because it is not relevant to the old being. You've probably heard me say it before, but I will say it again. The gospel is about as relevant to this age as an argument for love and fidelity and marriage in a brothel, about as relevant as buttermilk in a bar. We might profitably listen to the words of Luther in the opening to the greater Galatians commentary. Luther, who lived in those halcyon days when everyone supposedly had a bad conscience and was just a sitting duck for the gospel:

> The devil cannot do otherwise than attack this doctrine vehemently, with might and with craft; nor does he rest as long as he sees even a spark of it remaining. . . . For the Gospel is a doctrine that teaches something far more sublime than the wisdom, righteousness, and religion of the world. It leaves those things at their proper level and commends them as good creatures of God. But the world prefers those creatures to the Creator. Ultimately, through them it wants to abolish sin, to be delivered from death, and to merit eternal life. This the Gospel condemns. But the world cannot bear the condemnation of that which it regards as best. Therefore, it charges the Gospel with being a seditious and erroneous doctrine that subverts commonwealths, principalities, kingdoms, empires, and religions; it accuses the Gospel of sinning against God and Caesar, of abrogating the laws, of subverting morality, and of granting people the license to do with impunity whatever they please. With righteous zeal, therefore, and with the appearance of high service to God, the world persecutes this doctrine and despises its teachers and followers as the greatest plague there can be on earth.[1]

There are no easy assumptions there, certainly, about the "relevance" of saying it to the world, and its enterprises and needs! That the world should so react to the gospel is small wonder. But that the same reactions should be heard in the church should give us pause, I should think, and we must not join that conspiracy. Yes, indeed, the gospel of absolutely free grace is dangerous. But God has apparently decided to take the risk, to do a new thing. Who then will do the good? Who will attend to the pressing problems of the age? Don't we have to have some levers to move people? How can grace do it? The questions invite and entice to silence. If you really want to get things done, you had best not say it. But perhaps we would do well to listen to Luther's counsel in the *Bondage of the Will* on that score:

> As for your fear that persons of vicious inclination will abuse this liberty, this must simply be thought of as . . . part of the temporal leprosy

1. LW 26, 13-14.

that we must bear and the malady we must endure. But it must not be held so important as to warrant the removal of the Word of God in order to restrain their abuse of it. If not all can be saved, yet some are saved; the Word of God came for their sake, and they love it the more fervently and assent to it the more readily. What evil did the ungodly not do before the Word of God came? and what good did they ever do? Was not the world always full of war, deceit, violence, quarreling, and iniquity of every kind? . . . Yet now that the Gospel is come, people start blaming the world's wickedness onto it! — when the truth is rather, that the good Gospel brings the world's wickedness to light; for without the Gospel the world dwelt in darkness. So do the uneducated blame education for the fact that as education spreads, their own ignorance becomes apparent. Such are the thanks we return for the word of life and salvation! What fear may we suppose there was . . . when the Gospel freed all men from the Law of Moses? What scope did not this great liberty appear to give to evil people? Yet the Gospel was not, on that account, taken away; instead the godly were told not to abuse their liberty to indulge the flesh, and the ungodly were left to their own devices.[2]

In other words, why blame the gospel? Is it not incredible that we should make such a move? The conspiracy entices, fired by the disappointment, no doubt, that our words seem to have so little effect, and you will be sorely tempted by it again and again. But we cannot join it. Who will do the good? The question above appears so weighty and so pious. But it is a smokescreen under cover of which evil things are done. It is blown away by stiff breezes of the truth: Who ever did do the good? We are not doing so well now, are we? Can we ever really think that the truly good or just is going to be done without the gospel?

What then can we do about the conspiracy of silence? It is a subtle thing, a temptation that will never go away, as Luther knew well. There is nothing to be done but simply to break it and say it. For God's sake, say it! The agonizing thing about the gospel is that it leaves us quite without levers in this world. We should have no illusions about that. We can only say it and wait. "When the rabble," Luther observed,

---

2. Martin Luther, *The Bondage of the Will*, trans. J. I. Packer and O. K. Johnston (New York: Fleming H. Revell, 1957), p. 94.

hear from the Gospel that righteousness comes by the sheer grace of God and by faith alone, without the law or works, it draws the same conclusion always. . . . "Then let us not do any works!" And they really live up to this.

What then are we to do? This evil troubles us severely, *but we cannot stop it*. When Christ preached, He had to hear that He was a blasphemer and a rebel. The same thing happened to Paul and all the apostles. And so it is today and always will be. All right then, let it slander and persecute us. Still we must not keep silence. . .[3]

There *is* no real remedy against the conspiracy of silence except to go on saying it. We cannot stop it because it is the very gospel itself that arouses the complaint and fires the conspiracy. Whenever the gospel is preached, the conspiracy arises. To attempt to stop the conspiracy by proving one's self before the world would simply be to join it and to fall silent. But we must not keep silence. God has decided to do a new thing. Of that we must speak and prophesy. Here we have no abiding city, but we look for that which is to come. It isn't here yet. It's coming, but it isn't here. Therefore we must say it, prophesy it, promise it. The kingdom of God comes by the saying of it. Is that "pie in the sky bye and bye"? Perhaps the best reply to that is, "What's the matter, don't you like pie?" One cheap shot deserves another, after all!

Do I go too far? Is this not just too wild, too dangerous, too much of an exaggeration? I suppose that is the last temptation to silence. And it is the most subtle. It is the most subtle because it comes more from within than from without. It is the disquiet, the uneasy feeling, the insinuation of the conspiracy, that if you ever really do rear back and preach the gospel with no holds barred, that "now you've done it, now you've gone too far." You probably wrecked the building program or the fund drive! It is as though we have this marvelous institution called the church going, and all the grand concerns it involves, and the gospel is going to spoil it all! You had best trim your sails a bit and keep judicious silence about such things. Ah, but what is the institution for? What is the building program for, if it is not precisely to provide at least a temporary home for the saying of such wild, wild things?

No, we must not keep silence, for the silence is the darkness, and the

3. LW 26: 305.

darkness is the darkness of the tomb. But Jesus has been raised from the dead and has broken the silence forever. For God's sake, say it! Say it until we begin, at least, to get a taste for the kingdom of God and a hope for the new thing. There is a river, the streams whereof make glad the City of God! Don't be afraid; break the conspiracy of silence — you can't go too far. Let the bird fly. Let the bird of the Spirit take wing! It can't hurt us and you'll be surprised — it will be the power to save us, both now and forever.

You Are Witnesses (Ordination)

LUKE 24:44-49

We come together in our worship today to ordain James and send him out to be an ambassador for Christ in the work of his church. Whenever we do that, it is a good time for us to stop and ask who we are and why we do such things. From the world's point of view it might be regarded as a rather strange — maybe even an arrogant thing to do — to send someone out in that fashion. Who, as we might put it today, do we think we are? What are we up to in this world? What is the "bottom line" for what is happening here?

The text for today tells us flat out who we are. The risen Christ, our Lord, speaking to his astonished and somewhat bewildered and confused disciples says, "You are witnesses." As Christians, we are witnesses. That's the bottom line. We are, of course, a lot of things just like everyone else: mother, father, child, worker, but essentially we are witnesses. When you think about it, that is a rather strange thing to be in the world of religion and considering what religious people are supposed to be. You are witnesses. That is to say, we are not *essentially* religious beings, holy men or women perhaps (although we should seek to lead lives that are holy enough in their witness). But we are not, according to Christ's word, as Christ's disciples and followers, essentially the kind of holy men or women who go off to caves or mountaintops to practice holiness codes or purification rites or methods of meditation or whatever dazzles and impresses the world in its religious quest. By so doing we might indeed bear a kind of witness, but we would bear witness mostly to ourselves and our own religiosity. But we are not called to do that. We are witnesses not to ourselves but to Another.

You are witnesses. That is also to say that we are not gurus or something like that, religious geniuses who claim somehow to have found the secret to the inner life or the abundant life or the transcendent life or whatever it may be — geniuses who are willing to let us in on the secret (for a small fee, of course). The guru too tends mostly to call attention to the self and to get lost in the inner mazes of the psyche. We are not in that game. Even though we do care about the inner life of people, that is not the bottom line. We are witnesses to something else, to Another.

One could, I expect, go through a whole catalog of things we could be tempted to be in the religious cafeteria of our time, things even pastors might be tempted to become in order to be popular, to succeed, to pander to our religious foibles: counselors, group leaders, managers of some great religious organization, rulers of a great television empire with millions coming in daily, leaders of a religious crusade, or manipulators of people's need for religion. But these things get broken on this particular hard rock: You are witnesses — just witnesses. That is the bottom line. Whatever else we might aspire to be is fluff, window dressing, unessential. I think here of the famous altar painting by Grünewald of the crucifixion. The crucifixion scene itself is awesome. But to one side, under the cross, stands John the Baptist pointing his long, bony finger at the crucified one. Just pointing. Just a witness. That is finally the only real significance of his life. The inscription by him reads: "He must increase, but I must decrease." John did not exist to call attention to himself, but to Another.

Now that, of course, brings us to the crucial question. Why just witnesses? What can be so important about that? What can demand all that attention? The text tells us, of course, not just that we are witnesses, but that we are witnesses "of these things." The "these things" refers us back to the cross and resurrection of Jesus: ". . . that the Christ should suffer and on the third day rise from the dead." In the first place, to put it bluntly, just like a witness in a court of law, we are witnesses to a crime, specifically a murder. There is no point in quibbling; a murder is what it was. Jesus was killed. This man, sent from God, was executed. This is what we are witnesses to. And not only that, we have seen the shocking thing that it was the good religious people like us who killed him. Indeed, if we think on it rightly, we will realize that it was not merely someone else way back there who did it, but that we are all implicated. As it is put in one of our hymns:

Who was the guilty; who brought this upon thee?
Alas, my treason, Jesus, hath undone thee.
Twas I, Lord Jesus, I it was denied thee.
I crucified thee.

Here lies the deepest reason why we can only be witnesses. Seeing the crime and sensing our implication in it, we cannot pretend anymore. We cannot aspire to be religious holy people or gurus or paragons of virtue. We can only bear witness, shocked and stunned witness to the fact that the Christ, God's Messiah, was killed and cast out of our world — "wasted" as we would put it today.

But that, of course, is not the end — to our continued amazement. Had it ended only with that we could not, we would not, want to be witnesses. We would rather try to cover it up, forget it, hide it, bury it under the earth, put the body in a deep, deep tomb and roll a great stone over it, hoping that in time the world would forget it like all its other crimes. But God raised him up. When we had done our worst, God did his best! God turned the tables on us. He vindicated the one whom everyone rejected by raising him from the dead. Now the stone which the builders rejected has become the chief cornerstone of something entirely new. If our quest to be religious holy people ended there at Golgotha, God there began something new. Because Jesus was raised from the dead, our text tells us, *repentance and forgiveness of sins* should be preached in his name to all nations. God began his church, gathering a repentant and forgiven people to himself. Jesus, our text says, opened their minds to understand the Scripture. He brought them to see that just exactly this forgiveness is what God wants in the world. Everything written in the Law of Moses and the Prophets and the Psalms is fulfilled in the crucified and risen one. God has reached his goal. He wants a world, a people that lives on, lives from and acts on his forgiveness. He doesn't want or need self-styled holiness, or religious gurus, or self-appointed prophets. He wants a world that will repent, believe, and act on the word of forgiveness.

We are witness to these things. We have seen and heard it. And having seen and heard, we cannot be silent. We cannot be the same anymore. We must break the conspiracy of silence and tell the world of the good news of the forgiveness from God. But it is not only telling. Witnessing means a certain kind of life as well, but not that *we* are witnesses. We are witnesses to Another. That is the bottom line. That is what we are about here today when we come together to ordain James and send him out. We reaffirm who we are. We bear witness to the conviction that the word must be preached, that we cannot keep silent.

"But why so?" you might ask. "Doesn't everybody know it already? Doesn't everybody know that God is love, that God is a forgiving God?" Yes, perhaps they do — to some degree or another. Everybody knows that God is loving and forgiving *in general*. As H. Heine put it, "That's his business!" But you see, that is not good enough. The question is, "How do you know he forgives *you?*" Not just that he is forgiving in general, but the bottom line is that he forgives *you*. I might, for example, have the general reputation of being a nice person, loving and forgiving, but if you actually have a falling out with me, how can you be sure I forgive you specifically? Generalities don't help much in that situation. How do you know what God thinks of you unless someone with the authority and right to do so actually tells you, actually delivers the message? That, ultimately, is what the death and resurrection of Jesus was about — giving us the right, the authority to speak those precious words for God himself: I forgive you your sins for Jesus' sake. Not just to speak in generalities and platitudes about God, but to say "I forgive you," *for God.* Before Jesus, in the Old Testament especially, everyone knew that God was loving and forgiving in general. But Jesus came to say that word *in particular.* He had the nerve to say it: "I forgive you your sins." The result was that he got killed for it because everyone thought it was presumptuous and blasphemous. "No one," they said, "can forgive sins but God alone." So he was killed. But God raised him up. God put his stamp of approval on Jesus' preaching of forgiveness in particular. And it is he, the risen Lord, who speaks the words of our text to us, telling us and giving us the unheard-of authority to go and say the same thing for God. You are witness to these things. That is why he concludes with the words, "Behold, I send the promise of my Father upon you . . . you will be clothed with power from on high." This is what God wants done. The witness has the authority to say it to you and all the other "yous" in the world — not just that God is loving and forgiving in general, but that he forgives *you* for Jesus' sake.

As a Christian you have that authority. That is the bottom line. That is the witness. So James, as a witness of these things, we send you out with our prayers, our blessings, our hopes. Remember through all the many and varied things you will be asked to do, that you are the witness to Another. So witness to these things of His. Remember above all, that the promise of the Father, the power from on high is, above all, the power of forgiveness. Don't forget to claim that also for yourself. You are not called to carry the burden of the world on your back. You are not called to be religious megalomaniacs, gurus, or whatever. You are witnesses. You see, there is real, good news here for you too. You aren't called to do it all. Just to bear witness. God will take it from there. You will be clothed with power from on high. Speak that word of forgiveness! Preach it! Break the conspiracy of silence, and God be with you!

On Preaching Good News to the Poor

And the poor have good news preached to them.

Matthew 11:2-5

"And the poor have good news preached to them." What have we here? The blind receive their sight, the lame walk, the lepers are cleansed, the deaf hear, the dead are raised up. But the poor? They get a sermon. Surely that is one colossal, cruel, and unfair anti-climax to this catalog of remedies for human misery? Should it not rather go: The blind see, the lame walk, lepers are cleansed, the deaf hear, the dead are raised, and the poor get rich? Would that not be only fair and just? Surely the preaching of good news is hardly to be compared with all those other mighty and miraculous cures?

There is a good deal of talk about the poor these days, as indeed there should and must be. Abject, cruel, grinding, hopeless, unjust poverty is constantly before us and ought to be heavy on our consciences. And we must do something about it. But there is also, I fear, a lot of posturing about the poor. It has become something of a theological fashion to talk *about* the poor, and much of it, it seems, at the expense of the good news. It isn't all that important to preach the gospel, is it? Isn't it more important to be there and witness by deeds? After all, we can't have a Christ running about who saves us from our sin for nothing, can we? A Christ, perhaps, who even gets people off the hook and supposedly dissipates all our earnest zeal for the poor. It seems sometimes as though we had decided that the good news would really be bad news for the poor, so we'd better hold back on it lest it disrupt our important plans. So perhaps we should then rewrite the passage like this: The blind see, the lame walk, lepers are cleansed, the deaf hear, the dead are raised up, and the poor get a handout. After all, it is tax-deductible, you know. Or if in righteous indignation we are *really* going to do something it might go like this: The blind see, the lame walk, lepers are cleansed, the deaf hear, the dead are raised up, and the poor get automatic rifles so they can fight us for their bread — and no doubt replenish the depleted ranks of the blind, the lame, the deaf, and the dead? It seems sometimes as though we think that since the good news isn't all that effective, and Jesus isn't really the solution (and may even do some harm), we should best take him away and make a big present to the poor of ourselves and all our proposed remedies.

There is probably no more devastating attack on our attitudes and proposals than that puzzling and even embarrassing story about the poor woman who came to anoint Jesus with an alabaster jar of very costly nard. The onlookers, perhaps expecting approval from Jesus, complain at the great waste and protest that it should have been sold and the proceeds given to the poor. But Jesus refuses to go along with the scheme. He refuses to be the hero of the nice little plot. He acidly puts down all such gratuitous posturing. "The poor," he says, "you always have with you, and whenever you will you can do good to them; but you do not always have me." The poor you always have with you. Yes. I expect that is not so much cruel or pessimistic resignation as it is rather an accusation. You are the sorts that always have the poor with you, always causing poverty, always grinding someone in the dust. When the last political scheme has been tried, the last relief program completed, the last revolutionary shot fired, the poor will still be there — perhaps not the same ones as before; the characters change, but the plot seems always to stay the same. So why this pious indignation at the poor woman's beautiful act? Her one chance, one wild, extravagant gesture of hope — why shut that down? Is this our big move to help the poor? This kind of tokenism that wouldn't cost us anything anyway? To take from the poor to help the poor? "The poor you always have with you," Jesus says, "and whenever you will you can do good to them." Any time you want you can help the poor. There is no great mystery about it; no big miracle is required for that. They are always there waiting.

So why does it have to be at Jesus' expense? Or is the point exactly that it doesn't matter much at whose expense it is so long as it isn't ours? Is even Jesus expendable for the sake of our programs? "Are we free," Karl Barth asked once, "of the Satanism of the 'Grand Inquisitor', who, though he knows God, yet for the love of humanity refuses to know him, and would rather put Christ to death than allow the Word of the freedom of God to run its course?" Could it be that we have to get rid of Jesus exactly because he is so dangerous to our penny-ante schemes? I expect it is no accident that in Matthew's Gospel it is no longer the onlookers, but the *disciples* who launch the complaint about the woman's extravagance, while finally in John's Gospel it is Judas the betrayer of Jesus who poses as the great friend and advocate of the poor. Is that the way it is? The disciple, the would-be do-gooder who, like the Grand Inquisitor, wants to improve on Jesus, who at last sells him out?

That poor woman who anointed Jesus knows, of course, in her own way what is going on, even if we don't. "She," Jesus says, at least, "has done what she could; she has anointed my body beforehand for burying." She anticipates what will happen to Jesus in a world so full of free advice about what to do for the poor.

"The poor you always have with you . . . but you will not always have me." Yes, I expect that is the size of it. Or will we *ever* have him? Will the good news ever grasp and hold us? But if it doesn't, what chance will the poor have then?

So we come back to the Baptist John's searching question. Are you the one, Jesus? Are you the one who is to come, or do we look for another? Are you the answer to it all? Well, the only reply we will get is: "The blind see, the lame walk, lepers are cleansed, the deaf hear, and the dead are raised." And yes, "the poor have good news preached to them." And perhaps that is the greatest miracle of all. It might even be the best thing that could happen — both for them and for us. It might just be that were it to happen, we too might actually do something about the poor. Yes, indeed, Jesus says, the poor have good news preached to them; and blessed are they who take no offense at me.

A Voice from the Darkness

> What have you to do with us, Jesus of Nazareth? Have you
> come to destroy us?
>
> *Mark 1:24*

Epiphany is the season of light. Jesus is the light to the nations, the manifestation in whom we see God's glory. We celebrate the morning star, the star of Bethlehem, in our hymns for the season: "Brightest and best of the stars of the morning, dawn on our darkness and lend us your aid," and "Bright and glorious is the sky, radiant are the heavens high, where the golden stars are shining, all their rays to earth inclining, beckon us to heaven above." I like Epiphany. It is a joyous, enlightening, happy time. But now today, like a sour note in a chorus, a note of foreboding, an impending tragedy, we have this strange and disconcerting voice from the darkness — "What have you to do with us, Jesus? Have you come to destroy us?"

So in the midst of Epiphany, the season of light, the darkness announces itself. That voice from the darkness reminds us of several important matters we may easily forget as we bask in the light. It reminds us first of all that not everyone greeted the morning star with gladness. Not everyone was happy about the manifestation of Jesus' glory and power. It reminds us further of an even more disturbing thing: that it was really only this man with an unclean spirit who in a real sense *saw* Jesus in all his glory and power. He was the only one who knew what was going on really and

306

truly: "I know who you are, the Holy One of God." The others, the crowd and even the disciples, are more or less puzzled by Jesus and are not sure what to make of him. They are astonished at his teaching, we are told, because he taught with authority, not as the scribes. Even when he casts out the unclean spirit, they are "amazed," we are told, but could only puzzle about what was going on. "What is this?" they said. "A new teaching?" No, they didn't really know what was up. As for most of us, those strange proceedings there in the synagogue at Capernaum just didn't register on their scale of comprehension.

In the modern world we like to say that this business about demons and unclean spirits is outmoded. We don't know what it means. Well, it seems it was rather strange for those people back there too. They couldn't figure it out either. Like many today, they could only make sense of it as some kind of obscure teaching. They thought, apparently, that Jesus was a great new teacher, even one who taught with supreme divine authority. They were, perhaps, something like those who like to say that what is important and lasting about Jesus is his *teaching*. If only we would all get with it, and follow the teachings of Jesus, the world would improve and be a better place. Well, that is no doubt in some measure true, and we shouldn't knock it. But the disconcerting and disturbing voice from the darkness reminds us that the problem is much deeper and the stakes much higher. "What have you to do with us, Jesus? Have you come to destroy us? I know who you are, the Holy One of God." It is, you see, not merely a matter of teaching. It is a matter of a battle, a desperate battle. Someone is going to get hurt; someone is going to be destroyed. The voice from the darkness announces that the battle is under way.

But now, I suppose, we must ask, "Whence comes this voice?" Who is this strange man? What is the darkness out of which he speaks? A man with an unclean spirit, our text says. But what is that supposed to mean? Is he perhaps just a relic out of the past? Something that just doesn't occur anymore in our enlightened and modern world? Is he, perhaps, one whom today we would call mentally disturbed? Are there really such things as unclean spirits and demons about, or has modern science and knowledge banished them? That is a subject which would be interesting to discuss and could no doubt occupy us for many an hour. But such discussion would be a very dangerous business. Why? Because the nature of the battle is such that we cannot possibly win it with our talk. Our talk, our teaching, you see, is like that of the scribes. It has no authority. We think, I suppose, that we can talk, or teach the demons into, or out of, existence. But our talk has no authority, and we will end only by losing the battle.

How so? There is an old proverb that says that the demons can't see you until you look at them, and when you do, they've got you. That is, the more you talk about them, the more likely you are to be fascinated by them and start seeing them all around — most likely, of course, in other people. Every now and then we read tragic stories about people — usually religious people — who have become convinced that their children are demon-possessed and undertake to beat the demons out of them. But then, you see, the demons win after all. They can't see you until you look at them, and then they've got you! We can't win that battle; we can't fight them with our weapons. As another old proverb has it, if you try to cut a demon in two with your sword, you only produce two more of them.

Or we might, on the other hand, try to convince ourselves that there is no such thing anymore. After all, enlightenment and science, and so on, have banished the demons and unclean spirits. But can we really rest assured on such teaching? Does it have authority? As we look about in the world, can we be so convinced that there is not something terribly wrong? As it has been put, the devil's cleverest trick is to get us to believe he doesn't exist. Indeed, that is precisely what he wants. For then he would have everything to himself. If no one suspects he is there he has already won. In another place Jesus said that when the unclean spirit has gone out of a person it passes over waterless places seeking rest. When it finds none, it decides to return to the old home, and finding the house empty and swept clean, it goes and gets seven more demons more evil than itself, and settles in once again. And so the last state of such a person is worse than the first. Why is that? Because now the man doesn't even know they are there! We may try to convince ourselves there is no such thing about. We may try to empty the house and sweep it clean, but an empty house is a dangerous thing. There is no unoccupied territory in this cosmic battle. No, our talk, our teaching, cannot help us here. It has no authority. One way or another we can only lose.

Whence, then, comes that voice out of the darkness? I guess what scares me most about that voice is not that it sounds so odd, or crazy, so ancient or outmoded, but rather that it seems so reasonable, so modern, and so up-to-date: "What have you to do with us, Jesus? Have you come to destroy us? I know who you are, the Holy One of God." When we really begin to see who Jesus is and what he is up to, do we not begin to tremble?

Do we not know or at least dimly sense that the gospel is a mighty attack on our way of doing business? The unclean spirit, after all, is one who makes business out of sin, or capitalizes on it by accusing and adding to grace. It says: How can you run a world like this on forgiveness? What would happen if we were actually all to sell everything we have and give it to the poor? The economy would be wrecked overnight! So much for the "teachings" of Jesus. "I fled him," the poet Francis Thompson said. "I fled him down the nights and down the days and down the labyrinthine ways of my heart, for I was sore adread lest having him I might have nought beside." Can it be that that ancient and curious man in the text really speaks somehow for us all? Can it be that the darkness from which he speaks is the darkness dwelling deep in this world, indeed, in all of us? "What have you to do with us, Jesus? Have you come to destroy us? We know who you are, the Holy One of God!" But this is our world!

But if that is so, how shall such darkness be dispelled? In our text the question from the darkness can only be answered by the *light*, the commanding voice that gives no argument, no teaching as such — the voice of authority and so of new life. "Be silent," Jesus said, "and come out of him." The unclean spirit left, kicking and screaming. But this was, of course, only a preliminary skirmish in the battle. It went on until finally that voice from our darkness nailed him to the cross. He came to preach forgiveness and the absolutely free grace of God. But we couldn't let him do it. "What have you to do with us, Jesus? Have you come to destroy us? We can't let you do that. This is our world." So at last it comes down to the final battle between us and him. When he is about to be crucified he says, "Now, *now,* will the prince of this world be cast out." But when we did our worst, God did his best. He raised Jesus from the dead, casting down the unclean spirit from the world forever. Forgiveness is to be declared unconditionally to all. What have you to do with us, Jesus? Have you come to destroy us? The plain unvarnished truth is, of course, that he has. The unclean spirit knew. The darkness knows it can't live with the light. The situation is desperate enough so that it cannot be our friend without first being our enemy. The road to life can only lead through death. But in Jesus it *does* lead to life. "Whoever would save his life shall lose it; whoever loses his life for my sake shall find it." We shall find it. To be baptized, Paul says, is to be baptized into the death of Christ so as to be raised with him. That is why baptism is exorcism. We shall be raised, and so: "I have been crucified with Christ, and it is no longer I who live, but Christ in me." Luther too said it: "When

God makes alive, he does so by killing, when he justifies, he does so by pronouncing guilty, when he carries up to heaven, he does so by bringing down to hell." When Jesus enters into battle to defeat the demons he comes to put the old to death so as to raise up something absolutely new. The battle is over, the victory won. So it is, perhaps, not strange that we don't hear much of the demons anymore. But yet the voice lingers, so we should beware. The devil, the unclean spirit was right, but it had only half the story. It wants to convince us that there is no more to say.

But now, of course, the mopping-up operations still go on. The voice from the darkness still seems to linger and haunt us: "What have you to do with us, Jesus?" When we hear that we can only be saved by grace alone, there is still that pocket of resistance that rises up: "But, I have to do something, don't I?"

When we hear that God alone elects and carries it out in Jesus, we begin to fear for our own plans and freedom.

"Can't I say no?"

When we begin to see that he is the Holy One of God, we fear that he is going to ask too much of us. What will happen to us if we fall into the hands of the living God? The question is always near at hand — that voice from the darkness: "What have you to do with us, Jesus? Have you come to destroy us?" So now there is nothing left to say but what Jesus said: Be silent! Be gone! Come out! For once in your life, just be still and listen to the voice that speaks with authority, that casts out all the demons: It's all over! Believe it! Your sins are forgiven; Jesus bore the destruction and death himself. It was for you. There is nothing now for you but new life. The future belongs only to God and his Christ! The demons are defeated, and you belong to him.

A Gracious Neighbor or a Gracious God?

Let us fall into the hands of the Lord, for his mercy is great;
but let me not fall into the hand of man.

2 Samuel 24:1-5, 10-14; Romans 3:9-19; Matthew 5:43-48

It has become virtually a dogma in our time that what we moderns need
and seek is not so much a gracious God as a gracious neighbor. Since today
happens to be the anniversary of the birthday of that curious man, Martin
Luther, who believed that the quest for a gracious God was absolutely vital
for him and for human existence in general, it occurred to me that we
might stop and reflect a bit today on the success — or lack of it — of our
quest for a gracious neighbor. I must say that when I looked to Scripture
for a text to support such a quest I was not exactly encouraged. St. Paul's
catena of quotes from the Old Testament poses something of a roadblock
that is hard to get around: "None is righteous, no not one; no one understands, no one seeks for God. All have turned aside, together they have
gone wrong; no one does good, not even one. Their throat is an open
grave, they use their tongues to deceive. The venom of asps is under their
lips. Their mouth is full of curses and bitterness. Their feet are swift to
shed blood, in their paths are ruin and misery, and the way of peace they
do not know. There is no fear of God before their eyes."

Not every encouraging. But surely, we might be inclined to say that
that must be an exaggeration, hyperbole, the pessimism of some primeval

misanthrope. But if we don't want to take Paul's word for it, what shall we say when we look about in the world a bit? Perhaps I have been watching the news too much lately, or reading the papers and paying too much attention to the "real world," but I find it rather depressing: the possibility of nuclear holocaust is a constant companion with the fear that some maniac will set it all off and plunge us to our doom; PCBs (isn't it nice how we all get used to the abbreviations — it seems almost as if they are familiar friends!) — PCBs in the "fountains of the deep," sulfurous waste in the heavens and air we breathe; no jobs; inflation; hunger; drugs; handguns so we won't be cheated of the right to kill the neighbor should the impulse or occasion arise; Lebanon; South Africa; Afghanistan, Nicaragua — you all know the endless litany. Is there some grim and terrible irony in that list so much like the Apostles'? The television programs we watch are full of violence, pain, dirt, blood, and grime, but the ads at least speak of relief and happiness and cleanliness and righteousness and freedom from pain. No more tricks or treats on All-Hallows' Eve, there might be a dirty trick in your treat — and the world grows a little bit colder and sadder.

What's going on anyway? Here we are, always talking about the new freedom, beautiful people, meaningful relationships, community, celebrating the goodness of life, and Lord knows what all — all of which is supposed to be some sort of gospel, while all the signs point in the opposite direction. What do you suppose "the neighbor" out there is trying to say to us in all this? Perhaps that he or she just doesn't want our burden, and scornfully spurns our quest — that perhaps even he or she is just another terrifying mask of the *deus absconditus,* the God of wrath? Were you to ask, the neighbor may well protest: "having lost God, it's not fair to expect grace from me. I'm only dying, as you are! Gimme a break!" Therein lies the omnipresent contemporary plea for mercy: "Gimme a break!" Well then, if we can't find a world full of gracious neighbors, can we not find *some* at least? Where to look? Even among the people of God it seems no different; we find the same troubles among them.

Well, okay then, if the quest out there in the world seems discouraging, perhaps we can find *one* gracious one — one's beloved, perhaps. "Ah, love," says the poet,

> To lie before us like a land of dreams,
> So various, so beautiful, so new,
> Hath really neither joy, nor love, nor light,

Nor certitude, nor peace, nor help for pain;
And we are there as on a darkling plain
Swept with confused alarms of struggle and flight
Where ignorant armies clash by night.

Is that it? "Ah, love, let us at least be true!" Can you find someone, some beloved, who will be true, who will be the font of all grace and blessing? Well, maybe, if you are lucky — for awhile at least — while health, youth, and beauty last, perhaps. But really, when you think on it a bit, even should you succeed, is not even that somewhat preposterous? Is it fair to dump such a load of cosmic discontent on the beloved — joy, love, light, certitude, peace, help for pain — can she, can he bear it? Can he or she be a surrogate to you for God? Should not the beloved be simply loved and enjoyed for what he or she is? Oh yes, we are big on *talk* about "meaningful relationships," but what of the actuality? We tend more and more, it seems, to leave behind us a trail of broken hearts, broken promises, broken marriages, broken homes, not to say the battered and bruised bodies of our "loved ones." Why is that? Could it be that the quest is simply devastating and only makes the beloved the object of our disappointed rage?

If so, the possibilities are narrowed in our search for someone gracious. Where do we look? Well, how about the pastor? Now we are getting closer to home. Is not the pastor supposed to be a kind of professional gracious neighbor — one who somehow just exudes graciousness and heavenly unction by an "incarnational lifestyle," or some such marvelous business? I read somewhere the other day about how we are supposed to be "sacraments of salvation" for one another. My goodness! That all sounds nice, but what about when we get down to actual cases? Take me, for instance! Am I not impressive? Am I not reasonably clever with words? Are not these robes pretty? Am I not just the living end of your quest? Well, about all I can say is: "Don't count on it!" You get too close and you'll find I have bad breath or something. But that is only the prelude to some inevitable and greater putrification.

Who am *I*? I'm no sacrament, I fear! I am only dying too. Oh, yes, I will try to do my best. But how am I supposed to know where you are coming from? I have an idea where you are going, but I'll be hanged if I can tell half the time where you all are coming from. Oh, I will do my best. But in the end I suppose I will get caught with all my skills hanging out. I will grope in the dark night of your soul, for your "feelings," and probably blow it fifty ways from Sunday. I suppose I'm not supportive enough, or sharing and caring enough, and my language isn't inclusive enough, and I don't succeed in relating meaningfully, and goodness knows what all. What can I say? Except maybe to ask, "Is it fair to dump all that freight on me, one pastor? Gimme a break!"

Well, then, where are we? Could it be, after all, that we are not much farther along than old King David way back there when he got into big trouble for trying to put his trust in human strength? He took a census, you know, a body count, so as better to calculate his chances — even against the advice of his generals. (Where generals got such intelligence, I don't know! Things were different in those days, I guess.) When the prophet of the Lord came to settle accounts he gave David a choice: either to suffer at the hands of nature or of humans or of God. And David said, "I'll take my chances with God . . . I am in great distress; let us fall into the hands of the Lord, for his mercy is great; but let me not fall into the hand of man." Wise man, old David.

For that is about the sum of it at the last, is it not? "Let us fall into the hands of the Lord, for his mercy is great." You see, my friends, my only excuse for standing before you today is that I'm here to tell you about a gracious God. I am only a voice crying in the wilderness: "Prepare the way of the Lord!" I am here to try to tell you that your quest, whatever it is, is over. Jesus came and died and rose for you. What I am, or am not, is beside the point. (I suppose that is why I am covered by these fine robes.) I make bold to claim only that I bear an office, the preposterous claim that I am here to speak for a gracious God and to say that here you have fallen into his hands — your sins are forgiven. No, I'm no sacrament of salvation, but I am bidden to tell you that Jesus is, and to say that all you need to feel is the bread on your lips and the wine in your throat. Maybe, in the world's economy, that doesn't seem like much, but in the end, when it comes to grace, my friend, that's about all you've got!

But then, if you are at all grasped by that, perhaps you can turn back from your impetuous quest and look for that not-so-gracious neighbor and have pity. For, having a gracious God, you are not to lay *that* burden on anyone else: "For I say to you, love your enemies and pray for those who persecute you, so that you may be children of your Father who is in heaven; for he makes his sun to rise on the evil and on the good, and sends rain on the just and on the unjust. For if you love those who love you, what reward have you? Do not even the tax collectors do the same? And if you salute only your friends, what more are you doing than others? Do not even the Gentiles do the same? You therefore must be perfect, as your heavenly Father is perfect."

If we listen carefully, I think we can hear even in that thunder the promise of a gracious God who plans to have *his* way with us at last.

The Laborers in the Vineyard

I choose to give to this last as I give to you. Am I not
allowed to do what I choose with what belongs to me?

Matthew 20:1-16

What's this? They all got the same? Do you mean to tell me that what I do
doesn't matter? Scandal! Do you mean to tell me that all my hard-earned
religious cash isn't worth anything? Preposterous! Do you mean to tell me
that all those efforts, all those transporting and ecstatic experiences, all
that suffering, all that bearing the heat of the day — all that adds up to
nothing? Does it not count for something at least, if not here, then in the
great by-and-by? Appalling! Disgusting! Where is the justice in that? Do
you really mean it? But the answer comes back: "Yes, that's just what I
mean! You finally got the message!"

But how am I supposed to make sense out of that? How can that
have any relevance for my daily life? There is just something about a parable like this that makes it hard to get around, hard to fit in to what we call
"the scheme of things," or the way we go about doing things, or the way
we think about ourselves. We might, I suppose, even think we can penetrate the secret by some Herculean act of theological understanding so
that we could make it all quite reasonable and logical. We might tell ourselves that this is, after all, a parable about "the way God does things," or
about God's grace. And we would no doubt be quite right about that, as

far as theology goes. So we could all nod our heads wisely and go back to our business as usual. It's about God's grace alright. We all know about that, at least in theory.

But still it sticks in the craw somehow. They all got the same. I could understand it, I suppose, if it would fit nicely with what we would say about grace. Grace, we say, is for sinners. But the galling thing is that the parable doesn't seem to be about sinners really. It is about *workers* in the vineyard. They weren't *sinning* when they did that, were they? They were doing their bit for God. If the parable had said that there were some big sinners and some little ones, but God nevertheless dealt mercifully with them all, I could see my way clear toward buying that it is all about grace — especially if I were a big-time sinner! Yet the only real reason given why some come early and some late is that the master saw fit to do it that way; he saw fit to call them in that order: "Can I not do what I want with what is my own?" Isn't that shocking? Isn't that wild?

And so the only thing to do at last, I think, is just to sit back and listen. Listen! Maybe you will hear the music. They all got the same! Isn't that fantastic! There is a different world, a new one, just around the corner, just on the other side of all your calculations, your scheming, and your pious or impious games. You are forgiven for all that — all of it. God has acted in Jesus so that every mouth is stopped, and there is something new afoot. He has acted to expose all those who hold down the truth in unrighteousness. He has a new kingdom. It is as when Pilgrim approached the Celestial City — he heard all the trumpets blowing for him on the other side. There is something else calling you now. Here is the pure and untrammeled gift. Here is your chance, for once in your life, to catch hold of something without price, to act in freedom, without calculation, out of pure heart. It is pure, beautiful, and good. It is the Master's good pleasure to call you to that.

And if you don't find that "relevant" to your daily life, perhaps you'd better stop a bit and take stock. For it might just be that your daily life is irrelevant to what the Master has in mind. Do you begrudge him his goodness? Or as the King James Version put it, "Is your eye evil, because I am good?" There is nothing left to do but praise him. Praise him *because* they all got the same. Isn't that fantastic! Maybe you consider yourself an extraordinarily pious person. Forget it. It is nothing. Maybe you consider yourself an easy-going, liberated person. Forget it and praise him. Maybe you think it is something big to be an "evangelical," a real Bible-believing

Christian, or even style yourself a true charismatic. But is that anything in the final analysis? Forget it, for we are told, the last shall be first, and the first last.

So just listen. They all got the same. Just think of that! Fantastic, beautiful! Can you hear that? It is the Master calling. For when you hear, you can go back to work, with a chuckle, for God is great and good.

Yes!

Do I make my plans like a worldly man, ready to say Yes and No at once? As surely as God is faithful, our word to you has not been Yes and No. For the Son of God, Jesus Christ, whom we preached among you, Silvanus and Timothy and I, was not Yes and No; but in him it is always Yes.

2 Corinthians 1:17b-19

How would you like to take a bite out of the cross? Of course, most of them are made of metal now, so it would be rather hard on the teeth. In case you hadn't noticed, or had forgotten, this is Holy Cross day — a day that originated in the alleged rediscovery of the Cross in the rubble of Jerusalem when Constantine ordered the building of the Basilica of the Holy Sepulcher. The most intriguing bit of legend about that to me is the report by a Spanish Pilgrim, Egeria (ca. 385-388), that the deacons had to post guard so the pilgrims who came to kiss the cross wouldn't bite out splinters of it to take home with them! Imagine such a scene. One scarcely knows what is more wondrous, or pathetic (perhaps a little of both), the pilgrim who wanted a bite of the cross, or a church that stood guard to make sure they didn't get it!

What should we make of this? At the very least we can take it, I think, as a sign that there is a dangerous and fearsome power threatening to erupt here. In the words of the text set for the day, it is the power of the Yes. The cross stands, in the first instance of course, as our ultimate and final No — no to God, no to Jesus, no to everything he came to give. But God said Yes. Exactly through and in spite of our No, God said Yes. So now in Jesus, it is always Yes. All the promises of God find their Yes in him. Think of that! There is something, there is a speaking, in this benighted world in which there is at last not No, but only Yes!

But that is just the terror of it. Should I, can I, just say Yes? Must I not, must we not, as Paul says, make our plans like good and prudent worldlings, and be ready to say Yes and No at once — just to be safe? Yes, you can kiss the cross, but don't get carried away! No, you can't have a bite of it! I mean if everybody took a bite out of it, wouldn't it, like everything else in this age, soon be exhausted, splintered, scattered to the four winds? Isn't that what in fact happened? Of course, we are more sophisticated than that nowadays. Were we to try it we would no doubt be charged with vandalism for destroying religious art! But are we all that much different? Do we not hesitate, tremble, and even pull up in fear before the Yes? Are we not always ready with the No? Are we not inclined to dole out grace in doses just small enough so that no one will get what we consider to be the wrong idea? Are we not always ready to say Yes and No at once, just to cover our tracks?

But God said Yes. Holy Cross day was retained in the Lutheran calendar, it is said, so that there might be opportunity to reflect on and contemplate the glory of the cross apart from the solemn gloom of Lent and Good Friday. And perhaps that is well. For that fearsome and awesome power threatening to erupt here, the power we catch a glint of in the eternal Yes, is simply the glory of the Almighty. What we tremble and hesitate before is that glory ready to break upon us. As the spiritual has it, "He come from de glory!" Our real problem, as Paul could put it, is that all have sinned and fallen short — of the law? No! Of Glory. "Glory to God in the highest and on earth peace . . ." That is the way it began with the song of the angels. "And he shall come again in glory to judge the living and the dead!" So it shall end.

God said Yes! That is the glory of it. That's how the glory dawns in our darkness. So there is nothing to do but watch and listen for the dawning.

Did you say nothing to do?

Yes.

Do you mean it is an absolute gift?

Yes.

But isn't that dangerous?

Yes. After all, we killed him for it, but that only gave him the opportunity to say it again, Yes!

But might not someone get the wrong idea?

Yes, likely, but shall God turn off the glory for the sake of those who happen to be blinded by the light?

Do you mean I can be God's just by being washed in a little water and receiving some bread and wine?

Yes.

Do you mean it's all God's doing and not mine?

Yes.

Do you mean it's not my choice?

Yes.

Do you mean I can't say No?

Yes, how can you?

Or should I say yes and no at once? Do you mean it's irresistible?

Yes, after all that, I should think so! If God said Yes, how can I say No? No doubt it doesn't make sense yet, in this world of the Yes and the No, but hang on. You see, "he come from de glory!" It's Yes, Yes, Yes, all the way home. Yes, until you finally die of it and begin to whisper Yes! Amen! So be it, Lord. For thine is the kingdom, and the power, and the glory, Amen! Yes, Sink your teeth into it! There is nothing to stop you.

Amen, Yes.

Bibliography of the Writings of Gerhard O. Forde

Compiled by Amy Marga

This bibliography has been compiled first of all from By Faith Alone: Essays on Justification in Honor of Gerhard O. Forde, *edited by Joseph A. Burgess and Marc Kolden (Grand Rapids: Eerdmans, 2004), pp. 341-44. There the bibliographic references are listed in chronological order; here they are listed alphabetically. It also adds several items, including those printed or reprinted since then, as well as book reviews by Forde.*

Books

A More Radical Gospel. Essays on Eschatology, Authority, Atonement, and Ecumenism. Edited by Mark C. Mattes and Steven D. Paulson. Grand Rapids: Eerdmans, 2004.

Captivation of the Will: Luther vs. Erasmus on Freedom and Bondage. Edited by Steven D. Paulson. Grand Rapids: Eerdmans, 2005.

Free to Be: A Handbook to Luther's Small Catechism. Minneapolis: Augsburg, 1975; revised 1993. With James A. Nestingen.

Justification by Faith: A Matter of Death and Life. Philadelphia: Fortress, 1982.

Law-Gospel Debate, The: An Interpretation of Its Historical Development. Minneapolis: Augsburg, 1969.

On Being a Theologian of the Cross. Grand Rapids: Eerdmans, 1997.

Preached God, The: Proclamation in Word and Sacrament. Edited by

Mark C. Mattes and Steven D. Paulson. Grand Rapids: Eerdmans, 2007.

Theology Is for Proclamation. Minneapolis: Fortress, 1990.

Where God Meets Man: Luther's Down-to-Earth Approach to the Gospel. Minneapolis: Augsburg, 1972. This book has also been translated into German, Japanese, and Norwegian.

Articles, Chapters in Books, and Editorials

"A Call for Discussion of the 'Joint Declaration on the Doctrine of Justification,'" *dialog* 36 (1997): 224-29. With five other Luther Seminary faculty members.

"A Movement Without a Move? [Lutheranism's identity crisis, editorial]," *dialog* 30 (1991): 83-84.

"A Short Word [language use in the church]," *dialog* 20 (1981): 88-92.

"Beware of Greeks Bearing Gifts" [a reply to Carl E. Braaten and the ELCA], *dialog* 39 (2000): 291-92. With James Nestingen.

"Bound to Be Free," in *Encounters with Luther.* Edited by Eric Gritsch. 2 vols. Gettysburg, Pa.: Lutheran Theological Seminary at Gettysburg, 1976, vol. 2, pp. 67-80.

"Bultmann: Where Did He Take Us?" *dialog* 17 (1978): 27-30.

"Called to Freedom," *Lutherjahrbuch* 62 (1995): 13-27. Also in *The Preached God: Proclamation in Word and Sacrament.* Edited by Mark C. Mattes and Steven D. Paulson. Grand Rapids: Eerdmans, 2007, pp. 254-69.

"Catholic Impasse, The: Reflections on Lutheran-Roman Catholic Dialogue Today," in *Promoting Unity: Themes in Lutheran-Catholic Dialogue.* Edited by H. George Anderson et al. Minneapolis: Augsburg, 1989, pp. 67-78. Also in *A More Radical Gospel. Essays on Eschatology, Authority, Atonement, and Ecumenism.* Edited by Mark C. Mattes and Steven D. Paulson. Grand Rapids: Eerdmans, 2004, pp. 189-99.

"Caught in the Act: Reflections on the Work of Christ," *Word & World* 3 (1983): 22-31. Also in *A More Radical Gospel. Essays on Eschatology, Authority, Atonement, and Ecumenism.* Edited by Mark C. Mattes and Steven D. Paulson. Grand Rapids: Eerdmans, 2004, pp. 85-97.

"Christian Life, The," in *Christian Dogmatics.* Edited by Carl E. Braaten and Robert W. Jenson. 2 vols. Philadelphia: Fortress, 1984, vol. 2, pp. 391-470.

"Confessional Subscription: What Does It Mean for Lutherans Today?" *Word & World* 11 (1991): 316-20.

"Critical Response of German Theological Professors to the Joint Declaration on Justification, The," *dialog* 38 (1999): 71-72.

"Does the Gospel Have a Future? Barth's *Romans* Revisited," *Word & World* 14 (1994): 67-77.

"Exodus from Virtue to Grace, The: Justification by Faith Today," *Interpretation* 34 (1980): 32-44.

"Fake Theology: Reflections on Antinomianism Past and Present," *dialog* 22 (1983): 246-51. Also in *The Preached God: Proclamation in Word and Sacrament.* Edited by Mark C. Mattes and Steven D. Paulson. Grand Rapids: Eerdmans, 2007, pp. 214-25.

"Forensic Justification and the Law in Lutheran Theology," in *Justification by Faith.* Lutherans and Catholics in Dialogue 7. Edited by H. George Anderson, T. Austin Murphy, and Joseph A. Burgess. Minneapolis: Augsburg, 1985, pp. 287-303.

"Formula of Concord Article V: End or New Beginning?" *dialog* 15 (1976): 184-91.

"Full Communion?" *dialog* 28 (1989): 85-86.

"Infallibility Language and the Early Lutheran Tradition," in *Teaching Authority and Infallibility in the Church.* Lutherans and Catholics in Dialogue 6. Edited by Paul C. Empie, T. Austin Murphy, and Joseph A. Burgess. Minneapolis: Augsburg, 1980, pp. 120-37.

"Is Forgiveness Enough? Reflections on an Odd Question," *Word & World* 16 (1996): 302-8.

"Is Invocation of Saints an Adiaphoron?" in *The One Mediator, the Saints, and Mary.* Lutherans and Catholics in Dialogue 8. Edited by H. George Anderson, J. Francis Stafford, and Joseph A. Burgess. Minneapolis: Augsburg, 1992, pp. 327-38.

"Justification by Faith Alone," in *In Search of Christian Unity: Basic Consensus/Basic Differences.* Edited by Joseph A. Burgess. Minneapolis: Fortress, 1991, pp. 64-76.

"Justification by Faith Alone: The Article by Which the Church Stands or Falls?" *dialog* 27 (1988): 260-67.

"Law and Gospel as the Methodological Principle of Theology," in *Theological Perspectives: A Discussion of Contemporary Issues in Theology by Members of the Religion Department at Luther College.* Decorah, Iowa: Luther College Press, 1964, pp. 50-69.

"Law and Gospel in Luther's Hermeneutic," *Interpretation* 37 (1983): 240-52.

"Law and Sexual Behavior," *Lutheran Quarterly* 9 (1995): 3-22.

"*Lex semper accusat?* Nineteenth-Century Roots of Our Current Dilemma," *dialog* 9 (1970): 265-74. Also in *A More Radical Gospel. Essays on Eschatology, Authority, Atonement, and Ecumenism.* Edited by Mark C. Mattes and Steven D. Paulson. Grand Rapids: Eerdmans, 2004, pp. 33-49.

"Lord's Supper as the Testament of Jesus, The," *Word & World* 17 (1997): 5-9. Also in *The Preached God: Proclamation in Word and Sacrament.* Edited by Mark C. Mattes and Steven D. Paulson. Grand Rapids: Eerdmans, 2007, pp. 146-51.

"Loser Takes All: The Victory of Christ," *Lutheran Standard* (September 2, 1975): 3-5. Also in *A More Radical Gospel. Essays on Eschatology, Authority, Atonement, and Ecumenism.* Edited by Mark C. Mattes and Steven D. Paulson. Grand Rapids: Eerdmans, 2004, pp. 98-100.

"Luther and the *Usus Pauli*," *dialog* 32 (1993): 275-82.

"Lutheran Ecumenism: With Whom and How Much?" *Lutheran Quarterly* 17 (2003): 436-55. Also in *A More Radical Gospel. Essays on Eschatology, Authority, Atonement, and Ecumenism.* Edited by Mark C. Mattes and Steven D. Paulson. Grand Rapids: Eerdmans, 2004, pp. 171-88.

"Lutheran View, The," in *Christian Spirituality: Five Views of Sanctification.* Edited by Donald L. Alexander. Downers Grove, Ill.: InterVarsity, 1988, pp. 13-32. See also Forde's responses to the other views, pp. 77-82, 119-22, 155-57, 190-93. Also in *The Preached God: Proclamation in Word and Sacrament.* Edited by Mark C. Mattes and Steven D. Paulson. Grand Rapids: Eerdmans, 2007, pp. 226-44.

"Lutheranism," in *The Blackwell Encyclopedia of Modern Christian Thought.* Edited by Alister McGrath. Cambridge, Mass.: Blackwell, 1993, pp. 354-58.

"Martens on the Condemnations," *Lutheran Quarterly* 10 (1996): 67-69.

"Meaning of *satis est*, The," *Lutheran Forum* 26 (1992): 14-18. Also in *A More Radical Gospel. Essays on Eschatology, Authority, Atonement, and Ecumenism.* Edited by Mark C. Mattes and Steven D. Paulson. Grand Rapids: Eerdmans, 2004, pp. 159-70.

"Naming the One Who Is Above Us," in *Speaking the Christian God: The Holy Trinity and the Challenge of Feminism.* Edited by Alvin F. Kimmel. Grand Rapids: Eerdmans, 1992, pp. 110-19.

"Newness of the Gospel," *dialog* 6 (1967): 87-94.

"Newness of the New Testament, The," in *All Things New: Essays in Honor of Roy A. Harrisville.* Edited by Arland J. Hultgren, Donald H. Juel, and Jack D. Kingsbury. St. Paul: *Word & World* Supplement, 1992, pp. 175-80.

"Normative Character of Scripture for Matters of Faith and Life, The: Human Sexuality in Light of Romans 1:16-32," *Word & World* 14 (1994): 305-14. Also as "Human Sexuality and Romans, Chapter One," in *The Preached God: Proclamation in Word and Sacrament.* Edited by Mark C. Mattes and Steven D. Paulson. Grand Rapids: Eerdmans, 2007, pp. 204-13.

"'Old Synod', The: A Search for Objectivity," in *Striving for Ministry: Centennial Essays Interpreting the Heritage of Luther Seminary.* Edited by Warren Quanbeck et al. Minneapolis: Published under auspices of Luther Theological Seminary by Augsburg, 1977, pp. 67-80.

"On Being a Theologian of the Cross," *Christian Century* 114 (1997): 947-49.

"Once More into the Breach? Some Questions about Key 73," *dialog* 12 (1973): 7-14.

"One Acted Upon [Theological Autobiography], The," *dialog* 36 (1997): 54-61.

"Ordained Ministry, The," in *Called and Ordained: Lutheran Perspectives on the Office of the Ministry.* Edited by Todd Nichol and Marc Kolden. Minneapolis: Fortress, 1990, pp. 117-36.

"Place of Theology in the Church, The," *dialog* 22 (1983): 121-30.

"Power of Negative Thinking, The: On the Principle of Negation in Luther and Hegelianism," *dialog* 23 (1984): 250-56.

"Preaching the Sacraments," *Lutheran Theological Seminary Bulletin* 64, no. 4 (1984): 3-27. Also in *The Preached God: Proclamation in Word and Sacrament.* Edited by Mark C. Mattes and Steven D. Paulson. Grand Rapids: Eerdmans, 2007, pp. 89-115.

"Proclamation: The Present Tense of the Gospel," *dialog* 29 (1990): 167-73.

"Public Ministry and Its Limits," *dialog* 30 (1991): 102-10. Also in *The Preached God: Proclamation in Word and Sacrament.* Edited by Mark C. Mattes and Steven D. Paulson. Grand Rapids: Eerdmans, 2007, pp. 116-30.

"Radical Lutheranism: Lutheran Identity in America," *Lutheran Quarterly* 1 (1987): 5-18. Also in *A More Radical Gospel. Essays on Eschatology,*

Authority, Atonement, and Ecumenism. Edited by Mark C. Mattes and Steven D. Paulson. Grand Rapids: Eerdmans, 2004, pp. 3-16.

"Response to James Nestingen's Article," *dialog* 31 (1992): 34-35.

"Revolt and the Wedding, The: An Essay on Social Ethics in the Perspective of Luther's Theology," in *The Reformation and the Revolution.* Sioux Falls, S. Dak.: Augustana College Press, 1970, pp. 79-88.

"Robert Jenson's Soteriology," in *Trinity, Time, and Church: A Response to the Theology of Robert W. Jenson.* Edited by Colin Gunton. Grand Rapids: Eerdmans, 2000, pp. 126-38.

"Romans 8:18-27," *Interpretation* 38 (1984): 281-85.

"Sense and Nonsense about Luther [reply to H. Bauman]," *dialog* 10 (1971): 65-67.

"Some Remarks on [Ted] Peters' Review of *Christian Dogmatics*," *dialog* 24 (1985): 297-99.

"Something to Believe: A Theological Perspective on Infant Baptism," *Interpretation* 47 (1993): 229-41. Also in *The Preached God: Proclamation in Word and Sacrament.* Edited by Mark C. Mattes and Steven D. Paulson. Grand Rapids: Eerdmans, 2007, pp. 131-45.

"Theology as *modus operandi*," *dialog* 21 (1982): 175-79.

"Unity without Concord," *dialog* 20 (1981): 166-73.

"Viability of Luther Today, The: A North American Perspective," *Word & World* 7 (1987): 22-31.

"What Finally to Do about the (Counter-) Reformation Condemnations," *Lutheran Quarterly* 11 (1997): 3-16.

"What Next? [ELCA Ecumenism; editorial]," *dialog* 37 (1998): 163.

"What's in a Name? Eucharist or Lord's Supper," *Word & World* 9 (1989): 52-55.

"When Old Gods Fail: Martin Luther's Critique of Mysticism," in *Piety, Politics, and Ethics. Reformation Studies in Honor of George Wolfgang Forell.* Edited by Carter Lindberg. Kirksville, Mo.: Sixteenth Century Journal Publishers, Inc., 1984, pp. 15-26. Also in *The Preached God: Proclamation in Word and Sacrament.* Edited by Mark C. Mattes and Steven D. Paulson. Grand Rapids: Eerdmans, 2007, pp. 56-68.

"Word on Quotas, The," *Lutheran Quarterly* 6 (1992): 119-26.

"Word That Kills and Makes Alive, The," in *Marks of the Body of Christ.* Edited by Carl E. Braaten and Robert W. Jenson. Grand Rapids: Eerdmans, 1999, pp. 1-12.

"Work of Christ, The," in *Christian Dogmatics.* Edited by Carl E. Braaten and Robert W. Jenson. 2 vols. Philadelphia: Fortress, 1984, vol. 2, pp. 5-100.

Translation

Reinhard Schwarz, "Last Supper, The: The Testament of Jesus," *Lutheran Quarterly* 9 (1995): 391-403.

Book Reviews

Christianity and Humanism: Studies in the History of Ideas, by Quirinus Breen, *Lutheran World* 16, no. 2 (1969): 193-94.

Creation and Law, by Gustaf Wingren, *dialog* 1 (1962): 78-79.

Critical Issues in Modern Religion, by Roger A. Johnson, *dialog* 13 (1974): 232-33.

Dogmatics, by Hermann Diem, *dialog* 1 (1962): 69-70.

Eberhard Jüngel: An Introduction to His Theology, by John Webster, *Lutheran Quarterly* 2 (1988): 531-33.

Faith and the Vitalities of History: A Theological Study Based on the Work of Albrecht Ritschl, by Philip J. Hefner, *Interpretation* 21 (1967): 486-89.

Formation of Historical Theology: A Study of Ferdinand Christian Baur, by Peter Crafts Hodgson, *Una sancta* 24 (1967): 69-72.

God As the Mystery of the World, by Eberhard Jüngel, *Word & World* 4 (1984): 458-61.

Gospel and Church, by Gustaf Wingren, *dialog* 5 (1966): 150-53.

Göttingen Dogmatics, The: Instruction in the Christian Religion, vol. 1, by Karl Barth, Geoffrey Bromiley, trans., *Pro Ecclesia* 2 (1993): 240-42.

Luther and Staupitz: An Essay in the Intellectual Origins of the Protestant Reformation, by David C. Steinmetz, *Interpretation* 36 (1982): 196-99.

Luther in Mid-Career 1521-1530, by Heinrich Bornkamm, *Interpretation* 39 (1985): 436ff.

Place of Bonhoeffer, The: Problems and Possibilities in His Thought, by Martin E. Marty, ed., *dialog* 2 (1963): 334-35.

Reality of the Devil, The: Evil in Man, by Ruth Nanda Anshen, *dialog* 12 (1973): 156-58.

Revolt Against Heaven: An Enquiry into Anti-Supernaturalism, by Kenneth Hamilton, *dialog* 5 (1966): 312-14.

Structure of Lutheranism, The, 2 vols., by Werner Elert, *dialog* 3 (1964): 77-78.

Theology and Preaching, by Heinrich Ott, *dialog* 5 (1966): 150-53.

Theology and Proclamation: Dialogue with Bultmann, by Gerhard Ebeling, *dialog* 6 (1967): 299-302.

Word and the Spirit: Essays on the Inspiration of the Scriptures, by Regin Prenter, *dialog* 4 (1965): 304-6.

CPSIA information can be obtained
at www.ICGtesting.com
Printed in the USA
LVOW13s0915310118

564645LV00014B/187/P